Canada and the end of empire

Edited by Phillip Buckner

165101

Canada and the End of Empire

UBCPress · Vancouver · Toronto

15 14 13 12 11 10 09 08 07 06 05   5 4 3 2 1

Printed in Canada on acid-free paper

Library and Archives Canada Cataloguing in Publication

Canada and the end of empire / edited by Phillip Buckner.

 Includes bibliographical references and index.
 ISBN 0-7748-0915-9 (bound); ISBN 0-7748-0916-7 (pbk.)

 1. Canada – History – 20th century. 2. Canada – Relations – Great Britain.
3. Great Britain – Relations – Canada. 4. Postcolonialism – Canada. 5. Nationalism –
Canada – History. I. Buckner, Phillip A. (Phillip Alfred), 1942-

FC245.C348 2004   971.06   C2004-906056-2

Canadä

UBC Press gratefully acknowledges the financial support for our publishing
program of the Government of Canada through the Book Publishing Industry
Development Program (BPIDP), and of the Canada Council for the Arts, and
the British Columbia Arts Council.

This book has been published with the help of a grant from the Canadian Federation
for the Humanities and Social Sciences, through the Aid to Scholarly Publications
Programme, using funds provided by the Social Sciences and Humanities Research
Council of Canada, and with a grant from the Institute of Commonwealth Studies.

Printed and bound in Canada by Friesens
Set in Stone by Artegraphica Design Co. Ltd.
Copy editor: Jonathan Dore
Proofreader: Kate Spezowka
Indexer: Christine Jacobs

UBC Press
The University of British Columbia
2029 West Mall
Vancouver, BC V6T 1Z2
604-822-5959 / Fax: 604-822-6083
www.ubcpress.ca

Contents

Canada and the End of Empire

Introduction

Phillip Buckner

Sir John Seeley once wrote that the British Empire was acquired in 'a fit of absence of mind.' Whatever the truth of this comment, it is certainly arguable that the empire was dismantled in a fit of absence of mind. There have, of course, been numerous studies of decolonization, focusing on the political, diplomatic, and economic pressures behind the British decision to dismantle their empire and on the process of negotiation between British officials and those seeking independence.[1] But only recently have British historians begun to assess the significance to those who lived in Britain of the rapid disengagement from empire that took place after the Second World War. The topic remains a highly controversial one, since some British historians continue to insist that the mass of the British people had always been relatively indifferent to the existence of the empire. Bernard Porter has even claimed that the loss of the empire meant little to the British public because 'the mass of the people, as they had all along, cared very little.'[2] Yet it has become harder and harder to believe in this supposed indifference as more recent studies show the importance of the empire in virtually every area of popular culture in Britain. Particularly influential has been the Manchester University Press series on *Studies in Empire* edited by John MacKenzie.[3] As the significance of the empire to the evolution of Britain itself becomes increasingly apparent, British historians have been forced to re-examine the complex ways in which the 'end of empire' affected and continues to affect virtually every area of British life.[4]

The significance of the end of empire has also become an important subject of enquiry in many of the countries that were formerly part of the empire. Particularly relevant to Canadian historians ought to be the frequently heated debate taking place in Australia. Indeed, there are many common features between the approaches of Australian and Canadian historians to the imperial connection. Stuart Ward – one of the contributors to this volume – has recently written that 'Australian historians have tended to look for easily recognisable patterns of national behaviour, constructing an innate self-sufficient Australian nationalism as the primary force under-lying Australia's ambiguous progression towards independent nation.'⁵ Virtually the same could be said of Canadian historians. Until recently, most Canadian historians were self-confessed nationalists and, though many present-day historians would deny the label, they continue to write from a nationalist perspective little different from that of their predecessors. Like Australian historians, Canadian historians usually present the core dynamic of the relationship with Britain as being based on mutual antagonism, and assume as a given the existence of an innate and irresistible pressure to put an end to the outmoded, unnecessary, and distracting colonial relation-ship. To challenge this paradigm requires considerable courage, since to do so immediately lays one open to the charge of being an immature colonial, tied to the apron strings of the mother country. Thus, in Australia, Neville Meaney's assertion that until comparatively recently most Australians saw themselves as British and therefore did not seek to break the imperial con-nection has led to an intense and often bitter debate.⁶ Yet it is difficult to see how else one can explain why Australia (and the other colonies of settle-ment) moved so slowly to cut the umbilical cord with Britain. Not until the 1960s, Stuart Ward points out, was there 'a major re-assessment of the core precepts of the Anglo-Australian relationship,' and it was events in Britain that provided the catalyst for this re-assessment.⁷

In Canada we have yet to see even the beginning of a similar debate. The empire has come to be viewed as a complete irrelevance, and its signifi-cance to Canadians in the past is almost completely ignored. More than a decade ago, in my presidential address to the Canadian Historical Associa-tion, I asked the question 'Whatever happened to the British Empire?' and attempted to persuade Canadian historians to return imperial history to a central place in Canadian historiography.⁸ My plea fell largely on deaf ears. One prominent Canadian historian recently told me how surprised – and implicitly how disappointed – the audience was when I chose not to talk about Canadian history. This comment shows how completely the audi-ence missed the point of my address, which was to argue that Canadian history cannot be understood without recognition of the fact that Canada was for several centuries part of a 'Greater Britain' that extended around the globe. Until well after the Second World War, most English-speaking Cana-dians, Australians, New Zealanders, and English-speaking South Africans were the descendants of migrants from the British Isles, and they wanted to re-create a form of British society in the overseas dominions. They did not want to slavishly reproduce British society; indeed, the majority probably wished to create a 'Better Britain' than the one that existed at home – one free of the class, religious, and other constraints of the mother country.⁹ They also demanded, and were given, local self-government. In each of the old dominions there were those who sought some kind of closer imperial union with the mother country, but they were everywhere in the minority. But while the majority were opposed to any form of imperial federation, they were determined to maintain a close relationship with Britain, which they continued to think of as the mother country. This sentimental attachment to Britain and the imperial relationship did not preclude the evolution of distinct national identities in Australia, Canada, New Zealand, and South Africa, just as being British in Britain did not lead to the collapse of other national identities there. Certainly English-speaking Canadians had no difficulty in holding multiple identities. They saw themselves as both British and Canadian, and they saw the empire as belonging to them as well as to the British who lived in the mother country.

More recently I returned to this theme in a paper on 'The Rediscovery of Canada's Imperial Past,' delivered as the keynote address at a conference on the theme of 'Recasting Canadian History in the Wider World: Towards New Perspectives for the Twenty-First Century.'[10] Once again, the predominant reaction of the audience appeared to be shock – even horror – that I was calling for historians of Canada to return to a focus on a topic best forgotten. In part, this reaction reflects the desire of Canadians to gloss over the part they played in the making of the British Empire, both in the extension of British authority over the upper half of the North American continent and in the support they gave to the extension of British authority in other parts of the globe. Canadians did participate in imperial wars – most notably the South African War but also in other parts of Africa and Asia – and they clearly supported the imperial expansion across the globe. They were proud to see large parts of the map of the world painted red. But English-speaking Canadians would now prefer to ignore their imperial past. Anyone who calls for a re-assertion of the significance of the imperial relationship is dismissed as an imperial apologist, a reactionary who wishes to wallow in imperial nostalgia. This is patent nonsense. One does not have to believe that the empire was a 'good thing' to believe in its importance to generations of Canadians. But there is a deeper problem with the approach of Canadian historians. Because most are Canadian nationalists, they essentially approach the imperial relationship as a handicap that prevented Canada from reaching its potential. They therefore focus on the areas of conflict between Canada and Great Britain, and the gradual extension of self-government as Canada moved from colony to nation. In most Canadian history textbooks, therefore, the emphasis will be on the rebellions of 1837 and the 'struggle for responsible government,' the Confederation of the British North American colonies in 1867-71, the resistance to efforts at imperial centralization in the late nineteenth and early twentieth centuries, Britain's betrayal of Canadian interests in the negotiations over the Treaty of Washington and during the Alaska Boundary Dispute, the struggle for Canadian autonomy during and immediately after the First World War, the waste of Canadian lives at Vimy Ridge and Dieppe, and the failure of the British to consult the Canadian government adequately during the Chanak and Suez crises. Each of these events is seen as a stepping stone towards independence and the end of imperial entanglements.

Yet it is important to remember that this is not necessarily how these events were viewed by contemporary Canadians. After the failure of the rebellions of 1837, which were at least as much about who should rule at home as about home rule, there was never again a serious challenge to the imperial connection. Those who invented the term 'responsible govern-ment' and sought to have it introduced into the British North American colonies saw it as a means of strengthening and perpetuating the imperial connection – not weakening and shortening it. And they were, of course, correct in that assumption, since responsible government did give those living in the British North American colonies sufficient control over their own affairs to avoid any serious movement towards separation. Confedera-tion was an exercise in nation-building, but it was not designed to lead to the creation of an independent and autonomous state, only to the creation of a larger and more important British colony. Most of those who advo-cated Confederation – certainly most of the English-speaking Fathers of Confederation – viewed it as a measure that would strengthen and perpetu-ate the ties between Canada and Great Britain, not weaken them. John A. Macdonald may have been speaking to Queen Victoria when he declared that the Queen and her successors would be the head of the Canadian State forever, but there is no reason to doubt his sincerity. Macdonald was op-posed to any form of imperial federation, as were the vast majority of Cana-dians, for he believed that the empire could only survive if it gave to those colonies with a British majority the power to run their own internal affairs. But he also believed that there was a basic community of interest between the Britons at home and abroad. Most Canadians shared this view. While they may have been angered by the terms of the Treaty of Washington and the Alaska Boundary settlement, they did not abandon their faith in the value of imperial connection. Sir Wilfrid Laurier may have wanted to move Canada gradually towards independence, but he recognized that this was not what the English-speaking majority wanted. Indeed, English-speaking Canadians revealed their commitment to the empire in a small way during the South African War and in an even clearer way during the First World War.[11]

It is a pervasive myth – but a myth nonetheless – that Canadians emerged from the First World War disillusioned and alienated. Obviously some did, but as Jonathan Vance has shown, most Canadians did not accept that the war had been in vain, and they sought to defend the sacrifices that had been made.[12] Even in the interwar years there is no evidence that the major-ity of Canadians wanted to end the imperial relationship, although they did want the power to decide for themselves when they would follow British leadership, a power given them at the Imperial Conferences of 1923 and 1926 and confirmed by the Statute of Westminster in 1931.] During the 1920s and 1930s the proportion of Canadian trade with Britain and of British capital invested in Canada decreased while the proportion of trade with the United States and of American capital increased, but most English-speaking Canadians still considered themselves to be more British than American. The widespread enthusiasm surrounding the royal tour of 1939, the first to Canada by a reigning monarch, and the decision – taken virtually automatically and without substantial opposition in English Canada – to enter the Second World War, revealed how deeply English-speaking Canadians felt about their British heritage and their commitment to the mother country.

A stronger case can be made for the impact of the Second World War in ending this sense of belonging to a wider British World. In retrospect it seems clear that by the end of the war Britain had neither the will nor the ability to hang on to its empire and that Canada was rapidly becoming more Americanized in culture. Yet we must be careful not to let hindsight becloud our understanding of what Canadians thought at the time. In the 1940s and early 1950s the empire did not yet appear entirely a spent force. India achieved independence and became a republic, but large parts of Africa and Asia were still painted red on the maps of the world, which hung on the wall in every Canadian schoolroom (at least in English Canada). In 1949 the British Commonwealth of Nations became simply the Commonwealth of Nations, but this probably meant little to most Canadians, who saw little significance in the change of wording and who continued to think of the Commonwealth as essentially a club of self-governing British communities, as indeed it basically was until the late 1950s.[13] The majority ethnic group in Ontario, the Maritimes, and English-speaking Quebec were descendants of earlier waves of immigrants from the British Isles, and most of Canada's urban centres received a fresh wave of British immigrants in the immediate postwar period. Indeed, until the 1960s Britain remained the largest single source of Canadian immigrants. Moreover, most of the earlier non-British immigrants had no difficulty with the imperial relationship, particularly in Western Canada where the costs of assimilating into the British majority had long since been paid. Only in Quebec was there a strong desire to end the imperial connection, but just how strong must remain a subject of conjecture, since anti-imperial sentiment rarely expressed itself publicly in the 1950s.

Growing up in the 1950s, born in Canada but with English parents, I did not have any sense that the days of the empire and Canada's ties with Britain were numbered. Like the generation before me, I found in the public library the novels of G.A. Henty, John Buchan, and Rider Haggard, and unthinkingly absorbed their idealistic view of the empire. I was a cub scout and then a boy scout and then a rover scout, read *Scouting for Boys*, and viewed Lord Baden-Powell as a great imperial hero. I regularly participated in scout camps, which always included sitting around a camp fire singing imperial songs such as 'Marching to Pretoria,' and I can remember a boy scout jamboree in Quebec City in which thousands of Scouts from all across English Canada tramped across the Plains of Abraham arrogantly and thoughtlessly singing 'The Maple Leaf Forever.' I was also one of tens of thousands of school children who were lined up to see Princess Elizabeth when she came to Toronto in 1951, and who cheered and waved Union Jacks in her honour.[14] Like everyone else I viewed the Queen's coronation in 1953 with great enthusiasm and saw the ascent of Everest that year as a great imperial achievement, in which in some ill-defined way Canada shared. We learned in school as an article of faith the advantages of the British form of constitutional monarchy over the republican system of the United States, and were taught by Canadian historians like Donald Creighton, W.L. Morton, and even less imperially minded figures like A.R.M. Lower, that the commitment to the British system of government was one of the key characteristics distinguishing Canadians from Americans. Every year students from Toronto's public schools were selected to form two large city choirs, which performed on two successive evenings in Massey Hall. I was part of the delegation sent from Leslie St. School. The highlight of the concert was a rousing rendition of 'Land of Hope and Glory,' during which several hundred students marched onto the stage carrying alternating Union Jacks and Red Ensigns. Like most of the students present, I had no difficulty in seeing myself as both a Canadian nationalist and a British subject. I simply did not see these identities as incompatible. Of course, Toronto is not Canada, and it may be that the enthusiasm for empire was weaker elsewhere. But I suspect that I was not atypical of a majority of young English-speaking Canadians growing up in the 1950s. It is not that the empire impinged all that often upon our lives, but that there was a huge reservoir of emotional support for the continuation of the British connection, which could be drawn upon in moments of crisis.

The extent of this instinctive loyalty was shown during the Suez Crisis of 1956. We now know that British imperial power in the postwar period was an illusion and that the Suez Crisis revealed that Britain (and France) could no longer act like superpowers. When they attempted to do so in 1956, some Canadians did begin to reassess the value of the historic relationship with Great Britain. But while the Suez Crisis was a undoubtedly a major turning point in Anglo-Canadian relations – and in Lester B. Pearson's personal intellectual odyssey – it is far from clear that the majority of English-speaking Canadians shared Pearson's view of the crisis. It surely was not an accident that it was Ontario and the Maritimes, the areas of Canada with the highest proportion of people of British ancestry, which brought John Diefenbaker and the Progressive Conservatives to power in 1957. Diefenbaker was elected in part because he promised to restore good relations with Britain – which he naïvely and clumsily set out to do when he made his famous commitment to redirect 15 percent of Canada's trade away from the United States and towards Great Britain. This was an impossible goal. Indeed, the British decision to seek entry into the European Economic Community made clear that the Commonwealth was no longer a viable economic unit.

But the imperial relationship in the colonies settled by British immigrants (or more accurately, resettled after the native peoples had been cleared from the land) had always been based on more than economics. It had been based on a sense of shared ethnicity and values between the British in the mother country and the British in the dominions overseas. The Suez Crisis and the British application for entry into Europe certainly weakened this sense of a shared British identity among many English-speaking Canadians. Somewhat reluctantly, Lester B. Pearson, who had grown up in an intensely pro-British environment and who remained a committed anglophile, decided that it was time for Canada to reject the older symbols of Canada as a British nation – most notably the flag. He was also propelled by a growing fear of where the Quiet Revolution in Quebec might lead, and the need to adopt a series of national symbols that both French- and English-speaking Canadians could honour. In retrospect, those who opposed the new flag and sought to have the Red Ensign – or at least a flag that included the Union Jack – adopted as the official Canadian flag were clearly fighting a losing battle. But that again was not so clear at the time. Whatever his motives – and there is no particular reason to question Diefenbaker's motives any more than there is to question those of Pearson and the proponents of the new flag – Diefenbaker led a vigorous campaign against the new Canadian flag. It was unsuccessful, but it is worth remembering that it was Diefenbaker – not Pearson – who probably spoke for the majority of English-speaking Canadians. In both 1963 and, more significantly, in 1965, Diefenbaker and the Conservatives carried a majority of seats outside of Quebec and a majority of the seats in English-speaking Canada outside of a few urban centres. Diefenbaker did not speak for all Canadians; he did not even speak for all of English Canada. But he did speak for a very substantial number of English-speaking Canadians who saw their ethnicity as British as well as Canadian and who believed that the nation's symbols should incorporate that sense of a British-Canadian identity.

This all seems a very long time ago. Within a few years, partly because of the enthusiasm generated by the centennial celebrations in 1967, the new flag became almost universally accepted by English-speaking Canadians. In parts of rural Ontario, the Maritimes, and the rural West one used to see the

occasional Red Ensign, but it is very, very rarely seen now. Several generations of Canadians have grown to maturity knowing only the modern
Canadian flag. They know the words to 'O Canada' but not 'God Save the
Queen' – and certainly not 'The Maple Leaf Forever.' Younger English-
speaking Canadians now do have a strong sense of national identity and a
set of national symbols of which they are intensely proud. But the irony is
that Québécois nationalists – and they form a majority of the French-
speaking residents of Quebec – share neither the identity nor the commitment to these national symbols. The empire died giving birth to two national
identities in Canada, not one, and it is still an open question whether the
two can be reconciled within the bosom of a single state.

It thus seems an appropriate time to begin to examine the implications of
the end of empire for Canadians. Unlike most of the former British colonies
in Africa and Asia, which achieved their independence in the postwar period, frequently after an armed struggle, Canada – like Australia and New
Zealand – achieved independence gradually, through a series of steps. Indeed, it remains difficult to say precisely when Canada did become independent. An earlier generation of historians would undoubtedly have chosen
the passing of the Statute of Westminster in 1931 as the crucial turning
point. The statute gave Canada the right to run its own affairs, although the
constitutional amendment of the British North America Act was specifically excluded from the terms of the statute until an amending formula had
been agreed upon. This anomaly was finally resolved in 1982, and most
people today would probably see the patriation of the constitution in that
year as marking the end of the colonial relationship. Either date probably
places too much emphasis on the constitutional relationship between
Canada and Great Britain. The Statute of Westminster did mean that Canada
was effectively self-governing, even in the area of foreign policy, but it did
not alter the reality that a majority of English-speaking Canadians still considered Canada an integral part of the empire. Patriation of the constitution
did put an end to the problem of finding an amending formula – a problem
that was not resolved earlier only because the federal government and the
provinces had been unable to agree on a formula. But long before 1982 the
majority of Canadians had lost the sense of being part of a British World
extending around the globe. For some Canadians the critical turning point
was undoubtedly the Suez Crisis in 1956, when Canada rejected British leadership in external affairs and stood alongside the United States. Yet, while
Canada's actions during the crisis may have been warmly supported internationally and won Lester Pearson the Nobel Peace Prize, they were rejected
by a substantial number – perhaps even a majority – of English-speaking
Canadians, who continued to believe that a special relationship could and
should exist between Canada and Great Britain. The decision to adopt a

distinctively Canadian flag in 1964 was undeniably a critical moment when Canadians truly declared their symbolic independence. But historians tend to forget that the new flag was not greeted with universal enthusiasm, and that those who opposed the flag were just as proud Canadian nationalists as those who supported it. The issue was no longer whether Canada would have a flag of its own but whether that flag would be the Red Ensign – or at least a flag recognizing Canada's British identity. In this sense, even before the flag debate had begun, the vast majority of Canadians were already first and foremost Canadian nationalists. What is clear from the chapters in this volume is that there was no magic day on which all Canadians came to accept that the empire was over. The empire came to an end at different times and in different ways for different groups of Canadians. But the critical period was the decade from 1956 until 1967 when most English-speaking Canadians were compelled – some very reluctantly – to come to grips with the lingering death of the empire.

The chapters in this volume examine the various ways in which Canadians responded to the end of empire. In 'Imperial Twilight, or When Did the Empire End?' John Darwin examines the problem from the perspective of an historian of the British Empire and of decolonization, about which he has written extensively. As he shows convincingly, by the end of the 1940s the old British Empire had collapsed and could not be resuscitated. But this changed reality was to some extent concealed by the temporary weakness of the European economies and by the willingness of the United States in the early stages of the Cold War to shore up British power. Indeed, while imperial power may well have been based upon an illusion, it was an illusion that was not seriously threatened until well into the 1950s. In 1950 Britain was still the third-ranked world power, and not until the Suez Crisis were the limits of that power revealed. Two chapters in this collection focus on the Suez Crisis. In 'Canadian Relations with the United Kingdom at the End of Empire, 1956-73,' John Hilliker and Greg Donaghy examine Canadian attitudes towards Britain after the Suez Crisis from the perspective of the Department of External Affairs (now the Department of Foreign Affairs and International Trade). As late as 1956, they point out, Canada's relationship with Britain remained unusually close, which is why the British lack of consultation over Suez came as such a shock to Canadian Prime Minister Louis St. Laurent and Minister for External Affairs Lester B. Pearson. But old habits and attitudes persisted, and only gradually was the nature of Canada's engagement with British foreign policy reshaped, until by the early 1970s Britain was seen as just another country with whom Canada had relations. José Igartua, in '"Ready, Aye, Ready" No More? Canada, Britain, and the Suez Crisis in the Canadian Press,' approaches the Suez Crisis from a very different perspective. It is usually assumed that the Suez Crisis was a major turning point in shaping Canadian attitudes towards Britain, but Igartua shows through an examination of the English-language press that this was not the case, at least for most English-speaking Canadians. In fact, majority opinion in English Canada seems to have been generally sympathetic to the British actions in Egypt, and even those English-speaking Canadians who criticized the British government usually did so reluctantly, from a kind of kith-and-kin perspective. In 1956, Igartua concludes, the essential 'Britishness' of Canada was taken as a given by a substantial majority of English-speaking Canadians. My chapter on the 'Last Great Royal Tour: Queen Elizabeth's 1959 Tour to Canada' reaches much the same conclusion. Even as late as 1959, a tour by the Queen was still considered an event of considerable symbolic importance by English-speaking Canadians, who turned out in large numbers to welcome her. Clearly not all Canadians shared this commitment to the monarchy. The French-Canadian response was not hostile, but nor was it overly enthusiastic, as was the response of many 'new Canadians' (as they were called in 1959). Even many young native-born Canadians of British ancestry showed limited interest in the Queen's tour, which is one reason why it would be the last tour of its kind to Canada.

Although the Queen's visit in 1959 to open the St. Lawrence Seaway had originally been proposed by the government of Louis St. Laurent, Diefenbaker was in power when the tour took place. Diefenbaker had become prime minister in 1957 partly because he was able to tap into the residual loyalty of many English-speaking Canadians to the British connection. But he was aware that the old imperial relationship was gradually being eroded and that for British institutions to survive in Canada they must be Canadianized. Indeed, one of Diefenbaker's major concerns in 1959 was to Canadianize the monarchy, to persuade Canadians that the Queen was coming as Queen of Canada, and that she was a vital part of the Canadian constitution. Diefenbaker saw the British institutions and the British connection as a critical counterbalance to the growing influence of the United States. Yet the Commonwealth was an increasingly frail instrument for this purpose and ultimately, in the election of 1963, Diefenbaker lost power, partly because of his perceived anti-Americanism. The election of 1963 was a crucial turning point because the new prime minister, Lester B. Pearson, had no doubt that it was vital for Canada to retain good relations with the United States. As Gordon T. Stewart points out in '"An Objective of US Foreign Policy since the Founding of the Republic": The United States and the End of Empire in Canada,' the American State Department viewed with ill-disguised annoyance Diefenbaker's efforts to reduce Canada's dependence on the United States, and enthusiastically welcomed Pearson's election in 1963. On 23 May 1963 Pearson met in Ottawa with three top American officials and (according to their summary) assured them that the Commonwealth trading system was doomed. Stewart argues that from the perspective of the American government this meeting marked the end of empire in Canada.

By 1963 it was indeed apparent that there would be no recovery in Canada's trade with Great Britain. Five chapters in this volume deal with the whole issue of Anglo-Canadian trade. In 'Britain, Europe, and Diefenbaker's Trade Diversion Proposals, 1957-58,' Tim Rooth examines the failure of Diefenbaker's poorly thought-out efforts to divert a larger proportion of Canadian trade from the United States to Great Britain. In 'Customs Valuations and Other Irritants: The Continuing Decline of Anglo-Canadian Trade in the 1960s,' Bruce Muirhead takes up the story of the continuing decline of Anglo-Canadian trade, focusing particularly on the various negotiations between the British and Canadian governments aimed at removing barriers to trade. In 'Asleep at the Wheel? British Motor Vehicle Exports to Canada, 1945-75,' Steve Koerner looks at the decline in Anglo-Canadian trade from the British perspective, examining why the British failed to retain a substantial share in the rapidly expanding Canadian market for motor vehicles. Of course, what fatally undermined any hope of a recovery in Canadian trade with Britain (as opposed to British trade with Canada) was the British decision to enter the EEC. In 'Britain, Europe, and the "Other Quiet Revolution" in Canada,' Andrea Benvenuti and Stuart Ward look at the whole issue of trade from a broader perspective than the purely economic. They argue that the decision of the British government to apply for EEC membership in 1961, even though unsuccessful, had significant consequences in undermining the worldview of those English-speaking Canadians who still believed in a special relationship between Canada and Great Britain. Using a term coined by José Igartua, they describe the reaction in English Canada to the British decision as equivalent to the 'Quiet Revolution' in Quebec.

Yet the process of unravelling the remnants of the old imperial connection would be a slow one. As George Richardson points out in 'Nostalgia and National Identity: The History and Social Studies Curricula of Alberta and Ontario at the End of Empire,' until the 1960s the school systems of many Canadian provinces (and not just Alberta and Ontario) embodied an imperial vision of reality. It was a vision warmly embraced, as Paul Rutherford shows in 'The Persistence of Britain: The Culture Project in Postwar Canada,' by the English-speaking elite, which saw British culture as a necessary counterbalance to the vulgar popular culture of the United States. Yet by the 1950s and 1960s, even this battle was being lost as the mass media became increasingly American in inspiration and in content. Moreover, by this time, as Allan Smith points out in 'From Guthrie to Greenberg: Canadian High Culture and the End of Empire,' even Britain's stature as the cultural leader of the anglophone world in the fine, performing, and creative arts was being called into question. Canadian high culture also increasingly looked to the United States for models and for inspiration.

As Britain's economic, political, and cultural influence declined, Canada had inevitably to redefine its relationship with the United Kingdom. There was a growing desire to end the anomaly that prevented Canada from making any changes in the constitutional relationship between the federal government and the provinces without referring those changes to the British Parliament for approval. Between 1950 and the mid-1960s there were three unsuccessful efforts to find an amending formula. As Penny Bryden shows in 'Ontario's Agenda in Post-Imperial Constitutional Negotiations, 1949-68,' in 1967 it was the government of Ontario that took the initiative and forced Pearson to convene a series of first minister constitutional conferences, which made possible the final push towards patriation. But while constitutional issues were important, for many Canadians the adoption of a distinctively Canadian flag was a much more significant symbolic turning point. As Gregory A. Johnson argues in 'The Last Gasp of Empire: The 1964 Flag Debate Revisited,' the flag debate deeply divided Canadians. In '"One Flag, One Throne, One Empire": The IODE, the Great Flag Debate, and the End of Empire,' Lorraine Coops examines the part played in the flag debate by the Imperial Order Daughters of the Empire (IODE), one of the largest women's organizations in Canada. The IODE, which had been founded at the beginning of the twentieth century, was in favour of adopting the Red Ensign as the Canadian flag and bitterly opposed to a flag that was devoid of any British symbolism. Yet, after the debate was over, the leadership accepted that continued resistance was futile, though it is doubtful whether all of the rank and file endorsed reality so quickly. Certainly there were pockets of resistance. Many Canadian organizations – such as the Royal Canadian Legion – were far from happy with the new flag and the attempt to remove the signs of Canada's old imperial identity. As Marc Milner argues in 'More Royal than Canadian? The Royal Canadian Navy's Search for Identity, 1910-68,' The Royal Canadian Navy fought a futile rear-guard action to preserve the structure of an imperial navy tradition. For many, the collapse of the old imperial relationship had profoundly negative implications for Canada. Both Harold Innis and George Grant, Doug Francis maintains in 'Technology and Empire: The Ideas of Harold A. Innis and George P. Grant,' viewed the collapse of the British Empire as a disaster that would undermine Canadian independence. Their fears were shared by a host of other scholars, most notably the historians Donald Creighton and W.L. Morton.

Canada's First Nations had a rather different reason for resisting the collapse of the old imperial relationship. In 'Petitioning the Great White Mother: First Nations' Organizations and Lobbying in London,' Jim Miller examines the attitude of the First Nations to the end of empire. The First Nations had always insisted that their relationship was directly with the monarch in London, rather than with the Canadian government and parliament. Only after the patriation of the constitution made clear that there was no longer any point in appealing to London did First Nations' organizations abandon lobbying there. In an ironic sense the First Nations, who had suffered the longest and most from the creation of the British Empire in Canada, were one of the last groups in Canada to accept that the empire was really dead.

All of the chapters in this volume (except for my own on the 1959 royal tour) were originally given at a symposium held in May 2001 on the theme of 'Canada and the End of Empire' at the Institute of Commonwealth Studies, which is part of the School of Advanced Studies of the University of London. Unfortunately only a selection of the papers presented there could be included in this collection. There are also some clear gaps in the collection. We tried but failed to find someone to write a chapter on French-Canadian attitudes towards the end of empire. It is not surprising that this was a topic of greater concern to anglophone than to francophone historians. For earlier generations of English-speaking Canadians the British connection was part of their heritage and a key component of their national identity, while for French-speaking Canadians it was seen as a barrier hindering the evolution of a truly Canadian national identity. The major reason why Pearson decided in 1964 to introduce a new and distinctive Canadian flag was his desire to breach the 'two solitudes,' but for many Québécois this was a decision that came too late. Ironically it was English-speaking Canada, where opposition to the new flag had been strongest, which quickly came to embrace the new flag and the ideal of a Canadian national identity. Yet francophone historians are beginning to realize that the empire did affect the evolution of Quebec in a variety of ways both good and bad, that Quebec culture was partly shaped by the long connection with Britain, and that a history of Quebec, whether it is within Canada or without, has to be placed in the larger context of the history of the British Empire in North America.[15]

We also failed to find someone to write about the whole issue of immigration and the changing composition of Canadian society after the Second World War and its impact on Canadian attitudes towards the end of empire. We need more detailed studies of the attitudes of allophone Canadians (those whose ethnic origins were neither British nor French) towards British Canada and its institutions and symbols. These attitudes varied enormously from group to group and among individuals within the different groups, and they shifted over time. We also need more detailed studies of what the end of empire actually meant to those organizations that most strongly supported the British connection, such as the Boy Scouts, Veterans' Associations, and the Orange Order, as well as more studies of how the imperial relationship was maintained into the 1950s by the provincial education systems, by royal tours, and by public ceremonies. But what should be clear is that the transition from colony to nation was neither simple nor straightforward.

Notes

1 See, for example, John Darwin, *Britain and Decolonization in the Post-War World* (London: Macmillan, 1988), and D. George Boyce, *Decolonization and the British Empire, 1775-1997* (London: Macmillan, 1999).

2 Bernard Porter, *The Lion's Share: A Short History of British Imperialism, 1850-1995* (Harlow: Longman, 1996), 347. Porter is in the process of completing a book, which he claims will show that even at its peak the Empire was of interest to only a tiny minority of the residents of the United Kingdom.

3 See, in particular, John MacKenzie, *Propaganda and Empire: The Manipulation of British Public Opinion, 1880-1960* (Manchester: Manchester University Press, 1984) and John MacKenzie, ed., *Imperialism and Popular Culture* (Manchester: Manchester University Press, 1986).

4 See Stuart Ward, ed., *British Culture and the End of Empire* (Manchester: Manchester University Press, 2001).

5 Stuart Ward, *Australia and the British Embrace: The Demise of the Imperial Ideal* (Melbourne: Melbourne University Press, 2001), 5.

6 See Neville Meaney, 'Britishness and Australian Identity: The Problem of Nationalism in Australian History and Historiography,' *Australian Historical Studies* 32/116 (April 2000): 76-90, and the various responses, ibid., 128-36.

7 Ward, *Australia and the British Embrace*, 11.

8 P.A. Buckner, 'Whatever Happened to the British Empire?' *Journal of the Canadian Historical Association* 3 (1992): 3-34.

9 This is the fundamental problem I have with the chapter on the 'Dominions' in David Cannadine's stimulating study, *Ornamentalism: How the British Saw Their Empire* (London: Penguin, 2002). It is simply not true that all – or even most – of those living in the Dominions were in favour of replicating the British class structure. For the concept of 'Better Britain' I am indebted to James Belich.

10 The conference, organized jointly by the University of Genoa and the University of Toronto, was held at Sestri Levante, Italy, on 2-6 May 2001.

11 On Canada's participation in the South African War, see my chapter on 'Canada' in *The Impact of the South African War*, ed. David Omissi and Andrew Thompson (Houndmills: Palgrave, 2002).

12 See Jonathan Vance, *Death So Noble: Memory, Meaning, and the First World War* (Vancouver: UBC Press, 1997).

13 Even Pearson found it difficult to admit the significance of the change. See John English, *The Worldly Years: The Life of Lester Pearson*, Vol. 2: *1949-1972* (Toronto: Alfred A. Knopf, 1992), 27-28.

14 To be strictly accurate, the Union Jack is a naval flag and the correct description should be the Union Flag; however, Canadians have always referred to the Union Flag as the Union Jack and this usage has been retained throughout this volume.

15 See, for example, the work of Gérard Bouchard, especially his *Genèse des nations et cultures du nouveau monde: Essai d'histoire comparée* (Montréal: Les Éditions du Boréal, 2000).

1

Imperial Twilight, or When Did the Empire End?

John Darwin

'The three great dominatory powers of the world will be the three great empires,' pronounced the young 'red Tory' George Parkin Grant in 1945. 'The British Empire and Commonwealth will continue to encircle the globe.' In this three-power world, he went on, if Canada were 'cut off from the British nations,' it would soon be forced to join the hemispheric empire of the United States.[1] Three years later, W.L. Mackenzie King, on the brink of retirement as prime minister, warned his successor Louis St. Laurent against the danger that the Conservative leader, George Drew, would ignite the old fires of imperial patriotism in English Canada. 'You will probably need to fight all Sir Wilfrid's battles over again,' said King, referring to Drew's apparent enthusiasm for a more cohesive Commonwealth.[2] From their different points in the political spectrum, and from the varied standpoints of youthful visionary and wily pragmatist, Grant and King were in agreement that the British Empire-Commonwealth was still a powerful international combine, comparable to the emerging superpowers, and still capable of exerting (this was King's point) a fierce gravitational pull on Canadian politics. Indeed, it was precisely the gravitational pull, with its destabilizing effects on the Liberal party, of which King had always been so fearful.

But were Grant and King in their separate ways over-impressed by the surviving bulk of a floating museum, holed below the waterline, with its engines failing and its rudder jammed? It may have taken some time to sink, but was the British Empire condemned by 1945 to a lingering death? Or should we date its real demise either much later, or much earlier? Historians have fretted inconsequentially over this question. A generation ago, it was commonplace for British imperialism to be hustled towards its grave at the end of the First World War. Constitutional reform in India, the partition of Ireland, the surrender of naval supremacy in the Washington treaties, the Balfour declaration on dominion status, and the decline of the old industrial staples, were all taken as evidence that the Edwardian high noon had turned to a leaden evening. The end of empire impended. At the other extreme are those who insist that the Falklands War of 1982 was symptomatic of imperial recidivism and that only with the rendition of Hong Kong in 1997 was empire really laid to rest. It has even been possible (all things are possible) for a recent study of 'postcoloniality' to detect in the existence of 'British Gibraltar' the sinister fingerprint of a decadent imperialism. If even some of these interpretations are true, Canada has spent much of the greater part of its national existence living through the end of empire, and the phrase itself thus becomes void of useful meaning.

To restore some utility to the term, we need first of all to decide what we mean by 'empire.' There is of course no consensus. But what is striking is the tendency among writers on decolonization to equate it with territorial possession and its termination consequently with the renunciation of sovereignty by the 'imperial' power. This is despite the fact that for nearly fifty years historians of imperial *expansion* have acknowledged that it cannot be treated simply as the imposition of rule or sovereignty. An 'informal' empire of commercial, diplomatic or strategic influence was the *doppelgänger* of the 'formal' empire of rule and settlement.[3] It would be strange indeed to recognize the centrality of informal empire in the history of imperial *growth* but to discount it completely in the history of imperial *decay*. The absurdity of such a proceeding can be neatly illustrated by a country with which Britain's relations were exceptionally close and troubled. Egypt was occupied but not annexed in 1882. It was declared a protectorate in 1914 to terminate Ottoman sovereignty (recognized until then) and became an independent kingdom in 1922. But British troops still occupied Cairo and Alexandria, British officials still rendered 'advice' to Egyptian ministers, and the British high commissioner could still threaten the king with a premature retirement.[4] As late as the 1950s, some 80,000 British troops occupied the canal zone. At what point, then, did empire end in Egypt? If we cannot find a satisfactory answer for Egypt, whose future was debated more frequently and with greater urgency by British ministers than that of any territory in the formal empire save India, what hope have we of devising a more general formula for the British 'empire' as a whole?

What we need is a definition of empire that is capacious enough for the commercial and diplomatic realities but precise enough to reveal when empire ceased to be a working principle in international politics and become a shell or a sham. We might begin by acknowledging that the British version of empire was not unique or isolated but part of a larger order whose disappearance coincided with its own. The British, that is, contributed to and drew strength from a worldwide regime that we might call 'global colonialism' or, more elegantly, 'empire.' Empire was the longest lived of the global regimes we have seen since a single system of world politics emerged in the later nineteenth century. It was a Eurocentric regime dominated by a small club of 'world states': Britain, France, Russia, and Germany with their ambivalent 'junior partners' (after 1900), the United States, and Japan. It divided the world outside Euro-America into a patchwork of formal empires and a jigsaw of spheres of influence: some more or less clearly demarcated, some less so; some upheld by gunboats and garrisons, some by local self-interest. It imposed a European norm in international law, applying a 'standard of civilization' test before full admission to the family of nations.[5] Those outside were deemed incapable of guaranteeing the civilized treatment of foreigners and their interests, and consequently were liable to foreign intervention to protect or promote those interests. Empire assumed a division between industrial master nations and commodity-producing colonials and semicolonials. This division was enforced by the 'open economy,' which wedged open the markets of colonies or semi-colonies by rule (as in India) or unequal treaties (as in China). Empire meant a demographic order that sanctioned the transfer of European migrants to 'empty lands' or 'neo-Europes'; or justified their plantation among subject peoples as privileged agents of order and progress. And empire prescribed a hierarchy in which the capacity for spiritual, intellectual, and material advance was reserved for those who practised or adopted the cultural values of northwest Europe. By the late nineteenth century, this hierarchy was notoriously identified with biological or 'racial' characteristics, so as to fix in perpetuity a differential scale of cultural attainment. The whole grand edifice of diplomacy, rule, ideology, commerce, and culture was predicated upon the competitive coexistence of the imperial powers and their common loyalty to the imperial idea. Some modifications were required by the outcome of the First World War, when Germany was expelled from the colonial club, Russia declared ideological war on its members, and the United States declared a principled objection to formal colonialism. The League of Nations' mandates proclaimed standards for imperial 'best practice.' But the isolation or mutual antagonism of the 'revisionists' limited their influence. In the late 1930s, Japan denounced Western imperialism root and branch while vigorously practising its own Asian variety. Yet empire remained the rule of the road in international politics until the Second World War.

The British Empire was thus part of a larger system whose values and assumptions it embodied. The British model combined rule and influence, formal and informal empire. It was an economic, cultural, and strategic system. Its safety, stability, and legitimacy had been buttressed by the ubiquity of the colonial order, especially in Africa and Asia. But despite the restoration of colonial rule in Asia at the end of the Second World War, it was doubtful how long that order could survive the drastic weakening of its principal champions. Only Britain of the three victor powers of 1945 was sympathetic to the imperial idea. France, the Netherlands, Belgium, and Portugal, the remaining colonial powers, were heavily dependent on American goodwill. Of course, American policy swung round sharply in favour of colonialism at the end of the war, but only where colonialism seemed the best available barrier to communism.[6] The result, in some places, was to prolong colonial rule into the 1950s and beyond. But what we have to consider is whether, in the British case at least, what survived was the shadow rather than the substance of imperial power.

Since the second half of the nineteenth century, the British imperial system had depended upon the voluntary and involuntary cohesion of its four prime elements. The first and most obvious of these was the naval, industrial, commercial, and demographic strength of the British Isles. Capital and credit, maritime primacy, and the leverage Britain exercised in European politics, were indispensable to the strategic safety and economic development of the system as a whole. In the Eastern world, however, British power required the mobilizing of Indian resources, the second of these major elements. India supplied a great market for British manufactures, kept open by the imperial fiat of the London government.[7] It was a prodigal source of manpower, skilled and unskilled, that staffed the mercantile networks and plantation economies, without which British rule in much of the tropical world would have been economically stultified. But most of all India was a bank of military power. With an army of its own (140,000 men) and a garrison of British troops (typically some 70,000 men), both paid for by the Indian taxpayer, Indian revenues supported around two-thirds of the regular troops of the empire as a whole. The 'Army in India' – the Indian army and the British contingent – formed the strategic reserve for the British Empire east of Suez.[8] Troops sent from India allowed Britain to intervene across the world from the eastern Mediterranean to the Yellow Sea. They were the timely reinforcements that checked – just – the Boer dash for the sea in 1899. In the First World War, Indian troops were deployed in the Middle East and East Africa as well as on the Western Front – perhaps a million men in all.

British rule in India thus had an *ultima ratio*. It might promote economic development. It might even permit a crab-like progress towards representative government. But it must guarantee the funding of an army – indeed two armies – for imperial purposes. This 'imperial dividend' from India had a further value. It made possible the strange conventions of responsible government through which the third great component of British power – the settler states or 'white dominions' – were connected to the British system. Unlike India, the settler countries were exempt from a military tribute. Indeed, it is hard to imagine how responsible government, let alone the growth of a pan-British sentiment, could have survived an attempt to impose one. Instead (as dominion premiers liked to point out), the settler states became 'dominions of debt,'[9] mortgaging themselves to become markets and producers for the motherland. Settler self-government in North America, the South Pacific, and even (with more mixed results) South Africa proved an astonishingly successful mechanism for harnessing private energies to the task of developing vast regions for British occupation, and with British capital. By the turn of the twentieth century, economic maturation, strategic anxiety, and an emphasis on nation-building had sharpened their sense of imperial Britishness. In the era of two world wars, imperial patriotism in the British dominions was a crucial ingredient in the Anglo-dominion partnership, just as the loyal manpower and industrial strength of the white dominions was an indispensable element of British world power. Indeed, the white dominions contributed as many soldiers as did India to the imperial effort in the First World War.

The fourth component of British power was no less vital. Outside Europe and beyond the formal empire stretched the economic realm ruled or managed from the City of London. This was the commercial empire of foreign investment and business services. It was most visible in the banks, insurance companies, trading houses, railway and shipping lines, harbours, docks, tramways and water installations, cable and telegraph networks, mining enterprises, and oil concessions through which British interests promoted and exploited the growth of the international economy. The dynamism of this commercial empire had helped Britain find new markets as industrial competition in Europe and the United States grew hotter. It also contributed a large share to the huge invisible income Britain had built up by 1913: the secret of her payments surplus, the source of new investment, and the prop for a living standard that could not be sustained by exports alone.

Each of the overseas components of British power was a major source of strength, a means of projecting and paying for British influence. Together they made up a world system. But each was subject to centrifugal pressures. Even the early Indian nationalists raged against their military burden and envied the freedom of the white dominions.[10] Yet in those white dominions, London's domineering tendency in defence and foreign policy was a constant grievance; so in hard times was the greed of the British investor. In the commercial empire, public resentment at foreign-owned enterprise, the stresses of maintaining an 'open economy,' and the periodic temptation to financial default showed that the attractions of autarky could not be ruled out. Even in Britain, the normally muted hostility to the costs and risks of imperial power became more vociferous at moments of financial strain or diplomatic embarrassment. Yet, to a remarkable extent, the four great elements of British power had been buckled together by 1913 through a combination of cultural attraction, economic dependence, and political self-interest. Partly as a result, the First World War was a great imperial victory. After the dust had settled in the Middle East, and the British had retreated from the further reaches of Curzonian expansionism, a vast new strategic barrier now guarded the 'Southern British World' (Leo Amery's term) from the intrigues of the European powers. Even in East Asia, where the war had shrivelled Britain's military presence and diplomatic pull, an Anglo-American *pax* seemed a good guarantee for this promising province of commercial empire. And for all the damage inflicted by depression and the centrifugal politics of India and the dominions between the wars, the British world system had sufficient cohesion to survive the unparalleled geostrategic catastrophe that it suffered between 1940 and 1942. The question in 1945 was whether it could still be held together in the new geopolitical, 'geo-economic,' and ideological climate that set in at the end of the war.

British leaders were determined that it should, though they recognized that their postwar system would have to accommodate a fully self-governing Indian dominion. Nor was their outlook just a matter of prestige or inertia. The British wanted maximum influence when the postwar rulebook was written on international trade, the monetary system, and non-self-governing territories. They were desperate to exploit their tropical colonies to alleviate consumer austerity (and voter alienation) in Britain and to increase their exports to dollar countries, the only source of capital goods. They were also afraid that any premature withdrawal from their colonial empire would open the door to communist ideology and Soviet influence. Ironically, therefore, the period in which Britain's relative decline in wealth and power was felt most acutely at home – through conscription, austerity, and financial crisis – was also the period in which British governments showed the greatest energy in developing their colonial dependencies and (where they could) beating down their colonial enemies.

Of course, even in 1950, Britain was still the third-ranked world power. While Britain's material strength was dwarfed by that of the United States and was no match on land for that of the Soviet Union, it was still vastly greater than that of the next-most powerful state in a war-torn world. In fact, this flattering status concealed the splintering of the world system on whose cohesion British power had long depended. Its four great components had drifted apart or suffered irreparable damage. Britain's physical plant and infrastructure had suffered badly in wartime, and its society faced drastic impoverishment from the brutal demands of a war economy. The generation of domestic British wealth, on which the economic expansion of the imperial system had hitherto depended, was at a standstill. Meanwhile the extreme instability of European politics – the underlying cause of imperial weakness by the late 1930s – persisted in the aftermath of war. No less serious was the dramatic contraction of the commercial empire whose remittances had been so vital to the payments balance and British solvency. Drawn down heavily during the war, its remaining assets faced expropriation in Argentina, China (after 1949), and the Middle East (in Mossadeq's Iran). Refloating sterling as a convertible currency and rebuilding London as a rival centre (to New York) of international trade was in consequence a forlorn enterprise. The economic magnetism that, along with allegiance, cultural sympathy, and strategic dependence, had offset the centrifugal pressures of the imperial system, was hugely weakened. The British had been forced to concede the independence of India, but on terms more adverse than anything they had dreamt of before 1939. Far from retaining the support of a loyal, cooperative, and dependent dominion, the British were driven to acquiesce to the partition of India into two antagonistic successor states, between which the army was divided. The postcolonial subcontinent became a zone of local rivalry and strategic weakness, contributing nothing to Commonwealth defence. The Indian government insisted on republican status and drifted steadily towards non-alignment between East and West. The great strategic assets that had once underpinned British influence east of Suez were nationalized and confiscated. Henceforth the military burden of empire would fall mainly on Britain: on its exhausted taxpayers and the conscripts of its citizen army.

In these conditions, it was hardly surprising that the relationship between Britain and the white dominions should have also been transformed. In the great imperial crisis of 1940-42, Canada, Australia, and New Zealand had all turned to the United States to take Britain's place as their strategic guardian – in Canada's case, this shift occurred even before the United States entered the war in late 1941. After 1945, Canadian governments, not without misgivings, deepened their economic and strategic dependence on Washington. The Pacific dominions, still eager for British markets and migrants, and less confident of American protection, hoped that their imperial ties would shore up the new reliance on American power in the Asia-Pacific region. In South Africa, the shock defeat of Jan Smuts in the election of 1948 brought to power an Afrikaner government that was hostile to British influence in the region and introvertedly nationalist in outlook. Australia, New Zealand, and South Africa all remained part of the sterling area (which worked to their advantage). 'Commonwealth preference' in trade was a postwar version of the imperial bloc established at Ottawa in 1932. But the prewar assumption that, in matters of global politics, majority opinion in the overseas dominions would take its cue from Britain (an assumption that had been vindicated in September 1939) now held good only in the Pacific dominions. Even there it was qualified by the new landscape of regional power.

By the end of the 1940s, therefore, very little remained of the great imperial system with which the British had confronted the menace of German, Italian, and Japanese aggression. The commercial empire had shrivelled. India had been lost. The dominion idea (of automatic solidarity) had been discredited. The trident had crossed the Atlantic. British security at home now rested (after 1948) upon an American guarantee. Of course, a vast colonial empire remained. But reality belied appearance. This empire had little in common with the empire of Salisbury, Balfour, Curzon, and Lloyd George, or even of Neville Chamberlain.

Indeed, it is tempting to mark the difference by designating the empire that was left after 1950 as a 'fourth' British empire,[11] and to think of it as a case of 'late colonialism.' After all, the classic features of empire as a global regime that we identified earlier were by now in full retreat. Formal and informal empires were breaking up. Their legitimacy had been ruptured. The 'open economy' had (largely) broken down. Racial hierarchy had been discredited. The fourth British empire was launched in this hostile environment. It was the distinctive product of Churchillian statecraft: an empire underwritten by Atlantic partnership. It rested heavily on American support – material and diplomatic[12] – and upon British, not imperial, resources and manpower. Its territories and spheres were concentrated in regions regarded with trepidation or disdain by the previous generation of imperial leaders. Even after the loss of Palestine in 1948, British influence and prestige were heavily invested in the Middle East, an exposed salient in the middle of the world, dangerously vulnerable to Soviet influence and regional nationalisms. Nemesis was not long in coming. The imperial mission was refocused in tropical Africa, an undergoverned colonial hinterland where the apparatus of rule was much too flimsy to bear the sudden strain of breakneck economic transition. Here too the upper millstone of imperial exigency soon ground against the lower millstone of colonial resentment. The third great colonial zone was in Southeast Asia, already by 1950 a largely postcolonial region, destabilized by the fallout of communist revolution in China and Vietnam. The price of overcoming a communist insurrection was rapid independence for the anticommunist majority and (thereafter) an expensive commitment to regional defence.

While all these regions yielded *potential* benefits to Britain, their costs and liabilities loomed far larger than on the old balance sheet of prewar empire. Worse still, they had to be ruled, or influenced, after the mid-1950s in an international climate dominated by the growth of superpower competition, driving up relentlessly the military and financial burden they imposed. It was little wonder that by the end of the 1950s even official opinion had begun to doubt whether such an empire – even metamorphosed into 'Commonwealth' – was worth its keep. By comparison with the real thing, it had become a weightless substitute, an empire of the 'third way,' defying the laws of political gravity – but not for long. For by 1960 even under-governed Africa had become ungovernable. Under Harold Macmillan, Churchillian statecraft entered its rococo phase. The 'special relationship' and 'Commonwealth unity,' those twin pillars of British world power, were now to be supplemented by entry into (and leadership of) the European Economic Community. It was a rich if unpleasant irony that the illusions of the 'age of Churchill' were abruptly terminated by the '*non*' of de Gaulle.

Perhaps the conclusion to be drawn is that what is conventionally thought of as the end of empire, and located chronologically in the 1950s and 1960s, was really little more than the aftermath to the 'awful revolution' of British power. To all intents, the British world system had collapsed by 1950 as an independent political structure. Its vital elements had split apart. The war had wrecked its commercial circuits. The British lost control of India. Strategic independence was never recovered. British claims on the allegiance of their prewar satellites were at a discount. The legitimacy of colonial rule was denied by the new norms of international politics, while its practicality was threatened by the progressive unravelling of the colonial order. But for almost a decade the effects of this seismic change were masked by the early phase of Cold War politics. British leverage on American policy, the temporary eclipse of the European economies, and the delayed maturation of superpower rivalry prolonged Britain's status as the third-ranked world power, to which its postwar empire was stuck like an appendix. This period of grace explains much of the complacency with which the British experience of decolonization is so widely regarded. It may also explain why it is only now that its significance for British politics and culture is beginning to be noticed.[13]

Notes

1 George Parkin Grant, *The Empire: Yes or No?* (Toronto: Ryerson, 1945). For the full text, A. Davis and P. Emberley, eds., *The Collected Works of George Grant: Volume 1* (Toronto: University of Toronto Press, 2000).
2 National Archives of Canada, Mackenzie King papers, Microfilm C 11052, W.L. Mackenzie King to Louis St. Laurent, 3 October 1948.
3 The famous distinction made by J. Gallagher and R. Robinson, 'The Imperialism of Free Trade,' *Economic History Review,* 2nd series, 6/1 (1953): 668-72.
4 For an account of Egypt's quasi-independence, see J. Darwin 'Imperialism in Decline?' *Historical Journal* 23/3 (1980). For a brilliant portrait of Anglo-Egyptian diplomacy, see M.E. Yapp, ed., *Politics and Diplomacy in Egypt: The Diaries of Sir Miles Lampson, 1935-1937* (Oxford: Oxford University Press 1997).
5 See Gerrit Gong, *The Standard of 'Civilization' in International Society* (Oxford: Clarendon Press 1984).
6 The classic account is W. Roger Louis, *Imperialism at Bay, 1941-1945: The United States and the Decolonization of the British Empire* (Oxford: Clarendon Press, 1977).
7 India was thus the largest market in 1913 for Britain's largest export, cotton cloth.

8   This was the conclusion of the Welby Commission, formally the Royal Commission on the Administration of the Expenditure of India (1900).

9   'This is our paper city, built / on the rock of debt, held fast/ against all winds by the / paperweight of debt.' From 'Dominion' by A.R.D. Fairburn.

10 The constitution of the Indian National Congress, drawn up in 1908, prescribed constitutional equality with the white dominions as the goal of political struggle.

11 For the utility (or otherwise) of the 'third British empire' as an historical category, see J. Darwin, 'A Third British Empire? The Dominion Idea in Imperial Politics' in *The Oxford History of the British Empire*, Vol. 4: *The Twentieth Century*, ed. Judith Brown and W. Roger Louis (Oxford: Oxford University Press, 1999).

12 See W. Roger Louis and R.E. Robinson, 'The Imperialism of Decolonisation,' *Journal of Imperial and Commonwealth History* 22/3 (1994): 426-511.

13 For a pioneering study, see Stuart Ward, ed., *British Culture and the End of Empire* (Manchester: Manchester University Press, 2001).

2

Canadian Relations with the United Kingdom at the End of Empire, 1956-73

John Hilliker and Greg Donaghy

What is most striking perhaps about Canada's relationship with the United Kingdom in 1956 is that it was still so cordial and intimate. The United Kingdom remained Canada's second-largest economic partner after the United States, and the principal source of immigrants. On the international scene, consultation was close, frank, and frequent, both bilaterally and in the United Nations, NATO, and the Commonwealth. This collaboration was based on practices established before and during the Second World War, but it was made easier afterwards by the progress of decolonization. When planning for the war against Japan was under way in 1944, Prime Minister William Lyon Mackenzie King made it clear, with the support of most of his ministers, that Canada did not want to be involved in Britain's efforts to restore control over its dependencies in Asia, and the broadening of the Commonwealth after India and Pakistan became independent was welcomed in Ottawa.[1] It also helped that Mackenzie King, suspicious to the end of the mother country's intentions, retired from politics in 1948, and that Canada's foreign relations were dominated between 1946 and 1957 by Lester Pearson, who worked easily and confidently with the leading British ministers and diplomats of the day.[2]

The relationship with the United Kingdom was not only easygoing, it was also taken for granted, at least in Ottawa. Because it was going well, there was no pressing need to examine it; it would have been a major task to do so, since it was pervasive and involved many branches of government; and there was no focal point, for a British desk was not established in the Department of External Affairs until 1967. Even the most amicable of associations, however, was not immune from change and indeed from surprise, which is what occurred in 1956 when Canada and Britain parted over British policy in the Middle East.

The year 1956 opened on a quiet, perhaps even self-congratulatory note. The prospective independence of the Gold Coast, as Ghana, caused Ottawa to give some thought to a part of the globe that hitherto had not figured large in Canadian foreign policy. The subject was seen very much in Cold War terms, the most urgent requirement being to do something to offset the 'declining influence of the United Kingdom' in a region where there was a 'dangerous possibility' that the Soviet Union would seek to increase its influence. Although the proposed Canadian contribution – the establishment of a diplomatic mission in Accra and the development of an aid program – was modest, it marked the beginning of a deeper Canadian involvement in Africa that would not always make for easy relations with the British.[3]

More immediate difficulties developed in the Middle East, where Canada grew alarmed in early 1956 at the deteriorating situation in the area. Pearson, Canada's secretary of state for external affairs, had met Egyptian Prime Minister Gamal Abdel Nasser in late 1955 during a quick tour of the troubled region. Pearson described Nasser as an 'impressive and attractive personality,' who gave 'an impression of sincerity and strength, without any trace of arrogance or self-assertion.'[4] Pearson dismissed American and British suggestions that Nasser was likely to fall easy prey to Soviet intrigue. Instead, he saw Nasser as representative of a resurgent Arab nationalism, whose deep-seated opposition to European colonialism would make it difficult for either the West or the Soviet Union to influence developments in the Middle East. Officials in the Department of External Affairs shared this view, and argued that the leading Western powers – the United States, Britain, and France – should invite the Soviet Union into the Middle East, seeking regional stability through a quadripartite settlement, possibly guaranteed through the United Nations. Pearson agreed, but American Secretary of State John Foster Dulles, and British Prime Minister Anthony Eden, did not.[5] When Nasser nationalized the Suez Canal on 26 July 1956, the implications of this difference in approach quickly became apparent. Canadian officials and ministers were immediately alarmed at the sharp and strident tone of the British reaction, which seemed a hollow echo of an earlier imperial era. When informed of Nasser's actions on 27 July, Canada's high commissioner in London, Norman Robertson, urged Lord Home, the secretary of state for Commonwealth relations, to bring the matter to the UN. He added the hope that the United Kingdom 'would not be too quick to gather too many spears to its own bosom.'[6]

In Ottawa, Pearson and Prime Minister Louis St. Laurent shared Robertson's concern. On 28 July, Eden sent St. Laurent and the other Commonwealth Prime Ministers a tough and uncompromising message: 'We can not allow [Nasser] to get away with this act of expropriation and we must take a firm stand.'[7] Alarmed by Eden's obvious determination to bring Nasser to heel, Pearson dashed off a warning for Robertson:

I am deeply concerned at the implications of some parts of Eden's message; especially as I doubt very much whether he will receive strong support from Washington in the firm line which he proposes to follow ... Surely the UK Government will not do anything which would commit them to strong action against Egypt until they know that the US will back them.

I am also worried as to the meaning of Eden's words, 'we believe that we should seize this opportunity of putting the canal under proper international control.' Surely with the Russians dissenting and supporting Egypt, the UK do not think that this can be done, as they profess to hope, 'by political pressure' alone. There remains force – which they visualize as a last resort ... Any effort to use force, in fact, would in all likelihood result in an appeal by Egypt to the UN. That would be bringing the UN into the matter with a vengeance, and by the wrong party.[8]

St. Laurent sent a carefully couched reply to Eden, specifically endorsing Robertson's views as his own. To emphasize the depth of Canadian concern, Robertson also sent the more strongly worded draft of St. Laurent's message to Sir Norman Brook, secretary of the British cabinet. In a paragraph dropped from the final version as likely to offend British sensibilities, the prime minister's worry was almost palpable: 'I am sure that you appreciate that the use of force in present circumstances – even as a last resort – will be surrounded by risks and difficulties, one of which might be the submission of the matter to the United Nations by the wrong party.'[9]

Canadian criticisms angered Eden, his ministers, and officials. When the British High Commission in Ottawa reported that a University of Alberta professor had argued on a CBC program that the United States and Britain had provoked Nasser, the prime minister minuted with irritation: 'Lord Home: Please speak. This is Canadian govt again. We must react.'[10] Anger quickly gave way to disbelief, as senior British officials simply refused to accept Canadian misgivings as real. When Robertson's old friend, Gladwyn Jebb, the British Ambassador to France, passed on his warnings to the Foreign Office, they were dismissed by Sir Harold Caccia, the deputy undersecretary of state for foreign affairs, as 'more Robertson than Canadian Government.'[11] Unfortunately, Britain was uninterested in exploring the Canadian reaction further. Sir Archibald Nye, the British high commissioner in Ottawa, reassured London that 'I have held back from making any approaches officially in case we got reactions which didn't suit us.'[12]

Though skeptical of British policy, Ottawa was sympathetic and tried to be helpful. St. Laurent agreed to meet a British request to freeze Egyptian assets in Canada, even though the government had little legal basis for doing so.[13] Ottawa also supported British efforts to convene a conference of canal users in mid-August, but worried what would happen next. Pearson considered it unlikely that Nasser would simply agree to British demands for genuine international control of the canal, moving London one more step towards the use of force. As this possibility loomed larger, the question of Canada's reaction to any eventual military action moved to the centre of Anglo-Canadian discussions. On 15 August, Robertson met with British Commonwealth Secretary Selwyn Lloyd, who asked him directly 'whether, if we had to use force we could expect the support of the Canadian Government.' Robertson's answer was a simple 'no.'[14]

Eden exploded with anger. 'I think this should be taken up with the Canadian government,' he minuted, 'it is far worse than anything US Govt has ever said.' Lloyd counselled patience, dismissing Robertson as inconsequential. The Canadian high commissioner, he pointed out, had been ill recently and was probably still depressed. In any event, Robertson was a 'strong' UN man, whose views were not likely representative of Ottawa's. With simply breathtaking arrogance, Lloyd suggested that Eden avoid approaching St. Laurent, ostensibly in order to spare Ottawa the embarrassment of having rejected the use of force too precipitately: 'May there not be some danger of their giving us an answer which they might be sorry for later if and when some new aggression by Nasser ... makes the use of force the definite and immediate issue?' Eden agreed, adding that he saw 'no advantage in asking Mr. Robertson his opinions any more.'[15] Canada had ceased to matter.

Ottawa watched from a distance as Eden's confrontation with Nasser played out in the fall of 1956. Though Britain eventually asked the Security Council to rule on its dispute with Egypt in late September, Canadian misgivings persisted. 'Far from seeking a solution,' observed R.A. MacKay, Canada's Permanent Representative to the United Nations, 'France and the UK, but particularly the latter, seem bent on humiliating Nasser.'[16] MacKay was right. Shortly after the Israeli assault on Egypt on 29 October, Britain and France demanded a ceasefire; when the fighting continued, they moved to seize control of the Suez Canal, catching Canada completely off-guard. Obviously distressed by the British action, Robertson reported to Ottawa that he had been 'given no inkling' of London's plans and 'not the slightest intimation that anything extraordinary was planned.'[17] Robertson spent the whole day, 30 October, trying to see key British officials, but met only closed doors and busy telephones.[18] In a message to the Canadian prime minister that arrived after he had already learned of the Anglo-French assault from the press, Eden explained that France and Britain could not stand by while a war between Israel and Egypt was allowed to block the Suez Canal. If war did break out, London and Paris would issue a call for a ceasefire; if none was forthcoming, they would take military action to make both sides retreat from the canal. Intervention would be risky, concluded the British prime minister, but 'I know that we can look for your understanding and much hope for your support in our endeavours.'[19] Enraged and disgusted, St. Laurent reportedly threw the telegram at Pearson, asking 'what do you think of that?'[20]

Pearson, who was anxious to moderate St. Laurent's anger, took charge of drafting the reply. It rejected completely Eden's justifications for acting. Apart from the danger that war might spread throughout the Middle East, three aspects of the British decision to intervene especially alarmed and irritated Ottawa. First, the decision to act while the Security Council was still considering Egypt's complaint against Israel was a direct challenge to the UN's authority; second, the British action would almost certainly alienate India and cause 'a serious division within the Commonwealth'; and third, Ottawa bemoaned the impact of the British decision on Anglo-American relations, fearing that 'it will cause as much satisfaction to the Soviet Union and its supporters as it does distress to all those who believe that Anglo-American cooperation and friendship is the very foundation of our hopes for progress toward a peaceful and secure world.'[21]

London was 'aghast' at the tone of St. Laurent's missive.[22] Arnold Smith, minister at the Canadian High Commission in London, reported that 'the bitterness about the Canadian attitude on Suez was as great as that against the Americans.'[23] But there was little time for recrimination as the UN's deliberations moved from the Security Council, where Britain and France could hide behind their permanent-member veto, to the General Assembly, where debate on a US motion calling for a ceasefire and an immediate withdrawal was slated to open in the afternoon of 1 November. St. Laurent and Pearson were anxious to salvage the British position, restore the UN's prestige, and heal the breach in the North Atlantic alliance. Before leaving Ottawa for New York, Pearson asked Robertson to seek Britain's reaction to a plan to call upon the General Assembly to create an 'adequate UN military force to separate the Egyptians from the Israelis.' On his arrival in New York, Pearson learned that Britain was ready to 'hand over' the Suez Canal 'to a UN force strong enough to prevent the renewed outbreak of hostilities between Egypt and Israel.'[24] This slight concession was enough, and during the debate on the American motion, Pearson sat quietly until the small hours of the morning. Rising at 3 a.m. to explain Canada's abstention, he argued that the American resolution calling for a return to the status quo was not enough; what was needed was a 'UN force large enough to keep these borders at peace while a political settlement is being worked out.'[25]

After lunch with UN Secretary-General Dag Hammarskjöld, who was doubtful that Pearson's idea would work, the minister returned to Ottawa, where the cabinet endorsed his proposal for an international peacekeeping force. Ottawa and Washington soon agreed on a draft UN resolution appointing a five-member committee to 'plan for the setting up in the Middle East of an emergency international United Nations force recruited from national military forces immediately available.'[26] Pearson returned to New York late in the afternoon of 3 November, bringing the draft with him. There he learned that British reaction to the proposed resolution had been encouraging. Indeed, Lloyd had even given Robertson the impression 'that the resolution was welcome and that ... they might even be able to vote for it.'[27] Hopeful that the resolution might stop French and British troops from landing in Egypt, Pearson pressed ahead. After lobbying other UN members for support, he met with the US Permanent Representative to the United Nations, Henry Cabot Lodge, and decided to base his resolution on a simpler US draft that asked the secretary-general alone to develop plans for a UN emergency force. Another late-night session followed before the UN General Assembly adopted the Canadian resolution early in the morning of 4 November. Within forty-eight hours, the United Nations Emergency Force (UNEF) had begun to take shape, and London and Paris had agreed to a ceasefire. The worst phase of the crisis was over.

Although Pearson and Eden both suggested otherwise in their memoirs,[28] the crisis had a lasting impact on Anglo-Canadian relations. The British deputy high commissioner in Ottawa, Neil Pritchard, warned London shortly afterwards that 'the lack of consultation has left a permanent scar. After all, this was an action on our part which might ... have involved [the Canadians] in a war, and which has in fact involved them in sending a battalion and an aircraft carrier to the Middle East.'[29] The British High Commission also acknowledged that Canadian foreign policymakers were likely to revise their traditional high regard for British diplomacy. 'I fear,' wrote Sir Saville Garner, who took up his duties as high commissioner in the middle of the crisis, 'that we are bound to find that the Canadian Government will never again accept our judgement so readily as they have been prepared to do in the past.'[30] This was a verdict echoed by Robertson, who wrote in the summer of 1957 of 'his loss of confidence in British judgement and good sense, which derives from the whole handling of the Suez problem.'[31] In Britain, even among those who accepted and applauded Pearson's effort at the United Nations, the feeling of betrayal lingered. Britain should not hesitate, the British Ambassador to the UN, Sir Pierson Dixon, wrote soon after the crisis ended, 'about excluding the other two members of the Old Commonwealth [Canada and South Africa] from consultations with the two [New Zealand and Australia] who have proved to be our real friends.'[32]

Some members of the Liberal cabinet – notably Minister of Finance Walter Harris, and Minister of Public Works Robert Winters – had warned that open disagreement with the United Kingdom might be politically dangerous in Canada, and Harris had been consulted during the drafting of St. Laurent's message to Eden of 31 October. Discussion of the issue in the press and in Parliament soon indicated that the country was in fact divided, something that was confirmed to a limited extent by the only public opinion poll to ask if Canadians supported the Anglo-French action. Carried out by Gallup on 12 November, the survey was limited to Toronto. It showed that 43 percent of respondents agreed with the Anglo-French action, 40 percent opposed it, and 17 percent had no opinion.[33] Taken together, the public debate and the poll suggested a continuing strong attachment to the British connection that, since the government's position had been close to that of the United States, fitted into a larger context of anxiety about the extent to which Canada had moved into the American orbit. Foreign policy was by no means a dominant issue in the federal election of 1957, but there was a market for the warnings by the Progressive Conservatives under John Diefenbaker about dangers from south of the border, especially American domination of the Canadian economy.[34] The Conservative victory on 10 June 1957 suggested that some changes were in store.

Diefenbaker looked to the past, when British and American influences on Canada had been more evenly balanced, for a remedy to the problem that he had identified during the election campaign. The timing was good, for Eden's successor, Harold Macmillan, was busy mending fences with Britain's allies. Macmillan's initial impression of Diefenbaker was favourable and he was prepared to expend considerable effort cultivating his goodwill. Unfortunately, Diefenbaker's ideas about what he wanted to achieve in relations with the United Kingdom were not very precise. At the end of June 1957, he attended a Commonwealth Prime Ministers' meeting in London and on his return on 6 July he told a press conference that it was the government's intention to divert 15 percent of its imports from the United States to Britain. This took the British – as well as the prime minister's own officials and cabinet colleagues – by surprise. The United Kingdom, engaged in negotiations for the European Free Trade Area, was already looking for more promising markets than the Commonwealth. The proposal, nonetheless, was tempting, offering as it did the possibility of recovering lost ground in the Canadian market. The British government also had to be careful not to provoke criticism at home for failure to respond positively to a friendly and very public initiative from an obviously anglophile Canadian prime minister. Moreover, Macmillan did not want to disrupt a promising start to the relationship with the new government in Ottawa. The alternative the British proposed was a free trade area between Canada and the United Kingdom, but this was unwelcome in Ottawa, since the advantage in the short run would flow to the British, and Canadian manufacturers were nervous about the competition that would result. With the home audience in mind, the British made sure that their offer became public through a press leak during the Commonwealth Finance Ministers' meeting at Mont Tremblant, Quebec, in September 1957. Unable to accept, the Canadian government sought to save face by arranging for a large party of potential importers to visit the United Kingdom later in the autumn under the leadership of

Minister of Trade and Commerce Gordon Churchill. It was clear, however, that the idea of a shift in Canada's economic orientation towards Britain had died, and in a way not helpful to the transatlantic relationship. Diefenbaker's incautious statement of 6 July ended up causing irritation on both sides, and left the Canadians, outmanoeuvred by more skilful players, feeling bruised.[35]

Better-planned initiatives had more hope of success. This was so with the Commonwealth economic conference held, despite some hesitation by the British, in Montreal in September 1958. Unlike the trade diversion, this was something that Diefenbaker had planned from the start; he had gone to the Prime Ministers' Meeting in June 1957 with the objective of raising support for the idea. Described by Diefenbaker's biographer Denis Smith as the 'culmination' of Diefenbaker's early efforts to promote the Commonwealth, the conference also looked back to the Imperial Economic Conference of 1932, a landmark event in the career of Diefenbaker's Conservative predecessor as prime minister, R.B. Bennett. Gratifyingly for the government, it was a public-relations success and produced some positive outcomes, notably the Commonwealth scholarship and fellowship plan.[36] It would soon become apparent, however, that the Commonwealth was now likely to offer more challenges than opportunities to a Canadian government. Two challenges, both related to the end of empire, were particularly serious: South Africa, and the British decision to seek membership in the European Economic Community (or the 'Common Market,' as it was often known).

The issue of apartheid in South Africa was exceptionally difficult for Diefenbaker, both personally and politically. Although he had a fondness for the old Commonwealth, he was also a civil libertarian who found apartheid reprehensible. His cabinet was divided, with a number of ministers more influenced by a sentimental attachment to the long-established relationship with South Africa than by the racial policies of the government there. For a long time, Diefenbaker was able to deal with these conflicts using his favourite strategy of delay, but the Sharpeville massacre of 21 March 1960 increased the pressure to take a position against the apartheid regime. Matters came to a head at the Commonwealth Prime Ministers' Meeting in March 1961, when South Africa was obliged to reapply for membership as a result of its decision to become a republic. Diefenbaker had limited room for manoeuvre, for the cabinet, while ready to condemn apartheid, did not want Canada to sponsor a Commonwealth declaration of principles, a device that might force South Africa to withdraw. Diefenbaker remained free, however, to support the efforts of others to formulate a declaration, and this is what happened after he learned that India was prepared to take the lead. Diefenbaker's refusal to compromise on the wording of the proposed declaration, as Denis Smith has made clear, helped to make it impossible for Macmillan to find a solution that would enable South Africa to remain.

Diefenbaker's stand, Smith has written, 'marked a high point of his prime ministership,' earning him praise not only in Canada but also in the United Kingdom.[37] The outcome, however, was a disappointment for Macmillan, whose earlier regard for Diefenbaker turned sour. 'Poor old Dief,' Macmillan wrote, 'would have read the leading article in the Winnipeg something-or-other, and he would suit his actions to that. Without him, we could have got through – though we might have failed at the next conference.'[38]

Another cause of deep irritation was the Canadian reaction to the British decision in 1960 to seek membership in the European Economic Community. For the Conservatives in Ottawa, this represented an attack on one of their party's historic achievements, the system of tariff preferences originating in the Imperial Economic Conference of 1932; it threatened the second most important market for Canadian exports; and it put at risk the economic links helping to bind the Commonwealth. It was a subject of much concern to the high commissioner in London, George Drew (Diefenbaker's predecessor as party leader), who assumed a highly unconventional role as a defender of Commonwealth interests in the public debate in the United Kingdom. At a Commonwealth ministerial meeting in Accra in September 1961, the ministers of finance and of trade and commerce, Donald Fleming and George Hees, took the lead in mobilizing opposition to the British plans. Unfavourable attention in the Canadian press caused the Diefenbaker government to soften its position, at least to the extent of accepting the British decision as a fait accompli, and both the travelling ministers and the high commissioner received instructions to take a more moderate line. Diefenbaker placed his hopes in a Commonwealth Prime Ministers' meeting to discuss the subject, which took place in London in September 1962.

With support for the Common Market low in opinion polls in Britain, Diefenbaker hoped that the meeting might persuade the Macmillan government to change its mind. Unlike other leaders, he was not interested in contingency plans against the success of the British bid, concentrating instead on presenting familiar Canadian arguments about the possibility of expanding Commonwealth trade and the risk to the association if Britain joined the community. These arguments were no more persuasive than they had been in the past, and the British ensured that they were countered by negative press coverage. Britain would be kept out of the Common Market by a French veto the following January, not by domestic opinion in favour of the Commonwealth; but the conference left the Canadian side still feeling that the promise of consultation had not been fulfilled, and Macmillan with his opinion of Diefenbaker again revised downward.[39] He was not the only one on the British side to be disappointed. There was, recalled Sir Saville Garner, the British high commissioner in Ottawa, 'something ... awry' in the relationship.[40]

When the Conservatives were defeated in the election of 8 April 1963 by the Liberals under Pearson, it was Canada's turn to start mending fences. This Pearson had pledged to do with Canada's three major allies, the United States, the United Kingdom, and France, and he started in London, between 1 and 4 May. His reason was partly political, for he thought that if he began with the United States he would be accused of subservience. The choice also was a matter of personal preference: 'I felt so much at home in London,' he wrote in his memoirs, 'that I wanted to go there first.' He knew Macmillan well, along with 'at least half' of the cabinet, and the two prime ministers had a good personal relationship. Pearson had no detailed agenda, as his government, having just assumed office, had not yet begun to make policy decisions. 'I ... had some very good general talks,' he recalled, 'but nothing of great substance.'[41] Macmillan was more interested in discussing general international and 'cold war questions' than specifically bilateral issues, and Pearson was happy to oblige. The two deliberately skirted subjects – the growing imbalance in bilateral trade and differences over nuclear arrangements in NATO – where sharp differences might arise.[42] While most observers were delighted with the visit, the *Manchester Guardian Weekly* glumly observed that 'it is by no means clear to what lengths Anglo-Canadian partnership or Canadian compliance with the programmes on which the two foremost Anglo-Saxon nations are agreed, can be taken by Mr. Pearson.'[43]

The *Guardian* was only partly right. As Macmillan and Pearson discovered in their general *tour d'horizon,* there was still plenty of common ground between London and Ottawa, especially on matters related to the general problem of decolonization and Third World stability. As the likelihood of conflict in Western Europe receded, the Pearson government was anxious to carve out a more distinctive and independent international role for Canada in the unstable and unsettled postcolonial states of Africa, Asia, and the Caribbean.[44] With British encouragement, Canada embarked on an extensive aid program in the former colonies of the British West Indies. In Africa and parts of Asia, Canada often stepped in as Britain retreated, supplying military assistance in order to ensure a Western presence and encourage local stability.[45]

Africa continued to be the scene of the most contentious issues arising from the End of Empire after the unilateral declaration of independence by Rhodesia on 11 November 1965. Rhodesia was dealt with at two Commonwealth Prime Ministers' meetings in 1966. At the first, in Lagos in January, a Canadian initiative that led to the creation of a sanctions committee helped to bridge the gap between the United Kingdom and the African members. Sanctions had not proved effective, however, by the time of the second meeting, in London in September. The British came under heavy pressure from African, Asian, and Caribbean leaders not to grant independence to Rhodesia without majority rule, to support compulsory sanctions, and to endorse the use of force by the United Nations if sanctions failed to work. These propositions were unacceptable to British Prime Minister Harold Wilson, who wanted a negotiated settlement and favoured neither mandatory sanctions nor the use of force except as a last resort. Pearson took the lead in searching for a compromise, which was embodied in the conference communiqué. This included commitments by Wilson, if negotiations with Rhodesia did not succeed by the end of 1966, to recommend to Parliament that majority rule be a condition for independence and to join in sponsoring a UN Security Council resolution calling for mandatory economic sanctions. This outcome was helpful to Wilson, who admired Pearson's performance and declared that only 'Mike could have done it.'[46]

Closer to home, Anglo-Canadian relations were less amicable. Although naturally worried about losing Canada's share of the British market if the United Kingdom joined the European Economic Community, Pearson's government was much more ready than Diefenbaker's to acknowledge that post-imperial Britain belonged in Europe. As part of Europe, the Canadian argument went, Britain would reduce the EEC's tendency to look inwards, and would help strengthen the transatlantic ties between Canada and Europe: 'It would be in the Western interest for London to develop and maintain closer and frequent consultations ... with Paris and Bonn particularly, both with a view to exert[ing] a positive influence ... that would reflect the broader interests of the Atlantic community, and with a view to avoid[ing] cultivating on the Continent any impression that Britain's main or exclusive interests are in her North American ties, thus encouraging the "strictly Europe" tendency to develop further.'[47] This seemed especially important in the early 1960s, as French President Charles de Gaulle's hostility to NATO threatened to destroy its transatlantic character, leaving Canada alone in North America with the United States. Just as important, the Pearson government was determined to meet French-Canadian demands that its foreign policy reflect Canada's bilingual and bicultural reality.[48] Consequently, it had become very important for Ottawa to nurture and develop France's relationship with NATO, however difficult that might be.

It was soon clear to Pearson and his secretary of state for external affairs, Paul Martin, that Wilson's government did not entirely share their perspective. Ottawa was obviously disturbed at the declaration by London's new Labour government in November 1964 that Britain was not interested in joining the EEC, and at London's decision to cancel the Concorde project, a powerful symbol of Anglo-French cooperation (a decision that was reversed shortly afterwards).[49] Still worse, the Labour government plunged into the divisive debate in NATO over the alliance's nuclear arrangements with an ill-conceived proposal for an Atlantic Nuclear Force (ANF). The ANF was to be a new strategic nuclear force, based essentially on existing American and British weapons. It seemed to make little military or political sense, and

Canadian officials suspected that it was 'designed as an attempt to return to the World War II Anglo-American alliance.' In sum, Canadian officials concluded, the British proposals reflected 'a more narrow view of "Atlantic partnership" than our own.' Anglo-Canadian differences over NATO came to a head during Wilson's visit to Ottawa in December 1964. Martin was outspoken in his criticism of Britain's unhelpful approach to France and he attacked the ANF as 'pretty dangerous stuff.' Pearson too expressed concern at the state of relations between London and Paris. An exasperated Wilson replied, with a justified dig at de Gaulle, that 'it was extremely hard to begin until both parties were prepared to talk.'[50] Neither Pearson nor Martin was impressed. At a cabinet meeting the following day, Pearson described Wilson as 'apathetic about the problems facing the Alliance.'[51]

As Canada's concern with the future of French relations with NATO grew throughout 1965, Martin redoubled his efforts to align Ottawa with Paris, much to the irritation of London and Washington. However, his attempt to reduce France's isolation by drafting a ministerial declaration on the future of the Alliance failed when de Gaulle abruptly announced in March 1966 that France would withdraw from NATO's integrated military structure. Undeterred, Martin made sure that Canada's response to the French initiative was among the most moderate in the alliance. But Britain, itching for a showdown with France, quickly took charge of drafting a paper to establish the framework for the negotiations between Paris and NATO's remaining fourteen members. With Washington's blessing, it was determined to make de Gaulle finally pay for his intransigence. In early May, the British minister for NATO affairs, George Thomson, travelled to Ottawa to explain London's thinking. In addition to dealing with the technical issues raised by the French decision, the British paper was to provide an up-to-date justification for the alliance that could be published 'to demonstrate that de Gaulle was not right.' Thomson added that if 'the French chose to reject the position of the fourteen the responsibility for being "unreasonable" would lie with de Gaulle.'[52]

Martin and Pearson were appalled at Britain's determination to isolate Paris. They felt that the paper would simply give de Gaulle grounds to denounce NATO.[53] In Paris, Canada led the way in scuttling the British paper, which was eventually replaced with a much milder Norwegian draft. Canada's mediatory efforts were far from finished. At the June 1966 ministerial meeting, Martin pressed both sides to compromise. He convinced the other fourteen members to postpone a decision on moving the North Atlantic Council from Paris to Brussels, temporarily retaining a symbol of France's continuing political relationship with NATO. It was a difficult and thankless task, which won him few friends. Time and again, he was forced to confront the British foreign secretary, Michael Stewart, leaving both sides resentful. 'Among the fourteen,' Martin complained, 'the British and Germans were consistently the least flexible.' The effects of the disagreement over NATO lingered. A year later, in the spring of 1967, the Canadian High Commission in London observed that, as a result, 'there has been a noticeable gap in Canada House consultations with the Foreign Office.'[54]

Disputes over bilateral trade also disturbed relations under Pearson and Wilson. During the early 1960s, Britain's current account deficit with Canada had shown what British officials described as a 'sharp deterioration,' rising steadily from 166 million dollars in 1960 to 213 million dollars in 1962. Britain acknowledged that the dollar's lower exchange rate and the temporary import surcharges erected to defend the Canadian economy in May 1962 had had an unfortunate impact on British exports. Nevertheless, they tended to fix the blame on Canada's Customs Act, especially the provisions used to establish the value of imports for duty purposes, and to apply anti-dumping duties.[55] During the spring and fall of 1963, Britain made no secret of its mounting irritation. In a well-publicized speech in Montreal shortly after Pearson's election, British High Commissioner Lord Amory characterized Anglo-Canadian trade as 'rather seriously out of balance at present.' The refrain was picked up by several British ministers, and was repeated at the 1963 meeting of the United Kingdom-Canada Continuing Committee (UKCCC) and in written representations by the British high commissioner.[56]

In response to continued pleading from Amory's successor, Sir Henry Lintott, the Canadian minister of trade and commerce, Mitchell Sharp, finally agreed in the fall of 1963 to ask his senior officials to explore the problem in greater detail. Simon Reisman, the tough-minded and combative assistant deputy minister of finance, led the investigation. His June 1964 report rejected the key British demand for a change in Canada's anti-dumping legislation, believing that it would harm Canadian producers vis-à-vis the United States. Instead, and only very reluctantly, he recommended adjusting the provisions for valuation for duty that discriminated against British producers. He cautioned that this would provide 'no more than marginal assistance to the British exporter ... [and] will not solve the major problem, which is the lack of competitiveness of UK exports in the Canadian market.' Although the proposed change was minor, Reisman argued against acting precipitately, suggesting that the government might want to use the prospective amendment as a bargaining chip during the Kennedy Round of the GATT.[57]

The cabinet agreed with Reisman's unsympathetic approach. When Sharp and the minister of finance, Walter Gordon, visited London in late June 1964, they dangled the possibility of an amendment to the Customs Act in front of British ministers, explaining that the necessary legislation was still several months in the offing. British ministers were not impressed.[58] They were even less impressed when they learned in December 1965 that Canada and the United States were about to conclude a free trade agreement for automobiles and automotive parts. The timing could not have been worse, as the news came on the heels of a balance-of-payments crisis that forced the Wilson government to impose stiff measures to reduce imports and take immediate steps to increase exports. The British were understandably irritated with the new Autopact, which effectively eliminated the 17.5 percent preference enjoyed by British automotive exports. But London was also deeply upset by Ottawa's apparent unwillingness to consult. 'Canada was less forthcoming,' accused the under-secretary of the board of trade, 'than the USA.'[59] The British high commissioner told Sharp that he felt 'that Canada had not been entirely sincere in her efforts to assist Britain in her present balance-of-trade difficulties.'[60]

In February 1965, in what Pearson described as a 'sternly worded message,' the British prime minister acknowledged the necessity of the Autopact from Canada's perspective, but regretted the loss of Britain's preference. Echoing Canadian arguments that the agreement was intended to rationalize the North American auto industry and make it much more competitive, Wilson pointed out how ironic it was that Canada's anti-dumping laws would prevent Britain from meeting that competition. Instead, as Canadian and American producers grew more efficient and reduced their prices, Britain would be forced from the market. The UK did not want a hand-out, Wilson averred; it just wanted the chance to compete.[61] Although the Department of Finance dismissed British fears as 'exaggerated,' officials in the Department of External Affairs, worried about the growing strain on Canada's relations with Britain, suggested a more conciliatory approach.[62] Pearson agreed, and a committee of senior officials was put to work looking for a solution.

In late April, Jake Warren, the deputy minister of trade and commerce, led a delegation of senior officials to London for talks with the British. In his pocket, he carried one small concession. At long last, Canada was ready to implement its 1964 promise to adjust its valuation procedures. Indeed, as part of these changes in the Customs Act, Canadian officials also proposed a technical adjustment that would alter the basis on which British automobiles were valued for duty. Calculating the 20 percent discount normally applied to British automotive imports on the basis of the British tax-included price, rather than the pre-tax price, generated a slightly larger discount, and had the effect of reducing the final price to consumers by about 4.5 percent.[63] Warren's mission seemed to lift the cloud that hung over Anglo-Canadian economic relations. Wilson quickly thanked Pearson, declaring that the talks marked 'the opening of a new phase in trade relations between Canada and Britain.'[64] The Canadian view was more restrained – and rightly so. British exporters soon realized that these slight changes to Canadian valuation for duty regulations would not solve their export woes, and London again charged Ottawa with deliberately restricting its exports.

The dispute over NATO and the endless squabbling over bilateral trade worried Martin, who was concerned that Canada's relations with the United Kingdom were not as good as they could be. For the minister, whose familiarity with the British went back to the 1930s, the root of the problem seemed to go beyond specific issues on which the two governments disagreed. 'Something,' he wrote in his memoirs, 'was lacking. I could not put my finger on it, because I knew it had more to do with the appearance than the substance of our political relationships.'[65] What he seems to have missed was the intimacy of earlier days. There did not seem to be quite the degree of frankness of confidence that should exist, he told the British high commissioner in April 1966.[66] Canada's deputy high commissioner in London, Geoffrey Murray, also saw a need for improvement. The result was a decision to have the situation examined, both in Ottawa and by Murray in London.

The Ottawa study showed that the minister's concern was not shared by the Department of External Affairs. The Department acknowledged that over the years there had been both major divergences of international importance (the Suez Crisis being identified as a landmark event) and numerous disagreements on bilateral issues. But its preliminary conclusion was that, although consultation might be improved at both the official and ministerial levels, 'in terms of substantial policy differences our problems today with Britain are neither more numerous nor more serious than at other periods.'[67] Murray's report was more comprehensive, reviewing the weakening of traditional ties since the Second World War and then assessing the irritants that had emerged in the mid-1960s. The latter fell into two main categories: economic decisions by the Canadian government that the British found to be to their disadvantage; and Canada's concern that it was being excluded from Anglo-American consultations on matters in which it had an interest, such as NATO policy and the war in Vietnam. The best way of bringing about improvement, Murray thought, would be to create a Canada-United Kingdom ministerial committee, similar to one that existed between Canada and the United States. This recommendation, a less-precise version of which also appeared in the department's preliminary observations, was accepted, and the committee had its first meeting in London on 19 and 20 April 1967. This meeting was considered in Ottawa to have been a good start, although the ministers who took part were disappointed by the scant attention it received in the British press. An important reason, the High Commission suggested, was that the public's attention was focused on their government's plans to make a renewed approach to the European Economic Community (which after merging with two other European organizations became the European Community later that year). This was even more likely than in the past to weaken British links with Canada and the rest of the Commonwealth, for, the High Commission reported, 'general opinion here' was now in favour of joining.[68]

In these circumstances, the new committee, however useful, was likely to have only a limited effect. After taking up his posting as high commissioner in 1967, Charles Ritchie, another Canadian long familiar with Britain, commented on the loss of intimacy compared with earlier days. The affection for England was there, he wrote in his diary, 'but British influence was gone ... We and the British were excellent friends who had known each other for a long time, but we were no longer members of the same family ... There remained the bonds of the past, but our future was no longer any concern of theirs. If our preoccupations were with the United States, theirs were increasingly with Europe.'[69] Ritchie and his generation were now approaching retirement, and the first to go would be Pearson, who at the end of 1967 announced his intention to leave politics. In the Department of External Affairs, his impending departure was recognized as having important implications for the relationship with the United Kingdom. 'One of the changes that will occur following the Liberal leadership convention,' the Commonwealth Division noted, 'is that we will no longer have as Prime Minister a man who, by training and by nature, was able to follow events in Britain and interpret them for himself; he did this both as a professional diplomat who had served in London and as an historian imbued with a deep sense of British constitutionalism.' 'With the departure of Mr. Pearson,' the memorandum continued, 'the urgency of developing a policy vis-à-vis Britain ... is becoming more and more apparent.'[70]

Early in April 1968, the Liberal party chose Pierre Trudeau as Pearson's successor. Although he had studied at the London School of Economics, Trudeau was a newcomer to politics who, apart from an interest in the constitution, had not in his previous career as a lawyer and academic found it necessary to give much thought to Canada's relationship with the United Kingdom. Left to its own devices, it did not seem likely that his government would do so: the first meeting of the newly formed Canada-United Kingdom ministerial committee in April 1967 also proved to be its last. There was, however, another consultative body, at the official level: the United Kingdom-Canada Continuing Committee on Trade and Economic Affairs, which had been in existence since 1948.[71] The prospect of a meeting of this group, plus Trudeau's commitment to a review of foreign policy, including a special study of Europe, provided the Department of External Affairs with the occasion to give some attention to the United Kingdom.

The initiative was taken by the assistant under-secretary responsible for economic policy, James Langley. Like others, he was concerned about 'a persistent deterioration in the warmth and intimacy' of the relationship, but he was also troubled by unexpected 'bitterness' over matters of comparatively minor importance. The root causes he found in historic changes, including Canada's 'emancipation' from colonial status, its increasing closeness to the United States, and the United Kingdom's decline in international stature. He then reviewed the various irritants that had emerged in recent years, taking note not only of Suez and other hardy perennials, but also of economic issues and the Canadian government's recent preoccupation with the francophone world. The same 'careful thought and analysis' as this last subject had received, he suggested, should be given to policy toward the United Kingdom, with a view to developing 'a programme for restoring and enhancing those ties of common interest, economic, political, social and cultural, which will survive the process of change.'[72] Yet no program emerged, and the United Kingdom received only modest coverage – in a paper dealing with broader European issues – in the foreign policy review completed in June 1970. This outcome may have been disappointing, but in the eyes of critics it was of little importance by comparison with the major omission from the review, a paper on relations with the United States. Much more significant so far as Britain was concerned was the outcome of another review, dealing with defence policy. In April 1969, Trudeau had announced that his government had decided to cut back its military commitment to NATO, and in 1970 the Canadian contingent in Europe was reduced by half. This decision produced widespread concern in Europe, including a strong response from the British defence minister, Denis Healey.

Wilson's defeat by the Conservatives under Edward Heath on 18 June 1970 was not likely to bring about change. 'Mr. Heath's commitment to Europe is stronger than Mr. Wilson's,' Charles Ritchie warned, 'and there is [a] commensurate dilution of interest in [the Commonwealth].' Heath might have used 'less offensive language' than Healey about Canada's decision on NATO, but he had been equally troubled by it, and the doubts raised about Canada's commitment to Europe were causing problems of credibility. There was 'a tendency in [London],' the high commissioner continued, 'to think that [Canada] has not ... looked at the wider perspective of our relations with [Britain] nor sufficiently considered what value and effort should be attached to this relationship as a whole, when the advancing political and economic integration in Europe may threaten to lock us more tightly into a North American system and when our requirement for friends in the European courts may be that much more pressing.' In these circumstances, he advised, it was dangerous to take Britain for granted, and the relationship should be examined in the round, rather than piecemeal. There were strengths to build on. One of long standing was the frequency of consultation at the ministerial, parliamentary, and official levels. Another of very recent date was the rescue on 6 December 1970 of Britain's senior trade commissioner in Montreal, James Cross, following his kidnapping by members of the separatist Front de Libération du Québec. This, Ritchie assured Ottawa, had given the British a better understanding of Canada's domestic situation and had enhanced the stature of Prime Minister Trudeau.[73]

Working against following up immediately on Ritchie's recommendation was another issue in Africa related to the end of empire: The United Kingdom's announcement that it intended to resume certain arms sales to South Africa under the terms of the Simonstown Agreement. This decision, which was deeply troubling to African members of the Commonwealth, became a subject of disagreement between Trudeau and Heath prior to a Commonwealth heads of government meeting in Singapore in January 1971. The meeting itself, however, proved helpful to their relationship, for the British acknowledged 'a great debt of gratitude' for Trudeau's contribution to securing wording acceptable to all in a conference declaration dealing with regimes with offensive racial policies.[74] Although the Canadian attitude to African questions was something that Heath would continue to find 'sometimes ... difficult to understand,'[75] the improved atmosphere after the Singapore meeting was more favourable to Ritchie's recommendation. Several circumstances made it appropriate to do something. On 15 August 1971, President Richard Nixon, in response to a severe foreign exchange crisis, announced a series of measures adversely affecting exporters to the United States, causing Canada to search for means of offsetting its growing dependence on that market. Shortly afterwards, Jake Warren was appointed as Ritchie's successor. In his first call on the permanent under-secretary at the Foreign and Commonwealth Office, Sir Denis Greenhill, Warren was told that 'more thought was currently being given in Whitehall' to relations with Canada 'than had been [the] case in recent years.'[76]

The Department of External Affairs finally initiated a study of relations with the United Kingdom in April 1972. The High Commission in London, which submitted its views in August, thought that the timing was good, for the United Kingdom, like Canada, was searching for counterweights to the United States in the aftermath of Nixon's economic measures. The High Commission now defined the connection between the two countries very much in the context of Britain's entry into the European Community in 1972. Goodwill would be important not only to advancing Canada's remaining interests in the British market but also to making the community friendly to outsiders, and hence to enhancing its potential as an offsetting influence, political as well as economic, to dominance by the United States.[77]

The draft study prepared in Ottawa, ready by October, was somewhat less optimistic about the possibilities of the United Kingdom as an advocate within the European Community, but nonetheless thought they were worth pursuing. The paper accepted the British government's view that easier access to the European market was likely to strengthen the United Kingdom's economy and, as a side effect, to increase its political influence. Not surprisingly, in view of this assessment of Britain's prospects, the conclusion was that a major effort should be made to enhance Canada's relationship with the United Kingdom.[78] By now, however, the Trudeau government was campaigning for re-election. One of its platform documents was a review of relations with the United States that had come to the conclusion that Canada should seek greater diversification in its associations, but the United Kingdom was no longer seen as the key to this refocusing, as it once would have been. Instead, the alternative was to be sought in a broader range of prosperous economic partners, in Europe generally, and Japan.[79] This conclusion was supported by statistical trends. Briefly, in 1971 and 1972, the United Kingdom lost first place to the United States as the homeland of immigrants to Canada; in 1972, Japan moved into second place as a source of imports; and in the following year Britain fell behind Japan as a market.[80] It would still be desirable, the external affairs minister was told, to 'remove the element of "drift" from the Canada-UK relationship.' That relationship, however, would 'become increasingly subordinate to the overall Canada-Europe relationship and influenced by the state of Canada/US rapport. In that context, Canadian relations with the UK will be increasingly measured against our relations with other European countries, notably [the Federal Republic of] Germany and France.'[81] Examination, in other words, had starkly revealed the limitations of the relationship with the United Kingdom. For Canada, the days of empire were truly a thing of the past, and the former mother country was now seen as important primarily in the context of a changing Europe.

Notes

1 C.P. Stacey, *Arms, Men and Governments: The War Policies of Canada, 1939-1945* (Ottawa: Information Canada, 1970), 58-60; J.W. Pickersgill and D.F. Forster, eds., *The Mackenzie King Record*, Vol. 2: *1944-1945* (Toronto: University of Toronto Press, 1968), 72, 74-75, 112-13; Lester B. Pearson, *Mike: The Memoirs of the Right Honourable Lester B. Pearson* (Toronto: University of Toronto Press, 1973), Vol. 2: 106-7; Hector Mackenzie, 'An Old Dominion and the New Commonwealth: Canadian Policy on the Question of India's Membership, 1947-49,' *Journal of Imperial and Commonwealth History* 27/3 (1999): 82-112.

2 John English, *The Worldly Years: The Life of Lester Pearson*, Vol. 2: *1949-1972* (Toronto: Alfred A. Knopf, 1992), 86.

3 Under-Secretary of State for External Affairs (USSEA) to Secretary of State for External Affairs (SSEA), 9 December 1955, reprinted in *Documents on Canadian External Relations [DCER]*, vol. 22: *1956-57, Part 1*, ed. Greg Donaghy (Ottawa: Canada Communication Group, 2001), 1387-92.

4 L.B. Pearson, memorandum for SSEA, 20 October 1955, reprinted in *DCER*, vol. 21: *1955*, ed. Greg Donaghy (Ottawa: Canada Communication Group, 1999), 1236-38.

5 J.W. Holmes, memorandum for the USSEA, 8 March 1956, and R.A.D. Ford, memorandum by head of the European Division, 13 March 1956, reprinted in *DCER*, vol. 22: 5-12. On Pearson's conversation with Eden, see ibid., 1302-7; on his conversation with Dulles, ibid., 69-70. On the general shift in Canadian position, see John W. Holmes, *The Shaping of Peace: Canada and the Search for World Order, 1943-1957* (Toronto: University of Toronto Press, 1982), vol. 2: 351-52.

6 London to Ottawa, telegram 996, 27 July 1956, reprinted in *DCER*, vol. 22: 131-32.

7 PM of the UK to PM of Canada, 28 July 1956, reprinted in ibid., 132.

8 Ottawa to London, telegram J-1063, 28 July 1956, reprinted in ibid., 133.

9 Ottawa to London, telegram M-1064, 28 July 1956, and Ottawa to London, telegram M-1070, 30 July 1956, reprinted in ibid., 133-37. See also ibid., 138, n. 104.

10 Public Record Office, London (PRO), Prime Minister's Office (PREM) 12/1094, Eden minute on UK high commissioner in Canada to Commonwealth Relations Office (CRO), Telegram no. 734, 30 July 1956. The authors would like to thank Brian Hearnden for providing the British documentation on which this discussion is based.

11 PRO, Foreign Office (FO) 371/119088, Caccia's note on Gladwyn Jebb to Sir Harold Caccia, 31 July 1956.

12 PRO, Dominions Office (DO) 35/6314, Sir Archibald Nye to Sir Gilbert Laithwaite, permanent under-secretary of state for Commonwealth relations, 1 August 1956.

13 J. Léger, memorandum for the SSEA, 30 July 1956, reprinted in *DCER*, 22: 136-37.

14 PRO, PREM 11/1094, record of a conversation between the secretary of state for Commonwealth relations and the Canadian high commissioner, 15 August 1956.

15 Ibid., foreign secretary to the prime minister, 17 August 1956, and Eden's marginalia.

16 New York to Ottawa, telegram 755, 25 September 1956, reprinted in *DCER*, 22: 167-69.

17 London to Ottawa, telegram G-1418, 30 October 1956, reprinted in ibid., 179.

18 J.L. Granatstein, *A Man of Influence: Norman A. Robertson and Canadian Statecraft, 1929-1968* (Toronto: Deneau, 1981), 301.

19 PM of the UK to PM of Canada, 30 July 1956, reprinted in *DCER*, 22: 182-83.

20 English, *Life of Pearson*, Vol. 2: 134.

21 PM of Canada to PM of the UK, 31 October 1956, reprinted in *DCER*, 22: 187-88.

22 Memorandum from Commonwealth and Middle East Division to the USSEA, 2 November 1956, reprinted in ibid., 197-98.

23 Cited in English, *Life of Pearson*, Vol. 2: 135.

24 London to Ottawa, telegram 1501, 1 November 1956, reprinted in *DCER*, 22: 191-92.

25 Canada, Department of External Affairs, *The Crisis in the Middle East* (Ottawa: Queen's Printer, 1957), 10.

26 Arnold Heeney, memorandum for file, 3 November 1956, reprinted in ibid., 205.

27 Memorandum from Permanent Mission to the UN to SSEA, 3 November 1956, reprinted in ibid., 207-8.

28 Anthony Eden, *The Memoirs of the Rt. Hon. Sir Anthony Eden . . .: Full Circle* (London: Cassell, 1960), 541; Pearson, *Mike*, Vol. 2: 274.

29 PRO, DO 34/6334, Neil Pritchard to A.W. Snelling, 16 November 1956.

30 PRO, PREM 11/1097, Garner to the permanent under-secretary of state for Commonwealth relations, 14 December 1956.

31 Granatstein, *A Man of Influence*, 308.

32 PRO, FO 115/4545, Sir Pierson Dixon to Sir Ivone Kirkpatrick, 22 December 1956.

33 John Hilliker and Donald Barry, *Canada's Department of External Affairs*, Vol. 2: *Coming of Age, 1946-1968* (Montreal and Kingston: McGill-Queen's University Press, 1995), 125, 128; George H. Gallup, *The Gallup Poll: Public Opinion, 1935-1971*, Vol. 2: *1949-1958* (New York: Random House, 1972), 1455. There was a willingness at the time to accept the poll as representative of national opinion. *La Presse* (Montreal), 12 November 1956. Cf. James Eayrs, 'Canadian Policy and Opinion during the Suez Crisis,' *International Journal* 12/2 (1957): 98-108.

34 J. H. Aitchison, 'Canadian Foreign Policy in the House and on the Hustings,' *International Journal* 12/4 (1957): 285-87; John Meisel, *The Canadian General Election of 1957* (Toronto: University of Toronto Press, 1962), 273-77.

35 Alistair Horne, *Macmillan* (London: Macmillan, 1989), Vol. 2: 57; H. Basil Robinson, *Diefenbaker's World: A Populist in Foreign Affairs* (Toronto: University of Toronto Press, 1989), 14; Denis Smith, *Rogue Tory: The Life and Legend of John G. Diefenbaker* (Toronto: MacFarlane, Walter and Ross, 1995), 252-57, 299-301; J.L. Granatstein, *Canada, 1957-1967: The Years of Uncertainty and Innovation* (Toronto: McClelland and Stewart, 1986), 44-45.

36 Smith, *Rogue Tory*, 252, 254, 290.

37 Ibid., 353-66; also Hilliker and Barry, *Canada's Department*, Vol. 2: 163-66, and John Hilliker, 'The Politicians and the "Pearsonalities": The Diefenbaker Government and the Conduct of Canadian External Relations,' Canadian Historical Association *Historical Papers* (1984): 160-61.

38 Quoted in Horne, *Macmillan*, 2: 394. On this subject, see also Peter Henshaw, 'Canada and the "South African Disputes" at the United Nations, 1946-1961,' *Canadian Journal of African Studies* 33/1 (1999): 27-36.
39 Horne, *Macmillan*, 2: 356.
40 Robinson, *Diefenbaker's World*, 267; Hilliker, 'The Politicians and the "Pearsonalities,"' 161-64; Hilliker and Barry, *Canada's Department*, Vol. 2: 227-30; Smith, *Rogue Tory*, 421-25, 450. On economic relations in this period, see also Bruce Muirhead, 'From Dreams to Reality: The Evolution of Anglo-Canadian Trade During the Diefenbaker Era,' *Journal of the Canadian Historical Association* 9 (1998): 243-66.
41 Pearson, *Mike*, Vol. 3: *1957-1968*, 98-100; English, *Life of Pearson*, 2: 268-69.
42 NAC, Privy Council Office Records (RG2), vol. 6253, Cabinet Conclusions, 7 May 1963.
43 Cited in John Saywell, ed., *The Canadian Annual Review for 1963* (Toronto, University of Toronto Press, 1964), 315.
44 Greg Donaghy, *Tolerant Allies: Canada and the United States, 1963-1968* (Montreal and Kingston: McGill-Queen's University Press, 2002), 93-96.
45 Greg Donaghy, 'The Rise and Fall of Canadian Military Assistance in the Developing World, 1952-1971,' *Canadian Military History* (Spring 1995): 75-84.
46 English, *Life of Pearson*, Vol. 2: 370; Hilliker and Barry, *Canada's Department*, Vol. 2: 282-84.
47 NAC, Department of External Affairs Records (RG25), vol. 10042, file 20-Brit-1-3, Talking Points re: British relations with Europe, 2 February 1965.
48 See Greg Donaghy, 'Domesticating NATO: Canada and the North Atlantic Alliance, 1963-68,' *International Journal* 52/3 (1997): 449; see also Hilliker and Barry, *Canada's Department*, Vol. 2: 391-412, and Dale Thomson, *Vive le Québec Libre* (Toronto: Deneau, 1988), 106.
49 NAC, RG 25, vol. 3493, file 18-1-D-Brit-1964/1, brief on Europe for the visit of the British prime minister and the NATO ministerial meeting, December 1964; ibid., British proposals on an Atlantic Nuclear Force, 3 December 1964.
50 Ibid., record of a talk between the PM and the Rt. Hon. Patrick Gordon Walker [9 December 1964], and Meeting of the PM with the PM of Britain: notes of a discussion following dinner at the prime minister's on 9 December 1964.
51 NAC, RG 2, vol. 6265, cabinet conclusions, 10 December 1964.
52 NAC, RG 25, vol. 8839, file 27-4-NATO-12-1966-Spring, NATO to Ottawa, Telegram 939, 3 May 1966; Ottawa to NATO, Telegram DL-1359, 18 May 1966. See also NAC, Paul Martin papers, vol. 226, Summary record: discussion between SSEA and British ambassador for NATO affairs, 18 May 1966.
53 NAC, RG 25, vol. 8839, file 27-4-NATO-12-1966-Spring, Ottawa to London, Telegram, DL-1384 and DL-131, 20 May and 9 June 1966.
54 NAC, RG25, vol. 10042, file 20-1-2-Brit, notes on Canada-UK relations by Geoffrey Murray.
55 NAC, RG25, vol. 3500, file 19-1-BA-BRIT-1963, prime minister's briefing book: trade relations between Canada and Britain [May 1963].
56 Department of Foreign Affairs and International Trade [DFAIT], file 37-8-6, S.S. Reisman, memorandum to the cabinet committee on finance and economic policy, 16 June 1964. The renaming of the Department of External Affairs was announced in 1993. Files cited as at DFAIT had not been transferred to the NAC at the time of writing.
57 DFAIT, file 37-8-6, S.S. Reisman, memorandum to the cabinet committee on finance and economic policy, 16 June 1964.
58 DFAIT, file 37-7-1-USA-2, Lionel Chevrier to Paul Martin, 8 February 1965.
59 Ibid., London to Ottawa, Telegram 4428, 30 December 1964.
60 NAC, RG2, vol. 6265, cabinet conclusions, 18 February 1965.
61 Ibid.; see also DFAIT, file 37-7-1-USA-2, message from the Rt. Hon. Harold Wilson to the Rt. Hon. Lester Pearson, 15 February 1965.
62 DFAIT, file 37-7-1-USA-2, J.R. McKinney to A.E. Ritchie, 1 February 1965.
63 NAC, RG2, vol. 6274, memorandum for cabinet, 28 April 1965.
64 DFAIT, file 37-7-1-USA-2, Harold Wilson to Lester Pearson, 15 February 1965.

65　Paul Martin, *A Very Public Life* (Toronto: Deneau, 1985), Vol. 2: 407.

66　NAC, RG 25, vol. 10042, file 20-1-2-Brit, Basil Robinson (Deputy USSEA) to USSEA, 15 April 1966.

67　Ibid., USSEA to SSEA, 14 June 1966.

68　Ibid., London to Ottawa, 8 May 1967, Letter 789; Hilliker and Barry, *Canada's Department*, Vol. 2: 323-24.

69　Charles Ritchie, *Storm Signals: More Undiplomatic Diaries, 1962-1971* (Toronto: Macmillan of Canada, 1983), 90.

70　NAC, RG 25, vol. 10042, file 20-1-2-BRIT, Commonwealth Division to African and Middle Eastern Division and others, 4 March 1968; Hilliker and Barry, *Canada's Department*, Vol. 2: 325.

71　NAC, RG 25, vol. 8625, file 20-1-2-BRIT, R.M. Middleton to Bureau of European Affairs, 12 October 1972, and enclosure, 'Anglo-Canadian Relations,' n.d. We are grateful to Mary Halloran for providing much of the documentation on which this section is based.

72　NAC, RG25, vol. 8624, Canada's Relations with Britain, n.d.

73　Ibid., London to Ottawa, 11 December 1970, telegram 4044; also SSEA, *Foreign Policy for Canadians: Europe* (Ottawa: Information Canada, 1970), 17, 21.

74　Ibid., London to Ottawa, 28 January 1971, telegram 276.

75　Ibid., London to Ottawa, 21 September 1971, telegram 3170.

76　Ibid., London to Ottawa, 5 October 1971, telegram 3342.

77　Ibid., London to Ottawa, 10 August 1972, Letter 923, and enclosure, 'Anglo-Canadian Relations,' August 1972.

78　Ibid., R.M. Middleton to Bureau of European Affairs, 12 October 1972, and enclosure, 'Anglo-Canadian Relations,' n.d.

79　Mitchell Sharp, 'Canada–US Relations: Options for the Future,' *International Perspectives* (Autumn 1972): 1-24.

80　F.H. Leacy, ed., *Historical Statistics of Canada*, 2nd ed. (Ottawa: Ministry of Supply and Services, 1983), A385-416, G401-14.

81　NAC, RG25, vol. 8625, file 20-1-2-BRIT, USSEA to SSEA, 19 February 1973.

3
'Ready, Aye, Ready' No More? Canada, Britain, and the Suez Crisis in the Canadian Press

José E. Igartua

On 27 November 1956, the Progressive Conservative Foreign Affairs critic in the Canadian House of Commons, Howard C. Green, claimed that 'the United States would have far more admiration for Canada, Mr. Speaker, if this government stopped being the United States chore boy ... Now this government, by its actions in the Suez Crisis, has made this month of November, 1956, the most disgraceful period for Canada in the history of this nation.' Lester B. Pearson, secretary of state for external affairs, retorted: 'The hon. Gentleman who has just taken his seat talked about Canada being the chore boy of the United States. Our record over the last years, Mr. Speaker, gives us the right to say we have performed and will perform no such role. It is bad to be a chore boy of the United States. It is equally bad to be a colonial chore boy running around shouting "Ready, aye, ready."'

'Ready, aye, ready' no more, Pearson was saying. Since July 1956, he had grown increasingly disillusioned, discouraged, and even distraught at the British government's reaction to Nasser's nationalization of the Suez Canal Company. Pearson was a firm believer in collective security through the United Nations, and he wanted the Suez issue resolved in that forum through peaceful international agreement.[1] The St. Laurent government agreed with its secretary of state for external affairs.[2] Its position had been communicated to the British government in the summer of 1956. The British had led the Canadians to believe that they would rely on the United Nations and seek a resolution of the issue there.

Yet at the end of October 1956, the Eden government, together with that of France, colluded with Israel in creating a reason for military intervention in the canal zone. Israel invaded Egypt on 29 October. The next day, Britain and France issued an 'ultimatum' enjoining Israel and Egypt to stop fighting, or they would take 'such military action as may be necessary to compel the offender to conform,' as Eden wrote St. Laurent.[3] Twenty-four hours later, British and French armed forces began air attacks against Egypt, even while the United Nations Security Council was grappling with the Israeli invasion. Canada had not been apprised of the impending Anglo-French intervention, and the Canadian prime minister complained to Eden that 'the first intimation I had of your government's intention to take certain grave steps in Egypt was from the press reports of your statements in the House of Commons.' The Canadian government's policy was to 'shape our course in conformity with what we regard as our obligations under the Charter of and our membership in the United Nations,' St. Laurent indicated to Eden.[4] It would not be 'a chore boy running around shouting "Ready, aye, ready."'

Yet many Canadians were quick to rise to Britain's side. On the day after Nasser nationalized the Suez Canal Company in late July 1956, Progressive Conservative Opposition MP John G. Diefenbaker rose in the House of Commons to ask whether the Canadian government 'ought not to join with Britain in condemnation of what has taken place there in a perversion of international contracts, and also indicate to Britain and the other nations Canada's agreement with the stand which they are taking to meet this situation?'[5] Diefenbaker never intimated whether Canada's agreement with Britain should involve more than moral support, but he was not alone in believing that Canada should stand firmly with Britain. Perhaps the most forceful expression of this sentiment came when the Suez Crisis took a military turn. The day after Canada refrained from voting on the UN resolution condemning the Anglo-French aggression in Egypt, the *Calgary Herald* issued a vociferous condemnation of the Canadian position:

> Tuesday, October 30, will go down in Canada's history as a day of shock and shame.
>
> On that day the government of Canada chose to run out on Britain at a time when Britain was asserting the kind of leadership the world has missed, and needed, in these ominous times ...
>
> What degradation is this? ...
>
> The Liberals have been carefully preparing the way for years, discarding the ties of ancestry and Commonwealth one by one, selling out our natural resources and our industry to the highest US bidder.
>
> And now we have the ultimate sell-out.
>
> They have sold out our decency and our honor.[6]

The Suez incident became a litmus test of Canada's sense of place on the international scene, of Canadian values, and of national unity. It provoked both defenders and opponents of the Canadian position at the United Nations into arguments based on varying conceptions of what Canada was as a country, and what it should be. It quickly became the object of partisan debate in the press. Newspaper editors, and their readers, were sharply divided on the issue.[7] And interest in the issue went much beyond the editorial offices of newspapers or the pronouncements of habitual writers of letters to the editor. The Canadian public was generally well aware of the Middle East situation. A Canadian Institute of Public Opinion [Gallup] poll, in September 1956, indicated that 87 percent of the 1,970 respondents had 'heard of the Suez Canal dispute.' Regionally, this awareness ranged from a low of 72 percent in Newfoundland to a high of 97 percent in British Columbia. More than two-thirds of the survey's French-speaking Quebec respondents had also heard of it. Canadians did not, however, feel very exercised by the Suez issue. Gallup asked whether it was better to 'risk war or give Egypt control of Suez.' Less than a quarter were ready to risk war, a third were explicitly ready to allow Egypt to control the canal, and 40 percent could not express a clear opinion on the question. The regional variation was pronounced, with only 14 percent of Quebec respondents willing to wage war (76 respondents out of 543 – the rate for French-speaking respondents was only 9 percent), and up to 45 percent in British Columbia, where only 26 percent were willing to let Egypt control the canal.[8]

The Gallup poll taken the following month showed that Canadians on the whole remained favourably disposed towards Great Britain's foreign policy – more, in fact, than towards US foreign policy. The October 1956 poll asked whether US foreign policy was losing America friends. Of those who offered an opinion, 42 percent agreed with the statement, while only 39 percent agreed to a similar question about UK foreign policy. Only in Alberta was there a larger number of respondents agreeing with the statement about UK foreign policy than disagreeing with it, though the small number of Alberta respondents makes this a dubious measure. Opinion was evenly divided among Quebec's francophone respondents, but surprisingly, so was it among British Columbia's respondents. Ontarians had a more positive opinion of Great Britain's foreign policy, with two-thirds of those expressing an opinion believing that the UK was not losing friends because of its foreign policy. Overall, although 28.5 percent of the 2,040 Gallup respondents thought the United Kingdom's foreign policy was losing it friends, only 150 (7.4 percent) specifically alluded to the Middle East crisis as a reason for this.[9]

The Suez Crisis forced Canadians to reassess Canada's role in international affairs. While the Middle East situation did not directly involve Canada, it raised issues of foreign policy that affected the country's relationship with Great Britain, France, and the United States, the three most influential countries in Canada's development. Traditionally, these three countries had taken similar positions on international affairs, and Canada had fought alongside all three in two world wars. The Suez Crisis disrupted this pattern and forced the Canadian government out of its self-satisfied definition as the 'bridge' between the two great English-speaking countries. Indeed, the Suez Crisis constituted a significant juncture in the process I call 'the other

Quiet Revolution': the dissolution of English-speaking Canada's self-representation as a 'British' nation.

Like Quebec's Quiet Revolution, the 'other Quiet Revolution' in English-speaking Canada did not appear abruptly, or without warning. It was the culmination of a process that began during the Second World War and continued through the 1950s. It was viewed as an insidious Liberal plot by the *Globe and Mail*, by members of the Progressive Conservative party, and among part of the Canadian intelligentsia.[10] For the *Globe* and other Conservative-leaning newspapers, St. Laurent's administration was bent on dismantling the symbols of Canada's attachment to Great Britain. The creation of a Canadian citizenship in 1946,[11] the promise of a 'distinctive' Canadian flag in the 1948 federal election campaign, the abolition of appeals to the British Privy Council in December 1949, the nomination of a Canadian as Governor General in 1951, and the transformation of Victoria Day into a moveable holiday in 1953, were all seen as manifestations of this insidious plot, hatched by what the Ottawa *Citizen* called in 1946 the 'ultra-nationalists,'[12] a phrase left undefined but that obviously pointed to, in the code of the day, the French-speaking members of the Liberal party.[13] On the celebration of Victoria Day in 1956, the *Globe and Mail* reiterated caustically: 'Disrespect for Canada's past (especially that part of it which related in any way to Britain) is endemic in Ottawa. As the late Herman Goering reached for his pistol whenever he heard the word culture, so Ottawa reaches for the eraser whenever it sees words like Victoria and Royal and Empire and Dominion.'[14]

The defenders of a 'British' definition of Canada conceived of the country as blessed with the wisdom and greatness of British tradition embodied in its political and judicial system, in its educational and literary traditions, and in its manly defence of democracy and decency on the world stage. British immigration had sustained this noble heritage. This definition of Canada as 'British' implicitly and very often explicitly considered British political tradition as the greatest in the world: It had brought liberty and democracy to Europe, to the British Empire, and beyond. Implicit too in this view was that Canadians of other than British ancestry were less likely to make model 'subjects' naturally and had to be 'brought up' to the level of British civilization. This view, common enough in nineteenth-century Canada – witness the Durham report – still held sway among some English-speaking Canadians a century later, in part because of the values the education system had tried to instill in them. But other views of Canada were current as well. A view closely associated with Liberal supporters defined Canada as made up of two nations, the French and the British, who had developed the land in partnership. The nature of the partnership was seldom elaborated on, but it too rested on an 'ethnic' definition of the nation. The 'civic' view of Canada, on the other hand, remained a minority one in the 1950s. It was most often expressed by spokespersons on the left, in the

CCF but also in progressive circles that promoted a bill of rights for Canadians. These circles included the Canadian Jewish Congress, the Trades and Labour Congress, and the Canadian Congress of Labour, as well as the National Council of Women.[15]

This summary sketch of the competing representations of national identity expressed in English-speaking Canada suggests an internal coherence and a national 'essence' that would be hard to demonstrate. Trying to define 'the' English-Canadian national identity would be futile. Charles Tilly summarizes what he calls the emerging view of public identities as agreeing on four basic characteristics. The first is the *relational* nature of such identities. By this Tilly means that identities are located in 'connections among individuals and groups rather than in the minds of particular persons or whole populations.' The second element of this view is '*cultural* in insisting that social identities rest on shared understandings and their representations. [The third] is *historical* in calling attention to the path-dependent accretion of memories, understandings, and means of action within particular identities. The emerging view, finally, is *contingent* in that it regards each assertion of identity as a strategic interaction liable to failure or misfiring rather than a straightforward expression of an actor's attributes.'[16]

Tilly's characterization of public identities has a number of implications for the analysis of this type of discourse. First, collective identities are not fixed attributes of groups, but are historical constructs liable to evolve, as does the nature of the relations within and between groups that give rise to expressions of identity. Second, Tilly's model suggests that identities are enunciated for specific reasons at specific times. From this it follows that expressions of national identity will not necessarily be coherent, either internally or over time. Thus it is important to understand the circumstances of such expressions in order to assess their meaning. Finally, collective identities exist only at the cultural level, that is, as shared representations.

Benedict Anderson has defined the 'nation' as an 'imagined community,' founded in a *belief* in shared characteristics, a shared past and the hope of a shared future.[17] There are no tangible characteristics of nationhood that are shared by all members of the nation. Instead, nations exist when communities believe in their existence; they are grounded in the imagination more than in any objective sociological characteristics of their members. It follows that they have a historical, rather than an essential, existence: they can be born and they can die, when communities no longer believe in them. Likewise, national identity, or the definitions that a community gives of itself as a national entity, are historically constructed and thus are liable to evolve over time. The historical question therefore is to discover why certain forms of national identity are born and why certain forms fade away – specifically, in the present case, what are the processes and circumstances that produced a withering away among English-speaking Canadians of the definition of Canada as a British nation. 'English Canada,' for the purposes of this inquiry, refers to the communicational community, within the Canadian state, whose shared language was and is English. This communicational community has existed since newspapers, the telegraph, and the railway ('print capitalism,' in Benedict Anderson's phrase) first defined this communicational space. The focus is on language, rather than on ethnic or cultural origins, though a language of communication rests on the supposed sharing of cultural referents.

The Suez Crisis began with the invasion of Egypt by Israel on 29 October 1956, and the ultimatum Britain and France issued to Egypt and Israel the next day. On 1 November, Britain and France launched air attacks against Egypt. The United Nations Security Council was unable to deal with the crisis, as Britain and France vetoed the American resolution requesting Israeli withdrawal from the Sinai desert, and the matter was referred to an emergency session of the UN General Assembly.[18] The session began in late afternoon, 1 November, and early the next morning the General Assembly adopted an American resolution calling for a ceasefire. Canada abstained on the resolution rather than vote against it. Pearson flew back from the United Nations emergency session to a Cabinet meeting on Saturday, 3 November, where a Canadian position was agreed upon: Canada would propose the creation of a UN international police force to supervise the ceasefire and to ensure peace in the Middle East. Pearson returned to New York Saturday evening with the Canadian proposal. At 2 a.m. on Sunday morning, the Canadian resolution passed in the UN General Assembly. Canadians could listen to Pearson's speeches at the UN on the CBC network.[19] By Monday, the UN had agreed to the creation of an emergency force, under the direction of Canadian General E.L.M. Burns. But the British and French had sent troops into Egypt on Sunday and only agreed to a ceasefire on Tuesday 6 November.[20]

For the proponents of Canada as a 'British' nation, there was no doubting the fitness and courage of the Anglo-French action in Suez. The most vehement criticism of the Liberal government's position was expressed by the *Calgary Herald*. On 2 November, commenting on St. Laurent's apparent testiness with press-gallery reporters, the paper rhetorically asked:

> Could it be that he does not feel quite right about Canada's running out on Britain at a time of crisis, to hide behind the skirts of the United States?
>
> Does he, perhaps, fear that this time he has gone a bit too far and too fast in edging Canada out of its historic place in the Commonwealth? It was all right when he and his crypto-republicans dropped the 'Royal' out of 'Royal Mail.' It was all right when they bulldozed ahead and appointed a Canadian governor-general. It was all right when the word 'Dominion' disappeared from Canada's name ... But is it all right to sell out Canada's honor,

to run out on Britain openly in time of danger, to court Washington's smile so brazenly?[21]

The editorial's metaphors called into question St. Laurent's masculinity, virtue, and honour. On 3 November, the paper condemned Canada's abstention during the UN vote on the American ceasefire resolution. The paper did not believe that the UN could by itself effect a return to peace: 'The British and French forces already carrying the burden of the struggle are as good a U.N. force as anything. All they are lacking is a United Nations flag.' On 9 November, it again sided clearly with Great Britain and France: 'The world owes its thanks to Britain and France for their prompt intervention between Israel and Egypt in the Middle East.' On 21 November, it even attributed Anthony Eden's ill health in part to 'Canada's deplorable behaviour as the senior Commonwealth partner in the United Nations, [which] undoubtedly had much to do with the strain on the Prime Minister.' The title of the editorial, 'Free Men Are in Debt to Sir Anthony,' linked Britain's action to the defence of freedom, a virtue implicitly British in its essence. The paper's readers, however, were more divided on the issue. While a majority of letters to the editor endorsed the paper's editorial stand, a significant number (10 of 25) disagreed with it.[22]

The other newspaper in the Alberta Southam chain, the *Edmonton Journal*, took a similar, though less vociferous, position, but it too came to see the Liberal government's stand on Suez as an attempt to destroy the British tradition in Canada. On 5 November, it called the conduct of the St. Laurent government a 'disappointment to most Canadians, and especially to all those who value the ties to the Commonwealth.' It blamed the government for failing to mediate between the United States and Great Britain and for joining 'the chorus of misrepresentation and abuse.' Canadian governments, it reminded its readers, had always 'hastened to declare their full support ... when Britain has been confronted with a major crisis threatening her existence as a great power.' All in all, it was 'A Bad Week's Work,' as the paper titled its editorial. Three weeks later, just before Parliament was convened in special session, the paper condemned the government for creating 'deep and bitter resentment in Canada.' It had gained the impression that Americans considered 'that Mr. Pearson's action constituted a sort of declaration of independence – that Canada has now severed its links with the British Commonwealth, and given its allegiance to Washington. Nothing, of course, could be farther from the truth. Our ancient ties with Britain are not so easily broken, however much Mr. Pearson and Mr. St. Laurent may wish to do so.' It called upon the Conservative Opposition to put a motion of nonconfidence against the government, and personal censure against Pearson. The debates during the special session only confirmed its worst fears: the St. Laurent government was effecting 'a deliberate repudiation of the bonds of the Commonwealth.' It proclaimed that 'many government actions in the past decade fall into perspective. They were minor things in themselves – for example, the appointment of a Canadian governor-general, or the dropping of such words as "dominion" and "royal" – but they all had the effect of weakening the formal and symbolic links of the Commonwealth. The suspicion is now almost a certainty that Mr. St. Laurent and his colleagues saw in the complex and confusing Suez crisis a magnificent opportunity to finish the job and break with the Commonwealth altogether.'[23]

The Toronto *Globe and Mail* also used the Suez Crisis to attack the St. Laurent government. It defended Britain's actions and condemned the Canadian government's kowtowing to the Americans. On 2 November, it portrayed the Anglo-French invasion as a replacement for UN action: 'It would seem that the only nations willing and able to keep peace in the Middle East are the two who, at the moment, are so vehemently being denounced as "aggressors."' The paper could not oppose Pearson's proposal for a United Nations military force, as it had put the idea forward itself in the past. It condemned the Liberal government for not having pressed the issue harder at the United Nations: 'The Canadian government has been disastrously wrong in its timidity – first, turning a blind eye to the Middle East; then, when it did see the need to police the area, failing to press home its views in Washington and all of the time giving tacit approval to United States actions and attitudes which prepared the debacle here ... The chickens of apathy, irresponsibility and me-tooism have come home to roost at Ottawa; and it will take more than UN speeches to drive them away.' In the following days, the newspaper published a series called 'Readers' Views on Middle East Crisis' in which readers overwhelmingly expressed support for the British action. The paper cast its support of the British action as an endorsement of the fight for freedom against the tyranny of Nasser or of the Kremlin. Free peoples, it declared, have to choose. 'If they are cowards, who want peace at any price, let them say so ... But if they are men, who have broken the bones of tyrants before and will cheerfully break them again, let them say that instead. And let them say it frequently, firmly, in a voice loud enough to reach well into the Kremlin.'[24] Here again, national character was defined as masculine virtue.

Even the *Vancouver Sun*, ranked at that time among the 'independent' Liberal newspapers,[25] and cautious in its support of the Anglo-French action in Suez, grew increasingly critical of the Canadian government's stand at the United Nations as events unfolded. In its first editorial on the issue, on 1 November 1956, it averred that 'Canadians agree with External Affairs Minister Pearson in regretting "that Britain found it necessary" to send troops into Egypt in the face of the Israeli-Arab crisis.' But it was ready to grant the benefit of the doubt to Britain: 'Yet British governments haven't usually acted in this way without grave reasons. Until recently the British have been regarded as the sobering influence in world affairs.' It 'prayed' Britain and France 'know what they are doing.' The next day, it reflected on the effects among Canadians of the tension between Britain and the United States, 'a question that sharply divides their loyalties.' It called for a reconsideration of the smug Canadian position between our two allies. 'Canada will have to do some straight and sober thinking about her course. This country has toyed for a long time with the notion that we can be both British and American – a bridge between two great nations. The present break in Anglo-American understanding speaks of our failure. The reason may be that we haven't truly tried to consider Britain's point of view.' It was critical of Canada's half-hearted participation in the Commonwealth and began to criticize Canada's lack of support for Britain at the UN. On 3 November 1956, it expressed support for the idea of a UN peace-keeping force but doubted the UN could set one up 'in view of its present inability to make difficult decisions.' It disparaged American foreign policy and Canada's tacit endorsement of it. It supported the Canadian proposal of a UN police force but condemned Canada's failure to stand by Britain: 'the anti-British stand we took by the side of Russia and the United States was a sign of unbalanced judgement.' On 14 November it opined that 'The Liberal government in Ottawa took this attitude [opposing Britain at the UN] apparently in the sincere belief that the United Nations is more important than the Commonwealth and believing also that it had the majority of Canadians behind it. But neither of these things is at present certain.' It later rejected Immigration Minister Jack Pickersgill's statement that the Canadian position at the UN had not been against Britain and added that it might have also been 'against our own ultimate good.'[26]

In the main, however, Liberal newspapers supported the government. The *Toronto Daily Star* and the *Winnipeg Free Press* wholeheartedly stood with the St. Laurent government on the Suez issue. The *Star* had few editorials on the subject. On 5 November, it commended the Canadian government for having 'had the courage to put principles ahead of sentiment' by supporting the UN charter, 'which stands against force as a means of settling international disputes,' rather than following 'her feeling for Britain.' It rejected as sterile and unhelpful in resolving the crisis the position that 'right or wrong Canada should have stuck by Britain; indeed, this sentimental cry already is being echoed by some newspapers.' It again condemned this attitude when Earle Rowe, the Leader of the Opposition, expressed it in the Commons at the opening of the special session of Parliament, calling it 'a perfect exhibition of outdated colonial mentality.' That editorial, aptly enough, was titled 'Colony or Nation?'[27]

The *Winnipeg Free Press* condemned the Anglo-French action on Suez as an attempt on the part of Britain and France to 'appoint themselves "world policemen"' by quoting the British Labour leader, Hugh Gaitskell, as saying that they had no right to do so. It found the situation tragic, for 'to censure Britain is eminently distasteful. But for Canadians to turn their backs on the principles of collective security is unthinkable.' It approved Pearson's expression of 'regret' and hoped 'that his implied disapproval will even now have some effect on the Eden and Mollet Governments.' Yet the next day, its lead editorial was titled 'Be Fair to Britain': It affirmed that 'Britain's aim – to preserve stability in the Middle East against the ambitions of Mr. Nasser and everyone else – is the right aim for all the western nations.' An adjacent column by its London correspondent tried to throw some light on Eden's decision. Over the next two days, while debate was going on at the UN, the paper endorsed Pearson's position, heading its 2 November editorial with 'Mr. Pearson Speaks for Canada' and prodding the federal Cabinet the next day to endorse Pearson's proposal for a peacekeeping force, grandly adding: 'The Canadian Government can in this way render to the cause of peace a service almost unexampled in our history.' The *Free Press* vigorously condemned the Anglo-French troop landings in Egypt of 4 November as 'folly' and praised Pearson for getting the two powers to agree to a UN ceasefire force to replace their troops in Egypt. As a result of Pearson's efforts at the UN, 'this country has attained a new stature at the United Nations and throughout the free world.' It paid close attention to dissension within Conservative ranks in Britain concerning the Suez crisis, as a way of showing that Britain's Suez policy was opposed in Britain as well as elsewhere. Grant Dexter, the paper's Ottawa columnist, also singled out St. Laurent for special praise, noting that he 'took a much keener and immediate interest in these events than is commonly supposed.'[28]

Some Conservative newspapers in central Canada gave their support to the Canadian position at the United Nations. The *Ottawa Journal*'s first editorial on the issue, on 1 November, was apprehensive about Britain's action on Suez, being 'uneasy' about the precedent it was setting for circumventing the United Nations. At the same time, it warned its readers to be 'wary of making common cause with Britain's critics. Downing Street is not without sense, experience and courage.' It conceded that 'many Canadians are disturbed by what Britain and France are doing in Egypt,' and endorsed Pearson's and St. Laurent's 'clear and helpful' statements of Canadian policy regarding the Suez question and the Russian invasion of Hungary. The paper was careful to draw a distinction between Britain and France's willingness to let the UN take over the 'task of maintaining order along the Suez' on the one hand, and Russia's rejection of UN intervention in Hungary on the other. It characterized Canada's proposal of a peacekeeping force including Canadian troops as demonstrating 'the vigor and self-reliance of an independent, responsible nation.'[29]

The Montreal *Gazette*, another Conservative newspaper, had few editorial words on the Suez question, but on 5 November 1956, it endorsed the Pearson plan for the Middle East, while depicting Eden as an anti-appeaser from 1938 who believed British intervention was needed because the UN would be too slow to act. Four days later, commenting on the nomination of General E.L.M. Burns as head of the UN peacekeeping force, it observed that 'Canada's stature in world affairs has grown enormously with United Nations efforts to solve the Middle East crisis.' Some of its readers, however, expressed support for the Anglo-French action and condemned Canada's role at the UN, while others supported the Canadian stand.[30]

On the East Coast, the independent *Halifax Chronicle-Herald* also strongly endorsed the Canadian position on the Suez Crisis and condemned the British action: 'Great Britain has used the veto for the first time in the Security Council – and that to ignore the very basic principles of the United Nations itself.' It was the strongest condemnation of British action in the English-Canadian press. Nevertheless, it found the growing rift between Britain and the United States 'disturbing,' and applauded the 'cautious moving' and 'wise statesmanship' of the Canadian government, which it hoped all Canadians would support. Yet it agreed with Pearson that there was 'no parallel' between the Anglo-French action in Suez and Russia's 'criminal onslaught upon Hungary,' which Pearson had condemned at the UN. It considered 'Canada's Task' as taking the moral lead of the Commonwealth in showing 'a spirit of charity and decency and justice,' a task that, it noted, the *Manchester Guardian* had recognized Canada was undertaking.[31]

Editorial opinion in English-language newspapers was thus divided over the Anglo-French action in the Middle East and Canada's failure to support it at the United Nations. Those who supported Britain stressed the failure of the United Nations to act and the need to resist small-time dictators such as Nasser. Canada, they claimed, should have stood with Britain. Those who opposed the Anglo-French action, on the other hand, were disturbed that Canada was forced to disagree with Britain, but believed Canada had acted on moral grounds, an ethics inherited from the Commonwealth itself, as the *Halifax Chronicle-Herald* intimated. In both cases, 'British' values stood as the foundation on which editorial opinion was expressed.

In light of the fact that the Anglo-French action in the Middle East involved Canada's two 'mother countries,' it is remarkable that English-language newspapers made almost no specific comment about the role of France and about its alliance with Britain. The issue was cast solely as one of Canada's relationship with Britain and of the survival of the Commonwealth. Nor did the English-language press raise the issue of Quebec's opinion on the question.[32] The Quebec press wholeheartedly supported the St. Laurent government and endorsed the idea of Canadian participation in the peacekeeping mission, a departure from the isolationist stance of some French-language newspapers. But this was of no interest to the English-language press. What was at stake was its own self-definition as a British nation, for some a definition that was being abandoned, for others a definition that was being reaffirmed in spite of the failings of Britain itself.

The second major phase of the Suez debates in Canada occurred during the special session of Parliament convened to vote the necessary credits for the Canadian contingent in the UN Emergency Force and to vote as well some relief funds for Hungarian refugees fleeing communist repression. Two statements made by the government in the House drew sharp editorial comment. The first was St. Laurent's implicit inclusion of Britain and France among the 'supermen of Europe' whose time had passed, and the second was Pearson's answer to Howard Green, quoted at the beginning of this chapter, in which he rejected the idea that Canada should be a 'colonial chore boy.' The first provoked near universal condemnation in the English-language press, while the second drew approval in some papers and condemnation in others.

For the *Calgary Herald,* the special session of Parliament was a renewed occasion to condemn Canadian foreign policy in the strongest terms. 'The special session now under way has already proven to the country the futility of its government's policies, and the folly of its impulsive and erroneous judgement of Great Britain and France,' it wrote on 28 November. As for St. Laurent, he was 'displaying that petulance the country has come to expect whenever Mr. St. Laurent finds himself in a tight corner he can't wriggle out of with a well-turned phrase or two. His only contribution has been a meaningless diatribe against the "big powers."' The same editorial snickered at the 'familiar platitudes' the government 'so often uses to cover up its blunders.' The platitudes included the government 'following an "independent" course, free of the shackles of "colonialism,"' an allusion to Pearson's remarks about chore boys. On the same page, the paper published a letter from a 'fourth generation Canadian' who found it 'interesting to note that much of the senseless criticism of Britain comes from Canadians of European or Quebec background. They scorn everything British except the freedom they enjoy under a British flag which permits them to employ that freedom in reviling Britain.' St. Laurent's ethnic origins undoubtedly explained, for this reader, his 'senseless criticism.' The paper returned to its condemnation of St. Laurent when the latter was congratulated by the *Chicago Daily Tribune* on the independence of Canada's foreign policy: The *Tribune,* wrote the *Herald,* 'has long been known for its malicious condemnation of anything British in war or in peace,' and now regarded Canada as being a 'member of that not-too-exclusive band of Britain-haters, thanks to Mr. St. Laurent.' It predicted that 'his words about the "supermen of Europe" will live long in the minds of Canadians as a shocking memorial to the infamous behavior of his government as long as it holds office. Even many of those who have been in agreement with Canada's record in the Middle East found his words too much to stomach.'[33] The *Edmonton Journal* was more forthright in attributing Canadian foreign policy to St. Laurent's personal 'rancor and bitterness' against Britain. 'One gets the impression, reading his speech, of the stored-up hatred of a lifetime suddenly coming to the surface.'[34]

The *Globe and Mail* was more temperate in its criticism of the government. It did not take St. Laurent personally to task. It simply called St. Laurent's remark 'his own, special contribution' to Canada's foreign policy. On 28 November, its editorial 'Men and Supermen' chose to believe St. Laurent was referring not to Britain and France, but to Russia. Yet, assessing the special session in its editorial of 1 December, it recalled St. Laurent's 'spiteful criticism of Britain and France' but emphasized Conservative External Affairs critic John Diefenbaker's call for an international conference made up of France, the United States, and Commonwealth members in Quebec City. On 4 December, it reproduced the *Chicago Daily Tribune*'s editorial of 29 November, which quoted the 'supermen of Europe' remark, ironically labelling the editorial 'a tribute to Canada's Prime Minister'; for the paper, the *Tribune* endorsement confirmed St. Laurent's detestable pro-American leanings. The *Globe and Mail* agreed with Pearson that Canada should be no one's 'chore boy,' insisting that 'nobody has suggested that we should. What is being suggested is that we ought to follow a positive and courageous course in international affairs. What has been established is that we did not.' It condemned Canada's foreign policy as being dictated by the United States: 'We are caught seeming to approve and go along with the confusion in Washington; seeming to assist, to cover up and to justify the US retreat into isolationism.' Canada's 'only real hope' and interest in foreign policy, it argued, 'is our membership in the British Commonwealth,' and Canadian foreign policy should be refashioned accordingly. In late December 1956, commenting on the forthcoming visit of Nehru to Ottawa, it reiterated its commitment to the Commonwealth: 'The British Commonwealth of Nations ... remains the most effective, perhaps the only effective international political organization in the world today.' It also alluded to the 'chore boy' remark with an appreciation of Canada's colonial links to Britain: 'We do not wish to be a British colony today; but we count ourselves fortunate to have been one yesterday.'[35]

The *Vancouver Sun* maintained its independent Liberal approach in its comments on the special session of Parliament. It labelled Canadian foreign policy 'amateurish,' the reason for St. Laurent and Pearson's 'pique in the Commons debates.' The editorial continues: 'They have betrayed what may be part of the motive – jealousy of Britain, the mother country, and perhaps a trace of the colonial resentment of a bygone age.' It labelled Pearson's 'chore boy' remark 'an astonishing revelation of Mr. Pearson's subconscious mind' and an indication that the government utterly lacked an 'understanding of Britain's situation.'[36] Like the *Globe and Mail*, it considered that Canada's foreign policy had been 'guided by American reaction to Suez' and that the Canadian government could help 're-establish Commonwealth solidarity' by waiving interest on the postwar loan made to Britain. The *Sun* rose to the defence of British values in an editorial reminding its readers of the 'flesh and blood ... English people who have ... been bloodied in the cause of freedom.' For the newspaper, British values included 'not only the high-faluting freedoms of right to worship, to speak and read freely, to assemble for discussion, to decide political destiny, but the freedom to live a common-place life in the pursuit of happiness and escape from boredom.' Besides these fundamental freedoms were a host of lesser ones which North Americans wished for, including drinking, gambling, and singing and dancing in pubs. 'Small points these, it may be said. But remembering them, it is easier to visualize the background to the news. We sometimes wish Mr. Dulles, Mr. Eisenhower, Mr. St. Laurent and Mr. Pearson would remember these things – if they ever saw them.'[37] Lumping St. Laurent and Pearson with Dulles and Eisenhower and implying their ignorance of 'British freedoms' amounted to calling into question the latter two's commitment to Britain.

Some Conservative newspapers were even more forthright in their criticism. The Hamilton *Spectator* angrily called for answers to the questions raised by St. Laurent and Pearson's statements in the House of Commons. It wanted to know who the Canadian 'colonial chore-boys' were and what part of Canada they came from. 'Is a "colonial chore boy" to be taken as identifying those Canadians who did not at once damn Great Britain and France for a step that even now seems to have been a bold precaution that may actually have prevented a major conflict? We are afraid this is the only inference.' As for lumping Britain and France together with Russia, as St. Laurent had done, 'is that to be taken as a slip of a skilled tongue or does it take us back to 1917 and 1944?'[38] The allusion to the conscription crises of 1917 and 1944 implicitly raised the issue of St. Laurent's French-Canadian origins and, by extension, of the French-Canadian people's lack of loyalty to Britain.

In Newfoundland, the St. John's *Daily News* was equally appalled by St. Laurent's 'scathing denunciation of Britain by inference.' It told St. Laurent that he did not speak for Canada in being scandalized by Britain's conduct. 'It does the Prime Minister no credit that he has refused to acknowledge that Britain has a case and it does him less than credit when he wilfully joins the myopic critics who try to throw on Britain and France the blame for the savage Soviet repression of the Hungarian revolt.' The prime minister, it suggested, 'seems to see Britain in the same light as less-enlightened nations. And he has done no good to the Commonwealth, no good to Western interests, and no good to the unity of Canada by his unhappy and ill-chosen innuendos at Monday's session of the House of Commons.' The next day, the paper's editorial columnist, 'Wayfarer,' called St. Laurent's state-ment 'unjust and irrational in all the circumstances.' St. Laurent's declara-tion 'could very well have the unhappy effect of dividing Canadians at a time when unity within the nation is essential for the good of the world.' On 30 November, the paper's editorial drew a distinction between the prime minister's 'ill-tempered and ill-founded attack upon Britain' and Pearson's 'more acceptable interpretation of Canada's policy on the Middle East ques-tion.' It foresaw a threat to 'the unity that is desired among the people of the Dominion of Canada' if Canadian foreign policy did not follow objec-tives consistent with Britain's goals in the Middle East.[39]

Given their usual strong support of the government, it is telling that nei-ther of the flagship Liberal papers came to St. Laurent's defence. In its edito-rial of 27 November 1956, the *Toronto Daily Star* chose to ignore St. Laurent's remarks of the previous day in the House of Commons and instead focused on the acting Conservative Leader, Earl Rowe, for his 'perfect exhibition of the outdated colonial mentality.' But the *Winnipeg Free Press* was not so lenient. Its own editorial, entitled 'Anger Is Out of Place,' understood that St. Laurent might have been provoked by 'some foolish Conservative criti-cisms,' but his giving way to anger 'makes this country's relations with its friends abroad more difficult. And it unnecessarily sharpens disagreements within Canada; it raises greater obstacles to that degree of national unity, among people of diverse origins and outlooks, which is necessary to a con-sistent and successful policy for Canada's dealings with the world.' St. Laurent was 'wrong and unfair to lump together the "Great Powers" as a group.' The paper regretted that 'the tragedy of Mr. St. Laurent's speech is that it was angry and immoderate when actual Canadian policy has been understand-ing and moderate.'[40]

The *Halifax Chronicle-Herald* was the only paper to resolutely approve of St. Laurent's remarks: 'What Mr. St. Laurent said at Ottawa on Tuesday will be applauded by a very large majority of the Canadian people who, like him, have been "scandalized more than once by the attitude of the big powers" toward the smaller nationalities and the United Nations itself. It is not the Canadian way to find satisfaction in regimentation of the small and weak by the great and powerful, nor in defiance of the UN by any of the great powers for their own purposes and to advance their own interests.' According to the paper, Canada's foreign policy was governed by the moral imperative of duty, 'by refusing to go along with the Mother Country of the Commonwealth when it felt that its acts were wrong. Canada was hailed again as a peacemaker and to its record was added the title of moral leader.'[41]

The Suez Crisis gave rise to varying political positions among the edito-rial writers of English-speaking Canada's daily press. A tally of the twenty-six English-language dailies revealed an even split between those who supported the government and those who approved of the Anglo-French intervention.[42] But in nearly all the newspapers examined here – those of the major metropolitan centres – editorial positions took the close links between Britain and Canada, and Canada's role in the Commonwealth, as a given. The arguments either for or against Canada's stand at the United Nations were very often expressed in the language of the moral values of freedom, justice, and loyalty. These values were invoked as part of the British political heritage of Canada. If this heritage led some to disagree with British action in the Middle East, so be it. Indeed, support for the Canadian refusal to back Britain at the UN was bolstered by reference to opposition to the Eden government's position both by the Labour party in Britain, and within the Eden government itself. Among both those who opposed Britain's intervention in Suez and those who approved of it, or at least 'understood' the need for it, the frame of reference was Canada's self-definition as a 'British' nation. There never was any questioning of Canada's participation in the Commonwealth, though occasionally the conservative papers made some disparaging remarks about those members of the Commonwealth not part of the 'older' (i.e., white) dominions. The solidarity of culture, political tradition, and of 'race' was the foundation of Canada's role in the Commonwealth.

Other values linked with the 'British character' were invoked in the debate, especially among those who sided with Britain. The first was independence, a corollary of 'British freedom.' For newspapers such as the *Vancouver Sun* or Toronto's *Globe and Mail*, 'independence' meant independence from the foreign policy of the United States and the freedom to align Canada's foreign policy with that of Britain. The second value invoked by editorial writers was that of virility, a gender trait also deriving from Canada's 'British' origins.

The English-language press almost never bothered to comment on the specific role of France in the Suez Crisis. The military intervention in Egypt was always called the 'Anglo-French action' but the behaviour of France never elicited any substantial editorial comment and Canada's relationship with France was never broached. It is not surprising, therefore, that French-Canadian opinion on the Canadian stand at the UN was not discussed in the English-language press. French-Canadian ethnicity was only invoked by those newspapers who wanted to suggest explanations for St. Laurent's lack of 'loyalty' to Britain.

The Suez Crisis was the occasion for English-speaking newspapers to offer representations of Canada as a 'British' nation. This was not the exclusive self-representation of Canada among editorial writers, but at this particular juncture it was the most important representation to invoke in public debate. As such, it is a powerful indication that it touched an important common cultural trait among English-speaking Canadians. This trait had been high-lighted ten years earlier in the parliamentary debate over the Canadian Citizenship Act. It was still persistent in 1956. Yet, a scant eight years later, during the flag debate of 1964, the 'Britishness' of Canada was no longer assumed to be essential to English-speaking Canadians' representations of themselves as a nation. How this transition occurred remains to be elucidated.

Acknowledgments

The author wishes to thank Pascale Ryan, Manon Leroux, and Julie Landreville for their exemplary work in gathering newspaper material. Research for this chapter has received the financial support of the Social Science and Humanities Research Council of Canada, and travel assistance was provided by the Faculté des sciences humaines, Université du Québec à Montréal.

Notes

1 See Lester B. Pearson, *Mike: The Memoirs of the Right Honourable Lester B. Pearson* (Toronto: University of Toronto Press, 1973), Vol. 2: Chapters 10 and 11 for Pearson's account of his role in the Suez crisis.

2 The cabinet had its pro-British advocates. According to Dale Thomson, 'opinion among members of the Canadian cabinet was divided concerning the call for a conference of users of the canal [in August 1956]. Several members shared the Progressive Conservative view that they should stand by the mother country, if only to avoid giving the official opposition an opportunity to accuse them of making Canada, in Diefenbaker's words, "a mere tail on the American kike [sic]." Walter Harris and Robert Winters both expected that an independent Canadian stand at the UN would cost the Liberals seats at the next election.' Dale Thomson, *Louis St. Laurent: Canadian* (Toronto: Macmillan, 1967), 460, 465.

3 National Archives of Canada [NAC], MG26 N5, vol. 40, [Pearson] Memoirs, Vol. 2, Chapters 11 and 12. Suez. External Affairs Documents. Nov.-Dec. 1956, Eden to St. Laurent, 1 November 1956.

4 NAC, MG 26 N1, vol. 37, St. Laurent to Eden, 31 October 1956; on St. Laurent's reaction, see also Pearson, *Mike*, Vol. 2: 238.

5 Ibid., extract from *Hansard*, Saturday, 28 July 1956, 6607.

6 *Calgary Herald*, 1 November 1956.

7 Helen Patricia Adam, 'Canada and the Suez Crisis, 1956: The Evolution of Policy and Public Debate' (MA thesis, Acadia University, 1988) takes a careful look at editorial opinion and letters to the editor of twenty-nine Canadian dailies (twenty-six English-language and three French-language) during the months of October through December 1956, in an attempt to gauge public opinion. She used the letters to the editor because she did not find any public opinion polls she considered reliable (see Chapter 2, p. 30, and n. 33 for reference to a Gallup poll in Toronto [only] from 12 November, which was much debated at the time).

8 Carleton University Library Data Centre, Canadian Institute of Public Opinion [Gallup] poll #251k, September 1956, file cipo251k.por, portable SPSS file.

9 Carleton University Library Data Centre, Canadian Institute of Public Opinion [Gallup] poll #252, October 1956, file cipo252.por, portable SPSS file. Unfortunately, the data from the November 1956 poll are unreadable, according to the director of the Carleton University Library Data Centre, Wendy Watkins.

10 Among the Tories, George Drew was probably the most ardent defender of British tradition in Canada; among the intellectuals, Donald Creigthon, W.L. Morton, and John Farthing.

11 On the representations of Canadian identity during the debate surrounding the Canadian Citizenship Act of 1946, see José E. Igartua, 'L'autre révolution tranquille: l'évolution

du nationalisme canadien-anglais, 1945-1971,' in *La nation dans tous ses états: Le Québec en comparaison*, ed. Gérard Bouchard and Yvan Lamonde (Montreal: l'Harmattan, 1997), 271-96.

12 *Ottawa Citizen*, 16 April 1946.

13 For a preliminary survey of editorial opinion on these issues between 1946 and 1960, see José E. Igartua, 'The Quieter Revolution: Evolving Representations of National Identity in English Canada, 1941-1960' (paper presented at a joint session of the Canadian Historical Association and the Association of Canadian Studies, St. John's, Newfoundland, 8 June 1997). The paper is available at <http://www.er.uqam.ca/nobel/r12270/textes/cha97index.htm>.

14 *Globe and Mail* (Toronto), 21 May 1956.

15 For expressions of these definitions of the nation, see Igartua, 'The Quieter Revolution' and 'L'autre révolution tranquille.' On the genesis of the Canadian Bill of Rights (1960), see Christopher MacLennan, 'Toward the Charter: Canadians and the Demand for a National Bill of Rights, 1929-1960' (PhD thesis, University of Western Ontario, 1996).

16 Charles Tilly, 'Citizenship, Identity and Social History,' *International Review of Social History* 40, supp. 3 (1995): 5-6.

17 Benedict Anderson, *Imagined Communities: Reflections on the Origin and Spread of Nationalism*, 2nd ed. (London: Verso, 1991).

18 See Pearson's account in *Mike*, Vol. 2: Chapters 10-11. See also Geoffrey A.H. Pearson, *Seize the Day: Lester B. Pearson and Crisis Diplomacy* (Ottawa: Carleton University Press, 1993), 146.

19 The speeches led the CBC Ontario director, Ira Dilworth, and historian A.R.M. Lower to write Pearson to congratulate him. Lower asked Pearson to 'give me the least possible assurance that Eden and Company are not the damn fools that they appear to be ... The whole thing is tragic.' NAC, MG26 N1, vol. 38, Ira Dilworth to Pearson, 5 November 1956, and A.R.M. Lower to Pearson, 6 November 1956.

20 Pearson, *Seize the Day*, 150-52. See also John English, *The Worldly Years: The Life of Lester Pearson* (Toronto: Alfred A. Knopf Canada, 1992), Vol. 2: 133-40. The National Archives of Canada's holdings of CBC audio-visual archives do not contain these speeches.

21 *Calgary Herald*, 2 November 1956.

22 Ibid., 3, 9, 21 November 1956. See the letters of 7, 9, 12, 14, and 19 November.

23 *Edmonton Journal*, 5, 24, 28 November 1956.

24 *Globe and Mail*, 2, 3, 6, 8, 10, 12 November 1956.

25 According to the *Directory of Newspapers and Periodicals, 1956*, N.W. Ayer and Son (Philadelphia, n.d.), cited by Adam, 'Canada and the Suez Crisis,' 182.

26 *Vancouver Sun*, 1, 2, 3, 9, 14, 21 November 1956.

27 *Toronto Daily Star*, 5, 27 November 1956.

28 *Winnipeg Free Press*, 31 October, 1, 3, 5, 7, 13, 14 November 1956.

29 *Ottawa Journal*, 1, 5, 8 November 1956. Note again the appeal to the masculine virtue of 'vigor.'

30 *Gazette* (Montreal), 5, 9 November 1956. See the 'Letters from Our Readers' section of the editorial pages of 19, 24, and 27 November 1956.

31 *Halifax Chronicle-Herald*, 1, 5, 6, 13, 14, 15 November 1956.

32 *Globe and Mail* columnist Robert Duffy summarized in sarcastic tones the editorial position of Quebec newspapers on 4 December 1956.

33 *Calgary Herald*, 28 November, 10 December 1956.

34 *Edmonton Journal*, 28 November 1956.

35 *Globe and Mail*, 28, 29 November, 1, 4, 18 December 1956.

36 'Canada Must Redeem Itself,' editorial, *Vancouver Sun*, 29 November 1956.

37 *Vancouver Sun*, 6, 15 December 1956. The 6 December editorial recommended that Canada should waive the payment by Britain of interest on her postwar loans. The payment amounted to $22 million. By their stand at the UN, the editorial argued, Canada and the United States had contributed to Britain's financial troubles.

38 *Spectator*, 28 November 1956.

39 *Daily News*, 28, 29, 30 November 1956.
40 *Winnipeg Free Press*, 27 November 1956.
41 *Halifax Chronicle-Herald*, 28 November, 8 December 1956.
42 Adam, 'Canada and the Suez Crisis,' 181.

4

The Last Great Royal Tour: Queen Elizabeth's 1959 Tour to Canada

Phillip Buckner

On 18 June 1959 Queen Elizabeth II landed in Newfoundland to begin a forty-five-day visit to Canada. She would travel 15,000 miles, leapfrogging across the country by car, train, ship, and plane and then back again to Halifax, in the process shaking 5,000 hands, delivering two TV broadcasts and fifty speeches, and attending sixty-one formal and eighty-one informal functions.[1] A press release proudly proclaimed that it was 'the longest tour of Canada any reigning monarch has made.'[2] This was not claiming much. There had been only two previous visits to Canada by a reigning monarch – King George VI's tour in 1939, which had lasted nineteen days (five of which were spent in the United States), and Elizabeth's brief three-day visit to Ottawa in 1957. But Elizabeth's 1959 tour was very different in scope from her 1957 visit – indeed, it was Buckingham Palace officials that suggested it should be called a 'royal tour' rather than a 'royal visit' (as her 1951 tour as princess had been described).[3] This change was designed to indicate that the Queen was not a mere visitor but was 'equally at home in all her realms.'[4] But it also indicated that what was intended was a royal progress on the scale of the previous great royal tours of Canada by her grandfather (George V, while Duke of Cornwall) in 1901, her uncle (Edward VIII, while Prince of Wales) in 1919, her father in 1939 and herself in 1951. In fact, the 1959 tour would be the last great royal tour to Canada, since it would more closely resemble the great royal tours of the past than the shorter and more limited royal visits of the future. Elizabeth would return to Canada again and again, but never again would she tour the whole country and never again would there be a Canadian tour on the elaborate scale of 1959.

In several important respects, however, the 1959 tour was unlike all previous royal tours to Canada. Each of the previous major tours, in 1901, 1919, 1939, and 1951, had taken place before or in the aftermath of a war, and their purpose was to shore up Canadian loyalty to the imperial connection or to thank Canadians for the military support they had given to the mother country.[5] Each tour thus had a strong imperial dimension and was taken, at least in part, to serve an important interest of British foreign policy. However, neither the brief 1957 visit (which was tacked on to a visit to the United States) nor the lengthy 1959 tour had any particular imperial significance, or for that matter served any specific need of British foreign policy. In 1959 the Queen travelled with a comparatively small royal party, and she relied for advice on Sir Michael Adeane, her private secretary, and on Edmund Butler, her Canadian-born press secretary. Butler had graduated from the University of Toronto, served in the Royal Canadian Navy during the Second World War and worked for the federal government before joining the governor general's staff in 1955. He had been helping to organize the Queen's 1957 visit to Canada when he was invited by Adeane to transfer to London to assist in making the arrangements for the 1959 tour. The 'ruggedly handsome six-footer,' who had twice escorted Princess Margaret to charity balls, was 'at the Queen's elbow throughout her trip across Canada.'[6] The Queen also had the constant advice of representatives of the Canadian government, but no official representative of the British government accompanied her.[7] Undoubtedly the British government must have hoped that the royal presence in 1957 would help to relieve some of the tensions created in Anglo-Canadian relations during the 1956 Suez Crisis. Undoubtedly it also approved of the Queen's presence alongside the American president, Dwight D. Eisenhower, at the opening of the St. Lawrence Seaway in 1959 as a symbol not just of American-Canadian but of Anglo-American harmony. But by 1959 the British government had come to the conclusion that the old empire was dead, and was moving towards decolonization in Africa and Asia and towards joining the European Economic Community. There was a great deal of unofficial British interest in the 1959 tour, which was extensively covered in the British press, but this was more a reflection of the continuing British fascination with the royal family than a concern with the empire in general or with Canada in particular. British official interest in the 1959 tour was confined largely to the one-day visit to Chicago, which was included on the tour because a British trade fair was being held there.

It was the Canadian government – not the British government – that wanted the tour. The Liberal government of Louis St. Laurent initially made the request that Queen Elizabeth and Prince Philip come to Canada to open the St. Lawrence Seaway upon its completion in 1959. Although some younger Liberals wished to remove the symbols of the old imperial connection, including the monarchy, from the country's constitution, this was not the view of those who led the party (and probably not yet of the majority of its supporters). Louis St. Laurent apparently bemused the cabinet in February 1953 when he told them that he was 'a devoted admirer of the Royal Family in general and [Elizabeth] in particular' and that he believed 'the monarchy is more solidly established [in Canada] than ever.'[8] The minister of external affairs and St. Laurent's heir apparent, Lester B. Pearson, was also a committed monarchist. Both men were anglophiles and both believed that the institutions Canada had inherited from Britain helped Canada to maintain a sense of distinctiveness vis-à-vis the United States. But if the monarchy were to survive as a Canadian institution, they also believed that the Queen must be viewed by Canadians not simply as the Queen of England, but more specifically as Queen of Canada, a title formally bestowed on the Queen by the Canadian Parliament in 1952. St. Laurent and Pearson also felt that it was important for the Queen to come to Canada to perform her constitutional functions in person whenever possible, which is why the Liberal government enthusiastically encouraged the Queen to visit Canada en route to the United States in 1957 so that she could open the Canadian Parliament, the first time a monarch had done so in person. But St. Laurent was also concerned with ensuring that this would not interfere with her promise to open the St. Lawrence Seaway when it was completed, and he wrote personally to the British prime minister, Harold Macmillan, to ask him to confirm that the Queen would return in 1959.[9]

Ironically, by the time the Queen arrived in Canada in 1957, St. Laurent had been defeated in an election by John Diefenbaker, who was even more deeply committed to British institutions and symbols than his predecessor. During the 1957 and 1958 federal elections Diefenbaker castigated the Liberals for being pro-American and anti-British, and promised to take measures to strengthen the British connection. He saw Queen Elizabeth's visit in 1957 as an opportunity to emphasize the significance of Canada's British heritage, and he eagerly anticipated her return to Canada in 1959. At Diefenbaker's request the Queen agreed to extend her visit to open the Seaway into a royal progress that would include all parts of Canada, including the Yukon and Northwest Territories. In retrospect, Diefenbaker is frequently seen as a pathetic figure – at best a buffoon trying to hold back the forces of change and inevitably being overwhelmed by them. But this is not how he was viewed by Canadians in 1958 when they re-elected him with what was then the largest majority in Canadian history. Far from seeing him as the voice of 'Canada Past' they voted for him in 1958 because he presented them with a vision of a future and greater Canada. It was not an accident that the Queen would spend a considerable amount of time in 1959 visiting industrial sites and symbols of the new economy, like the new international airport at Gander, the Arvida plant of the Aluminum Company of Canada, the International Nickel Company in Sudbury, the Algoma Steel Corporation in Sault Ste Marie, and the new Canada and Dominion Sugar Refinery, selected because it was the first major industry brought to Toronto by the St. Lawrence Seaway.[10] (At one stage it was suggested that the Queen should visit the A.V. Roe Company in Toronto but this was not included on the final itinerary, presumably because, with the cancellation of the Avro Arrow jet interceptor in 1958, the company was headed for disintegration.)

Nor was it an accident that the tour included a lengthy visit to the North, to places like Yellowknife and Uranium City, which were added to the royal itinerary at Diefenbaker's insistence.[11] This 'practical tour' was, the *Financial Post* declared, designed to show that 'we are not just the fifty-first state of the Union.'[12] While Diefenbaker sought to strengthen ties with Britain, he was not prepared to do so at the expense of Canadian self-interest, as he showed in trade negotiations with the United Kingdom. Nor was his commitment to the monarchy based upon simple anglophilia. 'I am a Canadian, first, last, and always,' he wrote in his memoirs, 'and to me the monarchy remains a vital force in the Canadian constitution.'[13] Diefenbaker rather naïvely believed that a royal tour on a grand scale would make Canadians accept that Elizabeth was their Queen, and that she was, in fact as well as in theory, Queen of Canada.

To emphasize this relationship Diefenbaker arranged for the Queen to preside over a cabinet meeting during her 1957 visit. During the thirty-minute meeting the members of the cabinet were introduced to the Queen, and the cabinet then ratified a convention with Belgium for the avoidance of double taxation and briefly discussed the speech from the throne that the Queen was to read (but into which she had no real input). The purely formal meeting ended with a group photograph.[14] During the 1959 tour Diefenbaker insisted that the Queen must be accompanied at all times by a Canadian cabinet minister in case she needed advice on any pressing matter – in other words to maintain the fiction that while the Queen was in Canada she was an active part of the constitution. When a motorcade was organized in British Columbia in which no federal minister was to participate, the organizers were reminded that a minister 'must be present on all public engagements.'[15] Diefenbaker was also determined to make it 'quite clear' to the Americans that the Queen was visiting the United States as Queen of Canada and that 'it is the Canadian embassy and not the British Embassy officials who are in charge' of the Queen's itinerary.[16] The Queen's speeches in Chicago, written by her Canadian ministers, 'stressed steadily the fact that she had come to call as Queen of Canada.'[17] But Diefenbaker did not want the American visit to distract attention from the Canadian tour and so he opposed an extended visit to the United States. Initially a visit to Detroit had also been included on the itinerary, but when the palace queried why the visit to Detroit had been omitted from the tour, Diefenbaker simply responded that he was 'not prepared to advise any change in the Itinerary at this time.' On the 'advice of the Prime Minister,' the Department of External Affairs also informed the American government that there would be no call at Milwaukee en route from Chicago to Sarnia.[18] It was also Diefenbaker who insisted that the Queen give a TV broadcast to the nation on 1 July, over the objections of the tour organizer who felt that the Queen's program in Ottawa was already too full.[19] But Diefenbaker believed in the symbolic importance of the Queen speaking to her subjects on Dominion Day. Similarly, before leaving Canada, at Diefenbaker's request, the Queen also presided over a special cabinet meeting in Halifax, Nova Scotia, called solely to confirm that the next Governor General of Canada would be Georges Vanier.

To organize the tour Diefenbaker recruited Lieutenant-General Howard Graham, a distinguished soldier who had risen from the rank of private in the Canadian army during the First World War to serve as chief of the General Staff from 1956 to 1958. On the last weekend of October 1958 Graham met Diefenbaker at the Bessborough Hotel in Saskatoon. Diefenbaker was 'lying on a couch with his feet elevated and a mass of papers on a coffee table beside him,' and for an hour or so the two men discussed the 'sketchy plans' already prepared for the Queen's visit. Graham then met on 31 October with Prince Philip, who was in Ottawa attending a conference of the English-speaking Union. Philip's advice 'was to make the tour as personal as possible. The Queen would like to see some industries, some forms of entertainment enjoyed by Canadians, some houses and farms of ordinary people.' Philip warned Graham that in preparing the itinerary he should 'allow time for hair-dressing, changing frocks, resting, with one day free each week, if possible, and Sunday, except for church' and expressed the hope that Graham could travel to London by early December with 'an outline of the plans.'[20] Early in November 1958 Diefenbaker, while on a visit to London, met with Queen Elizabeth and Prince Philip and they agreed on a rough outline of where the tour would go.[21] In preparing a more detailed plan, Graham had the assistance of a cabinet committee chaired by George Hees, the minister of trade and commerce, which met every few weeks, largely to rubberstamp Graham's decisions, and a special interdepartmental committee composed of high-level civil servants from all the federal departments involved, which met much less frequently, still largely to rubberstamp Graham's decisions. In practice, Graham reported directly to Diefenbaker; they met several mornings a week when the prime minister was in Ottawa. Graham also met regularly with Governor General Vincent Massey, because he was aware that the relationship between Diefenbaker and Massey, a life-long Liberal, was not entirely cordial. One of the few arrangements made by Graham that Diefenbaker queried was the decision that the tour would include a weekend at Massey's country home, although in the end Diefenbaker did not prevent the visit.[22]

Initially Graham had a very small staff to assist him. H.F. Feaver, chief of protocol at the Department of External Affairs, acted as his deputy; T.D. Hayes served as secretary to the Special Interdepartmental Committee; Major General M.L. Brennan, formerly Adjutant General of the army, became Graham's chief executive officer; and Major J.M. Barry was seconded to arrange the advance booking of accommodation (an especially onerous task since 5,000 rooms had to be booked for the ceremonies at the opening of the Seaway). One registry clerk, two stenographers, and one messenger were borrowed on temporary loan from other government departments. The cabinet committee, to which Graham reported, approved these arrangements at its first meeting on 6 November 1958. It also agreed to send a photographer to London to obtain a formal portrait of Queen Elizabeth and Prince Philip, asked to see a proof of the special stamp the Post Office intended to issue on the occasion of the royal visit, and requested an estimate of the cost of presenting a commemorative medallion to every school child in Canada (an idea abandoned at the next meeting). Very quickly it became apparent that Graham and Diefenbaker had underestimated the complexity of the arrangements that had to be made.[23] Working out the details surrounding the opening of the Seaway necessitated lengthy negotiations with the American Ambassador to Canada and with the American State Department, as did the details of the Queen's one-day visit to Chicago. All of the details of the provincial programs had to be approved, and Graham was responsible for seeing that the royal party actually moved from place to place on schedule. Graham borrowed officers from the army, the navy, and the air force to help in planning the logistics of the tour, and he co-opted an official from Canadian National Railways to organize the timetable for the royal train. Discovering that no satisfactory automobiles would be available in many of the small towns to be visited, Graham persuaded the large automobile manufacturers to provide free cars, especially modified to meet royal needs, and he arranged to have the cars leapfrogged across the country ahead of the royal party. To ensure security Graham borrowed Assistant Commander D.O. Forrest from the RCMP. To handle public relations he secured the services of R.C. MacInnes, chief of public relations at Trans-Canada Airlines. But Graham's support staff remained inadequate, and the idea of simply recruiting personnel from other government departments as needed did not work. He repeatedly appealed to Diefenbaker to allow him to hire more help. Frustrated by Diefenbaker's failure to provide him with the staff he required, Graham complained at one point that 'the problem of securing staff is even more difficult than planning the tour.'[24]

Part of the reason why Diefenbaker procrastinated (other than sheer incompetence) may have been a concern over the costs of the tour. By the spring of 1959, the Canadian economy was heading into a recession and unemployment was rising. During a parliamentary discussion early in 1959 of a special grant of $110,000 for the expenses connected with the visit of Princess Margaret to Canada in 1958, several members of parliament asked the government to indicate the precise costs for which Canada was responsible for visiting royalty.[25] From the time the 1959 tour was first proposed, there were those who queried whether this was a sensible time to spend even more lavishly on a major royal tour. Graham was aware of the government's concern and he sought to keep costs down: 'While I do not want to "chisel" or do things on the cheap,' he wrote to the head of the CNR, 'still I am interested in getting value for every dollar spent on this Tour.'[26] He complained bitterly when charged $100 to rent a room at the Chateau Lake Louise for forty minutes, and another $60 for hors d'oeuvres for fourteen people.[27] The government also sought to emphasize the value of the tour to the tourist industry, printing 100,000 copies of the royal tour itinerary for circulation by the federal government travel bureau.[28]

The concern to be perceived as avoiding extravagance led the Canadian government to embrace eagerly a new policy in regard to the gifts that would be given to the visiting royals. Instead of giving the visitors expensive trinkets to add to the already vast collection of royal jewels, the Queen suggested that the money used to buy gifts might be devoted instead to endow a worthy cause that would benefit Canadians, such as a scholarship fund for young Canadians. Initially Diefenbaker was sympathetic to the idea but the cabinet feared that this would antagonize the provinces – especially Quebec – since education was a provincial responsibility.[29] So in the end the Queen Elizabeth II Foundation was established with a federal grant of $1,500,000 to support research into children's diseases. Pressure was put on the provincial governments and municipalities to follow suit. Most of the provinces established scholarships either to universities or to teachers' colleges, but Quebec gave $250,000 for research into heart disease, Prince Edward Island and Newfoundland made donations to assist in the education of mentally retarded children, and the Social Credit government of British Columbia handed out $1.5 million as a one-time grant to the aged, the needy, and the handicapped.[30] Many municipalities also established scholarship funds or gave grants to worthy causes such as the Cancer Foundation, and so did the occasional individual, such as the timber magnate H.R. MacMillan, who donated $50,000 to the University of British Columbia for graduate scholarships, in honour of the royal visit.[31] There were also a number of corporate gifts. Dominion Stores presented 2,000 portraits of the Queen to schools across Canada, while the Hudson's Bay Company established bursaries at the University of Manitoba.[32]

This policy did not rule out token gifts to the Queen and her family, and the royal yacht sailed home with a collection of silver and gold cigarette cases, desk sets, cuff links, bracelets embossed with pictures of mounties and maple leaves, and even a silver maple sugar jug.[33] Most were gifts from the various city and provincial governments, but many were the result of public subscription. In Calgary the prime minister personally thanked three young cub scouts for raising $13.06 for the Queen's gift by collecting and selling coat hangers and empty pop bottles.[34] Most of the gifts were really souvenirs: several Canadian books (including a three-volume history of the University of Saskatchewan and a two-volume history of Three Rivers, both of which can probably be found somewhere in the royal library with their pages uncut); a number of oil paintings and watercolours of power plants, the Toronto waterfront, and the Long Sault Rapids (none of which are likely to be prominently displayed in the Queen's Gallery); several items of sporting equipment (Prince Philip may well have used the fibreglass boat he was given but it is unlikely that Prince Charles found much use for the snowshoes, the Canadian football, the baseball and bat, or the hockey and lacrosse sticks); a variety of items of clothing, including four Cowichan sweaters, two Moosehide beaded jackets, and a cowboy hat for Prince Philip (none of which probably got a lot of wear); and a small menagerie of animals, including two falcons and a pony. The latter was a surprise presentation from the city of Windsor, Ontario. Initially the Windsor city council had been one of the few municipalities that decided not to give the Queen a welcoming gift, but this decision was taken while Mayor Michael Patrick was absent, and upon his return he overruled the city council and offered the Queen the pony. It was accepted even through the donors had not followed proper procedure and ensured that the gift was approved before it was presented.[35] In fact, virtually every gift was approved so long as the presentation was not seen as 'an occasion for advertising the product,' though in the case of some gifts – such as the fibreglass boat – it is hard to see how this could have been avoided.[36] A few of the gifts were of considerable value, such as the desk set made out of 150 ounces of BC gold and 100 ounces of BC silver.[37] Nonetheless, compared with earlier royal tours, the Queen returned home with much less bounty than usual, while many Canadians did benefit directly or indirectly from the medical and educational endowments made as a result of the royal visit.

This did not prevent the issue of the cost of the tour from continually resurfacing in letters to the editor of various newspapers, even from those who were in favour of the monarchy.[38] A number of letters were sent to Diefenbaker personally, and he took them seriously. He even asked Donald Fleming, the minister of finance, to reply personally to one letter from a Fred Bogden of East Kildonan, Manitoba, who asked to know how much the tour had cost.[39] The official final bill for the tour was $383,119.65. The largest single expense had been the royal train ($125,908.68), followed by the royal yacht ($63,065.92), the salaries of Graham and his staff ($61,897.05), and other travelling expenses ($53,556.23) of the royal party and the organizers.[40] The bill for the royal train was more than 25 percent higher than predicted, 'causing me some disquiet,' Graham noted. Nonetheless, Graham felt that the cost of the 1959 tour compared 'favourably' with the $82,896.95 spent on the 1939 tour of George VI or the $335,236.90 spent on Princess Elizabeth's 1951 tour.[41] Yet, as Fleming honestly admitted in his letter to Bogden, the official bill did not include the expenditures of a number of departments of state, including public works, national defence, and the RCMP, each of which had absorbed a substantial part of the costs in their own budgets, and he estimated the real cost (exclusive of the fund sent aside for research into children's diseases) at between $528,000 and $704,000, which he expressed as being between three and four cents for every Canadian. Even this was a considerable underestimate, since Fleming was only concerned with the federal government's contribution. This did not include any local costs, which had to be absorbed by the provincial governments and the municipalities visited by the royal party. The City of Montreal alone spent $100,000 on its ball, the fifteen minutes of fireworks in Victoria cost $5,000, and an estimated $150,000 was made by the companies that produced flags and bunting.[42] One of the most expensive private displays was the fifty-foot model of a logging camp, erected by the Bowater Pulp and Paper Company at a cost of $100,000. It is impossible to estimate the true cost of the tour to Canadians, but it was substantially more than three to four cents per capita.

Clearly the fear of costly expenses did not prevent local communities from demanding a share of the Queen's time. As soon as the Queen's visit was officially announced, there was a flood of requests to be included on the itinerary and appeals were made to the prime minister (who somewhat disingenuously claimed he was adopting a hands-off policy and leaving the decisions to Graham), to cabinet ministers and MPs, to Buckingham Palace (by those who were not aware that all the real decisions would be taken in Ottawa), and to Graham personally. In some cases an extensive letter-writing campaign was organized. So determined was Nelson, BC, to be included that Graham received letters from the local MP, the mayor, the City Council, the Chamber of Commerce and the Junior Chamber of Commerce; the chairman of the Nelson School District; the Kiwanis Club, the Rotary Club, and the Lion's Club; the Ladies' Auxiliary Branch no. 51 of the Canadian Legion, the Kootenay Lake General Hospital Women's Auxiliary, and the Kokanee Branch of the IODE; the Nelson and District Boy Scout and Girl Guide Associations; and the local Soroptimist Club. All were to no avail, since Graham wrote to inform them that he had had to 'omit this and other beautiful parts of Canada in order to make it possible for Her Majesty to see cities and towns which she had not hithertofore visited.'[43]

Even after the itinerary was announced, there were disagreements over what the Queen should do at the places she was to visit. Each city or town had to submit its plan to a provincial coordinator, who then submitted the provincial plan to Graham, who submitted it to the Palace. The Palace had laid down some general guidelines. Requests to unveil monuments to John Cabot in both Newfoundland and Cape Breton (since both claimed to be the place where Cabot had first landed) were both turned down because the Queen did not want the tour to become 'a progression of "unveiling" ceremonies.'[44] Even this rule was not rigidly followed, since in Ottawa the Queen did unveil a monument to the Commonwealth Air Training Plan. At the Queen's wish virtually all requests to open new buildings were turned down, even the new civic theatre in Vancouver, which had been named 'The Royal Elizabeth' after a considerable controversy.[45] She did open the new power plant named in her honour in Saskatoon (which was, of course, in Diefenbaker's home province). But while the Liberal Premier of Newfoundland, Joey Smallwood, was 'very keen' to have the Queen lay the cornerstone for the Confederation Building in St. John's, that request was rejected. So too was Smallwood's desire to name a new highway the 'Prince Charles Road,' since the Queen did not want the names of her children to be used for public purposes until they were older.[46] Smallwood and Diefenbaker were such bitter opponents that they were not even talking to each other, and so Smallwood could hardly appeal to the prime minister to overrule Graham. But Mayor Lloyd Jackson of Hamilton, Ontario, also a Liberal, appealed to Diefenbaker as a fellow Baptist and a friend to override Graham's refusal to have the Queen lay the cornerstone of the new city hall in Hamilton. Diefenbaker, aware that 'the Queen prefers NOT to lay cornerstones,' upheld Graham's decision.[47] The Palace also made clear that the Queen did not want to unveil memorials to George VI or to herself and requested that 'every opportunity should be taken to organize functions such as Theatres, Sports Meetings and so forth where people could see the Visitors, rather than luncheons and dinners' where only the invited guests would be able to see them.[48]

Graham preferred to leave such decisions to the provincial and local committees but he was repeatedly forced to interfere to ensure that the program was not too strenuous or too complex and that sufficient time was allowed to move from one event to the next. In the case of the Regina program, for example, this meant omitting a visit to Kiwanis Park and to the HMS *Queen* for reasons of time, deleting a drive in an open carriage because horses should be avoided where there were large crowds, changing the route to the hotel to provide more of a cushion between the morning program and lunch, and extending the visit to Taylor Park from four to ten minutes so that baseball equipment could be presented for the use of the Prince of Wales. 'All in all,' Graham wrote to the provincial coordinator, 'I think the programme is a good one but if we left it as the Mayor would wish, I feel it would spoil the whole thing by trying to do too much.'[49] Sometimes changes were made to increase the number of people who could see the Queen; thus the Toronto committee was asked not to move her by subway since that would deny most people a chance to see her.[50] Sometimes it is not clear why an event was vetoed. Graham tersely wrote to the Edmonton committee to 'delete chicken dance demonstration.'[51] Whatever the 'chicken dance demonstration' consisted of, it is hard to believe that it was a serious loss to the program. On the other hand, Graham was enthusiastic about including square dancing, 'which I like to refer to as Canadian folk dancing.'[52] But in general, Graham played a negative role in vetting the provincial plans, trying to contain the enthusiasm of local committees, although in doing so he sometimes created discontent. When he rejected the suggestion that the Queen should take a scenic drive through Winnipeg at 9 a.m. – a suggestion that ran directly counter to the Queen's wish that nothing begin before 10 a.m. – the Manitoba tour coordinator resigned in protest.[53]

Graham's political judgment was not always wise. The president of the Saint-Jean-Baptiste Society, supported by the mayor of Quebec City and the Speaker of the Quebec Assembly, asked that the Queen light the bonfire on the eve of Saint-Jean-Baptiste Day, which would take place while she was visiting Quebec. The request was turned down, although it was decided that the Queen should lay a wreath at the foot of the monument to Wolfe and Montcalm.[54] The decision was a bad one and led to complaints when the royal party drove past the bonfire without stopping.[55] Graham was not insensitive to French-Canadian feelings. Indeed, it was he who pointed out to George Hees that, of the twenty-four Canadian guests invited to dine on the royal yacht during the opening ceremonies of the St. Lawrence Seaway, none was a French Canadian.[56] But with Duplessis still in power and with no knowledge of the deluge to follow after Duplessis' death later in 1959, Graham was not overly concerned about French-Canadian nationalism.

Nor was he overly concerned about the plight of Canada's Native peoples. In Newfoundland there were no Beothuks for Queen Elizabeth and Prince Philip to meet, but one of the tableaux they passed in Cornerbrook was a picture of Native people receiving gifts from the white settlers. In Labrador several hundred Native people watched the Queen arrive at the airport, and several were interviewed by reporters, but the only meeting the Queen had was with the hereditary chief of the Montagnais, who presented her with a pair of moosehide beaded jackets.[57] In the Gaspé two Native people presented Queen Elizabeth and Prince Philip with deerskin jackets, but there was no official meeting with any Native representatives. Indeed, the limited Native representation during the ceremonies surrounding the opening of the Seaway was noted in the press.[58] In Ottawa a Native man from the Caughnawaga Reserve handed over to royal officials the gift of a 200-year-old wampum (worth an estimated $12,000) but was rewarded only with a sight of the Queen who walked by without noticing him.[59] At the last minute the Department of Northern Affairs did arrange for the Queen to meet with three Inuit at Stratford, Ontario – the first time a member of the royal family had met an Inuit. The meeting could hardly have greatly increased royal understanding of the difficulties faced by the northern First Nations. At the meeting Prince Philip asked most of the questions in 'rapid-fire Style,' but when he asked: 'What did the western Eskimo carve ... There's no carving, he was told. Beadwork and similar handicrafts are the rule.'[60] In Brantford, Ontario, Graham declared that the Queen would not have time to visit the Mohawk chapel to sign the historic Six Nations' Queen Anne Bible, but he did agree that the Queen might sign it during a brief train stop since, 'with the Indians forming the background, a very colourful ceremony can be developed.'[61] In Stoney Creek, Ontario, however, 'five full-feathered chief and twenty braves and their consorts' who came 'with a letter about their troubles for Her Majesty' were not allowed through the line to see her.[62]

Throughout the Western part of the tour, Native leaders were included on the welcoming platforms in many cities and towns, but the largest concentrations were in Calgary and Nanaimo. At the Calgary Stampede more than three hundred people from the Blackfoot, Sarcee, and Stoney First Nations had erected some thirty teepees in which some 'specially chosen' individuals stayed. They 'staged a war dance of welcome' for the Queen and the Prince, who 'spoke briefly to Chief Walking Buffalo and Chief Jacob, two young descendants of the original plains Indians,' and then spent three to four minutes visiting the village.[63] In Nanaimo there was a much lengthier meeting with the Salish nation at which the title 'mother of all people' was conferred on the Queen. This was followed by a welcoming dance and a visit to a 'replica' of a First Nations village, where the royal couple had conversations with some two hundred people, spending forty-five minutes instead of the allotted twenty-five. In the process they learned something about how to make fluffy candy from soap berries, how to carve a totem pole, and how to spin wool – but nothing about treaty issues or issues of land rights.[64] As the Calgary *Albertan* noted, the purpose of having Native peoples on the program was to add colour to the local show.[65]

Certainly the program needed more colour. In announcing the tour the government emphasized that the purpose was to allow the Queen 'to meet the people and see the country' and that 'formality and pomp will be kept to a minimum.'[66] From the beginning many were skeptical, including Pierre Berton, then a columnist for the *Toronto Daily Star*, who wrote on 18 December 1958 (when the tour was announced) that 'I've heard that song before. It's from an old familiar score played before every royal visit.' He then made fifteen savagely funny predictions about the reality of what would happen, almost every one of which came true to some extent. These included that the Queen would shake 180,000 hands, 169,578 of them belonging to aldermen, politicians, ward heelers, society matrons, bishops, staff officers, King Scouts, and 'stuffed shirts' (not an entirely inaccurate description of those she did meet); that during the tour there would be an outcry that the Queen was not meeting the people, and a spontaneous visit would be organized to the home of a 'typical Canadian farmer' (in fact, she visited two 'typical' farms and one 'typical' miner's house); that reporters would complain that the Queen looked tired and that the tour should cease at once (precisely what did happen); that the Queen would be given twenty-three illuminated addresses, fifteen silver cigarette cases, fifty-four examples of native wickerwork, and a plastic moose; that in British Columbia 'an old and toothless prospector will endear himself to almost everybody by greeting the Royal Couple with the phrases "Hi, Queen" and "Hello, Dook"'; that the Duke would be taken down seventeen mineshafts from Nanaimo to Sydney and it would be reported that he had shown a 'keen interest in the operations and asked several penetrating questions'; and that at the end of the tour 'the whole affair will be pronounced a huge success, but newspapers will deplore the fact that the Royal Couple were surrounded by a curtain of dignitaries and stuffed shirts.'[67]

General Graham was aware of Berton's predictions and sought to ensure that Berton would be proved wrong. But in vain. When the detailed program for the first stop of the tour at Gander, Newfoundland, arrived, Graham wrote to the provincial coordinator that he was 'a little disconcerted ... that some eighty-five "Government Officials" and others will be presented [to the Queen]. I had in mind perhaps half a dozen workmen who had been employed in the construction and a dozen or so representatives of air lines. I hope we are not going to, at the very beginning, get inundated with "officials." This will be a dreadful way to start the tour.'[68] This problem was to dog the tour right across the country. Despite the best efforts of Graham and the Palace to encourage innovation, each component of the tour tended to follow the same lines as all previous tours. In Vancouver the *Province* referred scathingly to the 'striped-pant curtain,' which meant that the Queen would be 'afflicted with 61 formal presentations at each of which she will shake an average of 60 sycophantic hands.'[69] Yet there was little that Graham could do since effective control of the local arrangements was in the hands of provincial and municipal officials, who vied with each other to gain invitations to the receptions and who used their status to gain access for their family and friends. In Montreal 2,000 prominent Montrealers were invited to a banquet and a royal ball, but 6,000 people attended a protest in the park, not against the Queen's visit but against subsidizing through taxation the formal ball from which the general public was excluded.[70]

An effort was made to incorporate into the ceremonies some of those who would not have been invited in an earlier era, most noticeably popular athletic stars. In Montreal Jean Beliveau of the Montreal Canadiens and Sam Etcheverry, the quarterback for the Montreal Alouettes (the latter an American) were invited to dinner with the royal party and happily conversed with Prince Philip about hockey and Canadian football (not that the Prince knew much about either). In Ottawa the Queen met 'Rocket' Richard, the Canadian hockey legend; in Toronto, Punch Imlach, the manager of the Toronto Maple Leafs; and in Winnipeg, Bud Grant, the coach of the Blue Bombers. One paper enthusiastically announced that the Queen and 'the Rocket were on first-name terms.'[71] In Ottawa an effort was made to include artists and intellectuals, and in Toronto a pretty representative sample of the city's elite was included in the formal reception. But virtually all of those invited were middle-class and usually middle-aged males and their wives (interestingly, the Palace's rule at that time was that when a husband and wife were presented, the husband was always presented first, regardless of whose status was higher). And those presented were virtually always native-born Canadians or emigrants from the British Isles. Indeed, the *Toronto Daily Star* examined the initial list of 1,100 invitees to the Toronto reception and pointed out that it included many businessmen but few labour leaders or public-school teachers. Even Graham, who had been absent when the list was submitted to his office, was unhappy with the overrepresentation of 'business magnates' and the neglect of people from 'the Arts and Sciences.'[72] Moreover, the initial list included only five or six 'ethnic figures,' even though 'ethnics' formed a third of Toronto's population.[73] There was a wave of protest from the ethnic press and the list was expanded to 1,500 to give greater – though certainly not proportional – representation to the ethnic minorities in the city.[74] There was also criticism of Mayor Nathan Phillips personally for selecting his granddaughter to present the bouquet of flowers to the Queen (as she had done to Princess Margaret the previous year).[75] In Western Canada there were far more non-English names on the reception lists but these were, of course, mainly native-born descendants of earlier generations of migrants, who had prospered and been effectively integrated into the British majority.

In the smaller towns along the route, where there was at most a very short stop, the reception committee inevitably consisted of the town council and city employees, with representatives of the towns' leading citizens or founding families, a few veterans, a local band, and some schoolchildren (in the form of a choir if the stop was long enough for a performance). Ironically the royal couple met most frequently with the very young or the very elderly. They met with 'more Boy Scouts and Girl Guides than ever attended a jamboree,' shook hands with ancient veterans who had served in the First World War, the Boer War, the Zulu War, and the Riel Rebellion, and chatted with the founding members of various organizations, such as the Women's Institute (represented in Stoney Creek by four ladies with a combined age of 235).[76] As June Callwood reported to the readers of the *Toronto Daily Star*, 'few functions along the tour lend themselves as poorly to informality as the 10-minute Stops so frequently scheduled at city halls or crossroads. God Save the Queen must be played, while the tableau freezes, mayors must be introduced ("We are so honored you could come"), then the shuffling lines of bobbing, shy citizens, the little frightened girl who presents the bouquet of pink roses, signing the guest book and leaving, waving to cheers and forests of flags.' Nonetheless, as Callwood admitted, Queen Elizabeth and Prince Philip did 'their inventive best to lift the ceremonies from their slough of Stiffness,' talking to children and inquiring about the health of old people.[77] For all the 'stiffness' of these small-town ceremonies, another reporter observed, 'the Queen and her subjects were literally rubbing shoulders,' whereas 'big-city conditions inevitably produced big-city precautions' and 'a red-tape, on-the-dot atmosphere ... that was almost depressing.'[78]

In the cities, most of the ceremonies were also predictable. In Edmonton, for example, the four-hour proceedings began with 'three florid speeches,' two by the mayor and one by Premier E.C. Manning. Then, before a crowd of some 5,000, 'while the Edmonton schoolboys' band emitted the slushy notes characteristic of boys' bands the world over,' the Queen met seventy-one representatives of twenty-four local associations, threw three shovelfuls of earth on a new oak tree, visited the Colonel Newburn military hospital and chatted with an eighty-eight-year-old 'veteran of the relief of Chitral (India),' and lunched at the Legislative building with 1,800 Albertans while the RCAF band played Handel.[79] In Regina the ceremony lasted five hours and was 'predictably pompous': long – very long – speeches by the mayor and Premier Tommy Douglas; 161 hands to be shaken; gold medals and certificates to be presented to girl guides and boy scouts; a thirty-minute stop at the Provincial Museum of Natural History to view stuffed birds and animals ('a lot less stuffy than the reception that preceded them,' one reporter noted); a brief visit to see part of a little-league football game; a grandstand performance of square dancing, Highland leaps, and a Hungarian polka; and then back on the train.[80] In the larger cities of Toronto, Montreal, Winnipeg, and Vancouver the visits were longer but differed only in degree, with the addition of a military parade, a visit to an especially important factory, large-scale fireworks displays, and some kind of cultural activity, such as a visit to a museum, an art gallery, or a concert. The latter were not always a success. During the combined performance of a symphony concert and a ballet in Winnipeg, both Queen Elizabeth and Prince Philip appeared to be bored: 'The Queen fumbled with her diamond necklace and adjusted her tiara and the Duke slouched in his chair in the hot, humid and smoky arena.'[81] On the other hand, they did appear to enjoy a performance of *As You Like It* at the Stratford Festival and seemed thoroughly to enjoy themselves at the running of the Queen's Plate and at the Calgary Stampede.

As the Palace had requested, there was an attempt to include a visit to the homes of 'ordinary people.' In Schefferville, Quebec, the Queen visited 'a small prefab home of a company clerk whose expectant wife proudly showed the Queen her oven and other electric appliances while the Duke discussed wages and rent with his host.'[82] In Tuxford, Saskatchewan, they visited the farm of the Wells family, and in Prince Edward Island the Prowses, where the Queen enquired about the kind of feed supplied the cows, and the Prince inspected the twelve-year-old Ernest Prowse's coin and gun collection. They then sat for a few minutes in the parlour but drank no tea, even though 'Mrs. Prowse had set out her silver service on the dining-room table, just in case.'[83] If anything, these events served only to emphasize the social and cultural gap between the Queen and 'ordinary' Canadians.

The repetitive nature of many of the events meant that the huge gang of reporters and photographers following the tour very often had little to report or to photograph. Graham had been aware that the job of handling the press would be 'a stinker,' partly because of the logistics. In previous tours the royal party had travelled by train, so it was easy to make arrangements for the press, but in 1959 the arrangements were much more complex since the royal party travelled by 'air, ship, air, train, air, train, ship, etc.'[84] Moreover, the number of accredited press representatives had been swelled by radio and television personnel to over 5,100 (from 3,000 in 1951). The number actually accompanying the royal party under Graham's auspices had to be limited to fifty: seven representatives of the CBC, and ten British, three American, twenty-nine Canadian, and one Australian journalist (though another 200 or so followed the tour everywhere by making their own arrangements). For the first time the journalists accompanying the royal party were asked to pay $1,500 each to cover their expenses instead of travelling at government expense and so, of course, they had to work even harder to justify these costs.[85] The relationship of the journalists with the government officials running the tour was frequently strained; they resented restrictions on their access to the crown, and security measures that stood in the way of a good photo-opportunity, and some of them complained bitterly about the standard of rooms and meals provided, as well as the price of a gin and tonic on the royal train.[86] In an attempt to promote good relations with the press the royal couple for the first time held an informal press reception on board the royal yacht *Britannia,* on the understanding that everything discussed during the reception would be kept private. When Prince Philip indicated in his usual off-the-cuff fashion that the Palace was wondering whether big royal tours really had outlived their usefulness and ought to be replaced by shorter, more focused regional events, the temptation was too good to resist and the Prince's remarks were quoted widely in the press, thus breaking the gentlemen's agreement about the reception.[87] No more such events were organized and for the rest of the tour Prince Philip would make critical comments about their profession to any reporters who crossed his path.

Ironically the Prince's repeated gaffes were welcomed by the press since these gave them something to write about. In Stephenville, when the automobile carrying the royal party would not start, Prince Philip leaned over to the driver and said: 'Too bad you haven't got an English car. They work better.'[88] In Ontario his attack on the province's antiquated liquor laws embarrassed the provincial government and led to an enormous outcry from the temperance movement across the country.[89] In a speech to the Canadian Medical Association he pronounced that 'people in Canada are not as fit as they might be.'[90] In Toronto he described the controversial design for the new city hall as looking 'like a boomerang.'[91] In Regina, while visiting a museum, he stepped inside an exhibit showing life-sized waxworks of Native people, picked up an ancient rifle, and took aim at the waxworks.[92] Yet, as the press admitted, with his 'infectious grin' Philip remained a 'crowd pleaser' and a 'glamour boy.' In receiving lines the Queen frequently said little but Philip 'stops about every fourth or fifth man – he seldom talks to women – and evinces interest in them whether he feels it or not.'[93] In visits to industrial plants he entirely stole the show. And for all the complaints by the reporters about lack of access, it was deliberate policy to allow them closer access to the royal family than in previous tours. This was not an unmixed blessing. One of the journalists travelling with the tour lamented: 'One of the aspects of royal tour reporting which has grown to disturbing proportions is the business of attempting to get any small tidbit of private or inconsequential conversation that can be heard where the royal couple are concerned, and then blowing it into headlines.' Much of the reporting of the royal tour had 'turned into a job of private detective work and peeping Tomism.'[94]

The British journalists were particularly negative in their criticism of the local arrangements and in their comments about the tour, thus arousing the antagonism of the Canadians, who condemned the British newspapermen for looking 'down their Fleet St. noses with disdain on Canada and Canadians.'[95] The Canadian papers eagerly reported the errors made by ignorant British journalists, pointing out to the *Times* that Canada's population was not 16,000,000, but 17,340,000.[96] Gerald Clark, the Montreal *Star's* staff correspondent in London, declared that the problem with the British press coverage was that 'Canadian achievements have been overlooked, while inside space is devoted rather to attempts to make Britons feel that Canadians are really a bunch of aborigines.'[97] The Canadian reporters were particularly annoyed by the London *Daily Mail*, which, Scott Young declared, was 'tired of our Indians and Eskimos, tired of our liquor, our food, our air conditioning, our inefficient telephone and telegraph arrangements, the gates that are always closed to the press bus, our accents, our ideas, and our cloddish refusal to accept the gospel according to the London *Daily Mail*.'[98]

At least one group of journalists were, however, very happy with their coverage. This was the large contingent, totalling nearly 900, employed by the CBC, which spent $500,000 covering the tour. It even hired Joy Davies, a former actress and model, to brief the male radio and TV announcers on how to describe the Queen's wardrobe.[99] The CBC had televised the Queen's visit in 1957, but its efforts then had been overshadowed by the National Film Board, which used the Queen's visit to explore the role of the Crown in a constitutional democracy by producing a film entitled *The Sceptre and the Mace*, which was used for educational purposes not only in Canada but throughout the Commonwealth. The CBC also dutifully covered Princess Margaret's rather uneventful – not to say boring – tour in 1958. In 1959, however, they adopted a new approach. Although they filmed brief items for the daily news, they focused their coverage around a series of the more colourful events – such as the opening of the St. Lawrence Seaway and the Calgary Stampede.[100] Their own surveys showed large and enthusiastic audiences for their programs, and the ninety-minute visit of the Queen to the Calgary Stampede was recommended by the critics as a best bet on television.[101] For those who missed the TV coverage, there was always a thirty-minute National Film Board documentary, *Royal River*, which was shown in cinemas after the tour was over.

Indeed, although there were criticisms of details of the arrangements and the repetitive nature of the many of the ceremonies, the majority of the press did think that the tour had been a success. As the *Times* noted, the repetitive nature of the ceremonies was not really an issue for the people involved in them since, unlike the journalists, each group only participated in the event once.[102] Not only did the television coverage attract large audiences, but also the royal visitors attracted large crowds everywhere they went. In Newfoundland, where the tour began, this was no great surprise, although in St. John's the city's population was swelled by a third, which made the Montreal *Star* wonder 'who was left at home to watch the procession on TV.'[103] Even in Quebec very large numbers welcomed the Queen. In Quebec City, June Callwood noted, French Canadians 'did not greet the Queen and Prince Philip even as warmly as they did eight years ago,' and 'only a relatively few adults showed genuine affection for her.' But even Callwood, perhaps the most critical of the Canadian reporters accompanying the tour, admitted that Montreal was a 'triumph.'[104] Charles Lynch estimated that 750,000 people – half the city's population – turned out, and he noted with relief that a very substantial proportion were French-speaking.[105] Astutely advised, the Queen delivered all of her speeches there in French. Indeed, at the public events in Quebec City alongside Maurice Duplessis and the representatives of the Roman Catholic hierarchy she spoke only in French rather than, as in other speeches, in a mixture of French and English. And in her speeches – prepared for her by her Canadian ministers – she extolled the virtues of a bicultural society. Not surprisingly the coverage of her tour by the French-Canadian press was overwhelmingly positive, many French-Canadian editors pointing out that English Canadians would do well to follow her example. *Le Montréal-Matin* declared that 'sa sympathique personnalité et sa délicatesse vers les Canadiens de langue française l'ont rendue très populaire chez nous. En plusieurs circonstances, en effet, elle eut à l'endroit de notre race des paroles manifestant une compréhension que nous ne ressentons pas toujours même sur le sol canadien.'[106]

Ironically it was in English-speaking Canada where the Queen's visit would attract the most negative publicity. Joyce Davidson, the twenty-four-year-old host of a popular CBC program, unleashed a furious controversy when, during an interview on American television, she declared that she, like most Canadians, was 'indifferent' to the royal tour. The CBC was inundated with telephone calls, mainly denouncing Davidson, and with letters, which were more sympathetic, if not to her comment (though many were), at least to her right to have an opinion.[107] The editorial pages of most English-language papers debated the issue and carried highly emotional letters denouncing or supporting her. Some prominent Canadians, like the CCF MP Frank Howard, publicly expressed their agreement; many more publicly disagreed. Davidson took a temporary holiday from her employment at the CBC and ostentatiously took her own children to view the Queen.[108] When the Press cars and buses appeared in Ottawa, some members of the huge crowds in the street called out, 'Do you think we're indifferent now?'[109] The newspapers ran polls to see whether Davidson was correct. The *Vancouver Sun* claimed that its poll showed that 70 percent of the people were interested in the tour (though it also admitted that only 52 percent believed that the government was warranted in spending money on the tour).[110] A Gallup poll indicated that while 64 percent of those polled thought Davidson was wrong, only 48 percent of those polled were themselves 'very interested' in the tour (compared to 23 percent not 'very interested' and 19 percent not interested at all).[111]

Certainly there can be no question that the crowds grew larger and more enthusiastic as the tour gathered momentum in Ontario and then in the West. In Ottawa 40,000 people requested seats for an event in Lansdowne Park, where only 15,000 seats could be provided.[112] In Toronto 200,000 people turned out, 300,000 in the towns of western Ontario, and another 200,000 in the Georgian Bay and Muskoka area.[113] In the Prairies in particular there can be no denying the warmth of the welcome extended to the Queen. Virtually the whole population appears to have turned out in Saskatchewan; in Saskatoon, the crowds soared to 125,000 and in Regina the crowds were estimated at 100,000, equal to the city's population. In Manitoba the crowds were nearly as large; some small communities had influxes up to ten times their population to meet the royal train, and in Winnipeg, nearly half the city's population turned out. The Queen, the Regina *Leader-Post* proclaimed, 'was a bigger smash than the Winnipeg Blue Bombers when they won the Grey Cup last fall.'[114] Calgary had a population of 230,000 only, but the royal visit, combined with the Calgary Stampede, led to an estimated crowd of 400,000 and 'the biggest and noisiest welcome of the royal tour.'[115] In British Columbia, the welcome was also warm. The *Vancouver Sun* reported that 'women with babies in their arms, some still wearing aprons, others with hands covered with soap suds, smiled and waved from every tiny clearing and settlement as the 16-car special train snaked through the Rockies into BC.' Wherever the train stopped, 'there were cheering, waving, smiling crowds to meet them.'[116] These numbers were especially impressive given the unseasonably hot temperatures that dogged the tour. The hottest day of the tour was in Fredericton, New Brunswick, where the Queen shook hands with 250 people, including the entire Provincial Assembly.[117] Even the unseasonable heat did not discourage Maritimers from turning out in large numbers.

Ironically (again as Berton had predicted), the latter part of the tour was marred by a different kind of controversy. From the beginning there had been those who argued that the tour was too long and would put too much stress on the Queen. Graham was aware of the criticism but pointed out that 'on the surface I suppose it looks a bit of a rat race but in fact it is not going to be the great strain on Her Majesty that some others have been,'[118] since for much of the trip the Queen would be on the royal yacht, many of her evenings were free, and there were frequent days of rest. What Graham did not know, and in fact what Diefenbaker did not know until he had a private conversation with the Queen in Kingston, was that she was pregnant. Diefenbaker immediately offered to curtail the tour but the Queen refused and swore him to silence, which he maintained even after she fell ill in Whitehorse. She was forced to cancel one day of activities, but then returned to the schedule, again declining Diefenbaker's offer to cut short the tour and continuing to deny rumours of her pregnancy. The result was that Diefenbaker faced a growing volume of abuse both in the British and in the Canadian press for designing a tour that was too strenuous for the Queen's health. He was particularly annoyed by the report in the London *Daily Herald* that he had pressured the Queen to continue with the tour,[119] but he could not even defend himself until after the Queen had returned to London and announced her pregnancy.

Partly for this reason the press almost unanimously predicted that there would never again be – indeed should never again be – a tour to Canada of this duration. The *Ottawa Citizen* proclaimed that the 'day of the gruelling transcontinental tour ... is about over.'[120] Royal progresses of this kind were, the Calgary *Albertan* proclaimed, 'hopelessly outdated' and 'anachronistic.' They were inevitably 'so embroiled in protocol and red tape, honor guards, government dignitaries and official functions from which all but a select few are excluded that it ceases to have any meaning to the Canadian people as a whole.' The *Albertan* understood the problem: 'The fact is that royalty has no roots in Canada. And if roots must be put down they certainly should be of a different kind than those which are historically proper for Britain.' It saw the solution as consisting of more frequent and less formal visits and predicted: 'Any more of these ponderous royal visits to Canada and the last vestiges of monarchical popularity are likely to be wiped out.'[121] The *Albertan* perhaps overstated the case; indeed, at least one subscriber cancelled his subscription because of the 'anti-British tone' of its coverage of the tour.[122] The Vancouver *Province* was less extreme. The problem with the tour, it declared, was that 'it has tried to adapt to an air age a type of royal progress fitted to older and more leisurely forms of travel.'[123]

But there was another and more important reason why this would be the last great royal tour to Canada. The tour had revealed a growing division within Canadian – particularly English-Canadian – society between those who viewed the Queen as Queen of Canada and those who did not. The government had done everything in its power to Canadianize the monarchy. For the first time during a royal visit the flag of choice almost everywhere was the Red Ensign, not the Union Jack. At the Seaway ceremony the official sequence of flags laid down by the Canadian government was the Red Ensign, the American flag, and the Union Jack, and elsewhere on the tour, the Red Ensign, the Union Jack, and the appropriate provincial flag.[124] Only in Newfoundland, where the Union Jack was also the provincial flag, did Union Jacks predominate.[125] In the rest of Canada the Ensign was more frequently flown, and where this was not the case there was an outcry. One writer to the *Vancouver Sun* protested that at the opening of the Queen Elizabeth Auditorium, there were displayed 'over 50 Imperial flags and two Canadian ensigns. Long live servility.'[126] In Vancouver the *Province* was extremely critical of the local committee for buying equal numbers of Union Flags and Red Ensigns for the children to wave, pointing out that 'there is a Canadian flag.'[127] The reality, of course, was that there wasn't, and that for a growing number of Canadians even the Red Ensign was no longer an adequate symbol for Canada. What was needed, letters to the editor in newspapers from Halifax to Vancouver proclaimed, was a 'truly Canadian flag,' one 'which consists of Canadian symbols only.'[128] In Quebec this was not such a burning issue, since the provincial flag was more frequently flown than the Ensign.[129] But along the Saguenay a number of young French Canadians planned to hold up signs welcoming the Queen but lamenting the lack of a national flag. Indeed, several Quebec papers carried articles declaring that it was the sign of 'un infantilisme patriotique' that the country had neither a national flag nor a national anthem of its own.[130]

The government also sought to encourage the singing of Canada's then-unofficial national anthem, 'O Canada,' whenever possible on official occasions. But 'God Save the Queen' had to be given priority whenever the Queen was present, although Graham wrote to the provincial coordinator for Ontario to complain that the playing of 'God Save The Queen' on three occasions was 'overdoing it a little,' suggesting that on at least one of these occasions 'O Canada' might have been sung.[131] The Queen's own behaviour was impeccable. The royal yacht prominently displayed the Red Ensign and 'at every place across the land where "O Canada" was played or sung the Queen rose to her feet and stood until it was finished.'[132] In Winnipeg she even joined twenty-five children in singing 'O Canada' before 15,000 on-lookers.[133] The 1959 tour did put an end to one historic tradition. In all previous visits one of the favourite tunes played to welcome the Queen was 'The Maple Leaf Forever,' but in 1959 it seems to have been played only once, in Midland, Ontario, by the Princess Royal Girls' Sea Ranger band.[134] The days when Canadians wanted 'Britannia's flag' and Britannia's anthem were gone. One letter to the editor of the *Vancouver Sun* queried why 'when abroad we hear "O Canada" played at official functions as our national anthem (not "God Save the Queen")' while at home 'we seldom hear it but [instead hear] the anthem of England.'[135]

The contradiction inherent in welcoming the Queen as Queen of Canada and yet having to display royal symbols that were clearly British in origin was not lost on many Canadians. A letter from a second-generation Canadian (and there were many others like it) declared: 'Let's cut the racket [probably not the word he used in private conversation] and start acting like loyal citizens of our own country instead of like a bunch of displaced limeys.'[136] One 'displaced limey' – a fifty-year resident of Port Alberni – echoed this statement: 'No disrespect is meant toward England; but as we live in B.C., Canada, let us be and think and act like Canadians.'[137] 'Let's not make Canada a "Little Britain,"' declared S. Aitken of Scarborough, Ontario, while W. McDonald, a sixth-generation Canadian, declared: 'To say the least, we are indifferent to the British flag and to the British national anthem and British royal tours with all the attendant gush and drivel and knee-bending … Let's be what we like to say we are – a Canadian nation – with a little self-respect.'[138] This sentiment was most strongly expressed in Toronto and Vancouver, which were growing rapidly in the postwar period, partly because of high birth rates and partly because of an influx of immigrants (at this stage still largely from the British Isles and continental Europe). Many of the postwar immigrants who flooded into Canada's urban centres, including many of those coming from Britain, sought to leave behind the Old World and its symbols.[139] This was not a universal sentiment. The crowds welcoming the Queen did include many 'New Canadians' and especially among those from 'behind the Iron Curtain' there was considerable support for the Queen and disdain for 'the inconsequential statement of Miss Joyce Davidson.'[140] Robert Badanai, the Italian-Canadian MP for Fort William, declared 'as a non-Anglo Saxon' that 'the non-Anglo Saxons are more keen about the Queen than the Anglo Saxons.'[141] But the reality was that most of the more recent immigrants simply did not have the same sense of the Queen as being *their* Queen as had generations of English-speaking Canadians of British origin.

Nor, for that matter, did many younger native-born English-speaking Canadians, who had trouble identifying the Queen as a Canadian, even if she had 'seen far more of Canada in a few weeks than most Canadians do in a lifetime.'[142] It is noticeable that among the polls organized by those who sought to prove or disprove the validity of Joyce Davidson's comment, the one that most strongly supported her was one taken by CHUM radio in Toronto, a station that appealed to the teenage market. The organizations that most strongly and enthusiastically welcomed the Queen – such as the Imperial Order Daughters of the Empire, the Orange Lodges, and the Veterans' Associations – were composed of an ageing membership, who were more likely to wave Union Jacks and carry signs saying 'There'll always be an England.'[143] Indeed, one of the great problems the tour's organizers repeatedly faced was to get children and young people involved, and at a number of events organized for them the turnout was smaller than anticipated.[144] Some blamed this on the fact that the tour took place during the summer holiday. But it seems more likely that members of the baby-boom generation, then working their way through the school system, simply did not share, in this area as in so many others, the values of their parents. It is debatable whether Joyce Davidson (or June Callwood or Pierre Berton) spoke for the majority of adult English-speaking Canadians, who had grown to maturity in what was essentially a British world and who had participated in at least one and in some cases two world wars to preserve the British connection. But Davidson probably did speak for a growing number of the next generation, whose attitude to the monarchy ranged from indifference to outright hostility.

As the *Toronto Daily Star* indicated, the controversy over the royal visit, 'like a flash of lightning' had 'suddenly illuminated a great chasm between Canadians on the question of their identity – how they see themselves and what they want to be, as a people.' For the pro-tour people the Queen was 'one of the few meaningful symbols uniting Canadians and giving them identity, tradition, and a meaningful brotherhood within the Commonwealth'; for them Davidson's comment had struck 'at the only conception of Canada that holds much meaning for them.' The anti-tour Canadians, on the other hand, were not of one mind. Some were 'simply fed up with the stuffy formality and social-climbing aspects of the tour,' while others had a 'deeper objection. They yearn passionately for this nation to have symbols that it can call its very own – an entirely distinctive flag and anthem, for example. They fear that frequent royal visits may stifle this home-grown Canadianism, that the symbol of the Crown will smother the native symbols.' Yet, the editor of the *Star* pointed out, out of the 'deluge of letters' which the paper had received, very few had opposed the institution of monarchy or suggested the creation of a Canadian republic. In reality, most Canadians believed that Canada needed a form of government distinct from that of the United States: 'It might even be said that if we did not have the Queen, it would be necessary to invent one, in order to preserve our nationhood.' But it was pointless to pretend that 'one could transplant to Canadian soil the British conception of the royal image and royal behaviour.' Instead of long, formal visits there should be shorter, less frequent, and less formal visits, which would 'emphasize the symbol rather than the person.'[145] Even the Toronto *Telegram*, a fiercely conservative and pro-monarchy newspaper, agreed that the tours were no longer serving the purpose for which they were intended, suggesting that the Queen should consider residing for part of the year in Canada.[146] There were no newspapers in Canada in 1959 (at least none that I was able to find) that called for the abolition of the monarchy, but the main argument used for retaining the Queen as head of state was her position as head of the Commonwealth, 'a mighty force in a free world face to face with communism.'[147] The very fact that the argument had to be constructed in these terms revealed that the tour had failed in its primary purpose: It had not convinced the Canadian public that the Queen's roots were or could be made Canadian.

The major lesson drawn from the 1959 tour was not to have another one. Pearson, who replaced Diefenbaker as prime minister in 1963, remained committed to preserving the monarchy, but he felt that members of the royal family should in future 'come for a specific occasion, not for a tour' and should 'return home when the event was over. I had been anxious to abandon the "Royal Trans-Canada Tour" idea, and so had the palace.'[148] Ironically the Queen's next tour, in 1964, although it lasted only ten days, was a disaster. Brought out to commemorate the hundredth anniversary of the Charlottetown and Quebec conferences, which had led to Confederation, the Queen's visit, far from uniting English Canadians and French Canadians, served only to divide them. Most French-speaking Québecois ignored the tour; the Queen was booed in Quebec City; and Quebec's Minister of Natural Resources René Lévesque boycotted the official banquet. The overreaction of the Quebec provincial police made martyrs of those separatists who sought to protest the Queen's visit.[149] Ironically, partly as a reaction to the events in French Canada, English Canadians turned out in unusually large numbers to welcome the Queen to Ottawa. For the Queen the 1964 tour was 'as testing emotionally as 1959 had been physically.'[150] From Pearson's perspective the Queen's visit during Canada's centennial celebrations in 1967 was more successful, at least compared with the controversy that surrounded de Gaulle's visit. But by then even Pearson, for all his monarchical sympathies, had to admit that it might be better to abandon the constitutional fiction that the Queen was Queen of Canada, and to consider her as the sovereign of Britain and Head of the Commonwealth rather than 'an absentee monarch endeavouring ... to live up to a designation which is theoretical rather than exact.' In effect, he noted, this would mean Canada would become a republic with a Canadian head of state and with 'no formal relationship to the Crown, but an association with the Crown through the ties of history and tradition and through the Commonwealth.' Pearson actually discussed this issue with the Queen during a private interview in London, where the Queen expressed her concern that 'the monarchy, or any controversy over it, should not become prejudicial to Canadian unity, or a source of division.'[151] But no decision was taken.

The Queen would continue to make periodic visits to Canada; indeed, I believe she has made more visits to Canada than to any other country. In theory these are visits taken by the Queen of Canada to meet her subjects. But fewer and fewer Canadians turn out to see her because, as Pearson had predicted, fewer and fewer Canadians really view her as Queen of Canada. As Queen of the United Kingdom and as Head of the Commonwealth – though that too is an organization that has less and less emotional appeal to Canadians – she could, and can, still attract a reasonable crowd, especially in those areas where the British-born or their descendants form a substantial part of the population. But the attempt by successive Liberal and Conservative governments in the postwar period to turn the Queen into a Canadian monarch inevitably failed. In retrospect what is perhaps surprising is their belief that there was any ever any real chance it could succeed.

Acknowledgments

I would like to thank the Government of Canada and the Canadian High Commission in London for a faculty research program award, which made the research for this chapter possible.

Notes

1 *Ottawa Journal*, 21 July 1959, 32.
2 National Archives of Canada [NAC], RG7 MG23, vol. 25, Staff Meeting no. 4, 4 February 1959.
3 NAC, RG7 MG23, vol. 25, Staff Meeting no. 4, 4 February 1959.
4 University of Toronto Archives [UTA], Vincent Massey papers, box 436, file 10, Michael Adeane to Vincent Massey, 22 January 1959. I would like to thank the Master and the Librarian of Massey College for granting me access to the Massey papers and for allowing me to quote from them.
5 For a discussion of the 1901 tour, see Phillip Buckner, 'Casting Daylight upon Magic: Deconstructing the Royal Tour of 1901 to Canada' in *The British World: Diaspora, Culture, Identity*, ed. Carl Bridge and Kent Fedorowich (London: Frank Cass, 2003), 158-89.
6 *Telegram* (Toronto), 11 June 1959, 7.
7 *Gazette* (Montreal), 18 June 1959, 2.
8 Quoted in John English, *The Worldly Years: The Life of Lester B. Pearson*, Vol. 2: 1949-1972 (Toronto: Alfred A. Knopf 1992), 77.
9 NAC, Diefenbaker papers, MG26 M, vol. 107, 91658-59, Harold Macmillan to St. Laurent, 2 June 1957.
10 *Globe and Mail*, 30 June 1959, 2.

11 NAC, RG7 MG23, vol. 26, Graham to Sir Michael Adeane, 5 January 1959.

12 Quoted in the *Gazette* (Montreal), 10 July 1959, 13.

13 John G. Diefenbaker, *One Canada: Memoirs of the Right Honourable John G. Diefenbaker,* Vol. 2: *The Years of Achievement, 1957-1962* (Toronto: Macmillan, 1976), 61.

14 UTA, Massey papers, box 353, file 01, cable from Department of External Affairs (Ottawa) to High Commission (London), 8 October 1957.

15 NAC, RG7 MG23, vol. 28, Graham to L.J. Wallace, 12 June 1959.

16 NAC, RG7 MG23, vol. 25, first meeting of the special cabinet committee, 6 November 1958; ibid., vol. 26, Graham to H.F. Feaver, 16 January 1959.

17 *Toronto Daily Star*, 7 July 1959, 3.

18 NAC, RG7 MG23, vol. 25, Commissioners' Office, staff meeting no. 7, 23 March 1959.

19 NAC, RG7 MG23, vol. 26, Graham to prime minister, 26 January 1959.

20 Howard Graham, *Citizen-Soldier: The Memoirs of Lieutenant-General Howard Graham* (Toronto: McClelland and Stewart, 1978), 246-47.

21 NAC, RG7 MG23, vol. 25, first meeting of special cabinet committee, 6 November 1958.

22 Graham, *Citizen-Soldier*, 248.

23 NAC, RG7 MG23, vol. 25, secret minutes of cabinet meeting, royal visit 1959, 6 November 1958.

24 NAC, RG7 MG23, vol. 26, file 13090-2-1, Graham to F.H. Miller, 10 March 1959.

25 See Canada, House of Commons, *Debates*, 18 February 1959, vol. 1, cols 1159-60.

26 NAC, RG7 MG23, vol. 28, Graham to S.F. Pringle, 10 June 1959.

27 NAC, RG7 MG23, vol. 28, Graham to D.A. Williams, 7 August 1959.

28 *Ottawa Citizen*, 16 June 1959, 4.

29 UTA, Massey papers, box 436, file 10, Adeane to Massey, 3 February 1959 and Massey to Adeane, 7 and 21 February 1959; NAC, Diefenbaker papers, MG 26 M, vol. 107, 92252-53, Diefenbaker to Miss M.E. Ritchie, 5 May 1959.

30 See *Halifax Chronicle-Herald*, 20 July 1959, 4; *Globe and Mail*, 24 June 1959, 8; *Guardian* (Charlottetown), 1 August 1959, 1; *Daily Colonist* (Victoria), 1 July 1959, 13.

31 *Province* (Vancouver), 23 July 1959, 1.

32 *Toronto Daily Star*, 2 July 1959, 3.

33 *Albertan* (Calgary), 10 July 1959, 1; *Vancouver Sun*, 18 July 1959, 17.

34 *Albertan* (Calgary), 11 July 1959, 3.

35 *Gazette* (Montreal), 4 July 1959, 1.

36 NAC, RG7 MG23, vol. 27, Graham to J.A. Phillips, 24 March 1958.

37 *Vancouver Sun*, 18 July 1959, 9, 17.

38 See, for example, *Toronto Daily Star*, 23 June 1959, 6.

39 NAC, Diefenbaker papers, M26 M, vol. 107, 92410-11, Donald Fleming to the prime ministers, 6 August 1959, enclosing Fleming to Bogden, 6 August 1959.

40 NAC, RG7 MG23, vol. 33, File: final statement of accounts.

41 NAC, RG7 MG23, vol. 33, File: train, Graham to S.F. Dingle, 1 June 1959; ibid., vol. 28, File: finance-general, Graham to E.R. Beddoe.

42 *Toronto Daily Star*, 18 June 1959, 3; 24 June 1959, 11; and 18 July 1959, 3; *Guardian* (Charlottetown), 11 July 1959, 4.

43 NAC, RG7 MG23, vol. 26, Graham to Mrs. J.I. Whimster (Corresponding Secretary, Soroptimist Club of Nelson), 26 January 1959. Similar letters to all the other organizations can be found in vol. 26.

44 NAC, RG7 MG23, vol. 27, Graham to Hon. J.S. Munro, 3 February 1959.

45 NAC, RG7 MG23, vol. 27, Graham to W.M. McIntyre, 18 February 1959, and to A.T. Alsbury, 3 March 1959.

46 NAC, RG7 MG23, vol. 27, Graham to J.K. Chalker, 17, 22 April 1959.

47 NAC, Diefenbaker papers, MG26 M, vol. 107, 91756, 91751-52, Lloyd Jackson to Diefenbaker, 14 January 1959; Graham's memo to Diefenbaker with the latter's annotations, and Diefenbaker to Jackson, 22 January 1959.

48 NAC, RG7 MG23, vol. 26, notes for Group Captain Richards, 5 January 1959.

49 NAC, RG7 MG23, vol. 27, Graham to H.S. Lee, 30 April 1959.

50 NAC, RG7 MG23, vol. 27, Graham to Col. F.F. MacEachern, 6 February 1959.

51 NAC, RG7 MG23, vol. 27, Graham to Hon. A. Russell Patrick, 19 March 1959.
52 NAC, RG7 MG23, vol. 27, Graham to Frank Ross, 4 March 1959.
53 *The Evening Telegram* (St. John's), 17 June 1959, 9.
54 NAC, RG7 MG23, vol. 27, Graham to G-M Pelletier, 27 February 1959.
55 *Toronto Daily Star*, 25 June 1959, 3.
56 NAC, RG7 MG23, vol. 27, Graham to George Hees, 21 April 1959.
57 *Globe and Mail*, 22 June 1959, 17.
58 *Telegram* (Toronto), 2 July 1959, 6.
59 *Saskatoon Star-Phoenix*, 2 July 1959, 2.
60 *Evening Telegram* (St. John's), 3 July 1959, 1; *Star* (Montreal), 3 July 1959, 21.
61 NAC, RG7 MG23, vol. 27, Graham to H.M. Jones, 9 March 1959.
62 *Toronto Daily Star*, 3 July 1959, 3.
63 *Vancouver Sun*, 10 July 1959, 1 and 11 July 1959, 2.
64 *Province* (Vancouver), 17 July 1959, 19; *Toronto Daily Star*, 17 July 1959, 3
65 *Albertan* (Calgary), 'Stampede Edition,' 3 July 1959, 17.
66 NAC, RG7 MG23, vol. 28, Graham to T.L. Hill, 19 May 1959.
67 *Toronto Daily Star*, 18 December 1959, 13. In a later column Berton triumphantly quoted editorials to prove his predictions had been correct. See ibid., 24 July 1959, 21.
68 NAC, RG7 MG23, vol. 28, Graham to F.T. Collins, 10 June 1959.
69 *Province* (Vancouver), 16 June 1959, 4.
70 *Saskatoon Star-Phoenix*, 19 June 1959, 2 and *Toronto Daily Star*, 26 June 1959, 11.
71 *Hamilton Spectator*, 2 July 1959, 2.
72 UTA, Massey papers, box 354, file 5, Graham to Adeane, 8 May 1959.
73 *Toronto Daily Star*, 19 June 1959, 6.
74 *Globe and Mail*, 19 June 1959, 8; *Telegram* (Toronto), 25 June 1959, 4.
75 *Toronto Daily Star*, 26 June 1959, 1.
76 *Globe and Mail* (Toronto), 29 July 1959, 1 and 27 June 1959, 8; *Telegram* (Toronto), 3 July 1959, 26.
77 *Toronto Daily Star*, 29 June 1959, 5.
78 *Globe and Mail*, 27 June 1959, 8.
79 *Toronto Daily Star*, 22 July 1959, 3.
80 *Toronto Daily Star*, 24 July 1959, 3.
81 *Ottawa Citizen*, 28 July 1958, 5.
82 *Globe and Mail*, 22 June 1959, 25 and *Toronto Daily Star*, 22 June 1959, 3.
83 *Toronto Daily Star*, 31 July 1959, 3.
84 NAC, RG7 MG23, vol. 27, Graham to F.H. Miller, 10 March 1959.
85 *Gazette* (Montreal), 25 June 1959, 8.
86 *Calgary Herald*, 1 August 1959, 13.
87 *Hamilton Spectator*, 24 June 1959, 35 and 4 July 1959, 2; *Vancouver Sun*, 10 June 1959, 4.
88 *Leader-Post* (Regina), 20 June 1959, 1.
89 *Toronto Daily Star*, 7 July 1959, 6 and *Daily Gleaner* (Fredericton), 13 July 1959, 4.
90 *Gazette* (Montreal), 1 July 1959, 1.
91 *Toronto Daily Star*, 29 June 1959, 1.
92 *Leader-Post* (Regina), 23 July 1959, 5.
93 *Saskatoon Star-Phoenix*, 3 July 1959, 1.
94 *Toronto Daily Star*, 4 July 1959, 3.
95 *Globe and Mail*, 1 August 1959, 8.
96 *Vancouver Sun*, 18 June 1959, 5.
97 *Albertan* (Calgary), 3 July 1959, 3.
98 *Ottawa Journal*, 24 July 1959, 6.
99 *Gazette* (Montreal), 15 June 1959, 12.
100 See NAC, CBC Archives, RG41, vol. 246, file 11-37-14-8, part 8, highly confidential memorandum from T.F. Benson, executive producer, royal visit 1959, 26 January 1959.
101 *Vancouver Sun*, 9 July 1959, 53.
102 *Times* (London), 18 July 1959, in Diefenbaker papers, NAC, MG26 M, vol. 107, p. 92433.
103 *Montreal Star*, 19 June 1959, 2.

104 *Toronto Daily Star*, 34 June 1959, 3 and 26 June 1959, 3.
105 *Province* (Vancouver), 26 June 1959, 2. But other estimates put the crowd at around 500,000. See *Leader-Post* (Regina), 26 June 1959, 3.
106 *Montréal-Matin*, 23 June 1959.
107 *Gazette* (Montreal), 22 June 1959, 2; *Ottawa Journal*, 19 June 1959, 5.
108 *Toronto Daily Star*, 18 June 1959, 1.
109 *Winnipeg Free Press*, 2 July 1959, 29.
110 *Vancouver Sun*, 20 June 1959, 2.
111 *Toronto Daily Star*, 27 June 1959, 7.
112 *Ottawa Citizen*, 20 June 1959, 7.
113 *Telegram* (Toronto), 29 June 1959, 1 and *Toronto Daily Star*, 6 July 1959, 3.
114 *The Leader-Post* (Regina), 31 July 1959, 5.
115 *Albertan* (Calgary), 9 July 1959, 3; 10 July 1959, 1.
116 *Vancouver Sun*, 11 July 1959, p. 1.
117 *Toronto Daily Star*, 29 July 1959, 3.
118 NAC, RG7 MG23, vol. 26, Graham to Laurie McKechnie, 22 January 1959.
119 *Province* (Vancouver), 22 July 1959, 1.
120 *Ottawa Citizen*, 17 June 1959, 4.
121 *Albertan* (Calgary), 13 June 1959, 4.
122 'British' to the editor, n.d., *Albertan* (Calgary), 25 June 1959, 4.
123 *Province* (Vancouver), 21 July 1959, 4.
124 NAC, RG7 MG23, vol. 25, staff meeting no. 7, 23 March 1959 and 'Further Notes for Guidance on Planning Royal Tour of Canada 1959,' 26 March 1959.
125 *Hamilton Spectator*, 19 June 1959, 1.
126 G.B. Bow to the editor, n.d., *Vancouver Sun*, 8 July 1959, 4.
127 *Province* (Vancouver), 11 June 1959, 4.
128 R.K. Johnston to the editor, n.d., *Halifax Chronicle-Herald*, 23 July 1959, 4; 'Veteran' to the editor, n.d., *Province* (Vancouver), 29 June 1959, 4.
129 *Hamilton Spectator*, 23 June 1959, p. 1 and *Toronto Daily Star*, 24 June 1959, 1.
130 *L'Action Populaire* (Joliette), 1 July 1959, 1 and *Montreal Star*, 13 July 1959, 12.
131 NAC, MG23 RG7, vol. 27, Graham to Lt Col. F.F. to McEachern, 23 March 1959.
132 *Saskatoon Star-Phoenix*, 27 June 1959, 2.
133 *Telegram* (Toronto), 25 July 1959, 23.
134 *Toronto Daily Star*, 6 July 1959, 3.
135 'Canadian' to the editor, *Vancouver Sun*, 11 July 1959,4.
136 *Vancouver Sun*, 6 July 1959, 4.
137 '50 Year resident' to the editor, n.d., *Province* (Vancouver), 31 July 1959, 4.
138 *Gazette* (Montreal), 23 June 1959, 6.
139 See, for example, Barry Crewly to editor, n.d., *Province* (Vancouver), 25 July 1959, 4.
140 'European to the editor,' n.d. in *Montreal Star*, 3 July 1959, 8.
141 *Ottawa Citizen*, 22 June 1959, 35.
142 *Globe and Mail* (Toronto), 18 June 1959, 6.
143 *Ottawa Citizen*, 29 June 1959, 9; *Globe and Mail* (Toronto), 30 June 1959, 13.
144 For example, in New Westminster only 3,000 of an expected 9,000 schoolchildren showed up; *Vancouver Sun*, 15 July 1959, 16.
145 *Toronto Daily Star*, 23 June 1959, 6.
146 *The Telegram* (Toronto), 1 August 1959, 6.
147 *The Leader-Post* (Regina), 18 June 1959, 21.
148 *Mike: The Memoirs of the Right Honourable Lester B. Pearson* (Toronto: University of Toronto Press, 1975), Vol. 3: 291.
149 English, *The Worldly Years*, 298.
150 Elizabeth Longford, *Elizabeth R: A Biography* (London: Weidenfeld and Nicolson, 1984), 322.
151 *Mike*, 3: 300-1.

5

'An Objective of US Foreign Policy since the Founding of the Republic': The United States and the End of Empire in Canada

Gordon T. Stewart

Inventive historians can select many moments that may have marked the end of empire in Canada. The earliest possible choice would be the 1840s and 1850s when Britain gradually conceded internal self-government to the North American colonies, began withdrawing the imperial garrisons, and, by moving to free trade, terminated the commercial system that had undergirded the empire for the previous two hundred years. Another possible nineteenth-century date might be the 1871 Treaty of Washington, which settled the Anglo-American tensions caused during the American Civil War and, among other things, constituted a tacit British admission that the United States was the paramount power in North America. A more conventional choice would be the era between the two world wars of the twentieth century. Beginning with British recognition of the dominions' right to a role in war planning in the last two years of the 1914-18 war, running through to the Balfour Declaration at the 1926 Imperial Conference, which outlined dominion autonomy in the foreign policy arena, to the formal statutory confirmation of that change in 1931 in the Statute of Westminster, and culminating in Canada's own decision to enter the Second World War, these two decades witnessed much of the formal dismantling of Britain's imperial prerogatives and influence.

A specific North American marker of this change occurred in 1927 when Canada and the United States for the first time established direct and formal diplomatic ties between Ottawa and Washington, and so ceased working their relationship through the cumbersome channels of the British Colonial and Foreign Office. The Second World War is another obvious choice. R.D. Cuff and J.L. Granatstein observe that Canada's willingness to enter into permanent defence arrangements with the United States 'marked the shift of Canada from a British Dominion to Canada as an American protectorate.'[1] But several dates in the post-1945 era also suggest themselves: the appointing of Canadian-born Governors General from 1949 onwards, the break with Britain over Suez in 1956, and the patriation of the British

North America Act in 1982. All these occasions are plausible candidates for the end of empire 'moment' in Canadian history. But if officials in the US Department of State were called into this debate to make their choice they might well plump for one particular date – 23 May 1963.

There is no reason to regard this view as definitive – readings of developments in Canada by US administrations were frequently mistaken, since they naturally saw matters primarily in the light of their own assumptions and concerns. But American views are worth paying attention to because ever since the winning of independence from Britain, American policymakers had been particularly sensitive to the continuing imperial presence in North America. Indeed, the removal of the British imperial factor from North America had been a permanent goal of United States policy with respect to Canada ever since 1783.

For the first thirty years after independence, Americans viewed Canada as an active and aggressive agent of British imperialism that sought to check US expansion westwards. Even after the War of 1812 – 'this second war for our independence,' as Representative Israel Dickens of North Carolina put it – Americans still viewed imperial links with Native peoples from the Great Lakes to the Rockies with suspicion, and worried about British designs in the Pacific Northwest.[2] The Canadian rebellions of 1837 led Americans to think that Canada was finally following its geographic destiny by joining the United States and all the Central and South American republics that had thrown off European rule between 1811 and the 1820s. But those expectations were disappointed when, far from disappearing from the checkerboard of British possessions, the remaining North American colonies banded together to form the Dominion of Canada in 1867. Between 1880 and 1914 this strengthened and enlarged colonial state viewed itself as a vital link in the British worldwide empire. British capital backed a local Canadian expansionism that spread across the continent and for a time in the 1890s even seemed to constitute a rival to the American commercial presence in Hawaii and the Pacific.

The flag-waving rejection of the 1911 reciprocity treaty by Canadians on the grounds that Canada did not wish to undermine the imperial connection seemed to confirm that Canada's imperial orientation remained strong even in the first decade of the new century. Only in the interwar years, as Canadian politicians, historians, and artists paid attention to their North American roots and Canada developed full political autonomy from Britain, did the imperial option seem to begin finally dissolving. The intense collaboration between the US and Canada in the Second World War, and the integrative economic forces thereafter, seemed to put the imperial presence even further in the past, but just when the Americans thought the imperial era was over, it came roaring back during the Diefenbaker years between 1957 and 1963 as Canada balked on the issue of joint military defence of North America and called openly for a revival of the old Empire-Commonwealth trading system. That is why 23 May 1963 took on so much significance.

On that day a meeting took place in Ottawa between the new Canadian Prime Minister Lester Pearson and three top American officials – Secretary of State Dean Rusk, Secretary of Defense Robert McNamara, and the American Ambassador to Canada, W. Walton Butterworth. Pearson informed these three high-ranking Americans that the end of empire in Canada had finally come. He was blunt and left no room for ambiguity. As Butterworth reported:

> Perhaps the most noteworthy assertion of Pearson related to the British Commonwealth and the 'crisis' with respect to French Canada. As regards the former, Pearson frankly stated that the British Empire and Commonwealth, as it had previously existed, was in rapid dissolution by the emergence of colonial entities into independent states, and that the advent of African Commonwealth states doomed the Commonwealth system. He expressed the hope, but by no means confidently, that some special relationship would continue to be maintained between Canada, New Zealand, Australia and the United Kingdom and perhaps India. By implication he also sold the continuation of empire preferences short.[3]

The initial American reaction to the election of Pearson, and to his words on this occasion, was a huge sigh of relief. For the six years of John Diefenbaker's Progressive Conservative government, American officials had been concerned and then deeply worried that Canada's apparently comprehensively integrated relationship with the US, set in powerful motion by the military and economic cooperation during the Second World War and its aftermath, was about to be checked, perhaps even reversed, by the revitalization of Canada's imperial connection. Diefenbaker gave them plenty of evidence that this unanticipated reversal against the 'natural' course (in American eyes) of ever-increasing economic and military integration of the two North American neighbours was under way. American policymakers had thought that the empire bogey, which had frequently bedevilled US relations with Canada since 1783 and which had last reared its head with the trade-preference system set up at the Ottawa imperial conference in 1932, had receded into the history books. Because of the twin impact of those two catastrophic events, the Great Depression and the Second World War, Canada had agreed, first, to a reciprocal trade treaty with the US in 1935, undermining the imperial arrangements of 1932, and second, had committed itself to close military and economic ties with its neighbour during the war. But the Diefenbaker years had made American political leaders and officials wonder if they had been mistaken in their assessment that the imperial link was a thing of the past for Canada.

At the very starting point of modern American policymaking with respect to Canada, there was an acute awareness of the imperial dimension. A memorandum drafted in 1931 by Benjamin Wallace in the Office of the Economic Advisor excoriated the traditional American approach since the end of the Civil War of building up high tariff walls. This approach had simply forced Canada into imperial and nationalist alternatives. Wallace opened his paper by stating bluntly that 'the greatest error in the commercial policy of the United States has been the treatment of Canada. Canadians are of the same language and stock, and have essentially the same standard of living and the same political outlook and ideals as Americans. The boundary between us is largely artificial and Canada is so divided geographically that the natural trade routes are North and South. There is no military, or political, or economic reason for not treating Canada economically as part of the United States.'

He pointed out that because Canada was next to the United States it was exceptionally vulnerable to American tariff policies. 'Canada's difficulties in reaching other markets,' he argued, 'makes her peculiarly dependent on the United States, so that our tariff policy has hurt Canada more than it has hurt any other country. We have been in position to exploit the Canadians and we have done it ruthlessly. In no other country is there so much bitterness against the American tariff and so much reason for bitterness.' Wallace warned that sustained American protectionism always pushed Canada into the arms of the empire. He traced all of Canada's moves towards protection – John A. Macdonald's national policy initiated in 1879 and Wilfrid Laurier's introduction of imperial preference in 1897 – as reactions to prior American tariff hikes. 'After the [1914-18] war,' he maintained, 'the Liberal party of Canada made several successive reductions in the tariff but the hostile attitude of the United States discredited them, and their opponents made drastic increases after the recent revision of the US Tariff act and are proposing further large steps toward a union of the British Empire.' Wallace urged his masters to act quickly in an attempt to forestall further imperial binding: 'if anything is ever to be done to initiate closer trade relations between the US and Canada it should be done well before June 1932 when the next imperial conference meets.'[4]

Wallace's advice was not followed in 1931 because of domestic economic and political conditions in the United States. It is also very doubtful that any American action at that stage would have prevented the attempt by Prime Minister R.B. Bennett to follow through on his election slogans and attempt to solve the problems of the Depression by increasing intra-empire trade. But Wallace's proposed strategy was the one that took hold within the State Department over the next twenty-five years. The first harbinger of the new thinking, which was stimulated into actual policy because of the shock of the 1932 imperial-preference system, was the decision to explore an American trade treaty with Canada. In July 1933 William C. Bullitt, one of the American delegates to the 1933 London Economic Conference and soon to be appointed US Ambassador in Moscow, suggested to President Roosevelt the possibility of a reciprocal trade treaty so that 'via Canada we might make a hole in the Ottawa agreements.'[5] In February 1933 Pierre de Boal, American Chargé in Ottawa, reported a private conversation with Bennett in the course of which the Canadian prime minister had told him that he was willing to turn to the United States to 'free himself from the criticism that his economic policy in embracing the Empire had isolated Canada from its natural market, the United States.'[6] By the end of September 1934 there was an ad hoc British Empire Committee established in the State Department whose 'primary function was to determine the best means of undermining the imperial preference system.'[7]

A further sign that this new strategic thinking with respect to Canada had taken hold was the way in which academic experts entered the picture as advisers to the State Department officials responsible for Canada, and urged upon them the vital importance for the US of gaining access to Canadian markets and resources. A key figure in this respect was Professor W.Y. Elliot of Harvard's Department of Government. Elliot was the mentor of Henry Kissinger and also taught the future Canadian Prime Minister Pierre Trudeau (to whom he wrote in 1969 to complain about Canada's nationalist policies). A close relationship developed between Elliot and John D. Hickerson, Assistant Chief of the Division of Western European Affairs and the leading American expert on Canada in the 1930s and 1940s. In his letters to Hickerson, Elliot focused on the long-term goals of gaining access to Canada's minerals and natural resources and integrating Canada into the American-dominated North American economy by breaking the imperial orientation that Canada had once more opted for in 1932. He argued that 'from an economic point of view the resources of the northern and southern halves of the North American continent are in many respects complementary rather than competitive.' Canada was rich in non-ferrous metal resources and hydroelectric power but was deficient in iron, coal, and oil. Gaining easier access to 'Canadian mineral and power resources would directly aid in the solution of current economic and political problems such as those of dwindling international and national trade, of exchange transfer and debt payments, falling prices and monetary unsettlement, and extravagant economic nationalism and economic imperialism.' As Wallace had done, Elliot criticized the tendency of American policy, driven often by political forces in Congress, to cling to the shibboleths of protectionism, thus forcing Canada to turn to imperial solutions. 'Canadian participation in economic imperialism,' he told Hickerson, 'is based on resentment of American trade policy. Canada's natural economic ties are with the United States and are always quickly recognized when the opportunity is present. By allowing natural

forces free play, the completely artificial and extremely threatening structure of imperial economic antagonism to the United States would collapse.
The economic disadvantages to the United States of the Ottawa Empire
Conference are obvious; the damages to friendly relations and international
progress are incalculable.'

Despite the American tariff barriers that had been built up since 1866, the
economic ties between the United States and Canada had multiplied, which
proved to Elliot's satisfaction that economic integration was almost like a
force of nature. In spite of seventy years of ever-increasing American tariff
barriers, trade with Canada was 'by far the largest volume of trade which
the United States has with any one country,' and by 1931 the United States
invested more dollars in Canada than in all of South America, with the
amount now approaching the total US investment in all of Europe. To convey the scale of these economic links, Elliot pointed out that the interest
received by the United States on Canadian investments 'exceeded by 60
percent the total of similar interest, including all War Debt payments, received from any other country in 1931. In fact Canada is annually meeting
payments in New York far in excess of the total annual sums of both principal and interest due, paid or unpaid, from all the Allied War Debtors.' The
implications for US policy, concluded Elliot, were surely obvious. Negotiating a reciprocal trade arrangement that would lower tariffs and other obstacles to trade and investment would be 'an all important step in business
and monetary recovery and in dealing with current economic and political
problems such as the War Debts, and the economic imperialism of the British Empire.'[8]

This new thinking was one of the principal factors leading to the 1935
reciprocal trade treaty between the United States and Canada. That treaty
was much more limited than Elliot's grand strategic vision. This was because of the usual gap between the writings of academic advisers operating
purely in the world of ideas and statistics, and the practical outcomes in the
messy world where Congressional politics and international affairs came
together. Even though US experts like Hickerson saw the validity of the
points made by Wallace and Elliot, there were powerful political obstacles
to change. Above all, to allow – in the midst of the Depression – more Canadian grains and other farm products into the United States would have been
very hard to justify. It was telling that at one of the last meetings in connection with the 1935 treaty held in the Oval Office between President Roosevelt
and Hickerson and the two principal American negotiators (Henry Grady
and Francis Sayre) there was no grand visionary talk. The president was
concerned about steps taken to protect American agriculture from the reductions on the limited list of Canadian imports agreed to in the treaty, and
even took pains to ask about the impact on the dairy interests in his own
state.[9] Yet in spite of the limited nature of the 1935 agreement, American

policymakers believed they had made a good start (in difficult economic circumstances) at turning back the empire threat.

This reading of the course of events since the 1932 Ottawa conference seemed powerfully confirmed when William Lyon Mackenzie King was returned to office as prime minister following the 1935 election. The impression of American success in turning Canada away from Britain and toward the United States was strongly reinforced by the words and behaviour of King shortly after he took office. Norman Armour, the American minister in Ottawa, could hardly conceal his astonishment at the dramatic shift that had taken place. On 25 October 1935, the Canadian Thanksgiving holiday, the US minister was surprised by a visit from King, who had only taken office the night before. The new prime minister, Armour reported, 'insisted on coming to my house to see me although I assured him that I felt it was for me to come and see him.' King told Armour he had always been in favour of freer trade between the United States and Canada. In 1911 he had gone down to defeat with Wilfrid Laurier on that issue and in 1929 he had spoken to the then US minister, William Phillips, about possible tariff reductions. The Wall Street crash, followed by economic depression, had led to 'the disastrous Hawley-Smoot tariff and the defeat of Mr. King's own government' and the hiking of imperial tariffs in 1932. It was time to break away from these exclusionist policies. According to Armour, King continued in an even more effusive vein: 'He was himself, he laughingly remarked, accused of being pro-American. In fact they referred to him as "the American" and with a good deal of reason for so much of his life had been spent in the United States. He made it plain, as Dr. Skelton had done, that there were two roads open to Canada but that he wanted to choose "the American road" if we made it possible for him to do so. From every point of view, it was important that our attachment should be strong and our relations brought closer in every way, political as well as economic.'[10]

King's assurance that Canada was prepared to take 'the American road' seemed to become an irreversible course because of post-1935 trade patterns and, above all, the impact of the Second World War. The building up of an empire preference system in the wake of the 1932 Ottawa conference had led J. Pierrepont Moffat, then US Consul General in Australia (and later US minister to Canada), to expostulate that 'in matters of trade London is bitterly hostile ... I have reluctantly reached the conclusion that Britain is using her financial pressure to make preferential bargains, and that despite lip service to the Secretary's ideals she is fighting his theory ... to the last ditch.'[11] The reciprocal agreement with Canada seemed to stop this policy in its tracks in North America. In the four years after its signing, the American share of Canadian imports increased from 56.4 percent to 62.6 percent while the share 'supplied by the United Kingdom and countries outside the British Empire decreased proportionately.'[12] William Culbertson, vice-chairman of the US Tariff Commission, believed the Canadian treaty to be the most important of the series of reciprocal trade agreements the Americans had made in the 1930s.[13]

These trends were intensified by the war. Between August 1940 and April 1941 Canada entered into two agreements with the United States that tied the two countries closer than they had ever been before in economic and military matters. The Ogdensburg agreement committed Canada to a common defence policy for North America; the Hyde Park agreement set out the terms for economic collaboration to mobilize the resources of the continent. Together the two agreements set the stage for the post-1945 integration of the two countries' economies and defence policies. As Cuff and Granatstein remarked, the Hyde Park arrangements 'foretold the integration of the North American economies we live with today.'[14] After the war, continuing international economic problems, the devastation in Europe and Japan, and the advent of the Cold War drove the United States and Canada into an intimate working relationship. The tide reached its height in 1948 when discussions took place about eliminating all trade barriers between the two countries and setting up a complete free trade market for North America. The negotiators on the American side were Woodbury Willoughby, associate chief of the Division of Commercial Policy, and Willard Thorp, assistant secretary of state for economic affairs. The Canadian team was led by Hector Mackinnon, chairman of the Dominion Tariff Board, and John Deutsch, director of the Economic Relations Office in the Department of Finance. Both sides understood the far-reaching consequences of the proposal they had under discussion. Mackinnon and Deutsch viewed the free trade proposal 'if implemented, to be one of the most momentous decisions in their [Canadian] history.' On the American side Thorp explained that the phasing out of tariffs 'would result in the immediate elimination of all Empire preferences granted by Canada, with important economic and political implications for the United States.' This was, Thorp emphasized, 'a unique opportunity of promoting the most efficient utilization of the resources of the North American continent and knitting the two countries together – an objective of US foreign policy since the founding of the republic.'[15]

On all fronts the dozen years following the 1935 trade agreement were a huge success story for American policy with respect to Canada. In military and economic terms Canada was now solidly within the American sphere of influence. The fears that Canada might strengthen its imperial affiliations – fears that had surfaced in the 1880s and 1890s with Canada's robust territorial and economic expansion and association with imperial federation, fears that had concerned President William Howard Taft and Secretary of State Philander C. Knox in 1911, and fears that had caused acute concern as recently as 1932 – now seemed utterly remote. In a long confidential dispatch in November 1948, US minister in Canada Lawrence Steinhardt drew attention to the war-time and postwar developments that had tended 'to strengthen Canadian military integration with the United States.' Even as he wrote, the Canadian cabinet was pressing for more joint production agreements: This 'integration of military resources [was] the major change since before the war.' But on the economic front too the pre-war patterns had 'altered fundamentally.' Canada could no longer raise a sufficient surplus on her trade with Britain to support an adverse balance with the United States. The Hyde Park arrangements had addressed this problem for Canada and had set the stage for 'a closer integration of the economies of the two countries.' With Britain's exchange problems and general economic difficulties after 1945, Canada had nowhere to turn but the United States. 'One of the results of the changes in Canada's international trade,' Steinhardt continued, 'is that now three-quarters of Canada's total imports are from the United States compared to two-thirds before the war. Similarly, half of her exports are now marketed in the United States compared with two-fifths in the late 1930s.' The fact that it was the Canadians who took the initiative in the 1948 free trade talks was a sign that new modes of thinking had taken hold. The growing influence of American culture on Canada was another sign that the underlying trends were working in favour of American goals: 'Economically and militarily, Canada's orientation is shifting from Great Britain to the United States. The Commonwealth tie is still a cherished heritage for many but as Great Britain's economic and military power declines in relation to that of the United States, the Canadian government has tended to turn more to the latter as a source of economic welfare and military security. Improved means of transportation and communications have made the full impact of US culture felt in Canada so that in this regard as well a shift in orientation is discernible.'[16]

Inside the State Department there was evident satisfaction with this overview. William Snow, the assistant chief at the British Commonwealth desk, told Julian Harrington, minister at the US embassy in Ottawa, that he had taken Steinhardt's dispatch home and read it over the weekend: 'It is a fine piece of work, thoughtful, well-written, and timely.' Snow added that 'all indications we see at this end point to the fact that the British tie is not as strong as it was either before or during the war.'[17]

American complacency about the decline of imperial influence and the increasing economic, military, and cultural alignment of Canada with the United States received a further boost when the St. Lawrence Seaway agreement was made in 1953. From the American viewpoint the opening of a jointly operated seaway functioned like a zipper to draw the two economies into a continental whole. The question of the St. Lawrence navigation had first appeared back in the 1820s when the United States had pushed for free navigation from the lakes down the St. Lawrence to the Atlantic. Richard

Rush, on the instructions of Secretary of State John Quincy Adams, set out the American case to William Huskisson and George Canning, the British negotiators. Adams had urged Rush to rest the American case 'upon the sound and general principles of the laws of nature' and Rush took up that line of argument by proposing to the British that 'the river is the only outlet provided by nature for the inhabitants of several among the largest and most populous states of the American union. The right to use it as a medium of communication with the ocean rests upon the same ground of natural right and obvious necessity heretofore asserted by the government in behalf of the people of other portions of the United States in relation to the Mississippi.'[18]

In this American view the St. Lawrence, which ran through Canada, was to be treated in the same way as the Mississippi, to which the Americans had staked claims of navigation rights in 1783 (when the land it passed through was claimed by Spain) and which since the Louisiana Purchase of 1803 ran entirely through American territory (at least in its navigable part – it would take until the 1818 Convention to ensure that the whole course of the Mississippi lay in US territory). The Americans demanded that the St. Lawrence be open to Americans on the same terms as Canadians. Secretary of State Henry Clay summed up the American viewpoint in 1826, characteristically arguing 'that the interests of the greater population and the more fertile and extensive country above shall not be sacrificed to the jealousy and rivalry of the small population inhabiting a more limited and less productive country below.'[19] The American overtures were rejected on the grounds that to allow free navigation of the St. Lawrence to American ships would establish 'a perpetual thoroughfare through the heart of a British colony and under the walls of its principal fortress [Quebec].'[20] Such language simply confirmed to Americans that Canada was indeed a full-blown, armed, and troublesome imperial presence.

The issue died down after this burst of negotiation in the 1820s. The opening of the Erie Canal in 1825, the development of the Mississippi transport system, the emergence of railways after the 1840s, and the general growth of the internal American economy, which did not need to export to thrive, all helped make the St. Lawrence a minor issue. But it did remain an occasional irritant. In 1892, for example, Samuel Moffatt, chief editorial writer of the *New York Journal,* who prided himself on his knowledge of Canada and whose writings were read by Theodore Roosevelt, let this irritation rise to the surface. American policy, Moffatt began, 'is based upon the fact that the United States is, and intends to remain, the paramount power in the western hemisphere.' The one force working against this outcome was Canada, that expanding remnant of the British Empire in North America. Other European powers had demonstrated their acceptance of American hemispheric power by withdrawing from the continent, as Russia had done from Alaska in 1867, but Britain had remained and even augmented its presence. Indeed, through the creation of Canadian Confederation, Britain had embarked on a course of commercial rivalry. In the post-Civil War years the economic growth of the United States had led to the emergence of great industrial and port cities such as Chicago, Detroit, Cleveland, and Buffalo in the Great Lakes basin. Except for the position of Canada, Moffatt argued: 'They would rest in perfect security. No enemy could ever get at them ... Nowhere in the world is the key of one country's treasure thus left in the hands of another. The nearest position to such a situation is the position of Russia, with the Dardanelles in possession of Turkey. But Russia's interests in the Black Sea do not compare with those of the United States in the Great Lakes. Odessa, Batum and Sebastopol are a small stake beside Chicago, Cleveland, Buffalo, Detroit, Milwaukee, Toledo and Duluth.'[21]

These expressions of opinion had no policy implications at the time (although they did feed into the Republican determination in the 1890s to build the tariff walls even higher) but they did reflect the lingering American suspicion that Canada, backed by British capital resources, was continuing the old imperial game of checking American hegemony in North America. The St. Lawrence issue became a live one again in the 1920s when grain growers and shippers from Minneapolis and Chicago were seeking additional outlets for their exports. When the first US minister appointed to Ottawa was briefed on American priorities upon assuming office in 1927, top of the list was 'the negotiation of the St. Lawrence river project.'[22] But there was no movement forward because of domestic opposition in both countries. Canadian governments in the 1920s were much more interested in getting reductions in American tariffs and worried about construction costs. On the American side, railway interests, grain elevator companies, and grain shippers who used the New York and Baltimore outlets lobbied against the St. Lawrence project.

The talk about the St. Lawrence route to the sea petered out, but was revived after the Second World War. On this occasion, Under Secretary of State Dean Acheson sought to move things forward by sketching out the strategic significance of the St. Lawrence route in the light of the war experience and the new threats emerging in the postwar world. The National Security Resources Board had already pointed out that such a route would enable iron ore supplies to be brought to the United States from Labrador without exposing the ships to submarine attacks. Acheson himself, in his testimony before a Senate committee set up to examine the issue, echoed Moffatt's point made back in 1892. By this time the United States was more concerned about exports of manufactured goods than it had been in the 1890s, and the US industrial heartland needed a direct connection with the ocean. As Acheson explained to the senators: 'Almost unique among the highly industrialized sections of the world our middle western manufacturing areas have grown up far away from ocean transportation ... Since the First World War, this area has progressively grown into a surplus-producing area which now must ship its products not only within the United States but to foreign countries, and which must secure its raw materials not only from within the United States but increasingly from abroad. For all this a water route to the sea is needed.'[23]

Even with this kind of strategic overview the executive branch still had difficulties. The old railway and shipping companies were joined by power companies who worried about the impact of the new hydroelectric generating capacity that would be an offshoot of the seaway. But the Canadian economy was more prosperous by the 1950s and so the costs could be better borne than in the 1920s. Moreover, there was now an acute need in Canada's manufacturing heartland between Hamilton and Toronto for additional electricity. It was the determination of the Canadians to proceed with a seaway on their own that finally pushed things to the point of action in the United States. The US Joint Chiefs had already argued back in 1946 that from a national security standpoint it would not be acceptable to have a purely Canadian-controlled route into the American interior. Using these kinds of arguments to counter the remaining opposition in Congress, the Eisenhower administration finally succeeded in getting the Wiley-Dondero Bill passed in 1953, which committed the United States to joint construction and operation of the seaway. Thus a contentious issue that had first been identified back in the 1820s was resolved. Back then the enemy had been British imperial intransigence; since the 1920s it had been intransigence in the US Congress. Both these obstacles were overcome by the early 1950s in a manner that ensured American access to the Atlantic while at the same time tightening even further the economic bonds with Canada.

While American officials were always aware of the possible return of the Empire-Commonwealth option, they saw historical forces working in the American direction. Even when the allegedly pro-American St. Laurent government was defeated and the Conservatives led by Diefenbaker came into power in 1957, American policymakers saw no great danger that the historical clock would be turned back. Indeed, when Diefenbaker was first elected, he gave a similarly reassuring performance as King had done back in 1935. In 1957 the American ambassador, Livingston Merchant, telephoned to arrange his first meeting with the new prime minister at 10:30 a.m. that morning – a Saturday: 'Although a Cabinet meeting was in process, the Prime Minister courteously said that when I arrived at his office he would excuse himself from the meeting in order to receive me.' Diefenbaker did indeed leave his cabinet meeting when Merchant arrived. While they were together a telegram was brought in and handed to Diefenbaker. The rest of the story deserves to be told in Merchant's own words:

The Prime Minister then handed it to me with the remark that he didn't know what the protocol was in such cases but that since I was sitting there he wanted me to read it. It was a message of thanks from the Queen. The Prime Minister then said that 'the fact that within minutes of each other he had received these two personal messages was more than mere coincidence – it was prophetic.' He went on to say that this was a remarkable symbol of the ties of Canada to both Great Britain and the United States. He felt very strongly about both. The Prime Minister then started chatting on a variety of subjects in a thoroughly relaxed fashion and notwithstanding the fact that his chair was vacant in the Cabinet meeting in the next room ... I had the impression that he had deliberately seized the first opportunity for a long, informal talk with me (it lasted about forty minutes) with a view to helping to put Washington's mind at ease concerning future relationship with the new Government. He was blunt and obviously felt deeply about wheat. In all other respects and on other topics he reaffirmed in words and attitude his friendliness towards the United States, his recognition of the linkage of our destinies, and his basic assumption that there would be no change in the fundamental elements of Canadian foreign policy.[24]

This impression was confirmed by Secretary of State John Foster Dulles, who told Eisenhower in July 1957 that Diefenbaker 'is, I think, the kind of person we can get along with.' Dulles reported that at a dinner in Ottawa the new ministers

started out in a rather belligerent vein to the effect that 'you had better know once and for all that we intend to work in the Commonwealth with the United Kingdom and that will be the premise of all our action.' However, as we talked frankly and vigorously a good deal of the belligerency disappeared and we were talking realistically about practical problems ... I feel that my visit accomplished a great deal principally in enabling the leading members of the new government to blow off steam in friendly congenial atmosphere and I believe that Livie [Livingston Merchant] and I in the course of the conversation did a good deal to enlighten them and to make them realize that some of their off-hand thinking called for deeper study.[25]

This reading of Diefenbaker's government seemed powerfully confirmed when Canada agreed to the establishment of the North American Air Defense Command in 1957, which continued and intensified the joint defence course set for North America during the Second World War. Then in 1958 Diefenbaker's government agreed to accept the BOMARC weapon system. On the economic front American leaders did not take with any great seriousness Diefenbaker's threats about resurrecting Commonwealth trade.

The American ambassador in London, John Hay Whitney, pointed out that at the centre of the empire this possibility was regarded as a chimera. He reported that the United Kingdom would welcome any increased trade with Canada and would open trade offices and beef up advertising to accomplish that. The Diefenbaker initiative was therefore warmly welcomed as a means to increase British trade with Canada (and access to much needed dollars). But Diefenbaker's vision that this step could be part of a comprehensive plan to build up a Commonwealth trading system was, Whitney assured his masters in Washington, a non-starter for Britain. Diefenbaker had proposed a full Commonwealth trade and economic conference with an eye to developing an intra-Commonwealth trading system.

> The United Kingdom Government's attitude towards this suggestion is quite the opposite of enthusiastic ... The United Kingdom does not expect that a conference could achieve any significant increase in intra-Commonwealth trade or in availability of capital to Commonwealth members ... The United Kingdom has opposed as doomed to failure any inclusion as a conference agenda of tariff preferences. This is not only because of the United Kingdom's overall commercial policies and the rules of GATT, but also because the United Kingdom itself attempted without success in recent years to obtain concerted Commonwealth action on this subject. The newer members of the Commonwealth have not been interested in closer preferential ties ... there would not appear to be any easy means available to a Commonwealth conference for enhancing intra-Commonwealth trade.[26]

This reassuring assessment from London was one of the pieces of evidence that led American officials to discount Diefenbaker's rhetorical flourishes. The empire option seemed very much a thing of the past. In the Cold War world, the United States was anxious that Britain, Canada, and all the Western allies build up prosperous economies, and if trade increased between Canada and Britain, then so much the better. A briefing paper for the presidential visit to Ottawa in 1958 laid out this thinking as Dulles told the Canadians that the United States was 'not sensitive about Canadian discussions in the Commonwealth concerning economic matters. He said trade is not finite and can always be expanded ... The United States feels no concern at all regarding the Commonwealth conference.' On the other side, Canadian leaders continued to make reassuring statements in private to their American counterparts. Donald Fleming, the minister of finance, informed Dulles that 'it is obvious that the Conference cannot be like the Conference of 1932, as the world is now very different. No one is proposing any new Commonwealth trade preferences, but it is proposed to maintain the present system of preferences ... the Conference is not and never has been directed at the United States.'[27]

These early days of mutual reassurance deteriorated rapidly in the later years of the Diefenbaker government. The dramatic issue was in the defence arena. The Canadian government refused to have nuclear warheads on Canadian soil in spite of its acceptance of the BOMARC system, which was designed only for nuclear warheads. As Merchant pointed out in February 1962, the 'Diefenbaker government continues to procrastinate, with strong elements in Cabinet, particularly Foreign Minister Green, opposed to dirtying Canadian hands and reputation with nuclear weapons under any circumstances.'[28] The next day he told the State Department that 'Prime Minister Diefenbaker's remarks on nuclear weapons ... are nothing short of dismaying since they represent irresponsible treatment of a subject of vital importance to both Canada and the United States ... At the moment Diefenbaker is further than ever from the position we would like to see his government take on nuclear weapons.'[29] On 25 January 1963, in the aftermath of the Cuban missile crisis, Diefenbaker tried to explain Canadian policy in the Commons, in what the American assistant secretary of state for European affairs, William Tyler, called 'a long, rambling statement.'[30] The State Department issued a press release on 30 January that in effect challenged Diefenbaker's knowledge, competency, and honesty.[31] This in turn led the furious Diefenbaker to charge that the Americans, by issuing the statement and by cozying up to the opposition leader, Pearson (who had been invited to a White House dinner for Nobel Prize winners from the hemisphere, and spent some time with President Kennedy), were interfering in the upcoming Canadian election. He threatened to publish a note from the presidential advisor Walt Rostow written during Kennedy's visit to Canada, which spoke of the United States pushing Canada (the memo – an unofficial briefing note that Diefenbaker retrieved from a waste basket – listed things that Kennedy was to 'push' in his meetings with Diefenbaker).[32] That part of the story is well known, and became for several years a cause célèbre for Canadian nationalists. The more sober assessments of historians suggest that Diefenbaker was far from blameless.[33]

But if these aspects of the crisis in Canada's relations with the United States – the nuclear weapons issue and the alleged interference in Canadian elections – are widely discussed in the literature, there was a less well-understood aspect involving the Empire-Commonwealth that also fed into the crisis atmosphere. The trade issue, which had seemed so innocuous in the first three years of Diefenbaker's administration, had also entered a tense phase in the last three years, partly because Diefenbaker kept harping on the dangerous levels of American control of the Canadian economy. For example, when he met Kennedy and Rusk in Washington in February 1961, Diefenbaker refreshed the American leaders' knowledge of Canada by pointing out 'that the United States owns 75 percent of Canadian oil, 56 percent of Canadian manufacturing, and 50 percent of Canada's mineral resources.'

Moreover, Diefenbaker continued, Americans remained incredibly ignorant about Canada. He told Kennedy and Rusk that 'Canadian news gets less treatment in the United States than that from a "banana republic."' He predicted to Ambassador Merchant that the coming election campaign in Canada

> would be more bitter than it was in 1911 and he referred to Champ Clark's statement during the course of that campaign which it took the Canadians until 1917 to recover from. (According to my recollection, Champ Clark, the Speaker of the House of Representatives, said something along the lines that it was inevitable that the US should annex Canada. The basic issue of the campaign was the question of reciprocal trade agreement with the US and the outcome of the campaign was won and lost on the slogan of the Conservatives, 'No truck or trade with the Yankees').[34]

With such tormenting words Diefenbaker was forcing Merchant and other American policymakers to think once again in terms of Canada's imperial role. The reference to the 1911 election, which had turned on maintaining the connection with empire, was now being waved provocatively in the faces of American officials by the Canadian prime minister.

The Americans were surprised by this turning back of the clock, but such rhetoric did not alarm them unduly because they had come to expect such posturing from Diefenbaker. However, things took a more serious turn when the possibility of Empire-Commonwealth preferences became a serious policy concern for the first time since 1932. The change that made this a possibility was the decision by the British government to seek entry into the European Economic Community (popularly known as the Common Market) in 1961. This immediately raised the stakes for the United States. American officials were not in the least bit worried, in spite of Diefenbaker's high-blown speechifying, about increased Anglo-Canadian trade, but they were concerned that if Britain were to enter the EEC, taking Commonwealth preferences with them, this would threaten American trading interests by breathing new life into a world-wide preferential trading system linking Britain and its current and former colonies into the large European market. This was a different kettle of fish entirely from the prospect of small increases in bilateral Canadian-UK trade. In a memorandum to the president, George Ball, the under secretary of state for economic affairs, set out these American fears: 'The principal danger to the United States trading interests involved in the British move to adhere to the Common Market lies in the possible extension of Commonwealth preferences to the Common Market countries ... The United States Government has made it consistently clear both to the Common Market countries and to the United Kingdom that we cannot accept any arrangement which contemplates the extension of

Commonwealth preferences to the European Economic Community.'[35] Two months later Rusk wrote to the Embassy in London that 'I have been seriously disturbed by the impression I have received over the past few weeks that the British do not appear to take seriously our view on the need for ultimate elimination of preferential arrangements as an objective of United Kingdom-European Economic Community negotiations ... Do what you can to impress upon the top levels of the United Kingdom Government the importance we attach to arrangements arising out of these negotiations.'[36]

The old issue of Empire-Commonwealth tariffs that had seemed to be sinking into oblivion suddenly took on an urgent salience. Diefenbaker helped this sense of crisis along by tying the defence issue and the trade issue together in his free-wheeling attacks on American perfidy. During his tirade to Ambassador Merchant in May 1962, when he threatened to publish the Rostow note, he took some pleasure in letting Merchant know that he had passed on to the British his account of the note. Diefenbaker explained that 'he had told Macmillan most of this story, and that he [Diefenbaker] had also once been warned by prominent Conservative party members in Britain that the United States would support Pearson in Canadian politics because, through the latter's attitude towards the Common Market, the United States could secure the commercial benefits of the wiping out of Commonwealth preferences.'[37] Merchant proceeded to inform Ball that Diefenbaker had told him that 'he [Diefenbaker] was shocked by your [Ball's] recent speech or statement to the effect that the US wanted to get rid of Commonwealth preferences and that, hence, he concluded that we thought we could achieve this by supporting Pearson who was prepared to accept without argument Britain's unconditional entrance [i.e., without Commonwealth preferences] into the European Common market.'

Later in the year, Diefenbaker again complained about American officials sticking their oar in over the future of preferences: 'Diefenbaker dissertated [sic] at length about British statements,' reported the new American Ambassador Butterworth, 'and implied that our dislike of preferences was the source of the difficulty that Canada and the Commonwealth now faced.'

The trade issue naturally collapsed as a source of tension when French President Charles de Gaulle vetoed British entry in January 1963, but the way it had reared its head had worried Kennedy and Rusk. That was one more reason they would be glad to see the back of Diefenbaker. In his characteristically forceful language, Ambassador Butterworth, who had previously served as US representative to the EEC and who therefore knew the trade issue intimately, provided an appraisal of where things stood with respect to Canada in the wake of the State Department press release on defence and the American efforts to block Empire-Commonwealth preferences linking into the European market. He drew attention to the Canadian nationalist outrage against American interference but thought that the underlying trends were promising. His language gives some sense of the depth of American annoyance with Diefenbaker by this stage:

> In view our patient tolerance of unrealistic Canadian view of external world past half dozen years, witness Government of Canada foot dragging in vital matter of continental defense and pretentious posturing in various international arenas, our sudden dose of cold water naturally produced immediate cry of shock and outrage. Traditional psychopathic accusations of unwarranted US interference in domestic Canadian affairs, while violent, are subsiding quickly and both public and political leadership find hard realities, as set forth in Department release, are staring them in the face and cannot be ignored ... Preponderance of evidence available – news media, editorial comment, private citizens expression of views – indicate shift of public attention from US statement to clear recognition of Diefenbaker's indecisiveness, with frequent and widespread reaffirmation of identity of US and Canadian interests and explicit acknowledgment that Canada has somehow gone astray.[38]

In a concluding section, which showed how American officials, perhaps irritated by Diefenbaker's frequent reminders, viewed the historical context of these events, Butterworth claimed that the corner had now finally been turned: 'Not only is this not 1911, when "No trade or truck with the Yankees" was the slogan which won the election, but it is not even 1957 when Diefenbaker first came to power on a wave of anti-United States jingoism. The world has changed and Canadian people know it ... We look forward to closer Canadian appraisal of what our proximity means to them and greater Canadian realization of their need to cultivate good relations with us.'[39]

It was in this context that American leaders so warmly welcomed the Pearson statement of 23 May 1963, that 'the British Empire and Commonwealth ... was in rapid dissolution.' Those American policymakers who understood the fiscal and trade relations between Canada and the United States since 1935 and Britain's general economic position since 1945 had been slow to accept that a revival of an Empire-Commonwealth trade system was a possibility to be taken seriously. But Diefenbaker's words and actions dealt a sharp shock to the Americans. Presidents and secretaries of state and their staffs were surprised to see the old empire card being waved in their faces when they thought it had been removed from the pack. Pearson told them the card would never be played again.

It was by no means plain sailing for the Americans of course. In fact, they were astounded by the aggressively nationalist stance that the new Pearson government had taken on the issue of American control over the Canadian economy. Walter Gordon's proposals for a nationalistic budget that would seek to check the American presence in the Canadian economy 'came as a real surprise' to George Ball and his fellow policymakers at the State Department. 'The Department [was] extremely unhappy at these budget proposals,' Ball informed the ambassador in Canada.[40] But the central issue between the two countries was now different and clearer than it had been before 1963. Now the problem – from the US viewpoint – was purely one of Canadian nationalism, whereas right down to 1963 Canadian nationalism had always had the potential of being linked with the old Empire-Commonwealth dimension.

Even when routine trade matters had come up in the 1950s, the Americans learned they would have to take the imperial option into account. For example, in the summer of 1953, the counsellor in the US Embassy in Ottawa, Don C. Bliss, warned of Canadian dissatisfaction over the apparent protectionist surge in the US Congress, particularly with respect to dairy, farm, and fish products. He reported a warning from L.D. Wilgress, the under-secretary of state for external affairs (and former Canadian high commissioner in London), that

> if the United States were to introduce restrictions on oats and on fish fillets an almost inevitable result would be the emergence in Canada of a strong demand for closer trade relations within the Commonwealth. He recalled the course of events twenty years ago when the Hawley-Smoot Tariff of 1930 led inevitably to the 1932 Commonwealth Conference in Ottawa, to the establishment of Imperial Preference, and to a new set of trade relationships designed to exclude the United States. Even the passage of our reciprocal trade arrangements legislation in 1934 was not enough to reverse this trend and the consequences are still with us.[41]

Bliss informed his masters in Washington that 'in view of Wilgress' experience with international relationships in the economic field, his words of warning in this connection must be taken seriously.'[42]

After May 1963 the issue never came up in that way again. The United States no longer had to take the empire issue seriously – it had ceased to exist as a policy question in relation to Canada. When Secretary of State Rusk took stock of 'US-Canadian Problems' for President Lyndon Johnson in December 1963, the new conditions were put into sharp focus:

> Over the past few years, our relations with Canada have grown increasingly sticky. The Canadians have maneuvered themselves into an impossible dilemma. Their economic prosperity depends on the continual inflow of US capital. This necessarily brings with it control of their enterprises by US management. They could undoubtedly improve their standard of living if

they accepted the full consequences of this situation and permitted a gradual integration of the Canadian market with our own. But because they are so suspicious of the overwhelming size and power of the United States, they tend to pursue highly nationalistic policies – fearing that otherwise Canada would become, if not the 51st state, at least a neighbor heavily dependent on the US Colossus. The result is that no matter which party may be in power, every Canadian Government feels compelled to try to reduce the economic control that necessarily accompanies reliance on US capital ... The Pearson Government is, in spirit, friendly to us and, in principle, much more sympathetic with US objectives. But it too has felt compelled to take a series of measures that have kept relations on the edge of tension – measures that can, if carried too far, result in serious economic and political problems between our two countries.[43]

Attached to this memorandum was a 'Round-up of US-Canadian problems.' There were eleven items on the list, none of which mentioned any of the traditional Empire-Commonwealth issues. Americans understood they were now faced with pure Canadian nationalism. The empire that had loomed as a direct threat in the early days of the republic, and which had been a cause of sharp concern at various moments in the nineteenth century and an irritating presence well into the 1950s, was finally dead and, this time, buried.

There is a postscript, however, that raises broader questions about Canada and the end of empire. The kind of evidence used here to trace American official thinking on the end of empire in Canada sheds light largely on economic and political perspectives on that question. Even within this setting of the privileged diplomatic correspondence that shaped the world of high politics, traces of broader cultural patterns can be discerned. While the high fever that took hold during the waning months of the Diefenbaker premiership may have killed the last germs of imperialism in Canada in the economic, political, and diplomatic spheres, there may well have been a longer life for some cultural germs of empire in Canada.

A characteristic feature of European thinking during the 1815-1914 era, when the European empires extended their reach throughout Asia and then Africa, was the generally unquestioned assumption of European superiority – in terms of power, culture, and race. Remnants of those modes of thinking were still present in Canada even as it sloughed off the political and economic skin of its former imperial identity. One manifestation of these characteristic imperial mentalities surfaced in 1952 when the Canadian cabinet discussed the issue of American troops being stationed in Canada to defend and staff the new radar stations being established as part of the advanced warning system against possible Soviet attack. The cabinet was concerned about the presence of black troops in Canada. The cabinet minutes noted that

> the Minister of Defence reported that the United States wished to station army units in Canada for the manning of some of the radar stations and the units would include negroes integrated into white formations. They had enquired whether there would be any objection. There might well be objection to the stationing of negro units but it was difficult to take exception to units that included only a proportion of negroes. He suggested that the United States authorities be informed that the units could be brought in but that they be asked informally to ensure that the proportion of negro personnel did not exceed ten percent. The cabinet noted with approval the remarks of the Minister of Defence.[44]

Lest this be seen merely as a passing remark suggesting thoughtlessness rather than racial prejudice, it needs to be borne in mind that this was a full cabinet discussion, suggesting that the concerns expressed by the Canadian ministers reflected their deeply held (or at least conventionally held) beliefs on race hierarchies. Even more powerful evidence on this point comes from the very document written over a decade later that lies at the centre of the case made in this chapter – Pearson's statement to Rusk and McNamara in May 1963. In the course of assuring the Americans that the British Empire and Commonwealth was in rapid dissolution, Pearson elaborated his view that 'the advent of African Commonwealth states doomed the Commonwealth system.'[45] In Pearson's view the 'Commonwealth' consisted of the former white-settlement colonies – Canada, Australia, New Zealand (and historically South Africa, though it had withdrawn from the Commonwealth in 1961) – which had a special relationship with Britain. He allowed the possibility of India being counted in, presumably because of the size and importance of that country. But he could not in 1963 envisage the former British colonies in Africa fitting in at all. These attitudes changed over the following twenty years as Canada itself was transformed by immigration and a city such as Toronto changed from being a North American outpost of Anglo-colonial culture into a vibrant, cosmopolitan, multicultural metropolis. The international scene was also transformed as colonialism fell fully into disrepute and the newly independent states made their impact in the United Nations and other international venues. So Pearson's words looked back to the past rather than forward to the future, but the fact that such an enlightened prime minister could speak in those terms shows that empire mentalities had not entirely ended in Canada, even in 1963.

Notes

1 R.D. Cuff and J.L. Granatstein, *Canadian-American Relations in Wartime: From the Great War to the Cold War* (Toronto: Hakkert, 1975), 101.
2 Noble Cunningham Jr., ed., *Circular Letters of Congressmen to their Constituents 1789-1829* (Chapel Hill: University of North Carolina Press, 1978), Vol. 2: 912.
3 Memorandum of a conversation, Prime Minister Pearson, Secretary of State Rusk, Secretary of State McNamara, Ambassador Butterworth, Ottawa, 23 May 1963, *Foreign Relations of the United States* [hereafter *FRUS*], *1961-1963* (Washington, DC: United States Government Printing Office, 1994), vol. 13: 1207.
4 National Archives [NA], Washington, RG 59, State Department Decimal File [SDDF] 1930-1939, box 3178, Benjamin Wallace memorandum, Office of the Economic Advisor, 6 December 1931.
5 William C. Bullitt to President Roosevelt, 8 July 1933, quoted in Richard Kottman, *Reciprocity and the North Atlantic Triangle, 1932-1938* (Ithaca, NY: Cornell University Press, 1968), 77-78
6 NA, RG 59, SDDF 1930-1939, box 3178, Pierre de Boal to Secretary of State Hull, 21 February 1933.
7 Kottman, *Reciprocity, 1932-1938*, 121.
8 NA, RG 59, SDDF 1930-1939, box 3178, W.Y. Elliot to John Hickerson, 27 February 1933.
9 Ibid., box 3183, memorandum of Meeting at White House with President Roosevelt, Francis Sayre, n.d.
10 Ibid., box 3182, Norman Armour to Secretary of State Hull, 17 October 1935.
11 J. Pierrepont Moffatt to Norman H. Davis, 19 June 1936, quoted in Kottman, *Reciprocity, 1932-1938*, 8.
12 Grace L. Beckett, *The Reciprocal Trade Agreements Program* (New York: Columbia University Press, 1941), 91.
13 William S. Culbertson, *Reciprocity: A National Policy for Foreign Trade* (New York: McGraw Hill, 1937), 76-77, 238-39.
14 Cuff and Granatstein, *Canadian-American Relations*, 88.
15 Memorandum by Assistant Secretary of State for Economic Affairs Willard Thorp to Under Secretary of State Robert Lovett, 8 March 1948, in *FRUS 1948*, vol. 9: 406.
16 NA, RG 59, SDDF 1945-1949, box 5884, Lawrence Steinhardt to Secretary of State Marshall, 24 November 1948.
17 Ibid., William P. Snow to Julian Harrington, 8 December 1948.
18 John Quincy Adams to Richard Rush, 23 June 1823; Richard Rush to John Quincy Adams, 12 August 1824, printed in *American State Papers: Foreign Relations* (Washington, DC: United States Government 1859); vol. 7: 761, 759; Protocol between Richard Rush, William Huskisson, and Viscount Canning, 19 June 1824 in William Manning, *Diplomatic Correspondence of the United States: Canadian Relations 1784-1860* (Washington, DC: Carnegie Endowment for International Peace, 1942), vol. 2: 413.
19 Henry Clay to Albert Gallatin, 19 June 1826, *American State Papers: Foreign Relations*, vol. 7: 762.
20 British Paper on St. Lawrence, 24th. Protocol 'N,' ibid., vol. 7: 772.
21 Samuel E. Moffatt, 'How America Really Feels Towards England,' *The Living Age: A Weekly Magazine of Contemporary Life and Thought* (14 September 1901): 666-74.
22 Michigan State University Library, Frank B. Kellogg papers, microfilm reel 24, Secretary of State Kellogg to William Phillips, 18 January 1927.
23 Dean Acheson to Senate Subcommittee on St. Lawrence Seaway Project, 30 October 1946, *U.S. Congress. Senate Report 810, 80th. Congress, 2nd. Session*, 43, 100-1; Report of the National Security Resources Board, 24 April 1950, in *The St. Lawrence Seaway Manual: A Compilation of Documents on the Great Lake Seaway Project, U.S. Congress, Senate Document 165, 83rd Congress, 2nd Session*, 47-49, 54-55.
24 Memorandum of conversation between Prime Minister Diefenbaker and the ambassador in Canada (Merchant), 22 June 1957, in *FRUS 1955-1957*, vol. 27: 894-96.
25 Memorandum of a conversation with Prime Minister Diefenbaker, Secretary of State Dulles, and US Ambassador Merchant, 28 July 1957, in ibid., vol. 27: 906-7.

26 Dispatch from embassy in the U.K. (Whitney) to the Department of State, London, 9 September 1957, in ibid., vol. 27: 910-12.
27 President's visit to Ottawa (secretary of state, secretary of external affairs and others), 9 July 1958, in ibid., vol. 27: 701-2.
28 Telegram from US embassy in Canada to Department of State (Merchant), 26 February 1962, in ibid., vol. 27: 1166.
29 Telegram from US embassy in Canada to Department of State (Merchant), 27 February 1962, in ibid., vol. 27: 1167.
30 Memorandum from assistant secretary for European affairs (Tyler) to under-secretary of state (Ball), 29 January 1963 in ibid., vol. 27: 1193.
31 Department of State press release No. 59, Washington, 30 January 1963. United States and Canada negotiations regarding nuclear weapons, in ibid., vol. 27: 1195.
32 The American Ambassador sought to mollify Diefenbaker by arguing that the Rostow memorandum was unexceptionable and that the 'verb "push" corresponded to British "press" or Canadian phrase "seek to persuade."' Telegram from US Embassy in Canada to Department of State (Merchant), 13 May 1962, in ibid., vol. 27: 1179.
33 Robert Bothwell, Ian Drummond, and John English, *Canada since 1945: Power, Politics, and Provincialism* (Toronto: University of Toronto Press, 1981), 248-50 conclude that the US 'did not compel Canada or try to compel it to do anything in particular and therefore did not infringe its sovereignty.'
34 Letter from the ambassador in Canada (Merchant) to acting secretary of state (Ball), 5 May 1962, in *FRUS 1955-1957*, vol. 27: 1172-73.
35 Memorandum from under-secretary of state for economic affairs (Ball) to President Kennedy, 23 August 1961, in ibid., vol. 27: 32, 35
36 Telegram from the Department of State to the US embassy in the United Kingdom (Rusk), 17 October 1961, in ibid., vol. 27: 42.
37 Letter from the US ambassador in Canada (Merchant) to acting secretary of state (Ball), 5 May 1962, in ibid., vol. 27: 1174.
38 Telegram from US embassy in Canada to Department of State (Butterworth), 3 February 1963, in ibid., vol. 27: 1196-97.
39 Ibid., vol. 27: 1198.
40 Telegram from the Department of State to the US embassy in Canada (Ball), 28 June 1963, in ibid., vol. 27: 1209.
41 Counselor at US embassy in Canada (Bliss) to Department of State, 16 July 1953, in *FRUS 1952-1954*, vol. 6: 2095-96.
42 Memorandum from Secretary of State Rusk to President Johnson, 12 December 1963, in *FRUS 1961-1963*, vol. 13: 1217.
43 Memorandum from Secretary of State Rusk to President Johnson, 12 December 1963, in *FRUS 1961-1963*, vol. 13: 1217.
44 Extract from cabinet conclusions/Extrait des conclusions du cabinet, 28 November 1952, *Documents on Canadian External Relations*, Vol. 18: *1952* (Ottawa: Department of External Affairs, 1990), 1126.
45 Memorandum of a conversation (Prime Minister Pearson, Secretary of State Rusk, Secretary of Defense McNamara, Ambassador Butterworth), 23 May 1963, *FRUS 1961-1963*, vol. 13: 1217.

6
Britain, Europe, and Diefenbaker's Trade Diversion Proposals, 1957-58
Tim Rooth

On the eve of the Progressive Conservative election victory in 1957 there was nothing in the 'low politics' of trade and monetary relations between Canada and the United Kingdom to match the dramatic impact of the Suez Crisis on the broader relationship between the two countries. But although economic relations had not been subject to any such shock, Canada's economic links with the United Kingdom had been subject to prolonged erosion and were completely overshadowed by those between Canada and the United States. British exports to Canada, despite preferential treatment, had struggled in the postwar years. Although they had risen sharply between 1955 and 1956, they still accounted for only 8.5 percent of total Canadian imports in those years. This was approximately half the prewar share, still well below the level of the late 1940s, and dwarfed by imports from the United States, which accounted for 73 percent of the market. Britain was Canada's second most important customer, but a long way behind the United States, which had steadily grown in absolute and relative importance in the decade after the Second World War. Canadian exports to the United Kingdom constantly disappointed Ottawa, and an edge to Canadian frustration was provided by the persistence of dollar rationing and import licensing by Britain, which hampered Canadian sales. The Americans dominated inward investment.

During the election campaign John Diefenbaker had addressed these issues, expressing long-held anxieties about the economic penetration of Canada by the United States and the weakening links between Canada and the United Kingdom. His answer was to attempt to reinvigorate the Commonwealth and, in particular, its economic links, and he proposed a Commonwealth trade and economic conference to examine these issues. Diefenbaker was able to put this proposal to the other Commonwealth leaders when, almost immediately after the election, he departed for London to attend the Commonwealth Prime Ministers' meeting. Meanwhile, in Ottawa, cabinet meetings proceeded in Diefenbaker's absence. Donald Fleming, the minister of finance, reported to the cabinet on 25 June 1957 that the prime minister had been warned by 'all the officials with whom the matter had been discussed ... against expecting too much on the trade side.'[1] Diefenbaker, however, was given a huge welcome in London, especially from the Conservatives and from the Conservative press.[2] He also managed to gain agreement for his idea of a Commonwealth economic meeting, and he returned to Canada exhilarated by his trip. At a press conference on his return on 6 July he proposed that Canada should switch 15 percent of its imports from the United States to the United Kingdom, a transformation that he asserted could be achieved without harming the United States. In case there was any misunderstanding, he repeated this goal later in the month.[3]

This proposal caused consternation in Ottawa. Implementing Diefenbaker's scheme would mean reversing the long-term tendency for Britain's share of the Canadian market to fall. Instead, British exporters would have to raise their share of Canada's imports from 8.5 percent to nearly 20 percent – an increase of some 130 percent. Moreover, there was only a very limited range of products for which the United Kingdom had any hope of effecting this increase, since perhaps 60-65 percent of Canadian imports were of items that Britain was not in a position to supply. To meet the target in these circumstances, sales of product groups in which there was any real prospects of British advance would have to increase between three- and four-fold.[4] In London it was recognized that trade diversion even approaching this scale would be impossible without new tariff preferences or other radical departures in Canadian trade policy. Increasing preferences, however, ran counter to the international obligations of both countries – notably the GATT no-new-preference (NNP) rule – to reduce them gradually, and import-licensing schemes were also ruled out. In the absence of changes of this type it was thought the UK would do well to raise its exports by 25 percent, representing a switch of only 3 percent of Canadian imports.[5] The one hope of achieving anything remotely in line with the degree of trade diversion proposed by Diefenbaker, and consistent with GATT rules, was for Britain and Canada to form a free trade area. As this idea gained ground in Whitehall it was clear that support for it was influenced by its implications for the negotiations being held in Europe for the creation of an Industrial Free Trade Area (IFTA). It would do no harm for the Europeans to know that Britain had a line out to Canada, Sir David Eccles, president of the Board of Trade, suggested. He also noted that with the European negotiations about to proceed, in domestic political terms it was important not to have 'our imperialists dissatisfied.'[6] Looking further ahead, Eccles suggested that if the IFTA was eventually to materialize it might be useful to be able to say that Britain had put this idea to the Canadians. Informal soundings in Ottawa by the British high commissioner and other officials soon indicated, however, that the Canadians would oppose any such scheme: It would jeopardize the Canadian manufacturing industry and adversely affect relations with the United States.[7] Sir Saville (Joe) Garner, high commissioner to Canada, had warned that, because the free trade proposal would be unacceptable to the Canadians, 'we should try to avoid too formal or forcible approach on this idea.'[8]

Although amply warned that the idea would be rejected, British ministers decided to persevere nonetheless. But how should they proceed? Eccles preferred '*not* to see the idea put beforehand in the form of an aide-memoire. This would expose the plan to critical and sceptical scrutiny by Canadian officials before the wider political and economic aspects can be put to Mr. Diefenbaker direct.' The secretary of state for Commonwealth relations, Lord Home, wrote to the prime minister in similar terms.[9] A personal approach was considered the only one with any chance of success, and the job of persuading Diefenbaker of the benefits of a free trade area between Canada and the United Kingdom was given to Sir Derick Heathcoat Amory, the minister of agriculture, who was already scheduled to visit Canada. Sir Frank Lee (the permanent secretary of the Board of Trade) accompanied him. Amory first explained the British proposal to Diefenbaker and Fleming, following lunch at the Rideau Club on 9 September 1957.[10] In the afternoon, at a larger meeting chaired by Fleming and attended by senior Canadian officials, the idea was explored in greater detail. The Canadians, clearly well primed for the proposal, were uniformly hostile, arguing that the balance of advantage would be with the United Kingdom. Very much at the forefront of Canadian worries was the vulnerability of their industry to British competition. Wynne Plumptre asserted that 'broad areas of Canadian industry would probably be wiped out'; textiles and steel were thought to be particularly vulnerable. His colleague Simon Reisman suggested that if tariffs were scrapped perhaps two-thirds of increased British sales would be at the expense of Canadian industry rather than United States imports.[11]

Robert Bryce (secretary to the cabinet) and Kenneth Taylor (deputy minister of finance) emphasized to Lee that Diefenbaker's trade diversion announcement had come out of the blue, 'was unconsidered and unendorsed by his colleagues, and was probably the one major "brick" which the Government had dropped so far. There was no substance or programme behind it; the quest for the Holy Grail was well organised and far more hopeful in comparison.'[12] Writing to Macmillan two days after the first meetings, Amory reported that Diefenbaker 'was clearly scared stiff at the mere idea of free trade' and that he was now much keener on his Commonwealth conference idea than Anglo-Canadian trade diversion.[13] His minister of finance already regarded the 15 percent trade diversion proposal as an embarrassment.

Garner, although in favour of advocating a free trade area to the Canadians, had earlier cautioned against putting Diefenbaker on the spot politically.[14]

In the aftermath of Amory's abortive visit, the cabinet's deputy secretary, Burke Trend, also urged caution on the prime minister, pointing out that Britain did not want to start a brawl with the new Conservative administration in Canada and that 'it would be dialectically unwise to start an argument with them on how far Mr. Diefenbaker's statement of its intention to divert Canadian imports to United Kingdom represented a commitment which he had failed to honour; we are remarkably vulnerable to reply in kind – for example, about our intentions (still not carried out 12 years after the war) to remove discrimination and make sterling convertible.'[15]

The British cabinet was in a quandary. There had been counter-suggestions by Canadian officials that ministers might not be seriously troubled if the British government felt it necessary to state publicly that it had put forward the free trade proposals, which the Canadian government had felt unable to accept.[16] The British cabinet decided on 19 September not only to persevere with the free trade proposals if a suitable opportunity arose, but also to make sure they were publicized.[17] Influenced by the same considerations that had led them to advocate free trade in the first place, they had to be seen to respond to the Canadian offer in order to mollify their backbench imperialists while the European negotiations proceeded.

In Ottawa the free trade proposal had been dealt with discreetly and with a minimum of publicity. The minister of trade and commerce, Gordon Churchill, had been away when Amory visited. Nor was the British initiative discussed in cabinet until 20 September, eleven days after proposals had first been made and more or less instantly dismissed.[18] Churchill told Eccles that he considered it wrong to have rejected the proposal out of hand, and thought the new secretary of state for external affairs, Sidney Smith, would be of the same opinion.[19] At this point the UK government appears to have decided to make the free trade offer public. When the British and Canadian ministers next met in Canada later in September at the Commonwealth Finance Ministers' meeting in Mont Tremblant, following meetings of the International Monetary Fund in Washington, the British sent a strong team that included three ministers and four permanent secretaries. Fleming had succeeded in keeping the free trade proposal off the agenda. But during the course of the conference, details of the British scheme appeared in the *Financial Times* on 27 September. The probable source was Eccles in a briefing given to the paper in Washington.[20] The *Financial Times* piece and the *Montreal Star*'s afternoon coverage ensured lively interest in Canada. At a rowdy press meeting Peter Thorneycroft (chancellor of the exchequer) expounded enthusiastically on the free trade idea, while an embarrassed Fleming dwelt on its obstacles and difficulties.[21]

In the next days further lengthy discussions were held in Ottawa. The extent of Canadian embarrassment is indicated by the four hours the cabinet spent wrestling with the issue, much of the time devoted to producing a communiqué on the Anglo-Canadian discussions. At a meeting with British representatives late that same night, Canadian ministers appeared 'jaded, dispirited and worried.'[22] A formula was eventually found and a communiqué produced. Although the British insisted on reference to the free trade area being incorporated in the communiqué, they had accepted that it was virtually dead, now banished to realization 'over a period of 12 to 15 years.' It made a brief reappearance late in October when Fleming stated to the House of Commons that the United Kingdom had not proposed a free trade area until after the meeting at Mont Tremblant. This, at best, was disingenuous. Probably the main reason the British proposals were rejected was that they threatened jobs in Ontario and Quebec. As Diefenbaker explained, he 'could not possibly afford to fight an election on this issue,'[23] and as a minority administration, his government's immediate objective was to be re-elected with an overall majority. Garner emphasized this factor in his review of the reception of the free trade offer, but continued: 'If one adds to this the inexperience of Ministers and the mercurial temperament of the Prime Minister (who is almost completely lacking in economic expertise and shows little interest in more mundane details of trade), it is not wholly surprising that the United Kingdom proposal produced a combination of paralysis and alarm.'[24]

Did Britain gain anything from the economic discussions? With yet another sterling crisis blowing up in the autumn of 1957, nothing came of British hopes that Canada might be persuaded to hold sterling in its reserves, and it seems probable that they were warned off from making such a proposal formally. When Lee mentioned it in September, Governor of the Bank of Canada James Coyne had replied that he 'regarded this as rather fancy stuff.'[25] But in the late 1950s there *was* a measure of trade diversion to Britain. A Canadian trade mission visited the UK in 1957 with the aim of boosting British sales to Canada, and London maintained pressure on Ottawa to use government and Crown corporation spending to favour British products. As Table 6.1 reveals, British exports to Canada increased in the late 1950s in the face of an overall decline, and the United Kingdom share of Canadian imports rose from 8.5 percent in 1956 to 10.7 percent in 1960. Supplies from the United States fell but continued to dominate Canadian imports.[26]

After the brief flurry of activity over free trade, the main thrust of discussions at the Mont Tremblant meeting during the following ten months or so centred on holding a Commonwealth trade and economic conference (CTEC) in Montreal and the implications for the Commonwealth of Britain's negotiations for a free trade area in Europe. The holding of the CTEC had always been an integral part of Diefenbaker's program. The main Canadian objective at the Mont Tremblant meeting was to secure the agreement of other Commonwealth countries and this, albeit grudgingly, Ottawa achieved.

Table 6.1

Canadian imports, 1954-60 ($ million)

Year	From UK	From USA	Total	UK as % of total imports
1954	392	2,961	4,093	9.6
1955	401	3,452	4,712	8.5
1956	485	4,162	5,705	8.5
1957	522	3,999	5,623	9.3
1958	527	3,572	5,192	10.2
1959	597	3,829	5,654	10.6
1960	589	3,687	5,483	10.7

Source: M.C. Urquhart and K.A.H. Buckley, *Historical Statistics of Canada* (Toronto: Macmillan 1965), F348-56.

Diefenbaker had originally seen the conference as a means to increase Commonwealth trade. But the Canadian cabinet, debating the issue in mid-1957, also regarded an emphasis on Commonwealth trade as an essential offset to British European policy. A European free trade area would have injurious effects on Canadian trade and it 'was important, therefore, to raise the question of a Commonwealth meeting here as a counter balance. If it were agreed to hold discussions in Ottawa in September the British might not move so fast on the Free Trade Area front.'[27]

The British were not enthusiastic. Even before Diefenbaker arrived in London for the Prime Ministers' conference, Whitehall officials were trying to head the issue off, arguing not only that it was very doubtful whether such a conference would be useful, but that at present it 'might be dangerous.'[28] The British were very pessimistic about achieving anything on trade and feared that, in the absence of a trade initiative, attention would be switched to the unwelcome subject of development. Burke Trend subsequently argued that 'the likely agenda will hardly provide enough meat for a Conference at Prime Minister level; the possibilities of its succeeding are not great enough to induce us to have it in London, under a United Kingdom chairman; Delhi should clearly be avoided, since the Conference would then be diverted towards a discussion of assistance for under-developed countries.'[29] The British therefore saw the purpose of the conference as being primarily political: 'Although the material for a full-scale trade and economic conference appeared scant, we should support the conference proposal in view of the political importance of demonstrating the vitality of the Commonwealth conception.'[30] In particular, London needed to respond helpfully to the pro-Commonwealth initiative of the newly elected Canadian government. In Ottawa officials also appeared dubious about the future of the Commonwealth economic relationship. At a meeting of senior mandarins in Plumptre's house it was concluded: 'In economic terms there appeared to be little of real substance in the Commonwealth relationship and the trend was for the member countries to back away from such economic links as had at one time existed.'[31]

The process of preparing for the CTEC gave shape to growing doubts about the future of the Commonwealth economic relationship. One cause of the fragmentation of that relationship was British agricultural protection. Since the mid-nineteenth century the British food market had been open, and since 1932 Commonwealth countries had enjoyed the considerable benefits of imperial preference. But officials now admitted between themselves that the expansion of British agriculture since the war, stimulated by heavy subsidies, had been the single most damaging blow to Commonwealth trade in foodstuffs.[32] This not merely weakened the incentive for Commonwealth partners to smooth the path for British exports but positively encouraged a search for other markets. Although Australia and New Zealand were historically the keenest on imperial preference, both countries were now backtracking. This had been evident as early as 1952 when Britain had been unable to persuade other Commonwealth countries to push for the suspension of the GATT NNP rule. Antipodean disenchantment with imperial preference was made even more explicit when Australia insisted on reducing preferential margins on British imports in the 1956 Australian-UK trade agreement so as to free its hand in negotiations with other countries. Now New Zealand was pushing in the same direction, contemplating terminating its Ottawa agreement.[33] The days of imperial preference were numbered.

But if trade prospects looked bleak, the shifting composition of the Commonwealth was bringing to the fore new issues that were unwelcome to London. As decolonization gathered pace, the representation of underdeveloped independent countries at Commonwealth meetings was increased. Douglas Le Pan of External Affairs, in London to discuss the agenda for the conference, reported that the necessity for including development had been 'mentioned somewhat regretfully.'[34] Certainly Britain did not want development to dominate proceedings in Montreal.[35]

This concern reflected growing recognition of the inadequacy of British resources to fulfill their traditional role in financing Commonwealth economic development.[36] Vast domestic demands for capital – for steel, tankers, and nuclear power stations – had to come from the same resources as overseas investment, and some ministers were arguing that increased investment at home was more vital than overseas.[37] Furthermore, overseas investment imposed strains on the balance of payments and the value of sterling. As Thorneycroft explained to the powerful Economic Policy Committee: 'It was clear that our overseas investment objectives were too great for our present resources. In these circumstances it would be prudent to concentrate upon productive investment at home to additional investment in the Commonwealth, difficult though this might be to some sections of

opinion.'[38] But the sections of opinion resistant to the new emerging ortho-
doxy were well entrenched in government, and not merely on the back-
benches. The conventional wisdom emphasized the key role of finance and
trade in maintaining Commonwealth links, and argued that the more external capital came from sources other than the United Kingdom: 'The risk
will be increased of undue commercial, and hence political, penetration by
other countries, which could weaken Commonwealth ties.'[39] The Cabinet,
nonetheless, after long discussion, approved Thorneycroft's proposals for a
more restrictive policy on overseas investment and for the encouragement
of Commonwealth borrowing from other sources.[40] Tight monetary conditions and high borrowing costs had already deterred Commonwealth governments from raising money in London.[41] The ability to borrow from Britain
had been a fundamental feature of the sterling area, virtually a sine qua non.
British links with the Commonwealth were weakening and those with
Europe strengthening. But this was still a gradual process in the late 1950s.
Policy was driven less by shifting alignments than future prospects. *Privileged* access to Commonwealth markets was dying. Meanwhile developments
in Europe and the successful launch of the European Economic Community (Common Market) were seen as posing a huge threat to British trade.
Accordingly this became a major preoccupation of policy between 1956
and 1958, overshadowing preparations for the Commonwealth conference.

The British response to the Messina proposals and to the Treaty of Rome,
which established the EEC in 1957, was to push for the creation of an industrial free trade area (a proposal known as 'Plan G'). This was designed to
get the best of both worlds by fostering links with Europe without sacrific-
ing the Commonwealth. First, the plan envisaged was for a free trade area,
not a customs union, and would therefore allow Britain to keep its own
external tariff complete with free entry for the vast bulk of Commonwealth
supplies. Second, with a mind to protecting domestic agriculture and of
allowing preferential access for Commonwealth imports, agriculture was
excluded from the scheme. In proposing arrangements that left agriculture
out of account and allowed them to maintain tariff autonomy, the British
completely overestimated their bargaining power. They appear to have
thought that the six founder members of the EEC, along with the wider
membership of the Organization for European Economic Cooperation
(OEEC) would, in the words of one senior British official, R.W.B. Clarke,
'almost certainly jump at' the prospect of British participation in closer
European economic integration.[42] As Macmillan (then chancellor of the
exchequer) grandiloquently expressed it: 'Can we retain the leadership of
the Commonwealth world and at the same time seize the leadership of
Europe?'[43] Not all agreed with Clarke's view; some officials in both the Foreign Office and the Board of Trade warned that Britain was not offering big
enough bait.[44] The key ministers pushing the proposals in London were

Macmillan, initially as chancellor and later as prime minister, and Thorneycroft, in his role as president of the Board of Trade and subsequently as chancellor. Although they had a difficult task of persuasion to perform both in London and in continental Europe, the proposals were almost certainly shaped more by the need to override opposition to them in Britain than to attract support in the rest of Europe.

Certainly the IFTA in the form envisaged in London was perceived in the rest of Europe as giving Britain huge advantages. As Reginald Maudling, paymaster-general and head of the British negotiating team, explained to the cabinet in May 1958, Britain would have freedom of access to European markets, privileged access to Commonwealth markets, and, because of its tariff structure and Commonwealth free entry, a low cost base that would enhance its industrial competitiveness.[45] All this would make Britain very attractive to US investment. So what benefits did Britain's involvement on these terms hold out for its European partners? These were seen as essentially political. As Maudling emphasized, neither the French 'nor anyone else wishes to be left alone in Europe with Germany if they can avoid it. This is perhaps our greatest asset in the negotiations.'[46] In cabinet it was suggested that 'it would ... be desirable that the other European countries concerned should be reminded of the probable consequences to themselves if, as a result of their failure to satisfy our reasonable requirements in respect of the Free Trade Area, they compelled us to reconsider the scope and nature of our association with Europe and found themselves passing gradually under the dominance, both political and economic, of the Federal German Republic.'[47]

Yet it became increasingly apparent to the British government that they were not offering enough. As Reisman pointed out to his colleagues, the United Kingdom had probably overestimated its bargaining power at the outset.[48] As negotiations proceeded it became clear that the British needed more elbow room if they were to have any hope of bringing them to a successful conclusion. By March 1958 the major problems in the negotiations were identified as agriculture, the common external tariff (CET), and the attitude of France. The French had obtained a very good deal from the Treaty of Rome, and a high price had been paid by the others to secure French participation.[49] Maudling noted that 'the French attitude remains as hostile as ever. Based as it is on a combination of deep-seated protectionism and the insane jealousy of Britain and fanned by the vigorous propaganda activities of the French employers, it presents a formidable obstacle to agreement.'[50] Because of problems of 'trade deflection,' Britain was being driven to compromise its opposition to a common external tariff, particularly on items where it was likely to be a high one.[51] Any move on the CET, however, was certain to affect the exports of Commonwealth countries, especially for manufactured goods but also for basic materials. Canada was the most vulnerable because of its export structure. Indeed, Canadian chemicals posed special problems for the FTA negotiations. The French, believing that UK imports of chemicals from Canada would give US-owned production in Canada tariff-free access to the EEC, asserted this was clear proof that it was impossible to link the Common Market to the FTA.[52] Nor did other European countries want agriculture excluded; despite the expansion of British agricultural production since 1940, the United Kingdom was still the world's greatest food importer and potentially a highly attractive outlet for Continental surpluses. As the negotiations continued it became increasingly clear that Britain had overestimated its bargaining power and now needed to take risks if it was to persuade the more reluctant European countries to participate in an IFTA. Yet if Britain was to make concessions it needed the acquiescence of other Commonwealth countries before it did so.

Senior Commonwealth officials met in London in June 1958 to prepare for the Montreal conference. The implications of Britain's closer involvement with Europe dominated their discussions. The suspicions of other Commonwealth countries were given full vent. New Zealand at one stage had insisted on direct participation in the European negotiations. Although this was dismissed as impracticable, the rest of the Commonwealth was united in requiring the closest consultation with the UK as the European negotiations proceeded. Britain had general support for its initiative, but only if it could obtain its original terms. These might encourage an outward-looking, rather than a closed, Europe. But Commonwealth support was predicated on the Plan G terms that had safeguarded Commonwealth interests. Claude Isbister, the Canadian assistant deputy minister of trade and commerce, had spelt this out in June: 'The Canadian government's support has been postulated on the understanding that agriculture was excluded from F.T.A. proposal and on the formal assurances given by the United Kingdom Government that Commonwealth interests in the United Kingdom would be fully safeguarded.'[53] The Australians had expressed themselves even more forcibly. John Crawford reiterated the broad political support of the Australian government but said that as economic aspects of the negotiations came to the fore, the Australian government was increasingly concerned over the damaging economic effects: 'He felt bound to emphasise that the growing Australian concern regarding the economic aspects of the Free Trade Area negotiations might threaten their political support for the project.'[54] Commonwealth countries were faced with the prospect of 'reverse preferences' – of being discriminated against in the British market.

By the summer of 1958, British ministers, increasingly concerned about the possible failure of the free trade area negotiations, were beginning anxiously to discuss the alternatives. Eccles wrote to Macmillan sketching out possibilities: 'Some thought has been given to asking the Scandinavians to join with us in a Uniscan F.T.A. I do not like this. It would be a climbdown –

[like pursuing] the engineer's daughter when the general-manager's had said no. Would we be trying to make the Six jealous and take us back, or would we seriously contemplate life in the Scandinavian group over against the Six?'[55] During discussions in June with Commonwealth officials, Sir John Coulson talked about 'numerous if nebulous ideas' being discussed. One of these was Uniscan, of which he said, 'at first sight such an idea appeared open to considerable difficulties and disadvantages, and the United Kingdom had not thought it worthwhile to give it serious attention.'[56] Maudling agreed that there were no alternatives to the free trade area: He did not think much of the prospect of joining up with Scandinavia, which he agreed with Eccles, was 'an inferior idea.' He dismissed the Commonwealth: 'You know all the difficulties of the Commonwealth alternative. The more one studies the prospects of the Montreal conference the more obvious it is that no expansion of Commonwealth trade on a new preferential basis can be regarded as a possibility.'[57] Eccles pressed for something much broader, a North Atlantic free trade area in manufactures together with Commonwealth association. Maudling thought this fanciful, referring to Canada's rejection of free trade in 1957, and suggesting that US opposition would be equally strong. Britain had no choice but to carry on with the European free trade area discussions.

When the Commonwealth trade and economic conference was held in Montreal in September 1958 the European IFTA was unresolved. The meeting was more successful than many had feared. However, the British high commissioner, reporting on the broadly favourable reaction to the conference, not least by much of the Canadian press, emphasized that these assessments were coloured by the low expectations set by early doubts about prospects, the absence of any striking theme or idea, and 'the difficulties and tensions that emerged at the June meeting of officials.'[58] But the harmony achieved at the conference owed much to the greatly improved international economic environment in which it was held. The Mont Tremblant discussions had occurred in the midst of a sterling crisis, Macmillan writing at the time to his (absent) chancellor about the future of sterling in apocalyptic terms.[59] The prospect of an American recession and a world shortage of dollars had dominated much of the early preparations for the Commonwealth meeting, and was still casting a shadow over it as late as the summer of 1958.[60] But 1958, as it turned out, was to be the watershed between the postwar years of dollar shortage and an era of dollar glut. By the early autumn not only was the US economy recovering, but action on replenishing international currency reserves, and IMF reform, was also restoring confidence. The sterling-area balance of payments was also improving, and under these conditions Britain was able to announce, on the third day of the conference, some liberalization of import controls.[61] To the extent that the outcome of the conference was liberal and international in outlook, it stood in stark contrast to the Ottawa conference of 1932.[62] In the light of Diefenbaker's trade diversion offer the previous year, the Canadians had been at pains to reassure the US that Montreal 1958 would not be a repeat of Ottawa 1932: This was emphasized to Secretary of State John Foster Dulles, and arrangements made to ensure the US ambassador 'would be fully and quietly informed ... of the progress of the Conference.'[63] Despite the misgivings of the British, development featured prominently, and among the outcomes were a scheme for Commonwealth educational scholarships and for the bolstering of development funds, significantly with Canadian participation. But, as officials in Ottawa and London had correctly anticipated, the conference did not include measures for bolstering Commonwealth trade. Indeed, in the months following the conference, Britain did what Canada and Australia had long been pressing it to do, and announced the restoration of full current account convertibility for sterling, with effect from 1 January 1959. Most of the remaining quotas against dollar-area imports were scrapped in November 1959.[64] By the end of the 1950s the Bretton Woods system, envisaged in 1944, had at last become operational. Britain, by joining the 'one-world' economic system, had moved decisively away from the restrictive and exclusive policies that had characterized its relations with the Empire-Commonwealth since 1932. But that the internationalization of British economic policy, so keenly sought by Canada since 1945, failed to bring harmony to Canada-United Kingdom trade relations is made abundantly clear by Bruce Muirhead in Chapter 7 below.[65]

If one of the Canadian motives for holding the conference had been to distract Britain from the European project, it failed. But within two months of the conference, British ambitions for Europe were dead, killed by de Gaulle's veto in November.[66] Franco-German domination of the Common Market ensured that a largely protectionist and inward-looking Europe evolved, above all in its notorious Common Agricultural Policy.

Diefenbaker's trade diversion offer was made in pursuit of diversifying Canada's international trade and reducing dependence on the United States: He aimed at reinvigorating the Commonwealth connection and at distracting the United Kingdom from European involvement. The offer had all the hallmarks of the new administration, which, according to Canadian officials, characteristically tended to announce policy aspirations without thinking through their operational mechanics. The response to the British free trade offer revealed the deeply embedded strength of Canadian protectionism, especially in the electoral heartlands of Ontario and Quebec.[67] The British free trade proposal was probably all the easier to make because nobody seriously thought Canada would accept it. No detailed examination of its implications for the European negotiations or for other members of the Commonwealth appears to have been made. Neither the Anglo-

Canadian free trade area initiative nor plans for the Commonwealth conference succeeded in diminishing the strength of British overtures to Europe. Although it was clear that the United Kingdom would have to move away from its original Plan G, this was never put to the test. Maudling wanted elbow room in the negotiations but failed to obtain cabinet clearance. So no concrete proposals for higher tariffs (which Commonwealth countries would almost certainly have had to pay) or for opening up the British foodstuffs market to European competition had to be put to Commonwealth countries. Nor did they have to be put to the Macmillan cabinet, which, if it had approved them, would have had a difficult domestic battle on its hands. By the end of 1958 British trade policy was in disarray. Those responsible saw little economic future in the Commonwealth, and this was a view shared by influential figures in Ottawa. The European initiative was dead and, the general-manager's daughter having said no, the engineer's daughter was being pursued – though with a singular lack of passion (the little EFTA of the Seven became operational in 1960). But what had become clear by the end of 1958 was that there was no costless solution to Britain's European dilemma. In future Britain would have to choose between Europe and the Commonwealth.

Notes

1 National Archives of Canada (NAC), RG2/1892, cabinet minutes, 25 June 1957.
2 Denis Smith, *Rogue Tory: The Life and Legend of John G. Diefenbaker* (Toronto: MacFarlane, Walter and Ross, 1995), 250-52, and J.L. Granatstein, *Canada, 1957-1967: The Years of Uncertainty and Innovation* (Toronto: McClelland and Stewart, 1986), 43-45.
3 *Times* (London), 24 July 1957.
4 NAC, MG32 B9, Gordon Churchill papers, vol. 41, 'Diversion of Canadian Imports from the United States to the United Kingdom,' 9 August 1957.
5 Public Record Office (PRO), Cabinet (CAB) 129/88, C (57) 187, draft brief on Anglo-Canadian trade talks, annexed to note by Sir Roger Makins, joint permanent secretary to the treasury, 23 August 1957.
6 He was not advocating a free trade pact at this stage, and Commonwealth Relations Office officials thought his proposals distinctly unadventurous. PRO, CAB 129/88, C (57) 164, Eccles's note and attached letter to Macmillan, 16 July 1957. PRO, Dominions Office (DO) 35/8730, comments by H.E. Davies and A.W. Snelling in brief for secretary of state, 22 July 1957.
7 PRO, DO 35/8731, working group on preparations for 1957 meeting, 29 August 1957. The Canadian officials cited were Cabinet Secretary Robert Bryce and Mitchell Sharp of Trade and Commerce.
8 PRO, Premier (PREM) 11/2533, telegram, 30 August 1957. Earlier, officials had warned ministers that 'a free trade area would be more attractive to us than to Canada ... We can expect the idea to be rejected because of its difficulties for the Canadians ...' PRO, Cab 129/88, C (57) 187, draft brief on Anglo-Canadian Trade Talks, annexed to note by Makins, 23 August 1957.
9 PRO, PREM 11/2533, Eccles to Macmillan, 3 September 1957, and Home to Macmillan, 5 September 1957.
10 NAC, RG19/4192 8627/C212/U57. A.W.F. Plumptre to minister, 'History of British Proposal for a Canada-United Kingdom Free Trade Area,' 29 December 1961. Plumptre, assistant deputy minister of finance, was also present at the meeting.

11 NAC, RG19/4192, file 8627/C212/U57, draft minutes, 17 September 1957.
12 PRO, DO 35/8731, note of a discussion with Mr. Bryce and Mr. Kenneth Taylor, 10 September 1957. James Coyne, governor of the Bank of Canada, described ministers as 'almost inconceivably inexperienced.' PRO, CAB 129/89 C (57) 213, note by Lee, 10 September 1957, enclosed with memorandum by Thorneycroft, 17 September 1957.
13 PRO, PREM 11/2533, Amory to Macmillan, 11 September 1957.
14 PRO, DO 35/8730, minutes on meeting with Eccles, 26 July 1957.
15 PRO, PREM 11/2533, Burke Trend to prime minister, 18 September 1957.
16 PRO, DO 35/8731, note of a discussion with Mr. Mitchell Sharp and other officials, 10 September 1957.
17 PRO, CAB 128/31, CC (57), 69th conclusions.
18 NAC, RG2/1893, cabinet meeting, 20 September 1957.
19 PRO, DO 35/8731, minutes by Eccles on meeting with Churchill, 19 September 1957.
20 PRO, DO 35/8731, minutes by H.A.F. Rumbold (CRO official), 1 October 1957.
21 As the questions became 'more and more rude,' Fleming regretted the two-hour reception 'with free drinks' he had given for the press just before the press meeting. *So Very Near: The Political Memoirs of the Honourable Donald M. Fleming* (Toronto: McClelland and Stewart, 1985), vol. 1: 388-89.
22 A vivid description of the occasion is given in a note by Garner enclosed in a letter to Sir Gilbert Laithwaite, PRO, PREM 11/2533, 7 October 1957.
23 PRO, PREM 11/2533, meeting of British and Canadian Ministers, 2 October 1957.
24 PRO, DO 35/8731, Garner to Home, 18 October 1957.
25 PRO, CAB 129/89, C (57) 213, note by Lee, 10 September 1957, enclosed with memorandum by Thorneycroft, 17 September 1957. The Canadians nonetheless came to Mont Tremblant armed with briefs explaining why they would refuse any such request: NAC, RG32, Churchill papers, Series B9/25, 'Sterling in Our Reserves,' 16 September 1957. Similar suggestions by the United Kingdom in 1949 had met with very short shrift: T. Rooth, 'Britain's Other Dollar Problem: Economic Relations with Canada, 1945-50,' *Journal of Imperial and Commonwealth History* 27 (1999): 98.
26 Canada's external economic policy up to 1957 is thoroughly documented in Bruce W. Muirhead, *The Development of Postwar Canadian Trade Policy: The Failure of the Anglo-European Option* (Montreal and Kingston: McGill-Queen's University Press, 1992).
27 NAC, RG2/1892, cabinet meeting, 25 June 1957.
28 PRO, CAB 130/126, 'Proposals for a Commonwealth Trade Conference,' note by the Treasury, 24 June 1957.
29 PRO, PREM 11/2533, memorandum by Trend to prime minister, 18 September 1957. The 1958 IMF/World Bank meeting was scheduled for Delhi.
30 PRO, CAB 134/1841, ES (CE) (57) 21, draft brief for prime minister's Commonwealth tour; note by the Treasury, 11 December 1957.
31 NAC, RG19/4327, file 8262-03-1, meeting of officials, 25 February 1958.
32 PRO, CAB 129/88, C (57) 187, draft brief on Anglo-Canadian trade talks, annexed to note by Makins, 23 August 1957.
33 PRO, CAB129/94, C (58) 178, report by the ministerial committee on the Commonwealth Trade and Economic Conference, September 1958.
34 NAC, RG19/4327, file 8262-03/58-3, meeting of cabinet committee on the Commonwealth Conference, 8 May 1958.
35 PRO, CAB129/94, C (58) 178, report by the ministerial committee on the Commonwealth Trade and Economic Conference, September 1958.
36 PRO, T231/813, memorandum by M. Rudd (Treasury), 10 July 1957.
37 PRO, CAB 134/1676, EA (57) 52, Thorneycroft memorandum to Economic Policy Committee, 21 May 1957.
38 PRO, CAB 134/1674, Economic Policy Committee, 14th meeting, 29 May 1957.
39 PRO, CAB 134/1675, EA (57) 48, 'Report of the Committee on Commonwealth Economic Development: Provision of Capital.' The same report also suggested that any reduction in investment would be especially inopportune at a time when the UK initiative 'towards

closer economic association with Europe might encourage the misconception that this implies some weakening in the value which we place upon these ties.'

40   PRO, CAB 128/31, CC (57), 44th conclusions, 4 June 1957.

41   PRO, CAB 134/1675, EA (57) 47, 'Studies on Sterling – Capital Account,' memorandum by economic secretary (N. Birch), 17 May 1957. The sharp rise in the Bank rate in 1957 was the chief means of controlling capital exports: Gerold Krozewski, *Money and the End of Empire: British International Economic Policy and the Colonies, 1947-58* (Basingstoke: Palgrave, 2001), 156 and 159.

42   Note by 'Otto' Clarke (Treasury), 29 May 1956, cited by Martin Schaad, 'Plan G – A "Counterblast"? British Policy towards the Messina Countries, 1956,' *Contemporary European History* 7 (1998): 48. Clarke was referring to Plan F, a less ambitious scheme than G.

43   PRO, PREM CP (56), 208, Plan G, memorandum, 11 September 1956.

44   James Ellison, 'Perfidious Albion? Britain, Plan G and European Integration, 1955-1956,' *Contemporary British History* 10 (1996): 1-34.

45   PRO, CAB 129/93, C (58) 110, 'European Free Trade Area: Origin Problems,' note by Maudling, 16 May 1958.

46   Ibid., 27, note by Maudling, 30 January 1958.

47   PRO, CAB 128/32, CC (58), 5th conclusions, 14 January 1958.

48   NAC, RG19/4327, file 8262-03/58-3, meeting of cabinet committee on the Commonwealth Conference, 14 May 1958.

49   The French acknowledged this in private, foreign secretary Maurice Fauré informing Maudling that the greatest advantage to France was that such a high proportion of the cost of their colonial territories had been placed upon German shoulders; they also believed that they had obtained German undertakings to buy their agricultural produce at very favourable prices. PRO, CAB 129/93, C (58) 27, note by Maudling, 30 January 1958. De Gaulle may have been reconciled to the EEC because of this: F.M.B. Lynch, 'De Gaulle's First Veto: France, the Rueff Plan and the Free Trade Area,' *Contemporary European History* 9 (2000): 120-21.

50   PRO, CAB 129/92, C (58) 65, 'European Free Trade Area,' note by Maudling, 21 March 1958.

51   'Trade deflection' would be liable to occur when countries in a free trade area had differing external tariffs. To take a hypothetical example, if Britain had low or no tariffs on aluminum, and Italian importers were faced by high external tariffs, they might buy their supplies via the no-/low-tariff United Kingdom, causing trade to be 'deflected' from Italy.

52   A.S. Milward and G. Brennan, *Britain's Place in the World: A Historical Enquiry into Import Controls, 1945-60* (London and New York: Routledge, 1996), 248.

53   NAC, RG19/4328, file 8260-03/5(58), 'Brief for Montreal Conference: Canadian Position,' n.d.

54   NAC, RG19/4328, file 8262-03/4(58), second preparatory meeting of officials, 9 June 1958.

55   PRO, PREM 11/2531, Eccles to Macmillan, 14 July 1958.

56   NAC, RG19/4328, file 8262-03/4(58), third preparatory meeting of officials, 18 June 1958.

57   PRO, PREM 11/2531, Maudling to Macmillan, 5 August 1958.

58   PRO, DO 35/8482, Garner to Kilmuir, 17 October 1958.

59   PRO, PREM 11/2307, Macmillan to Thorneycroft, 28 October 1957.

60   NAC, RG19/4327, file 8262-03/58/3, discussions at cabinet committee on the Commonwealth Conference, 14 May and 9 July 1958.

61   Canada did not reciprocate. 'Once again, as so often in trade and tariff bargaining, Canada had tried to get without giving. This time it succeeded.' Robert Bothwell, Ian Drummond, and John English, *Canada since 1945: Power, Politics and Provincialism* (Toronto: University of Toronto Press, 1981), 206-7.

62   Grant Dexter, who had covered both events, vividly contrasted the setting and atmosphere of the two conferences. *Winnipeg Free Press*, 26 September 1958.

63   NAC, RG19/4327, file 8262-03/58/3, meeting of Canadian ministers with Dulles, 9 July 1958, and cabinet committee on the Commonwealth Conference, 8 September 1958.

64   Milward and Brennan, *Britain's Place*, 196.

65 See also Muirhead, 'From Dreams to Reality: The Evolution of Anglo-Canadian Trade during the Diefenbaker Era,' *Journal of the Canadian Historical Association* 9 (1998): 243-66: A considerable number of British imports from Canada continued to be subject to control (255).

66 Lynch, 'De Gaulle's First Veto'; J.W. Young, *Britain and European Unity, 1945-1992* (Basingstoke: Macmillan, 1993), 57-66; Jacqueline Tratt, *The Macmillan Government and Europe: A Study in the Process of Policy Development* (Basingstoke: Macmillan, 1996), Chapter 1.

67 Although Canadian public opinion supported the idea of a free trade area between Canada and the UK, with, according to a Gallup poll, all provinces showing a majority in favour. *Toronto Daily Star*, 14 December 1957.

7
Customs Valuations and Other Irritants: The Continuing Decline of Anglo-Canadian Trade in the 1960s
Bruce Muirhead

During the 1960s, the Anglo-Canadian economic relationship continued the inexorable decline that had characterized it since the war. Indeed, Britain seemed to largely disappear from the Canadian radar screen as Ottawa tuned in the United States more and more. By the end of the decade, imports from and exports to the United Kingdom accounted for only 5 percent and 9 percent, respectively, of the country's trade, and the two had grown apart to the extent that when London was successful in its bid for European Community (EC) membership as of 1 January 1973, it raised nary an eyebrow in Ottawa, a sharp contrast to the reaction to the United Kingdom's application to join the Community a decade before.[1] In short, what had once preoccupied Canadian decisionmakers – expanding trade with Britain – no longer did.

As the 1960s dawned, however, it was pretty much business as usual, or so it seemed. Indeed, that reassuring symbol of Anglo-Canadian economic relations, the United Kingdom-Canada Continuing Committee (UKCCC), a high-level forum where senior officials from both countries met to discuss mutual problems, gathered in June 1960 much as it had for the previous eleven years. Even many of the names had remained the same over the years. For the Canadians, Louis Rasminsky, then a deputy governor at the Bank of Canada, Kenneth Taylor from Finance, and James Grandy from the Department of External Affairs, all had long lineages with the committee. On the British side, Kenneth McGregor and Sir Robert Hall were among the longest-serving members. The agenda was eerily reminiscent of those from the late 1940s and 1950s – the General Agreement on Tariffs and Trade (GATT), the Canadian interest in the UK market, and overseas investment and aid. That said, this was to be the last of these meetings until October 1963, and the UKCCC, which was then briefly revived, was finally put to rest in 1967.

While some of the officials attending the meeting might have been comforted by the familiarity of the agenda and the discussion, the Anglo-Canadian economic relationship was changing; by the mid-1960s the British market was fading in importance for Canada, and no longer were hands wrung at emergency meetings convened in Ottawa, nor policy papers prepared in anticipation of a further decline. Much of the economic increase of the 1950s had been based on Canadian access to the US market, and it had been American dollars, pouring like a tidal wave of investment over Canada in that decade, which had helped to increase the gross domestic product and secure the sort of prosperity that had only been a dream twenty years before. And if there were nationalist concerns expressed every once in a while over the dependent relationship with the southern neighbour, they too were a reflection of the good times that the North American economic relationship had brought.[2]

And despite the kind words, sensible talk, and cooperative spirit that emanated from the UKCCC, the British, sensing that their future lay in Europe, were also in the process of investigating new economic angles and allegiances that did not necessarily include Canada. For example, they had taken the lead role in the establishment of the European Free Trade Area (EFTA) in November 1959, and in the initiative to forge some sort of link between the free trade area and the European Economic Community (as it was known until 1967). While the formal negotiations for a bridge between the two had failed in November 1958 (before the EFTA itself had become operative), informal talks had continued, to the dismay (and opposition) of the Canadians who remained very sensitive to anything that could compromise their exports to the United Kingdom. The British regretted the Canadian position, leading their high commissioner in Ottawa to write in January 1960, following a visit by F.J. Errol, the president of the Board of Trade, to explain the United Kingdom's Europe policy, that 'of any positive contribution of practical significance from their side, there is unfortunately no sign at present and, it is feared, a poor prospect in the future.' The main Canadian players, at least according to the high commissioner, were 'parochial protectionists' (James Roberts, deputy minister of trade and commerce), 'doctrinaire [free trade] ideologues' (Jake Warren, assistant deputy minister of trade and commerce, and Louis Rasminsky, deputy governor of the Bank of Canada), 'hard-headed and unimaginative' (Donald Fleming, minister of finance), or 'cautious' (A.E. Ritchie, an official from the Department of External Affairs, and A.F.W. Plumptre, assistant deputy minister of finance).[3] In the event of a British move into the EEC the Canadians wanted assurances that were not, and could not be, forthcoming. Indeed, during the visit to Ottawa, Errol had opined that Canada should support British efforts to establish a free trade area with some sort of link to the Community because the alternative might be the UK in a European customs union that would be even more detrimental to Canadian interests. This, or so some in Ottawa thought, 'seemed to amount to facing [us] with the invidious choice of whether [we] wished to be halved or quartered.'[4]

Quartered it was, as the British opted for negotiations in late July 1961 designed to lead to EEC membership. In Ottawa, at least among certain politicians, it was the moral equivalent of war, and John Diefenbaker, the prime minister, was particularly upset. Despite the fact that comparatively little of Canada's trade now went to the United Kingdom, and that he had turned down cold the British proposal for an Anglo-Canadian free trade area in September 1957, the prime minister did not appreciate the announcement. Some of his opposition lay in his fear of reduced trade if the United Kingdom joined the EEC, which was a restrictive customs union; the price of British entry, so Ottawa thought, would be '(1) a common tariff with the Six; (2) a common agricultural policy, and; (3) the disappearance of UK tariff preferences by the end of the transitional period.'[5] Surely, Diefenbaker told Duncan Sandys, the secretary of state for Commonwealth relations who had been sent on a tour of several Commonwealth capitals to explain the new policy, the end of the preference system that had been developed and implemented via the Ottawa Agreements of 1932 would destroy the Commonwealth. When the British minister demurred, suggesting that 'most of the new [member] countries did not regard preferences as the main basis of the Commonwealth,' the Canadian replied that if the old membership lost interest, then it would break up.[6] Diefenbaker's opposition probably reflected a nostalgia for an idealized Commonwealth that had never existed. British Prime Minister Harold Macmillan perceptively captured in his memoirs Diefenbaker's simplistic notions of imperial solidarity and his *Boy's Own* vision of the Empire-Commonwealth. After meeting the Canadian for the first time in 1957 Macmillan had confided to his diary that 'I fear that he has formed a picture of what can and cannot be done with the Commonwealth today which is rather misleading.'[7]

The Canadians went on the offensive (and were offensive) soon after the July announcement: UK trade with the Community accounted for only 14 percent of its total, they pointed out, as compared with the Commonwealth's 40 percent and the other 46 percent that went to neither the Community nor the Commonwealth. How were they going to square those figures with their fear that they were being left behind in the slipstream of history if they stayed outside? In September 1961 in Accra, Ghana, for a gathering of the Commonwealth's economic consultative council, the minister of finance, Donald Fleming, and the minister of trade and commerce, George Hees, blasted the British for wanting to join the EEC. Later, in November, George Drew, Canada's high commissioner in London, 'snubbed' the British when he did not attend an information session on UK-EEC negotiations. Finally, Diefenbaker himself gored Macmillan and his Europe policy at a prime ministers' meeting held in September 1962; his speech was 'very hostile' and, as the London Sunday newspaper the *Observer* noted, he was intent upon 'pulling [Macmillan's] recently-hoisted flag of Europe down.'[8] Through an increasingly bitter quarrel, Diefenbaker was convinced that the United Kingdom was 'hustling' Canada.[9]

The French veto over British entry on 29 January 1963 left it to the Canadians, they thought, to try to 'mend Commonwealth fences as quickly as possible' and to demonstrate that they had not been the cause of the refusal.[10] Indeed, the Canadian cabinet went on record as implying that Britain had refused to join the EEC because it could not secure terms that would protect essential Commonwealth interests. When this interpretation was rejected outright by Edward Heath, then lord privy seal and point man on the UK's entry bid, Diefenbaker had 'shown some hurt feelings, his line being that he was only trying to be a good Commonwealth man and to rally the Commonwealth to [Britain's] support[!]'[11] Surely the British heaved a sigh of relief when the Canadian Conservatives were defeated in the April 1963 federal election.

This disagreement, dragged out over a few years, was a damaging one for Anglo-Canadian relations. The political relationship had soured, while the economic one continued in freefall. It was also true that the Canadian position was dated. Whether or not the United Kingdom joined the EEC was not much of an economic concern for Canada (and a new Liberal government led by Lester Pearson) by 1963, but of tremendous importance to the United Kingdom. While that would become even more so as the years passed, it was also the case that once British entry had been rejected, they shifted their focus back to the Commonwealth 'partly because of the uncertainty about the future of trade with the European Community.'[12] A new Labour government in Britain, elected in October 1964 and led by Harold Wilson, supported this policy, at least initially. The new prime minister's 'personal preference was for a new emphasis on the Commonwealth, and an expansion of Commonwealth trade. [He] had an attachment to the old dominions which went back to his youth.'[13] That was the message relayed to British trade departments in the months following the Labour win and given some shape during the 1965 Commonwealth prime ministers' meeting. Although Wilson proposed a three-point plan for Commonwealth economic co-operation, very little was actually accomplished; he was 'acutely disappointed [that] there was virtually no willingness to improve intra-Commonwealth trading arrangements.'[14]

For Canada this was because its connection with the US now dwarfed all others in importance. By 1965, Canadian exports to the United Kingdom had increased only slightly, from CAN$915 million in 1960 to CAN$1.174 billion. On the other hand, sales to the US had gone from CAN$2.9 billion to CAN$5 billion, almost 60 percent of the country's exports, and were increasing at a rate of more than CAN$1 billion per year. British exports to Canada had stayed more or less static, at CAN$589 million in 1960 and CAN$619 million five years later; the United Kingdom held a mere 7 percent of the Canadian market, down from 9.5 percent in 1960. Britain's exporters were 'disillusioned' because of what they perceived to be the increasing difficulty of entering the Canadian market.[15] The Americans did not think so; their exports to Canada had held steady at roughly 70 percent of total Canadian imports. At the best of times, Canada had not been an easy place for British sales, especially given US competition, but that was now also complicated by the aftermath of Canada's financial crisis in May and June 1962. Then, Ottawa had devalued and fixed the value of the Canadian dollar at 92.5 cents US. It had also imposed temporary surcharges on about CAN$2.5 billion worth of imported goods, from which the British felt that they had suffered disproportionately. Canada, traditionally Britain's third- or fourth-largest market in the world, had dropped to seventh place by mid-1963. This situation had gotten so bad from the British point of view that in early 1963 the president of the Board of Trade, Edward Heath, wrote to Canada's secretary of state for external affairs, Howard Green, to draw attention to the serious lack of balance in the trade relationship and the growing British trade deficit with Canada, which had approached CAN$300 million in 1961 and nearly CAN$350 million a year later.[16] Labour and Conservative governments sang from the same hymn book on the trade-deficit issue, both pressing during their times in office for Canadian action.

But it also appeared that British business was largely uninterested in Canada. For example, the dynamics had not been good during a March 1964 meeting between Mitchell Sharp, the minister of trade and commerce in Pearson's Liberal government, and members of the Federation of British Industries. While Sharp had been there to learn about UK problems, 'there [had been] no real discussion or exchange of views.' The impression gained by the Canadian was 'that British businessmen were concerned to point out that Canada was only one market among many to which they exported and that they were reluctant to take special steps to get their products to meet the requirements of the Canadian market.' Sharp was particularly taken aback by the president of British Leyland, who had emphasized that his company had no intention of undertaking the 'special modifications that were required if Leyland buses were to meet Canadian conditions.'[17] Similarly, British bankers were largely uninterested in investing in Canada by the 1960s. That was the result, Assistant Deputy Minister of Finance Simon Reisman thought, of British ignorance. Their reluctance, he declared,

> stemmed from the fact that they had overestimated the ease with which large profits could be made during the Canadian boom of the Fifties; that

they had invested in Canada when the boom was at its height and had got their fingers badly burnt during the recession at the end of the Fifties, at which time better opportunities had opened up in Europe on which they were still concentrating; they showed insufficient awareness of the Canadian recovery that had been going on for three years; this was due partly to the fact that the recovery had been overshadowed by the 1962 crisis of confidence; all of this created a bad impression of Canada and tended to make the bankers lose sight of Canada's real economic position.

But it was also true that the British had their own list of legitimate complaints in dealing with Canada, which they brought up at every possible opportunity. These included 'devaluation; the temporary import surcharges; Canadian duty valuation practice and automatic anti-dumping duty; the shipbuilding subsidies; discrimination against Scotch whisky both in the Federal tariff and by Provincial liquor boards; the Ontario Trade Crusade; and the Ontario Special Place of Business Tax.'[18] British automobile sales to Canada, in particular, had taken a pounding, falling to approximately 18,000 vehicles, worth about £6.6 million in 1963, from 77,000 units valued at £38.5 million in 1960. While a part of that was due to the availability of more desirable American cars, some of them made in Canada, it was also a result of Canadian policy. Until 1960, there had been a special concession for British cars that had allowed them to be sold in Canada at the UK list price less 30 percent without attracting a dumping duty. This was modified to 22.5 percent because of the recession experienced in Canada in the late 1950s, and the government had refused to reinstate the more favourable treatment when the economic downturn had passed.

The British then tried another tack: to be allowed to give larger discounts to Canadian purchasers because of 'duplicated costs.'[19] Car manufacturers in the United Kingdom argued that the minimum Canadian price – list price less 22.5 percent, which was based on the British list price less trade discounts – should be adjusted to allow for the fact that the Canadian importer did not get as much for his money as the home distributor in the United Kingdom. The latter received with the vehicle certain facilities, the cost of which had been included by the manufacturer in arriving at the selling price. Those extras, including sales and service assistance from the factory and warranty claims administration, had to be provided in Canada by the importer, and an allowance should therefore be made for their duplication since they were charged for by the factory in the selling price on the UK home market – that is, the price on which the Canadian fair-market value was assessed. Ottawa declined to allow this, citing the success of Volkswagen, which had prospered relative to British manufacturers in Canada despite the handicap of a 17.5 percent preference in favour of Britain. The automobile issue, especially following the negotiation of the Autopact with the United States in 1965, was to continue to plague Anglo-Canadian economic relations.

The British reserved their special concern for the Canadian system of valuation for duty, coupled to an anti-dumping duty that was *automatically* imposed. As a memorandum to the president of the Board of Trade noted, if he had an opportunity in the meeting scheduled for 1 December 1964 with Mitchell Sharp, he might remind Sharp 'of the importance which we attach to changing certain aspects of the Canadian dumping legislation which bear unreasonably on our exports.'[20] The Canadian system did indeed work to the detriment of British exporters to a much greater extent than it did against most others, and especially the Americans. The Canadian formula for valuation was normally based upon the fair-market value of like goods sold in the exporter's home market. In addition, Canadian law provided that when goods of a class or kind made in Canada were sold in the country below the fair-market value, an anti-dumping duty *must* be imposed equal to the difference between the selling price and the fair-market value.[21]

This valuation system meant that goods from Britain, when dutiable, were often liable to higher duties than similar products from other countries, such as the United States, where a lower fair-market value had been established because there was an advantageous home-trade pattern and a distribution system similar to that of Canada. The disadvantage to Britain stemmed from differences in the distribution systems of Canada and the United Kingdom. In a compact, densely populated market like the latter, there were relatively few links in the distributive chain. When exporting to Canada, the manufacturer sold to an agent, who in turn sold to regional distributors. Therein lay the problem; exporters were prevented by the automatic dumping duty from reducing the price of their goods to take account of the overheads, which would have to be borne by the Canadian agents. And even though the Canadians had noted the barriers raised by these difficulties and had suggested that they would at least investigate their valuation system, that had not happened.

A large part of the reason was, indirectly, the United States. The valuation system had attained almost sacred status in Ottawa because it was viewed as 'essential as a protection against US [dumping] and [no Canadian] administration [was] prepared to abandon it.'[22] This Canadian fear of American dumping was well founded; Reisman, for one, thought the Americans were 'ruthless price cutters, particularly where marginal production was involved [and] could quickly swamp the Canadian market with dumped goods.'[23] While the British did not disagree with this analysis, they also thought that the rigidity of Canadian law meant that 'some British exporters find themselves severely penalized, not because they are damaging Canadian industry by dumping, but because of differences between British and Canadian trade patterns which bring them *technically* within the law's scope.'[24]

The large and growing British trade deficit with Canada continued to do just that, which the Canadians appreciated. The obverse of the British deficit was a Canadian surplus, which went part way towards cancelling out Canada's CAN$1 billion trade deficit with the United States.[25] Britain's adverse balance of trade with Canada amounted to some CAN$581 million in 1964, almost one-third of its overall balance-of-payments deficit. Nor did it seem likely that it would go away; there was a good chance, the first secretary of the newly created Department of Economic Affairs, George Brown, informed the new Labour cabinet during one of its first meetings, that the deficit with all countries could very likely exceed the staggering figure of £1.2 billion before the end of the day.[26] It was caused by a number of factors, but figuring prominently was a very large (and increasing) import bill not being offset by an equally large expansion in exports. The government had a few unpalatable choices; it could borrow to cover its current account deficit, it could restrict the flow of imports, or it could place a surcharge on imports. As had Canada in mid-1962, the United Kingdom resorted to the latter to redress its situation. Approximately 24 percent of Canadian exports to the United Kingdom were affected, primarily paper, chemicals, non-electric machinery, and iron and steel.

Given that two years before they had introduced their own import surcharges to address a similar problem, the Canadians should have demonstrated more sensitivity towards the British policy. London was particularly anxious that something be done about the unfairness of Canada's import valuation policy in order to assist UK exporters and, in the process, help to correct Britain's large trade deficit. Sharp, the minister coordinating Ottawa's response to the imposition of import surcharges, declined to help when asked because action on that front would mean legislation and the government was reluctant to contemplate that course. As well, given the reduced significance of the UK market in general, the Canadians could see no advantage for themselves in helping the British. There was, the president of the Federation of British Industries correctly mused, not much that Canada was prepared to do.[27] However, Sharp also believed that Canada's anti-dumping and valuation laws did not constitute the significant obstacle to British exports that London thought they did; other countries' exporters were, potentially, as badly affected as the United Kingdom, but they did much better. The main requirement 'was for British salesmen to show more drive and initiative and for British manufacturers to pay more attention to quality, delivery, and so on. It was these factors, rather than price, which were preventing British exports from expanding as much as they might.'[28] There was not too much hope from that quarter for UK exporters – and Sharp, unlike many of his colleagues, was a *supporter* of easing the effect of the legislation on UK exporters; indeed, he had told the high commissioner in Ottawa, Sir Henry Lintott, that he had been in favour of immediate action on the valuation front, but had been overruled in cabinet.[29] But perhaps Norman Robertson, chairman of a special committee to deal with Canadian preparations for the Kennedy round of GATT negotiations, and recently the under secretary of state for external affairs, got it right when he apprised Lintott of the political realities in Canada: 'He felt very doubtful whether the present Government, with its minority position, its dependence on Ontario seats, and its other current difficulties, would be all that anxious to introduce the necessary legislation.'[30] It was indeed an indication of a government 'concerned about protecting its immediate narrow [economic] interest.'[31]

Several months later, Alex Currall of the British High Commission in Ottawa reported that the Canadians were simply not moving. With exasperation pouring from every line in a letter written to Douglas Carter of the Board of Trade, Currall rehearsed all that he had done the previous week to make the Canadians pay attention. He had begun by telling Jake Warren that there were three areas that unfairly penalized British exporters: the general valuation and anti-dumping problem, the special case of motor vehicles, and Canadian government procurement policies. Not surprisingly, he had been turned down flat on valuation. The Canadians made reference to the Kennedy round whose object was to reduce tariffs. To participate in good faith there *and* to ask industry to accept any limitation on its other form of protection (that is, the valuation and anti-dumping duties) would not be feasible. 'Ministers,' the official explained, 'were reluctant to face up to [the British proposals] which involve them punching a large hole in the anti-dumping protection.' However, he held out some hope for action in the Canadian budget, to be introduced in the House of Commons in late April 1965.[32]

With respect to procurement policies, Warren also suggested that little could be done. He told Currall that by comparative international standards, Canadian procurement policies were not 'ungenerous' to the external supplier and it was, again, unrealistic to expect Canadian ministers to go further in the direction of meeting the British. At the federal level, the general rule seemed to be that a price advantage of up to 10 percent should be given to Canadian suppliers. In some areas, however, or so the British believed, 10 percent had become a minimum and premiums of as much as 50 percent were given to Canadian manufacturers. That was simply a political reality in Canada; C.M. Drury, the minister of industry in the second Pearson government, told Douglas Jay, the president of the Board of Trade, that 'preference for Canadian manufacturers [was] based on the need to give protection to Canadian industry.'[33] Similar margins applied to provincial and municipal purchases as well. Nor, the British thought, was there much prospect of improvement for them given the likely Canadian strategy in the Kennedy round. It had been the Canadian position in all postwar tariff negotiations to reduce most favoured nation rates without correspondingly increasing the rate of British preferential tariff discount, thereby reducing the margin of preference. As the same policy would presumably be followed in the current round, and given the fact that the British had very little with which to bargain in a tariff negotiation with Canada, British ministers assumed that their negotiations were going to make the Anglo-Canadian trading problem worse and not better. They were correct on every count.

On the valuation front, the Canadians did come through in the April budget and change their anti-dumping and valuation legislation to address some aspects that bore inequitably on British imports. The revisions proposed that where, on a report from the minister of national revenue, the Department of National Revenue was satisfied that certain provisions resulted in discrimination against a class of goods imported from one country as against the same goods imported from another, the government could, by order in council, provide that the value for duty be reduced. As a British comment on the proposed change noted with some perspicacity, 'much will depend on how the provision is administered.'[34] However much discretion it gave the government to determine cases, it did seem to be an attempt to get to the heart of the major British complaint of the mid- and later 1960s – that US exporters suffered less from the rules than did British because the scale and level of American sales in their domestic market and that of Canada were so similar. Walter Gordon, the minister of finance, emphasized in the House of Commons that the new powers would be used to remove discrimination against British goods. 'It is the hope of the government,' he ended this section of his budget speech, 'that this proposal will be taken by British exporters as a decisive response to their pleas that Canada give a clear signal that we welcome their goods.'[35]

Did it work out that way? Certainly not – and by the end of 1965, despite the promising beginning, the British were irritated at how the legislation (Section 37A of the Customs Act) had been interpreted. By December, of twenty applications for dispensation under the new rule, some of which had been made months earlier, none had been disposed of. Moreover, according to British manufacturers, the Department of National Revenue was demanding a large amount of irrelevant information as well as adopting a very narrow view of the provision, contrary to the spirit of Gordon's budget announcement. The British believed that 'there seems to be no question of the Canadian Department accepting any statement made by a British firm in a 37A application at its face value.'[36]

Following this brief lull in the war that followed the passage of Section 37A, Sir Henry Lintott thought that the United Kingdom should 'return to the attack on improvement of terms of entry for British exports.'[37] An important part of the strategy was to involve some Canadian ministers in favour of freer trade, like Mitchell Sharp, in the application process; otherwise, things got bogged down in the 'official machine which [was] geared to protectionist practices.' That characterization was certainly true, and the Department of National Revenue was rightly singled out for criticism. It was, British officials believed, 'clearly very inbred, [with] the Ministry of Finance and other Departments concerned with international trading relations often knowing little of what goes on in it and why.'[38]

There had also been some change in the Canadian political landscape that had not helped the British case. A federal election had been held on 8 November 1965, and the Liberals under Lester Pearson had been returned, albeit with an only slightly increased minority. This result, according to Lintott, was the worst possible. He believed that had Pearson been returned with a solid majority, the prime minister might have felt strong enough to take on some of the protectionist elements in his government and in the country at large. As events turned out, however, 'Pearson's position was weaker than before, and it would be more difficult to persuade Canadian Ministers to do anything effective.'[39] During the election, no political party or candidate had made much mention of Anglo-Canadian trade problems and issues, or even trade more generally. It was all Medicare, pensions, and improved educational and training facilities. Moreover, on 15 February 1965, a new Canadian flag had flown from the pole on top of the Peace Tower on Parliament Hill; the old Red Ensign was consigned to history. It was a symbolic departure from a past in which the United Kingdom had figured prominently. As J.L. Granatstein has written, 'the flag marked a new direction for Canada, a step into independence that ranked with the Statute of Westminster and the later patriation of the constitution.'[40] More and more, Britain was a country *comme les autres*.

By the end of 1965, the British were clearly at a loss. In a strategy session convened in Whitehall, several officials and Lintott discussed options relating to exerting pressure on Ottawa. One possibility was to cut down on purchases of Canadian wheat, but that threat was hollow. The Soviets and the Chinese were now buying millions of bushels of wheat from Canada and would continue to do so in the future. As well, the British noted that the strength of the Liberal party (the real enemy in all this, they assumed) did not lie in the prairies; indeed, those farmers were friends and were most sympathetic to the British cause. What was wanted instead was something that would hurt the growing Canadian trade with the United Kingdom in manufactured goods, and that meant Ontario, where Liberal members of parliament were very common. That went to the heart of the problem. Industrialization in Canada during the 1950s and early 1960s had continually reduced the number of items on which the British received free entry into Canada for their industrial goods, while at the same time increasing the value of Canada's preferences in Britain – about 96 percent of Canada's exports to the United Kingdom were duty-free, while only about 60 percent of

British exports to Canada enjoyed a similar status. However, for Whitehall to attempt to impose restrictions against Canadian manufactured goods was to run afoul of the GATT. It would be very difficult, if not impossible, to impose duties on Canadian manufacturers without also imposing them on similar goods imported from other Commonwealth countries.

It was decided that the only reasonable avenue open was to take any opportunity that presented itself to impress upon their Canadian counterparts the British concern about the state of their trade balance with Canada and the latter's unhelpfulness in efforts to correct it. While this was what they had been doing for many months, they were determined to make their case even more strongly to Ottawa. They intended to focus on the April 1965 budget and insist that it was of little value unless it was reinforced by a determination to make its valuation policy effective in the application, as well as the spirit, of the legislation. The British were appalled that in 1965 their *total* trade deficit with all other countries would be about equal to that with Canada. And while they had halved their deficit with the rest of the world during 1964, with Canada it had remained unchanged.[41]

The Labour government, with a more comfortable majority following the election of March 1966, was battling on a number of fronts. There was the increasingly serious balance-of-payments problem, partly fed by constant trade deficits, which would escalate into a crisis of confidence in sterling in 1966. On 20 July the government announced a restrictive package comprising an interest-rate increase, freezes on wages and prices, an increased purchase tax, cuts in government expenditure, limits on foreign travel allowances, and tighter hire-purchase regulations. However, none of these measures worked over the longer term and on 18 November 1967 the pound was devalued by approximately 14 percent. To make matters worse, a paper prepared for the cabinet by the eminent economist Nicholas Kaldor painted a depressing picture of British competitiveness. It began: 'The relatively low rate of growth of the real GNP [Gross National Product] in the UK (2.9 percent for the decade 1955-64 as against 4.6 percent for the average of the 18 member countries of the OECD [Organization for Economic Cooperation and Development]) is generally attributed to managerial inefficiency, bad industrial organization, restrictive labour practices, technological incompetence and insufficient domestic investment.'[42] These problems prompted the British to look once more to Europe for possible salvation. As the postmaster general, Anthony Wedgewood-Benn, has accurately noted in his diaries:

Defence, colour television, Concorde, rocket development – these are all issues raising economic considerations that reveal this country's basic inability to stay in the big league. We just can't afford it. The real choice is, do we go with Europe or do we become an American satellite? Without a conscious decision being taken the latter course is being followed every-where. For personal reasons, I would see much attraction in an English-speaking federation, bringing in Canada, Australia, New Zealand and Britain to a greater United States. But this is a pipe dream and in reality the choice lies between Britain as an island and a US protectorate, or Britain as a full member of the Six, followed by a wider European federation. I was always against the Common Market but the reality of our isolation is being borne in on me all the time.[43]

In May 1967 the Labour government made another formal application to join the Community. While success would not crown their efforts this time either, the very act of applying meant downgrading Britain's interest in the Commonwealth, and a good indication of that was the British response to letters received from the prime minister of Jamaica and the high commissioner of Trinidad and Tobago. They had requested that a committee be established to begin to explore the possibility of a free trade agreement between them and Britain; London's position was that any such initiative would 'now wait until there has been some definitive progress in the consultations in Europe.'[44] Commonwealth entanglements were to be avoided, at least those that might make the UK a less attractive partner in the European Community (as it became known in July 1967 when the EEC merged with European Coal and Steel Community and the European Atomic Energy Commission). Similarly, the United Kingdom-New Zealand trade agreement was renegotiated in June 1966 with an eye towards British membership in the EEC.[45] The sort of agricultural products that New Zealand was exporting to Britain were precisely those covered in the Community by the Common Agricultural Policy's import quotas and subsidies. The agreement with New Zealand was extended to mid-1970, since the UK 'could hardly be expected to join the Community before the beginning of 1968 at the earliest, and two and a half years from then could be regarded as a minimum transitional period.'[46] The thinking was that as Britain eased seamlessly into EC membership, the arrangement with New Zealand would expire.

Increasingly, the European Community figured into British calculations, and the Commonwealth concomitantly less. Mitchell Sharp, now the minister of finance, and Drury both noted in meetings they had with Douglas Jay, the secretary of state for Commonwealth relations, 'that working relations at senior official level seemed much closer in the early fifties, when they were Deputy Ministers.'[47] As well, Charles Ritchie, Canada's high commissioner in London from 1967 to 1971, caught the developing relationship in his diary: 'We and the British were excellent friends who had known each other for a long time, but were no longer members of the same family. If our attitudes had changed, so had those of the British. With their loss of influence [in the world] had come some loss of interest. There remained the bonds of the past, but our future was no longer any concern of theirs. If our preoccupations were with the United States, theirs were increasingly with Europe.' Moreover, Ritchie knew that 'there [was] no interest in Canada in tightening relations with the United Kingdom or in reporting on British policies.' In short, the British connection was 'far from popular' in Ottawa.[48]

Perhaps in an attempt to begin the resuscitation process, the Canadians proposed an annual gathering of senior ministers, using the same format as that with their American counterparts.[49] The idea for the committee had come out of discussions exploring ways to increase Anglo-Canadian trade that Robert Winters, the minister of trade and commerce, had had with several British ministers. Ironically, at the same time that Ottawa was exploring the possibility of regularized ministerial meetings, the United Kingdom-Canada Continuing Committee was quietly buried. That too was the fate of the ministerial committee; it met only once, on 19-20 April 1967. Similar Canadian arrangements with the US and Japan had had much longer lives, working effectively through the 1950s and 1960s.

The Anglo-Canadian trade relationship continued in the doldrums, the result of, from the British point of view, the 'vexed question of valuation.' By March 1967, of the fifty-seven applications submitted under Section 37A by UK exporters, only ten had been granted extra discounts and another ten had been granted concessions under other sections of the Customs Act. Nineteen applications had been refused by the Canadians, seven had been withdrawn by the British, and eleven remained under consideration.[50] Moreover, the dollar value of exports covered by the successful applications was depressingly low. The only possible solution seemed to lie in the negotiations taking place as a part of the Kennedy round in Geneva on an international dumping code. As a May 1967 British memorandum noted,

> Agreement on such a code has now been reached *ad referendum* and acceptance of the Code by the Canadians will mean radical amendment of Canadian legislation under which automaticity will be replaced by the introduction of material injury criterion. It is understood that the Canadians are thinking of making the legislative changes in their 1968 Budget and with the legislative changes the particular problem of valuation with which Section 37A aimed to deal could arise only if it could be established that dumped goods were causing or threatening material injury. The acceptance of a material injury criterion by Canada is a most welcome move. While we must see how the new arrangements – when introduced – will work in practice, the proposed change should go a long way to remove the anti-dumping problem created for United Kingdom exporters in the Canadian market.[51]

When Harold Wilson visited Ottawa in February 1968, he pushed the Canadians once again, raising 'the perennial question about the Canadian customs' handling and valuation of British exports.'[52] As he recalls, Pearson was embarrassed, covering it up and parodying a Whitehall brief: 'Yes,' he said, 'this is it. Canadian customs valuation. Defensive brief. The [Canadian] Prime Minister is advised not to raise this matter unless raised by the British Prime Minister. If it is raised, the Prime Minister is advised to say no more than.' Wilson took the point; there was little to be said that had not been gone over many times since 1964. British criticism of Canadian policy was finally met in the 1968 Canadian budget, tabled on 22 October 1968 with the revisions to take effect on 1 January 1969. The most significant change related to the provision that there had to be a formal inquiry into the impact of alleged dumping on production in Canada. Prior to this, tariffs had been automatically imposed by the Department of National Revenue. It would now not be so easy to impose penalties on suspected wrongdoers.

That, however, did nothing to slow the decline of Anglo-Canadian economic and political relationships. By the turn of the decade, the Canadians were contemplating the effects of the EC on their trade, and paid little attention to the United Kingdom. Indeed, Britain (and the Commonwealth) received virtually no mention in the white paper *Foreign Policy for Canadians.*[53] Anglo-Canadian trade figures had reached all-time lows, and Japan was now Canada's second-largest trading partner. Imports from Britain in 1970 and 1971 formed only 5 and 4.5 percent of Canada's total and Britain received 8 and 7 percent of Canada's exports, respectively. By comparison, imports from the US comprised 66 and 70 percent, respectively, of total Canadian imports, and exports 64 and 67 percent. When the British were invited to apply for European Community membership in 1970 (their nemesis de Gaulle having resigned as French president the previous year), Ottawa's official reaction was to regard it with faint interest, although the government of Pierre Trudeau, elected in June 1968, did undertake several studies of its potential impact and an interdepartmental committee was established to coordinate studies on the effect of EC enlargement on the country's trade policy. A.E. Ritchie, the under-secretary of state for external affairs, suggested to a high-level group of senior officials that the committee might look at issues that could arise concerning Canada's contractual relations under the GATT and also its bilateral rights with various applicants.[54] The under-secretary also thought the group should investigate where Canada would fit in a world dominated by two trading blocs, the EC and the United States. That was a much more worrisome issue for Canada than the fact of the United Kingdom entering the Community. The committee would develop papers on the effects and possible responses to the proliferation of EC preference agreements, as well as an assessment of how the Community's enlargement might affect Canada's dependence on the US market. That said, potential British entry did not arouse the same sort of hysteria in 1970 that it had a decade earlier; Ottawa could contemplate the further loss of the British market without being unduly disturbed.

The 1960s had not been kind to the development of Anglo-Canadian trade. Even the supposedly anglophilic Diefenbaker Conservatives ultimately demonstrated little concrete interest in encouraging trade. Nor did the Liberals who followed them in April 1963. Clearly, the United States had become the overwhelming interest in the consideration of Canadian trade policy development in a way that had not been the case in the 1950s and earlier. Canada had become a truly North American nation even as Britain was becoming European. It was bound to happen, and the Anglo-Canadian relationship, after some initial hesitation, evolved accordingly and in response to the rhythms of international trade as overseen by the General Agreement on Tariffs and Trade. There was nothing special about it now.

Notes

1 See Bruce Muirhead, 'From Dreams to Reality: The Evolution of Anglo-Canadian Trade during the Diefenbaker Era,' *Journal of the Canadian Historical Association* 9 (1998): 243-66.
2 While the North American economic relationship was denounced by the 'chattering classes,' resulting in a deluge of books and newspaper and magazine articles condemning it, the electorate ultimately seemed not to mind. Jack Granatstein caught that mood in a 1971 piece: 'A sneaking suspicion [exists] that Canadians preferred a prosperous existence – even as a satellite – to a poor but pure nationalism.' See J.L. Granatstein, 'Continentalism and the New Nationalism,' in *Canadian Annual Review, 1970,* ed. John Saywell (Toronto: University of Toronto Press, 1971), 349.
3 Public Record Office (PRO), Dominions Office Records (DO) 35, vol. 8381, 'Visit by the President of the Board of Trade to Canada,' January 1960.
4 PRO, DO 35, vol. 8682, UKCCC, 28-29 June 1960.
5 National Archives of Canada (NAC), Department of External Affairs Records (DEA-R), vol. 3448, file1-1962-1, 'British/EEC Negotiations: Specific Trade Objectives,' 31 August 1962. For an account of the advice given to Diefenbaker by the Canadian high commissioner in London, see J.L. Granatstein, *A Man of Influence: Norman A. Robertson and Canadian Statecraft, 1929-1968* (Toronto: Deneau, 1981), 335.
6 PRO, Treasury Records (T) 299, vol. 184, Ottawa to CRO, 14 August 1962.
7 Harold Macmillan, *Riding the Storm, 1956-1959* (London: Macmillan, 1971), 377.
8 J.L. Granatstein, *Canada, 1957-1967: The Years of Uncertainty and Innovation* (Toronto: McClelland and Stewart, 1986), 54.
9 PRO, T299, vol. 186, Commonwealth Conference, 11 September 1962.
10 PRO, Prime Minister's Office (PREM) 11, vol. 4121, brief for Mr. Diefenbaker's visit, February 1963.
11 John Campbell, *Edward Heath: A Biography* (London: Jonathan Cape, 1993), 125.
12 Mitchell Sharp, *Which Reminds Me: A Memoir* (Toronto: University of Toronto Press, 1994), 117.
13 Ben Pimlott, *Harold Wilson* (London: HarperCollins, 1993), 433.
14 Harold Wilson, *The Labour Government, 1964-1970: A Personal Record* (London: Weidenfeld and Nicolson, and Michael Joseph, 1971), 117.
15 PRO, Board of Trade (BT) 11, vol. 6056, brief for minister of state's visit to Canada – June 1963, 29 May 1963. See also Bank of Canada Archives, Louis Rasminsky Papers LR76-443-5, Canada's Trade with Britain, 1964.
16 In 1963, Canada's trade surplus with the United Kingdom was CAN$480 million, in 1964, CAN$600 million, and in 1965, CAN$451 million.

17 PRO, BT 11, vol. 6057, note for the record, 11 March 1964.
18 PRO, BT 11, vol. 6056, brief for minister of state's visit to Canada.
19 See PRO, BT 11, vol. 6269, UKCCC (64) A.7, 'Motor Cars,' June 1964.
20 PRO, BT 11, vol. 6414, 'Mr. Mitchell Sharp's courtesy call on the President, 1st December, 1964.'
21 PRO, BT 11, vol. 6056, The Canadian method of valuation for duty and their automatic anti-dumping duty, 25 June 1963. Emphasis added.
22 PRO, BT 11, vol. 6056, Lionel Lightman, confidential minute, 19 April 1963.
23 PRO, BT 11, vol. 6056, Lightman to Mervyn Trenaman, 29 April 1963.
24 PRO, BT 11, vol. 6353, note for a meeting between the president and the Hon. Lionel Chevrier, high commissioner for Canada, 13 November 1964. Emphasis added.
25 Bank of Canada Archives, Bank of Canada records, 4B-300, 'Projection of the Canadian Balance of Payments to 1970,' 30 December 1965. The current account deficit, which comprised a good portion of the country's overall trade deficit, had been the subject of study during 1965 when the minister of finance, Walter Gordon, had initiated a study 'to examine the character and cause of the current account deficit and consider what steps can be taken to correct it.'
26 PRO, Cabinet Conclusions (CAB) 128/39, 'Economic Situation.' See also PRO, PREM 11, vol. 851, UKCCC (65) 19, May 1965.
27 PRO, BT 11, vol. 6414, note of a meeting with Mr. Mitchell Sharp, 2 December 1964.
28 See PRO, BT 11, vol. 6310, Charles de Hoghton, Committee for Exports to Canada, 'Notes on a Visit to Canada,' December 1964. In an extended essay, de Hoghton records his impressions following a trip to Canada. Among the points he makes: 'The celebrated complaints about bad British deliveries may often be as fairly attributed to poor forward planning on the Canadian side as to sluggishness or maladministration on the British ... Essentially extraneous factors apart (the anti-dumping legislation), the toughness of the Canadian market could be significantly mitigated by greater understanding of what I have called the strategic questions, by greater use by smaller British firms of co-operative export efforts and marketing services offered by specialist firms and by a strengthening of our representation on the ground.'
29 PRO, BT 11, vol. 6058, minute to the prime minister from the secretary of state, December 1964.
30 PRO, BT 11, vol. 6058, 'Note of a Conversation with Mr. Norman Robertson, 15th October, 1964.'
31 Tom Keating, *Canada and World Order: The Multilateral Tradition in Canadian Foreign Policy* (Toronto: McClelland and Stewart, 1993), 142.
32 PRO, BT 11, vol. 6058, Currall to Carter, 25 February 1965.
33 PRO, BT 11, vol. 6761, 'Canada: Visit of the President of the Board of Trade from 25-27 May 1966,' 9 June 1966.
34 PRO, BT 11, vol. 6058, UKCCC, (65) 9, May 1965.
35 Canada, House of Commons, *Debates,* 26 April 1965, 438-39.
36 PRO, BT 11, vol. 6523, 'Meeting with Mr. L. Chapin, Minister/Counsellor (Economic) Canadian High Commission London,' 23 November 1965.
37 PRO, BT 11, vol. 6058, Lintott to secretary of state for Commonwealth relations, 16 November 1965.
38 PRO, BT 11, vol. 6525, C.W. Sanders, 'Visit to Canada, September 1966,' 23 September 1966.
39 PRO, BT 11, vol. 6523, Minute Sheet, W. Hughes, 15 November 1965.
40 Granatstein, *Canada, 1957-1967,* 205.
41 Nor would the Canadians go even part way, the British believed, in addressing this imbalance. An excellent opportunity for Ottawa to demonstrate goodwill would have been to purchase the HS-125, a British military aircraft. Instead, the government bought the more expensive French-made Mystère Falcon despite the (roughly) equal technical performance of the two aircraft. The Canadian purchase was the subject of a letter from Harold Wilson to Lester Pearson. The British thought that the HS-125 'provided a good opportunity for

the Canadian government to give a practical demonstration of its readiness to lessen the trade gap and seize an opportunity of influencing official procurement policy which they usually declare themselves ready to do in suitable cases.' See PRO, BT 11, vol. 6760, Ottawa to CRO, 16 May 1966.

42 PRO, PREM 11, vol. 852, Nicholas Kaldor, 'Causes of Low Rate of Economic Growth in the United Kingdom,' 12 April 1966.

43 Tony Benn, *The Benn Diaries* (London: Hutchison, 1995), 121.

44 PRO, BT 241, vol. 767, letters to R.C. Lightbourne and W. Andrew Rose, June 1966.

45 This agreement covered the duty-free entry into Britain of specified percentages of New Zealand dairy products, meat, apples, pears, and butter in return for Wellington's guaranteed margins of preference for certain UK products.

46 PRO, BT 241, vol. 767, Foreign Office to Bonn, 23 June 1966. However, given New Zealand's special relationship with Britain, it was also unanimously agreed by EEC governments that it would be given some sort of exceptional treatment following the UK's adhesion to the Treaty of Rome.

47 PRO, BT 11, vol. 6761, 'The High Commissioner's Dinner Party for Mr. Douglas Jay,' 27 May 1966.

48 Charles Ritchie, *Storm Signals: More Undiplomatic Diaries, 1962-1971* (Toronto: Macmillan, 1983), 90, 129, 114.

49 See John Hilliker and Donald Barry, *Canada's Department of External Affairs, Vol. 2: Coming of Age, 1946-1968* (Montreal and Kingston: McGill-Queen's University Press, 1995), 322-26.

50 PRO, BT 11, vol. 6525, F.P. Horne, minute sheet, 21 March 1967.

51 PRO, BT 11, vol. 6758, minute sheet, C.W. Sanders, 9 May 1967.

52 Wilson, *The Labour Government*, 503.

53 For another point of view, see John Holmes, 'Shadow and Substance: Diplomatic Relations between Britain and Canada,' in his *Canada: A Middle-Aged Power* (Toronto: McClelland and Stewart, 1976), 147-60. Holmes argues that despite a changing international context, Britain and Canada had much in common and should re-evaluate their relationship. The article, originally written in 1971, is clearly dated.

54 Rasminsky Papers LR76-543-33, Ritchie to Rasminsky, 30 October 1970.

8
Asleep at the Wheel? British Motor Vehicle Exports to Canada, 1945-75
Steve Koerner

On 30 September 1960 the Rover Motor Company presented a brief to the Royal Commission on the Automobile Industry (or Bladen Commission, after its chairman), which had been recently created by the Diefenbaker government. Indeed, in part it had been set up in direct response to concerns about increased levels of automobile imports, especially those from Britain.[1] The Rover Company brief claimed that the automobile trade between Canada and Britain was in certain ways representative, albeit on a smaller scale, of the wider trading relationship between the two countries. It explained that, because the best-selling Land Rover four-wheel drive light truck was manufactured from aluminum, the company had become one of the world's largest purchasers of Canadian aluminum. Thus Rover spent far more money in Canada than it earned from Canadian vehicle sales.[2] Up to a point, this was true. However, Rover's assertion about the nature of the Anglo-Canadian motor vehicle trade was only partially correct. In fact, prior to 1939, very few British motor vehicles of any kind entered Canada. Until well into the 1950s Canada was the only member of the British Empire and Commonwealth other than Britain itself with a substantial automobile industry. Indeed during the interwar period the Canadian industry was in the top league of the world's automotive exporters and during the 1920s was surpassed only by the United States.[3] And, whatever its fluctuations, the volume of British motor vehicles only periodically followed the general trend of trade between Britain and Canada.

There is a growing literature about the history of the British motor vehicle industry, especially for the years after 1945.[4] However, there has been very little study focusing on the activities of the industry in the export trade, including Canada, which was for a time one of Britain's largest postwar markets for automobiles.[5] Nor, for that matter, is there a full and comprehensive history of the Canadian automobile industry.[6] This chapter will examine whether or not British automotive manufacturers were 'asleep at the wheel' – whether they 'lost' the Canadian market through their own actions or were instead victims of events beyond their control. As such, it will look at the trade relationship between Canada and Britain through, as it were, a windshield, or over the handlebars of a motorbike.[7] Finally it will try and place this case study of Anglo-Canadian trade within the context of the postwar shift of Canadian trade away from the UK, a theme that has been explored in recent literature.[8]

Prior to 1939, the British motor vehicle industry was not the exporter it would become after 1945. Only 12 percent of automobiles produced in Britain were sent abroad and 85 percent of those went to destinations within the British Empire. A mere trickle of British-made automobiles and motorcycles entered Canada.[9] This was because British motor vehicles, mostly small and relatively underpowered, were simply not suitable for Canadian conditions, which were characterized by poor roads, long distances, and a severe climate. Canadian consumers preferred the larger, more powerful and robust domestically built vehicles or their counterparts imported from the United States, which dominated the Canadian market as they did many others.[10] Moreover, while comparatively large, the Canadian automobile industry was, nearly from its beginnings in the early twentieth century, a branch plant operation entirely owned by American and, more recently, Japanese manufacturers.

As their British rivals were all too aware, one of the main reasons why the Americans set up their manufacturing plants in Canada was to gain access to the lucrative empire and dominion trade, which would have been otherwise closed to them by tariffs.[11] Until 1932, British motor vehicle exports to Canada were themselves subject to Canadian tariffs. However, after 1932, as a result of the Ottawa Agreement, certain products (including motor vehicles and bicycles) could be brought in duty-free under the Imperial (later British or Commonwealth) Preferential Duty.[12] Yet, despite this advantage, British automotive imports scarcely increased. The few that did were mostly luxury or sports cars. As a representative from the Chrysler automobile company later recalled, during this period anyone who owned an imported car 'was considered to be either a wealthy man given to ostentation (if his car was a luxury model) or an eccentric (if he owned a small car).'[13]

This situation was paralleled in the motorcycle field. The British motorcycle industry, which dominated its world markets in much the same way as the American automobile industry did theirs, had barely any presence in North America.[14] Although, by the late 1930s, the once prolific American motorcycle industry had been reduced to just two manufacturers, Harley-Davidson and Indian, it was still able to hold on to at least 95 percent of the North American market. Nearly everywhere else, the British dominated. As with automobiles, the American-built machines were believed to be more suitable for the demanding conditions of North American roads, and this also contributed to the poor sales of British machines.[15]

Figure 8.1

Selected automobile exports to Canada, 1945-75

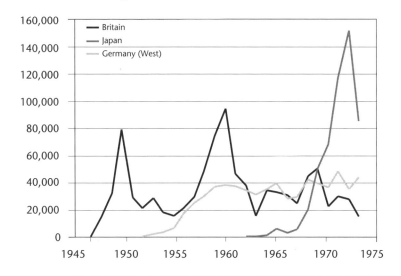

Source: Dominion Bureau of Statistics/Statistics Canada, Trade of Canada-Imports, various years.

After 1945 the situation changed radically. With domestic demand pent-up since 1939 because of wartime production policies, Canadian consumers were keen to acquire personal motor transport. The Canadian automobile industry was unable to meet this surge of demand, nor could imports from the US make up the difference. This created a sellers' market and a huge opportunity for British manufacturers. In response, British automotive exports to Canada sharply increased. In 1946 a mere 731 units entered; by 1950 this total had ballooned to 80,000, vastly more than from any other source (see Figure 8.1 and note 17 below). The fact that no duty was paid on them was undoubtedly a significant factor in their popularity and may have been one the reasons why British cars had become relatively more popular in Canada than the United States.[16] Nor should one discount the sentimental appeal of British products in a nation still very oriented towards the 'Old Country,' or the strong bonds forged between Canada and Britain during the course of two world wars. There was, moreover, virtually no other competition for the kind of vehicles the British were sending, and these imports enjoyed an additional price advantage after the 1949 sterling devaluation.[17] Finally, the British government itself provided various incentives to motor-vehicle manufacturers to export because of the dire financial state of the country, exhausted of its foreign exchange reserves by the war.[18]

Most British cars arriving in Canada at this time were re-designed but essentially prewar models that had been put back into production after 1945.

There were exceptions, such as the Morris Minor, one of the most popular models produced by Britain after 1945. Higher-performance sports cars, although comparatively expensive, were also successful among a certain stratum of Canadian car buyers. It may well be that British automobile exports during this period could have been greater than they were. Manufacturers were frequently plagued with materials shortages, and this held back production figures.[19] Still the volume was impressive, so much so that one car maker, AFN (Bristol), actually considered setting up an assembly plant in Canada.[20]

British motorcycle exports to Canada also dramatically increased during this period. Going from 153 machines in 1945, the number skyrocketed to 6,449 five years later (see Figure 8.2).[21] As with their four-wheeled counterparts, motorcycles were brought in on a duty-free basis. Nor did foreign competitors pose any serious challenge. Their main prewar rivals, the Germans, had been ruined by the war and the Americans were reeling from a huge influx of British imports that had knocked the Indian company out of business and forced Harley-Davidson to seek increased tariff protection from the American government. The bulk of Britain's motorcycle exports fell in the medium- to heavy-weight model categories (350cc to 500cc engine

Figure 8.2

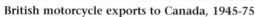

British motorcycle exports to Canada, 1945-75

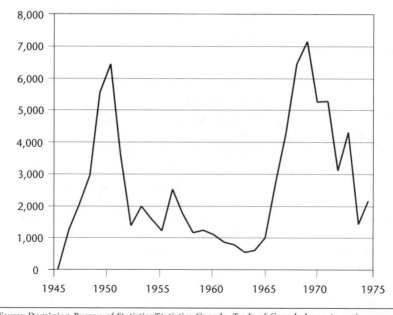

Source: Dominion Bureau of Statistics/Statistics Canada, Trade of Canada-Imports, various years.

capacity) and were mainly powerful sports-type models sold to enthusiasts. In contrast to the automobile industry, many of these machines, such as the Norton Dominator and the Triumph Thunderbird, were fresh designs, developed with the export trade in mind. Two-wheeled exports from other countries, such as scooters from Italy, tended to be far smaller than the British machines and were designed more for utilitarian purposes. In any case, they arrived in such small numbers that they barely dented the market.

The peak year of the initial postwar boom for British automobile exports to Canada was 1950 and was not to be exceeded until the end of the decade. Sales declined in part because the postwar buying spree had tapered off, but also because of the reassertion of the Canadian automobile industry in its home market. In 1949, for example, domestic automobile production had been 193,556 units; in 1950 it grew to 284,076. Annual production averaged between 280,000 and 350,000 units for the rest of the decade. Automotive importers also suffered from two recessions during the early 1950s, from credit restrictions imposed by the federal government, and from complaints about parts availability and service work in general provided to Canadian customers.[22] The latter were to become persistent complaints levelled against both British automobiles and motorcycles for long into the future.[23] During these years, few other nations exported significant numbers of automobiles to Canada. A major exception was West Germany, and particularly Volkswagen. Although only a handful of its Beetles were sold during 1952, its first year on the Canadian market, thereafter sales rose steadily.[24] Ironically, the Beetle, which posed a major threat to British car manufacturers throughout world export markets, had actually been offered to them in the immediate postwar years as part of German war reparations (the British occupying authorities controlled Volkswagen AG from 1945 to 1949). However, they turned it down as unsuitable for their purposes.[25]

What underlay the continuing popularity of imported cars, British or otherwise? One critical factor was the increasing affluence of Canadian consumers, as well as the burgeoning growth of suburbs, both of which contributed to a greater demand for cars. Indeed, for the first time, many Canadian families could afford two cars and, because of their greater fuel efficiency, ease of parking in congested urban areas, and general economy as compared to the domestic product, the second vehicle was often a British import. The increased affluence also underlay the appeal of sports cars such as the MG,[26] although saloon (sedan) cars and economy models tended to predominate and sales of Austins, Morrises, and Fords were strong, especially with women, who were believed by British manufacturers to have a significant influence in their families' automobile choices.[27] The smaller specialty producers also prospered. Land Rover in particular was a surprise success, finding a market niche, especially among institutional fleets such as provincial police forces, the geological survey, and the BC Forest Service.[28]

British automotive sales were not spread evenly across the country. British Columbia had by far the highest ownership of foreign-built automobiles with 42.7 percent of registrations, and Saskatchewan the lowest at 13.7 percent.[29] There were also some well-publicized failures, most notably Standard's Vanguard and Mayflower models. This was well known to the company, whose management noted that only fifty-nine of two hundred Vanguards stocked in Canada during 1954 had been sold.[30] As for the Mayflower, a company representative in Canada informed headquarters that they were 'rather outdated ... [and] difficult to sell.'[31] All this was despite the fact that they had been specifically designed for export markets. Both models were plagued with technical faults and never caught on with Canadian motorists.[32]

Such failures once again highlighted the general unsuitability of many British cars to the harsh and demanding driving conditions that characterized most of Canada, as well as the continuing consumer concerns about parts and servicing.[33] These in turn raised questions about how committed British car manufacturers were to the Canadian market. In 1954, for example, Standard Motors' director of export sales wrote to the company's spares manager that 'already British cars in general have an extremely bad reputation in this regard.'[34] In fact, judging from documents contained in the archives of the Federation of British Industry, complaints about cars reflected those made by Canadian consumers and suppliers about the sales and service of a number of other British products.[35] Nevertheless, by the late 1950s sales of car imports, 60 percent of which came from American branch plants located in Britain, were once more on the rise, particularly saloon models (see Figure 8.1). However, their popularity may have been incidental and was most probably stimulated by increased sales of the VW Beetle and other smaller economy cars brought about by changing patterns of consumer demand (see note 43 below).

What underlay this second upsurge in sales of imported automobiles? In part it was a backlash by a large number of Canadian consumers against the perceived excesses of the North American automobile industry, which persisted in building large, expensive, and gaudily designed models. Groups such as the Canadian Automobile Association and the Canadian Association of Consumers presented briefs to the Bladen Commission that excoriated the domestic industry and made favourable reference to the more practical and economical products that were arriving from Britain and Germany.[36] The consumer association was especially critical, charging that the domestic automobile industry churned out 'larger models ... flashier models – aimed to build up the prestige of the owner, all at a higher cost to the buyer.'[37] For their part, British car manufacturers claimed that their higher sales merely proved that they were filling a demand for a kind of market segment the domestic manufacturers had ignored, and claimed that they were not really competing head to head with the Canadian car industry.[38] All they were doing was providing Canadian consumers with vehicles that would otherwise have been unavailable.[39] The Bladen Commission also heard from advocates of the so-called 'all-Canadian car.' Many thought this type of vehicle, which soon came to be more popularly known as the 'Bladen Beaver,' would embody the ideals of economy and durability, features thought absent from products of both the Canadian and American car industries, but not from the imports.[40]

Canadian industry in general was divided over the growing influx of British automobiles. The forest industry in British Columbia, for example, which enjoyed a thriving export business with Britain, was opposed to import restrictions. These were unjustified, the Council of Forest Industries informed the Bladen Commission, because sales of Canadian wood products to Britain exceeded British motor vehicle imports by approximately $32 million.[41] However, others, particularly automobile manufacturers, domestic and foreign alike, who directly competed with the British, bitterly complained that they were at an unfair disadvantage because of the British (later Commonwealth) Preferential Tariff.[42] Indeed, Canadian auto makers claimed they were now caught in a two-way squeeze. On the one hand, they saw a flood of imports muscling in on their home market, while on the other, their own automobile exports, once an important aspect of the trade, were being shut out of market after market because of tariffs and import quotas. For example, General Motors claimed that while in 1929 it had sent 17,864 passenger cars and trucks to Australia, by 1959 this total had shrunk to only 2,066. The company blamed the decline on import quotas, Commonwealth content regulations, and discriminatory methods of establishing values for taxation purposes.[43] Because of this downturn in exports, Canada in the 1950s became, for the first time since the creation of the Canadian car industry, a net importer of automobiles. Nor was the automobile industry alone in suffering from increased British imports. The bicycle industry, which was dominated by one firm, CCM (Canada Cycle and Motor Company), also protested that its markets were being swamped by British bicycle imports.[44]

Inevitably the issue gained a political dimension and was discussed by the Diefenbaker cabinet, which even debated whether or not the federal government should continue to purchase imported vehicles for its own motor vehicle fleet. Obviously, there were sensitive political factors to be considered, especially in southern Ontario, the heartland of the Canadian auto industry, and indeed these were to be a major reason for the appointment of the Bladen Commission.[45] Although the Bladen Commission suggested some form of protection against imports for the Canadian car industry, the government was reluctant to follow its recommendations. In any case, pressure for punitive measures against British imports dropped away in

Figure 8.3

Production levels in the automobile industry for selected countries, 1945-75

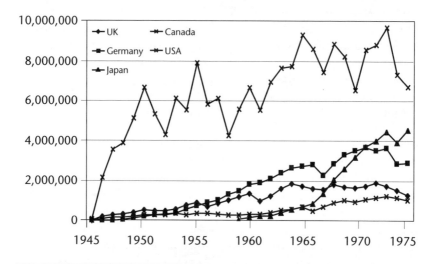

Source: SMMT, The Motor Industry of Great Britain, various years.

subsequent years as the British automobile industry entered an era of crippling turmoil.

Between 1960 and 1975 the British automotive industry suffered deep internal problems, highlighted by the creation of the British Leyland Motor Corporation, that would have severe implications for its export trade. Production levels fluctuated at the same time as international rivals' competitiveness intensified (see Figure 8.3). With the notable exception of models such as the BMC Mini and the Jaguar E-Type sports car, automobile design had stagnated, and this had a negative effect on sales in Canada and elsewhere.[46] In the first instance, after 1958 the British discovered that their models encountered increasing difficulty competing with the Canadian- and American-made 'compact' cars, which directly attacked their market.[47] Then, by the end of the 1960s, sales were sharply undercut by the arrival of Japanese competition (see Figure 8.1).[48] In response, the nature of their product mix changed. During the 1960s fewer and fewer British economy cars arrived in Canada. Instead, an increasing proportion became specialty cars, particularly sports cars such as the MGs and luxury marques such as Jaguar.[49] In the late 1960s and early 1970s, even when new economy models such as the Austin Marina did appear, they performed poorly in the Canadian market, suffering badly in comparison with better engineered and manufactured Japanese imports. Consequently, they were soon withdrawn from the Canadian market.[50]

Nor was the British stronghold in the sports car field secure. By the late 1960s the newly introduced Datsun 240Z, for example, easily outperformed the more venerable MG and Triumph models in both technical sophistication and sales.[51] And Land Rover was overwhelmed by the Toyota Land Cruiser in much the same way. Consequently, by 1975 Land Rover had withdrawn from the Canadian market, as did the sports cars several years later. British cars have continued to be sold in Canada since 1975. Imports reached a low point of 434 units in 1982. By 1999 they had risen to 3,179 but these were mostly in the luxury category, such as the high-priced Jaguar saloon cars. Land Rover re-entered the Canadian market in the early 1990s but now only sells its more expensive Range Rover and Discovery SUV models, which are nothing like the cheaper utilitarian machines it sold during the 1950s and 1960s.[52]

A similar pattern developed in the motorcycle field even though, in contrast to the car industry, motorcycle exports to Canada actually grew substantially, albeit briefly, in the late 1960s. Although only 1,102 British machines were imported in 1960, by 1969 they had reached an all-time peak of 7,152 mostly large and comparatively expensive machines (see Figure 8.4). However, in reality the British had simply been dragged along by

Figure 8.4

Selected motorcycle exports to Canada, 1945-75

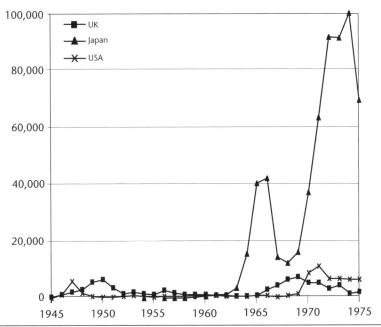

Source: Motor Cycle Association (Britain) and Honda Motor's *World Motorcycle Facts and Figures* (1997).

the huge rise in motorcycle sales largely created by the Japanese, who at first had exported small, cheap models – such as Honda Motors' 50cc Supercub – that dramatically stimulated the entire North American motorcycle market.[53] This inadvertently boosted the sale of British motorcycles, at least for several years. In 1960 the Japanese had sent 520 machines, all of them under 250cc, to Canada. Thereafter, their totals grew on a near-geometric basis. In 1964 they sent 15,551 machines, and the figure reached 69,183 in 1975. By contrast, after their peak in 1969, the British imports went into a sharp decline, dropping to 2,176 machines in 1975.[54] For several years there were virtually no British motorcycle exports to Canada, but these have since resumed in small numbers after the rebirth of the Triumph motorcycle company in the late 1980s.

What led to the collapse of British motorcycle exports to Canada? As with automobiles, by the mid-1960s British motorcycles suffered from outdated designs and factory-production technology. While the Japanese did not actually compete directly with the British until later in the decade, they gradually introduced larger, more powerful motorcycles that Canadian consumers not only found to be technically superior to their British counterparts but often cheaper as well. However, instead of trying to improve and upgrade their motorcycles, the British began a process that has been called 'segment retreat' and simply stopped making the medium-sized models in order to concentrate solely on the larger machines.[55] By the early 1970s, as the Japanese relentlessly moved into the 'Big Bike' markets, the British had reached the point where there was nowhere left for them to retreat. Within a few years virtually the entire industry was out of business, as the British government was unwilling to subsidize a two-wheeled equivalent to British Leyland. By 1975 the Japanese had taken over Britain's former position as the world's leading motorcycle producer.

So how to explain the failure of British motor vehicle manufacturers in the Canadian market? Is it fair to suggest that they had been 'asleep at the wheel,' losing out mainly through negligence? And does this case study reveal anything helpful about Anglo-Canadian trade generally during this period? Certainly there are the peculiarities of the Canadian market to consider, particularly the demanding climatic and geographical conditions with which British manufacturers had such difficulty coping, as they did with setting up parts and servicing networks. Moreover, Canada was the one Empire-Commonwealth market where British automobile (though not motorcycle) manufacturers encountered a strong domestic competitor. It was also unique in being outside the sterling area. The British did best during the late 1940s and early 1950s when they had the import field mostly to themselves. Subsequently, they had difficulties adapting to the pressures of a more competitive environment, even with the continuing advantages of the British or Commonwealth Preferential Tariff. Yet, at least up until the early

1960s, the British showed commendable skill and initiative with the introduction of imaginative and bold car and motorcycle designs. In certain instances with, for example, sports cars and the Land Rover, they literally created entirely new niche markets in Canada, although ironically these would ultimately be more fully developed by the Germans, the Japanese, and, to a lesser extent, the Americans. The British were even more relatively successful in the motorcycle field, where they benefited from the lack of a strong domestic competitor, or indeed from any serious competition until the late 1960s.

The failure of the British motor vehicle producers to maintain their hold on the Canadian market was as much a reflection of their own internal problems as it was of the challenges they encountered there. As a result, they were unable to press home their advantages over a longer period of time. The automobile industry, in particular, was either incapable or unwilling to develop models that were suitable for the Canadian market although, as proponents of the 'Bladen Beaver' had argued, this had also been the case with the domestic industry itself.

The British motor vehicle industry did not live up to the promise of its early successes in Canada after 1945. However, as a case study, its history highlights the importance of the supply side in Anglo-Canadian trade, especially how it and other British industries failed to come to grips with Canadian consumers, particularly in terms of quality control and service. Seen in this light, perhaps the Canadian motor vehicle market was, as the Rover company suggested in its brief to the Bladen Commission, symbolic of the larger trade relationship, but not entirely in the way they had originally intended it to be.

Acknowledgments
I would like to thank Paul Harris of Woodworks for preparing the four graphs used in this chapter.

Notes
1 The Commission's report was published as *Royal Commission on the Automotive Industry* (Ottawa: Queen's Printer, 1961), hereafter referred to as the *Bladen Report.*
2 See National Archives of Canada (NAC), RG33, box 45, vol. 2, brief 53, Rover Motor Co.
3 See Gerald Bloomfield, *The World Automotive Industry* (Newton Abbot: David and Charles, 1978), 315. In 1929, 39 percent or 103,000 motor vehicles out of a total of 265,000 were shipped abroad. See *The Canadian Automotive Industry: Performance and Proposals for Progress* [*Reisman Commission*] (Ottawa: Queen's Printer, 1978), 3.
4 See, for example, among the more recent, Roy Church, *The Rise and Decline of the British Motor Industry* (London: Macmillan, 1994); James Foreman-Peck, Sue Bowden, and Alan McKinley, *The British Motor Industry* (Manchester: Manchester University Press, 1995); and Timothy R. Whisler, *The British Motor Industry, 1945-1994* (Oxford: Oxford University Press, 1999). By contrast, there is no comparable published academic work that addresses the history of the British motorcycle industry.
5 There is some relevant literature for the United States; see, for example, James Rader, *Penetrating the U.S. Auto Market* (Ann Arbor: UMI Research Press, 1979), although it deals primarily with German and Japanese imports.

6 There is, however, Heather Robinson's *Driving Force: The McLaughlin Family and the Age of the Car* (Toronto: McClelland and Stewart, 1995) and two other popular histories of the industry, now somewhat dated. See James Dykes, *Canada's Automobile Industry* (Toronto: McGraw-Hill, 1970), and Hugh Durnford and Glenn Baechler, *Cars of Canada* (Toronto: McClelland and Stewart, 1973). For the early years of the industry, see Howard C. Aikman, *The Automobile Industry of Canada* (Montreal: McGill University Economic Studies No. 8, 1926).

7 This study is restricted to automobiles and motorcycles and will not deal with commercial vehicles such as trucks or buses.

8 See, most notably, Bruce Muirhead, *The Development of Postwar Canadian Trade Policy: The Failure of the Anglo-European Option* (Montreal and Kingston: McGill-Queen's University Press, 1992). See also R.D. Cuff and J.L. Granatstein, *American Dollars: Canadian Prosperity* (Toronto: Samuel-Stevens, 1978).

9 See Whisler, *The British Motor Industry, 1945-1994*, 307.

10 This point was well known to British government policymakers at the time. See, for example, Public Record Office (PRO), MT 34/55, memo 'R.V. 755' dated 31 December 1929, and also PRO, BT 59/24/589/20, a report entitled 'Motor Cars' prepared by C.E. House.

11 See House report, ibid.

12 Inexplicably, the Canadian government granted this concession without any commitment of similar reciprocity from the British; see *Bladen Report*, 6-7 and *Reisman Commission*, 8.

13 See NAC, RG33, box 45, file 37a, brief from the Chrysler Corporation, dated October 1960.

14 See Steve Koerner, 'The British Motor Cycle Industry during the 1930s,' *Journal of Transport History* (March 1995): 55-77.

15 This point was, once again, well understood by the British government and motorcycle manufacturers. See Modern Records Centre (MRC), University of Warwick, MSS 204/3/1/16b, *Notes on the Cycle and Motor Cycle Trade in Canada and the US* (Coventry: British Cycle and Motor Cycle Manufacturers and Traders, 1929), and PRO, BT 59/24, sub file 589, paper entitled 'Cycles and Motor Cycles' dated December 1938.

16 See Whisler, *The British Motor Industry, 1945-1994*, 312.

17 In 1950, only 4,700 vehicles were imported from the United States, 126 from France, 19 from Italy, and 774 from other unspecified countries. Figures are drawn from Table IV of the *Bladen Report*, 104.

18 For an overview of the postwar British automobile industry, see Jim Tomlinson, 'The Government and the Car Industry, 1945-70,' *Journal of Transport History* (March 1999): 17-29; and Nick Tiratsoo, 'The Motor Industry,' in *Labour Governments and Private Industry*, ed. H. Mercer, N. Rollings, and J.D. Tomlinson (Edinburgh: Edinburgh University Press, 1992), 162-85.

19 See various files contained in PRO, SUPP 14/331, entitled 'Motor Industry Steel Allocations, 1951, Part 1.'

20 See PRO, SUPP 14/328, H.J. Aldington (AFN Ltd.) to Stafford Cripps, 16 November 1948. Because of its high sales in Canada, motorcycle maker Norton Motors considered opening an assembly operation in the Montreal area at around the same time, although, for reasons unknown, neither it nor AFN ever did.

21 See Dominion Bureau of Statistics, *Trade of Canada: Imports*, various years, 1945-50.

22 See MRC, MSS 226/ST/3/0/CA/12, memo dated 3 July 1951 prepared by the Canadian distributor for Standard-Triumph. The memo went on to say that, for them at least, the Canadian market had essentially collapsed.

23 See, for example, MRC, MSS 226/ST/3/0/CA/1, memo from A.C.L. Mills (Standard Motors of Canada) to K. Aspland, secretary, Standard Motors Co., Coventry, 15 March 1951. Several years later the Canadian distributor for Standard Motors wrote to the company's British headquarters attributing problems with dealers, as well as the high price of the cars in comparison with used Canadian vehicles, as the main cause for lower sales levels. See MRC, MSS 226/ST/3/0/CA/5, F.W. Morris to K. Aspland, 26 May 1954.

24 Sales went from 49 during 1952 to 1,160 in 1953, 22,377 in 1957 and 27,574 in 1959. See the Volkswagen Canada brief, listed as Exhibit 24 to the Royal Commission on the Auto-

mobile Industry, dated September 1960. Copy on deposit at the National Library of Canada, Ottawa.

25 A description of the evaluation of the Beetle by British car firms is contained in the British Intelligence Objectives Sub-Committee, final report no. 998, item no. 19, *Investigation into the Design and Performance of the Volkswagen or German Peoples' Car* (London: Bios, n.d.). See also Martin Adeney, *The Motor Makers* (London: Fontana, 1989), 209.

26 See PRO, SUPP 14/332, 'Market for British cars in the USA. Report by embassy, Washington,' dated July 1950. The report covered Canada as well as the US.

27 The role of women in car sales was specifically addressed by the British embassy report, see ibid., 4. A statistical breakdown of British automobile sales by manufacturer between the years 1952 and 1958 is contained in MRC, MSS 226/ST/3/0/CA/20.

28 See Rover Motor Co. brief 53, Bladen Report.

29 See NAC, RG 33, box 45, vol. 3, brief 75, Province of Saskatchewan, Economic Advisory and Planning Board, dated February 1960. British Columbia was the best sales region for Standard Motors, see MRC, MSS 226/ST/3/0/CA/5, Morris to Aspland, 26 May 1954.

30 See MRC, MSS 226/ST/3/0/CA/5, Aspland to A.S. Dick, 21 July 1954.

31 See MRC, MSS 226/ST/3/0/CA/7/2 (product liability files), memo, F.W. Morris to R.J. Twigg, dated 5 May 1955.

32 See Nick Tiratsoo, 'Standard Motor 1945-55 and the Post-war Malaise of British Management,' in *Management and Business in Britain and France*, ed. Youssef Cassis, Francois Crouzet, and Terry Gourvish (Oxford: Clarendon Press, 1995), 91-95, and Adeney, *The Motor Makers*, 207.

33 Points that were addressed in some detail in the British embassy's report on the North American automobile market, op. cit. (note 27), 4-7.

34 See MRC, MSS 226/ST/3/0/US/2, memo, W.J.R. Warren to H.E. Pugh, 8 March 1954. While the remark referred to the US, the situation in Canada was little different.

35 See, among others, MRC, MSS 200/F/3/D3/8/8, letter about suppliers to FBI Director Norman Kipping from Julian Piggot, Chairman of the British Jewellery and Silverware Council, 24 April 1951; MRC, MSS 200/F/3/D3/8/10, memo from John Bonus, General Manager of the British Trade Council in Toronto to Kipping, 27 April 1956; and MRC, MSS 200/F/3/D3/8/12, minutes of a meeting between the Dollar Export Board and the Dollar-Sterling Trade Council, 19 January 1956.

36 The CAA commented that the 'increased sales of foreign cars is an indication that a great many Canadians are convinced that they can buy better economy, equal convenience and safety for a great deal less money.' See NAC, RG33, box 45, vol. 1, file 45, cab. 11, drwr. 1.

37 See ibid., file 107.

38 See brief from the Society of Motor Manufacturers and Traders, dated November 1960, on deposit at the National Library of Canada as well as NAC, RG33, box 45, vol. 16, brief 73 from the Dollar-Sterling Trade Council.

39 See briefs to the Bladen Commission from the British Motor Corporation, 30 September 1960 and from the Society of Motor Manufacturers and Traders (SMMT), November 1960, both on deposit at the National Library of Canada.

40 See NAC, RG33, box 45, vol. 6, news clipping entitled 'All-Canadian Made "Beaver" Answer to Auto Problems?' *Ottawa Citizen*, 29 October 1960.

41 See NAC, RG33, box 45, vol. 2, brief 30, Council of Forest Industries of BC, dated September 1960. The council also noted that a significant proportion of the Canadian exports were plywood products used by British car companies as packing cases for their exports.

42 See, for example, NAC, RG33, box 45, vol. 1, brief from the Canadian Automobile Chamber of Commerce, file 1, cab. 11, drwr.1, brief 53 from the Ford Motor Co. of Canada and brief 51 from the Studebaker-Packard Company of Canada, dated 3 October 1960. Volkswagen imports were affected by the 17.5 percent tariff, although this did not seem to affect their competitiveness.

43 See NAC, RG33, box 45, vol. 2 (briefs), brief 41, General Motors of Canada, dated October 1960. This was a puzzling complaint on the part of the General Motors Corporation since presumably any automobiles made in their Canadian factories that were exported

to Australia would have qualified for protection under the same imperial/Commonwealth preference tariff reductions.

44 See NAC, RG79, vol. 72, file 118-7-16, CCM to David Sims, deputy minister of customs and excise, 8 November 1954.

45 The matter of British car imports was discussed at Cabinet meetings held on 15 July, 11 and 24 August, and 11 October 1960. See NAC, RG2, vol. 2747, 1960 Cabinet Conclusions, vol. 83, 82.

46 See Church, *The Rise and Decline of the British Motor Industry*, 82-90; Whisler, *The British Motor Industry, 1945-1994*, 307-12; Foreman-Peck et al., *The British Motor Industry*, 160-63.

47 These so-called 'compacts' included models such as the GM Corvair, AMC Rambler, and Ford Falcon. See 'Cars of the 1960s,' *Financial Times*, 2 December 1960, contained in NAC, RG 33, box 45, vol. 7. Nor was the threat restricted to the compacts. The introduction of the Ford Mustang in the mid-1960s, for example, threatened the British sports car market. See MRC, MSS 226/ST/3/0/CA/10/2, minutes of the meeting of the directors of Standard-Triumph Motors (Canada), 19 January 1965.

48 As early as 1965, concern was raised about the growing numbers of smaller Japanese economy cars appearing in North America and the lack of updated British models to meet them. See ibid., minutes of a meeting of the directors of Leyland-Triumph Motors held in Toronto, 18 August 1965.

49 The vast proportion of sports-car production for models such as the MG and Austin-Healey went to North America; see Jonathan Wood, 'Export or Die,' in *Britain's Motor Industry*, ed. Nick Georgano (Sparkford, Somerset: G.T. Foulis, 1995), 143.

50 See Foreman-Peck et al., *The British Motor Industry*, 162, and Jonathan Wood, *Wheels of Misfortune: The Rise and Fall of the British Motor Industry* (London: Sidgwick and Jackson, 1988), 176-77.

51 See Whisler, *The British Motor Industry, 1945-1994*, 349.

52 See SMMT, *The Motor Industry of Great Britain*, 1983 and 2000.

53 For an analysis of Honda's North American motorcycle export drive, see Jun Otahara, 'An Evolutionary Phase of Honda Motor: The Establishment and Success of American Honda Motor,' *Japanese Yearbook on Business History* 17 (2000): 110-35.

54 See Dominion Bureau of Statistics, *Trade of Canada: Imports*, various years.

55 This process was investigated at some length in a government-sponsored study; see Boston Consulting Group, *Strategy Alternatives for the British Motor Cycle Industry* (London: HMSO, 1975). See also Steve Koerner, 'The British Motorcycle Industry, 1935-1975' (PhD thesis, University of Warwick, 1996), 300-65.

9
Britain, Europe, and the 'Other Quiet Revolution' in Canada
Andrea Benvenuti and Stuart Ward

This chapter is concerned with the political culture of Canada's changing economic and political ties with Great Britain in the end of empire era. The unravelling of the British nexus brought material consequences that had widespread repercussions in Canada. But even more significant was the way in which Britain's dwindling world role forced Canadians to reconsider their primary interests and allegiances in the post-imperial world. This had been a recurring feature of Canada's relations with Britain throughout the 1940s and 1950s. A range of issues such as the introduction of separate Canadian citizenship in 1946, the retention of India in the Commonwealth as a republic in 1949, the appointment of a Canadian as Governor General in 1951, the Suez Crisis of 1956, and the 'trade diversion' episode of 1957 had revealed a growing divergence of view as to the appropriate relationship between Canadian nationhood and the traditional attachment to Great Britain. Yet these disputes were not so much concerned with the relevance of Britain as such in the Canadian imagination. Rather, they represented a struggle between competing conceptions of Britishness – between the notion of a 'British inheritance' in the form of certain political rights and values on the one hand, and a more conservative emphasis on loyalty, kinship, and community of interest on the other. While there was considerable overlap between these views, there was little questioning among English-speaking Canadians of the basic idea that Canada was in some sense a 'British country' – a status that not only conferred special privileges and obligations in relation to the mother country, but also set Canadians squarely apart from their American neighbours.[1]

One issue that vividly exposed the tensions and contradictions inherent in Canada's British sensibilities was the Macmillan government's decision of July 1961 to seek membership in the European Economic Community. The prospect of British entry into the newly integrated Europe seemed incompatible with Britain's traditional role as leader of empire and Commonwealth, and signalled a major shift in British policies and priorities. The

Canadian outlook on the world had long been conditioned by the notion of a worldwide community of British countries, but it was difficult to see how this concept could be adapted to accommodate the emerging political realities of the 1960s. The Macmillan government's European aspirations underlined the widening gap between sentiment and self-interest in Britain's ties to the old dominions. The drawn-out negotiations between Britain and the European 'Six' throughout 1962 engendered unprecedented levels of distrust between the Canadian and British governments. Although the negotiations culminated in Charles de Gaulle's infamous veto of British EEC membership in January 1963, the issue nonetheless served to erode the instinctive sense of mutual identification that had traditionally characterized Commonwealth relations. As such, it provided a major impetus to what José Igartua has termed the 'other Quiet Revolution: the dissolution of English-speaking Canada's self-representation as a "British" nation.'[2]

In order to appreciate the impact of Britain's first EEC membership bid in 1961, it is necessary to consider the peculiar sense of dual identification that had long characterized English Canada's ties to Great Britain. On the one hand, Canadians had always shown a natural inclination to defend vigorously their own distinctive interests in times of dispute with the United Kingdom. But while a sense of Canadian distinctiveness had provided a useful framework for advancing Canada's material self-interest, it was rarely articulated in terms of an exclusive Canadian cultural identity, divorced entirely from its British moorings. The national aspirations of the Confederation era did not necessarily give rise to a self-sufficient national myth. The sentiments, qualities, and attributes widely thought to be distinctively 'Canadian' were more a variant of the imperial frontier myth, where peculiarities of climate, frontier conditions, and the struggle with the natural environment were said to have forged a community of 'Better Britons.' A deep attachment to a wider British ideal – 'Greater Britain' as Charles Dilke termed it in the 1860s – ensured that English-Canadian interests and identity were inevitably viewed through the sentimental prism of 'race patriotism.' Beyond an abiding awareness of Canada's more immediate, particular interests and concerns, there prevailed a powerful sentimental assumption that the interests of the various parts of the British world ought ultimately to coincide. As J.W. Dafoe put it in the 1920s, throughout the white settler empire there prevailed an 'instinctive sense of a common destiny.'[3]

Eric Hobsbawm has emphasized that individuals can maintain any number of multiple allegiances, often only becoming aware of the fact when these identities come into conflict.[4] But in the case of the British settler colonies, it is not sufficient merely to point out that they had a 'dual identity.' Britishness was the ethnic marker that inscribed the inner contours and outer limits of Australian, New Zealander, and English-Canadian identities. What Henry Parkes of Australia described as 'the crimson thread of kinship that runs through us all' was not an Australian kinship (despite the fact that he was referring to an Australian community), but rather a sense of common British ethnic origins. It was precisely this collective Britishness that held Queenslanders, Victorians, Tasmanians, and others together as a coherent 'Australian' grouping. Likewise in Canada, the very need for the term 'French Canadian' derived from the assumption by English-speakers that other Canadians were bound together by a common culture and ethnicity that was not French, but British. Thus the 'dual identity' of settler communities was not merely a case of switching hats as the need and occasion arose, because the hats were conceptually interwoven in such a way that made it difficult to conceive of them as distinct, self-sufficient ornaments. This explains, for example, why so many English Canadians – even as late as 1964 – could not contemplate a national flag that did not feature the Union Jack in some way.[5] As Douglas Cole has argued, Australian and Canadian identities had never become 'full blown nationalism,' expressing an exclusive loyalty to distinctive settler-colonial ethnic communities, because these communities were 'so vitally dependent upon Anglo-Saxonism and Caucasian racialism.'[6] 'Greater Britain' provided a sense of collective belonging that transcended the boundaries of the settler-colonial state, but it also furnished the very framework for celebrating a more limited colonial distinctiveness.

But although settler-colonial *nationhood* could not so easily be disentangled from its British ethnic foundations, the realities of separate *statehood* ensured that the material interests of Britain and the dominions frequently came into conflict. This was the core dilemma of the settler-colonial experience – how to reconcile political and economic differences with a mother country whose very existence was vital to the imagining of a settler-colonial identity. Periodic disputes were the very stuff of Canada's relations with Britain, whether it was the recurring rancour of the imperial conferences of the 1920s, the cynical horse-trading of the Ottawa tariff negotiations in the 1930s, or the yawning gap between rhetoric and reality in 'imperial defence cooperation' in the 1940s. The idea of settling these 'family' disputes in a gentlemanly fashion was an article of faith in empire relations, and a key mechanism for insulating the British myth against the occasional shocks of imperial discord. But as the earlier chapters in this volume have shown, the rapid decline in Britain's political and economic fortunes in the era after the Second World War tended to accelerate and intensify the divergence in UK and Canadian assessments of their material self-interest. This, in turn, called into question the sentimental certainties of the Greater British ideal.[7]

The Suez Crisis in particular is routinely regarded, both in Canada and Britain, as emblematic of the parting of the ways between the two countries. The Canadian government's steadfast and very public condemnation of Suez was widely resented in Britain, marking the first time that 'the traditional assumption that the Commonwealth was an asset came in for questioning.'[8] This remains true, but more recent studies indicate that the impact of Suez on popular conceptions of empire and Commonwealth, as opposed to the world of high politics, may not have been as immediate or far-reaching as has been assumed.[9] In many respects, the trauma of Suez derived more from heated disputes within Commonwealth countries, rather than from any fundamental breakdown in the sense of mutual identification between Commonwealth countries. José Igartua's chapter in this volume makes this point particularly vividly in the case of Canada, where Suez generated at least as much public opposition to the St. Laurent government in Ottawa as it inspired mass revulsion with the Eden government in London.

But even more significantly, the immediate post-Suez years illustrate the extent to which the 'British genius for compromise' was still available as a means of reconciling the discordant experiences of 1956 within a wider sense of organic British community. Both Harold Macmillan and John Diefenbaker voiced their determination to mend the cracks in the Commonwealth façade – a common conviction that promptly led them into further difficulties in the fiasco of the proposed United Kingdom-Canada Free Trade Agreement. Here, Diefenbaker's hopelessly impractical vision of diverting 15 percent of Canadian imports from the US to Britain derived more from a sentimental hankering for the old certainties of Canada's Britishness than from any rational appraisal of whether such a scheme was economically possible (or even desirable). In other words, even at the height of the tensions caused by Britain's dwindling power base in the world, the underlying tenets of 'Greater Britain' could still be called upon to explain (or explain away) the material changes affecting Canada's ties to Britain.

It is here that it becomes possible to identify the significance of Britain's EEC membership bid in the early 1960s. Harold Macmillan's European aspirations by no means represented the first major conflict between the material self-interest of the Canadian and UK governments. But it signalled a conflict of interest of an entirely different kind from those that had disrupted Commonwealth harmony in previous years. The prospect of British adoption of a European common tariff, and the long-term political implications of European unity, raised fundamental questions about the material and ideological foundations of a 'Greater Britain.' It seemed to imply a permanent reorientation of the British conception of community, away from the traditional emphasis on the worldwide British 'family' and towards a new basis for British power and influence in the world as a leading partner in an economically dynamic and politically united Europe. The very symbolism of Britain abandoning the Commonwealth in favour of an entirely incompatible grouping was enough to underline the magnitude of the changes taking place in Canada's world. In stark contrast to Suez, it wasn't a case of the Canadian government breaking ranks with the United Kingdom but the other way around – the Mother Country instigating changes that were bound to undermine the cohesion of the entire Commonwealth. Far from representing yet another awkward moment in a long line of internal disputes (calling on the customary reserves of mutual goodwill), it raised the prospect of the complete disbanding of the Commonwealth club.

The Macmillan Government's reasons for turning towards Europe have been well documented.[10] In essence, the decision to apply for EEC membership boiled down to a feeling that Britain's future outside a European context was one of steadily diminishing global influence, both politically and economically. Early skepticism about the prospects for the successful integration of Europe seemed a major miscalculation by 1960 – so much so that talk began circulating about Britain having 'missed the bus' and 'vegetating in a backwater.'[11] That this picture began to emerge at a time of increasing difficulties in Commonwealth relations – particularly over the thorny issue of South Africa – is no coincidence. The declining political and economic utility of the Commonwealth seemed to underline the extent of Britain's missed opportunity, and in the spring of 1960 Macmillan set in train a major policy rethink. By June 1961 the government was ready to take the leap.

But it was a leap taken with a heavy conscience and a number of encumbering qualifications. Most fundamentally, Macmillan felt bound publicly to uphold the fiction that Britain would never join the EEC on terms harmful to Commonwealth economic interests. This was regarded with some skepticism among Commonwealth countries, and with every justification. Macmillan and his senior ministers were well aware that the founding members of the European Community, particularly the French, would be extremely unwilling to concede any special economic favours to rival Commonwealth producers. On the eve of Britain's application, officials in the Commonwealth Relations Office laid it on the line: Britain's bargaining position was weak, and the best that could be achieved on behalf of the Commonwealth was a phasing out of Commonwealth trade preferences over a transitional period. Commonwealth secretary Duncan Sandys was under no illusion that this would be acceptable to Commonwealth countries, and he therefore proposed a purely tactical display of loyalty in the hope that the experience of negotiation with the EEC might ultimately secure the acquiescence of Commonwealth governments. He emphasized that 'if we tried to get the Commonwealth to agree to accept what we now thought might eventually be negotiated, we should risk doing serious damage to Commonwealth relations while there was still no assurance that we might negotiate satisfactory arrangements with the Six.'[12] Clearly, the Macmillan government had begun to discard sentimental notions about Britain's wider duties and obligations to the Commonwealth 'family.' But equally, there remained a keen awareness of the perils of disturbing such deeply held assumptions, not only among Commonwealth countries but also in Britain itself.

Thus, before announcing any formal decision to apply, the Macmillan government felt bound to make some effort towards 'consulting' Commonwealth governments. In late June 1961 it was agreed that senior ministers should be dispatched to the far reaches of the Commonwealth to explain Britain's position. The task of reassuring Canada, Australia, and New Zealand that their interests would not be harmed fell to Duncan Sandys. His task was far from simple. Not only was he charged with convincing Commonwealth leaders of a case that he did not believe in himself (i.e., that Britain could go into Europe on terms agreeable to the Commonwealth), but it was also widely anticipated that he would be subjected to a thorough grilling. As the *Economist* observed on the eve of his departure, Commonwealth countries were determined to 'make as much noise as possible to assert their interests.'[13]

Not surprisingly, therefore, Sandys was greeted by a cool response in Ottawa, and clearly failed to impress the Diefenbaker government.[14] In spite of his reassurances that the British cabinet had not yet decided to join the EEC, the Canadian ministers gained 'the impression that [Britain] had already reached a decision to negotiate.'[15] As a result, they wasted no time in expressing their concerns about the implications of any formal negotiation between Britain and the EEC.[16] The Canadians impressed upon Sandys their view that British entry would not only cause serious damage to the economy of Canada, but would also have wider political repercussions.[17] In economic terms, they pointed out that 76 percent (CAN$691 million worth) of Canadian exports to the UK would be put at risk should Britain accede to the Treaty of Rome unconditionally.[18] As for the political repercussions, the Canadians feared that British membership in the EEC would irredeemably weaken the Commonwealth and draw their country into the political and economic orbit of the United States. The press communiqué from these talks stated bluntly that 'Canada's assessment of the situation is different to that put forward by Mr. Sandys,'[19] while the Canadian press described the government's stance variously as 'frigid,' 'angry,' 'terse,' and 'the stiffest of the older Commonwealth countries.'[20]

Sandys' visit to Ottawa set the tone for what proved to be a remarkably awkward period in Anglo-Canadian relations. From the formal announcement of the Macmillan government's decision to seek EEC membership on 31 July 1961, to General de Gaulle's veto some eighteen months later, the relationship between the Diefenbaker government and London was marred by a climate of mutual suspicion and ill regard. If the British regarded the Diefenbaker cabinet as 'one of mediocrities' who 'seldom take [a] broad view on any issue and are obsessed by short-term domestic consequences,'[21] the Canadians were certainly no less disdainful of the Macmillan government. In response to Sandys' assurances that Britain would enter the EEC only if satisfactory terms could be obtained to secure the interests of Commonwealth countries, Canadian ministers pointed out 'the problem the UK would face in dropping out of negotiations once they had started.'[22] Indeed, from the very outset the Canadian government suspected that Macmillan was seeking 'to obtain the support of Australia and India and some other member countries before approaching Canada and New Zealand.'[23] From a Canadian point of view, not only were the British hiding their real intentions, but they were also intent on playing a dishonest game by dividing the Commonwealth camp. In reality, these suspicions were completely unfounded (Macmillan was equally intent on deceiving the Australian government),[24] but the very fact that the Canadians were speculating along these lines is indicative of their rapidly diminishing reserves of trust in the British government.

Canadian frustration with British tactics emerged more fully in September 1961 at the Commonwealth Economic Conference in Accra, when Canada's Finance Minister Donald Fleming and Trade Minister George Hees launched a frontal assault on Britain's European aspirations. Fleming demanded to know whether Britain's repeated assurances to the Commonwealth, voiced publicly over several years, were simply to be thrown 'out the window.' He stated bluntly that 'the United Kingdom cannot have its foot in each group and retain the freedom of action necessary to its leadership of the Commonwealth.' Hees voiced similar fears about the future of the Commonwealth, warning that 'if the great masses of the people who make up the Commonwealth believe that the leading member, the United Kingdom, has taken action which – though beneficial to itself – has adversely affected their standard of living, there will be a proportionate weakening of the ties which hold the Commonwealth together ... to a point where it exists in name only.' Fleming summed up the Canadian government's anxieties: 'Doubt and uncertainty remain. Hope is not enough. Good intentions are not enough ... There is no substitute for the Commonwealth. Is it to be dropped for the illusory shadow of who can tell what?' Although Fleming and Hees subsequently attempted to play down their criticism of British policy,[25] there was no mistaking the aggressive and provocative tone of their pronouncements. Fleming's performance in Accra, which prompted other Commonwealth delegates to air their grievances too, was described by the British delegation as 'a tirade as much as a speech.'[26]

Yet the Canadian ministers were by no means greeted at home with unstinting praise for their robust defence of Canadian interests. On the contrary, there prevailed a seemingly endless reservoir of trust in the assurances of the British government that vital Commonwealth interests would be protected. Public faith in British government assurances became a major thorn in the side of the Diefenbaker government in its efforts to secure a fair deal for Canadian exporters. The Toronto *Globe and Mail* was among the most vociferous critics of the government, accusing ministers of 'screaming before she is hurt,' and claiming that it would 'be wiser for Ottawa to reserve judgement until the actual effect on Canadian trade is known.'[27] The *Vancouver Sun* was even more scathing in its criticism of the government's performance at Accra: 'This pathetic bleat that we're being deserted by mother Britain – of whom, incidentally, we have been most anxious to show our independence – is tiresome and even more unproductive than some of our industry.'[28] The more conservative *Calgary Herald* assured readers that 'the United Kingdom has not lost sight of its responsibilities' to the Commonwealth, and that 'there should be no suggestion or accusations that Britain is going "outside the family."'[29] It warned the Canadian government against taking too hostile an approach to Macmillan's EEC aspirations, stating that 'friendship with Britain is a mighty thing to Canada and its continuance must not be impeded.'[30] Often, these assessments were based either on a failure to comprehend fully the commercial implications of British entry into a protectionist European trade bloc, and/or the misguided belief that Canada could somehow apply for associate-member status.[31] In support of the government, the *Ottawa Journal* urged that 'some among us shouting for Britain's entry into the Common Market, accusing the Diefenbaker Government of "dragging its feet" will take the trouble of finding out what the Common Market is about. They might begin by reading the Treaty of Rome.'[32]

The Liberal opposition, led by Lester Pearson, accused the government of having taken the lead in ganging up against Britain, and declared their unconditional support for Britain's EEC membership application. Yet Pearson, too, qualified his position with the vague assertion that Canada should somehow become 'associated' with the British move.[33] At no stage did he specify how Canada might achieve associate status with an enlarged EEC, and the idea was never tabled seriously in London, Brussels, or Ottawa. Indeed it is unlikely that Pearson ever took the idea seriously himself.

Diefenbaker was also reported to have been upset by his ministers' display in Accra, although his response was probably conditioned by the generally hostile reaction of the Canadian press. He criticized Fleming and Hees for having gone 'a long distance in endeavouring to destroy the British Commonwealth.'[34] In reality, however, they had merely given voice to anxieties that the prime minister shared fully. Although the government defended its handling of the Commonwealth Conference in the House of Commons, Diefenbaker subsequently warned against too strong a stance towards Britain. On 26 September 1961 he told his cabinet that 'it would not do for Canada to be held responsible for a socialist government coming to power in Britain.'[35] Clearly, Diefenbaker wanted to prevent Canada not only from being singled out as the most vocal opponent of British entry, but also from being held responsible for any eventual failure in Britain's negotiations with the Six. As the Cabinet recognized in the aftermath of Accra, 'the impression was abroad that Canada had given Britain but two alternatives – in or out – and had been anti-British.'[36]

The British high commissioner in Ottawa, Derick Heathcoat Amory, was positively embarrassed by the degree of understanding and support in Canada for Britain's EEC membership bid.[37] He informed Macmillan in March 1962: 'I think public opinion has been almost unreasoningly favourable to our case, with a tendency to oversimplify the issue and underestimate the effects of exchanging a preference *in favour* for a tariff *against* on (some) Canadian products.'[38] Donald Fleming made comments along similar lines during the visit to Canada of the chief British negotiator in the Brussels negotiations, Edward Heath, in March 1962. He told Heath candidly that 'public affection for Great Britain is so strong in this country that people tend to assume that anything the British Government does must be for the best.'[39] This reluctance to conceive that Britain might abandon Commonwealth interests was the other side of the coin of the Canadian response to the Common Market crisis. Regardless of whether one considered British entry an unmitigated disaster for Canada or took a more complacent view, the prospect of a major rupture of the old Commonwealth nexus was widely thought to be unthinkable.

In this awkward political climate, Fleming was forced to repudiate publicly the suggestion that Canada had behaved in a hostile manner towards the United Kingdom. He explained his government's cool response to the EEC question in a speech at Winnipeg: 'Like all families, we have had our differences; like all human associations ours is not a perfect one, but by and large our aims have been common, and where they have diverged we have brought our differences to the conference table and discussed them as members of a family.'[40] Thus, Fleming was placed in the extraordinary situation of having to defend himself against the charge of disloyalty to the Greater British ideal. But the real problem lay in how to define 'anti'- or 'pro'-British in the context of the EEC issue. The Diefenbaker government's opposition to Macmillan's European ambitions represented a determined effort to resist the steady erosion of Canada's British identity. Yet paradoxically, in order to defend Canada's Britishness, the UK government itself had to be opposed. On the other hand, any outright obstruction of the UK government's European ambitions could just as easily be construed as 'anti-British,' and prove equally harmful to Canada's British ties. This line of reasoning was skilfully deployed by Pearson in the Commons, where he mocked the government for having forgotten 'the old Chinese proverb ... "The wise man does not use a hatchet to kill a fly on the forehead of his friend."'[41] On this point (as in many others) the *Ottawa Journal* jumped to Diefenbaker's defence:

> In the matter of wanting to join the Common Market, what is meant by
> Britain? Not the British people, surely, seeing that according to all the sur-
> veys made, more of the British people are against the Common Market
> than for it. And this of course makes nonsense of the cry, heard from some
> in Canada, that when the Canadian Government takes the stand it is tak-
> ing on the Common Market it is 'opposing Britain.' What the Canadian
> Government is opposing is a position being taken by Prime Minister
> Macmillan and his ministers. Which is something different.[42]

Both sides of the argument, it seemed, were somehow implicated in the
Greater British mindset, and it should not be assumed that Canadian supporters of the Macmillan government had fully embraced the post-imperial
era.

What remains certain, however, is that the entire issue acted as a severe
drain on UK-Canadian understanding and goodwill. Senior British ministers became particularly infuriated by the maternal hankerings of the Commonwealth through the course of Britain's EEC membership negotiations.
Minister for Labour John Hare, for example, publicly accused Commonwealth countries of 'behaving in some respects like children.' While these
countries were quite happy when they were getting their own way, he complained, they became aggrieved when 'mother' decided to do what she
thought was right. What is significant about Hare's comments is that he
drew on the very language and symbolism of the Greater British family, but
in such a way as to dispute its relevance in a post-imperial age. These sentiments were echoed by the *Financial Times,* which claimed that Hare was
merely using the 'wrong words' to express a fundamental truth: 'Britain,
like all other Commonwealth countries, is independent, too, and must take
her decisions in the light of what is best for Britain.'[43] The editorial in Lord
Beaverbrook's *Daily Express,* by contrast, castigated Hare and demanded to
know whether Gallipoli, Vimy Ridge and the D-Day landings were also childish.[44] This kind of reminder of the wartime sacrifice of the dominions was a
recurring irritant for the Macmillan government, so much so that Edward
Heath issued a 'don't mention the war' directive to the British high commissioner in Ottawa in February 1962. Amory had sought permission to
refer publicly to the contribution of the Commonwealth during the Second
World War, and to reassure Canadians that 'the British people owe it to
their sense of honour to send a message no less loyal to the Commonwealth
... for at the end of the day we go into the Common Market if and only if we
believe we can get a square deal for you.'[45] But Heath cautioned strongly
against any official statement or public speech that celebrated Canada's
wartime contribution. 'Our main purpose now,' he advised, 'must be to
bring the Commonwealth public along with us as we go – not hoist the
banner even higher.'[46]

There is every indication that the British government's determination to join the EEC prompted a more resigned and philosophical perspective in Canada. Press opinion began to emphasize the futility of relying on British assurances, and the need for an alternative approach. The *Montreal Gazette* cast doubt on the political value of the modern Commonwealth and posed the question: 'What is really left but the ties of sentiment?'[47] The comments of the *Globe and Mail* were typical: 'We live in a world of change – changing trade, changing alliances, changing balances of power – and we must be adventurous and adaptable to survive. It is unthinkable that Canada, through lack of vision and selfish insistence upon present advantage, should attempt to resist great and beneficial changes in Europe.'[48] A similar line of argument appeared in a report entitled 'The Impact of European Integration on Canada' by the leading Canadian economist L.D. Wilgress in the spring of 1962. Wilgress recognized that 'the maintenance of the status quo is untenable in the face of the winds of change' and suggested that 'the passing of the good old easy days' might expose the Canadian economy to some healthy competition. He concluded his report on an optimistic note by saying that 'the stimulus afforded by this necessity may make Canada a stronger nation and a nation better fitted to achieve its destiny.'[49]

It was around this time that the Canadian government began to recognize the inevitability of Canadian trade sacrifices in the Brussels negotiations. This raised the political problem of how Canada might acquiesce in Britain's EEC membership without inviting the charge of 'selling particular interests down the river.'[50] As a way around this problem, Canadian ministers Donald Fleming, Howard Green, and George Hees entered into a bizarre clandestine agreement with Edward Heath in March 1962. During a series of meetings in Ottawa, Fleming explained to Heath that nearly all senior Canadian officials had been appointed during the Liberal party's twenty-two years of power (1935-57), and all of them still had the closest connections with the Liberal leaders. Therefore any written views on the merits of particular British proposals, even at the most confidential level, would be brought to the notice of their political opponents 'within a matter of minutes.' He therefore asked Heath to refrain from asking the Canadians for their official views on developments in the Brussels negotiations. The Canadians, in turn, would refrain from criticizing the performance of the British negotiators, either in public or in private. The rationale behind this deal, from the point of view of the Diefenbaker government, was to cloak the EEC issue in a shroud of silence and thereby remove it from the agenda in the forthcoming election campaign (which was expected to take place in June 1962).[51]

Thus, in a remarkable display of political expediency, the Canadians offered to soft-pedal their grievances, in return for British cooperation in making the Common Market a non-issue in Canadian electoral politics.

Heath could hardly believe his good fortune, and quickly accepted the offer on the condition that the Canadian government would not attempt to veto any decisions ultimately agreed upon in Brussels, nor claim at any future date that they had not been properly consulted. The outcome was a subtle, but nonetheless significant change in the tone and frequency of Canadian statements on the EEC issue. Rather than openly criticize the British government, Canadian ministers preferred to emphasize their reliance on British assurances, and deferred judgment on specific points until a more complete package of terms had emerged.[52]

In keeping with this newfound reticence, Diefenbaker instructed the Canadian representatives in London to 'give the "facts," listen to the United Kingdom ideas, but not to comment.'[53] Furthermore, while Australia and New Zealand sent high-level teams to Brussels in order to plead their case (Australia even demanded to sit at the negotiating table), Canada refrained from doing so. The Canadian government feared that its representatives could be dragged into the negotiating ring, thereby enabling the United Kingdom 'to bargain on Canada's behalf with the EEC.'[54] From a Canadian point of view, this presented two main dangers. First, it would facilitate Britain's negotiating task and increase the chances of reaching a final deal with the EEC – an outcome that the Diefenbaker government plainly did not want. Second, if an agreement with the EEC were reached that failed to meet Canada's demands, the British could always claim that their proposals had been discussed and agreed upon in advance with the Canadian representatives.[55] In short, Ottawa wished to make it extremely hard for Britain to escape responsibility for any failure to protect Canada's interests.

Consequently, Diefenbaker retained a tight grip on Canadian policy throughout the course of Britain's application. The prime minister's office kept in constant touch with the Canadian high commission in London, which closely monitored Britain's negotiations with the Six. In London, Diefenbaker could rely on his high commissioner, George Drew, who took 'a major and sustained interest' in the British application and had no trouble following his government's preferred line.[56] Like Diefenbaker, Drew was politically and emotionally troubled by the prospect of British entry, advising the prime minister in April 1962 that Britain was 'engaged in the unilateral planning of the fragmentation of the Commonwealth ... all the King's horses and all the King's men may never be able to put it together again.'[57]

Yet despite his agreement to refrain from formally criticizing the British government in public, Diefenbaker nonetheless took the opportunity to convey his concerns to Macmillan in private. Macmillan's visit to Ottawa at the end of April 1962 provided one such occasion. Here Diefenbaker stressed the importance of trade preferences 'in maintaining the cohesion of the Commonwealth' as a whole, and for Canada in particular 'as a means of staving off United States domination.' He underlined that the Canadian government 'was keenly concerned with the preservation of the Commonwealth and feared that its future would be endangered by the political implications of United Kingdom entry.' Should the United Kingdom become drawn into closer political and commercial relations with the Europeans, he feared, 'the basic buttress of the Commonwealth might go.' George Hees chimed in along similar lines, pointing out that 'for an increasing number of Canadians, the United Kingdom was not the mother country. Trade thus was of continuing importance in cementing the relationship.'[58] These comments reveal the extent of Canadian anxieties concerning the less tangible aspects of British entry into Europe – the unravelling of the British world raised acute awareness of the 'other quiet revolution,' and posed difficult questions about Canada's sense of place and purpose in the post-imperial world.

By the end of July 1962, the Macmillan government had abandoned formally any remaining hopes that Commonwealth trading arrangements might be preserved in an enlarged EEC. Duncan Sandys wrote to all three dominion prime ministers: 'We are being reluctantly forced to the conclusion ... that there is virtually no prospect of retaining the existing Commonwealth preferences after the transitional period and that we shall probably have to accept that they should be phased out by 1970.'[59] This amounted to the clearest admission on the part of the British that they would be unable to meet the requirements of the Commonwealth governments in the Brussels negotiations. And by implication, the British government conceded that it did not consider this sufficient reason to remain outside the EEC. Sandys' tactics accorded precisely with his original objective of bringing Commonwealth governments around gradually, after the experience of negotiation had demonstrated the futility of pressing for genuine safeguards. The dominion governments were given clearly to understand that the United Kingdom could ill afford to be deflected from what had become a primary national objective. Within two weeks of Sandys' message, the British government reached a broad outline of agreement with the Europeans for a phasing out of virtually all Commonwealth preferences by the end of the decade. The only encouragement for the dominions was a commitment on the part of the Europeans to work towards 'world-wide commodity agreements' as a long-term solution to their trading problems, combined with a remarkably vague undertaking to 'offer reasonable opportunities' for exporters of temperate foodstuffs.[60] It had thus become perfectly clear that where fundamental British interests collided with those of Commonwealth countries, the former would naturally prevail in the British government's decisions.

The final hurdle for the Macmillan government in securing Commonwealth acquiescence in these developments was the Commonwealth Prime Ministers' Conference of September 1962. In the weeks preceding the conference, the Canadian cabinet gave Diefenbaker 'a free hand to use his own discretion' in advocating Canada's position.[61] The Canadian prime minister used this free hand to mount a strong criticism of Britain's decision to go into Europe. Interestingly, the British high commissioner in Ottawa, Derick Heathcoat Amory, had reported on the eve of the London meeting that Diefenbaker would 'not seek deliberately to raise hell or engage in battle with Britain.'[62] But this prediction was not borne out by Diefenbaker's actions in London. Speaking on 11 September (his address immediately followed Macmillan's), Diefenbaker rejected Macmillan's claims that Britain would be able to influence the evolution of the EEC in directions more congenial to Commonwealth interests. He also angered the British delegation by quoting a number of past British statements in which ministers had ruled out British membership of the EEC in the light of Britain's continuing obligations to the Commonwealth. He reiterated his views on the implications of British entry for the future of the Commonwealth, and insisted that the terms negotiated thus far were unsatisfactory as a means of safeguarding Canadian and Commonwealth interests. Finally, he proposed that a further Commonwealth Prime Ministers' Conference be convened when the Brussels negotiations ended.[63] The British ministers were clearly taken aback by the force of Diefenbaker's protest. Amory surmised that the Canadian prime minister had become 'intoxicated by the evidence he got on arrival in London about the strength of Commonwealth objections,' and suddenly grew determined to 'outchampion the rest in the role of chief objector.'[64]

Yet, despite these fighting words, Diefenbaker was unwilling to sabotage British entry completely. British officials were relieved to find that when it came to drafting the final communiqué for the conference, Diefenbaker 'raised few difficulties and specifically stated that he would not press for the inclusion of his earlier proposal for a further meeting of prime ministers.'[65] In the end, the Commonwealth Prime Ministers' Conference, while failing to give its blessing to the British bid for membership, agreed that the decision whether to join the EEC was one for the British government alone to take. The final communiqué emphasized that various Commonwealth interests had not yet been satisfactorily safeguarded in the Brussels negotiations, but did not demand that any particular issue be renegotiated. Likewise, while stating that any final judgment on the part of the Commonwealth countries would not be possible until Britain's negotiations with the EEC were over, the communiqué fell short of advocating another Commonwealth Prime Ministers' Conference.[66] In practice, the British Government could resume its negotiations with the Six without having its hands tied.

But while the British government had secured its main objectives as far as the EEC negotiations were concerned, this came at considerable cost in terms of the future viability and even credibility of the Commonwealth association. As the *Globe and Mail* commented in the immediate aftermath of the conference: 'Despite the genial communiqué on Wednesday and benign comments on it by various prime ministers, it must be obvious to everyone that the past ten days at Marlborough House have done the Commonwealth no good at all. The Commonwealth concept (or is it a myth?) has in fact been perceptibly damaged – just how badly and with what prospects of repair only the future can tell.'[67] For the *Vancouver Sun*, the upshot of the conference was 'a bitterness which no events will quickly erase.'[68] The *Ottawa Journal* put it even more graphically: 'Both sides of the communiqué gave out with the old con – the ten days of talks had all been buddy buddy. This was eyewash. Blood had been spilled.'[69] Lester Pearson summed up the situation more moderately in the House of Commons in October: 'Certainly it is a fact, and the London conference underlines this fact, that the nature and character of the Commonwealth of nations has now changed as its composition has changed and as its membership has increased. Perhaps the old informal clubbish atmosphere of pre-World War II, and immediately after that war, when a few prime ministers sat around a table in Downing Street has gone forever, and this involves problems and creates new challenges for the new Commonwealth.'[70]

In this changing climate, the discussion about vital Commonwealth interests and the value of British assurances gave way to a widespread feeling of resignation. As the British high commissioner reported on the mood in Canada after the Prime Ministers' Conference: 'The general view seems to be that the Prime Ministers collectively gave the British a hard hammering but had no alternative to propose. That being so, the British have firmly made up their minds to go into Europe and Canada has to make the best of the situation.'[71] Diefenbaker henceforth showed every sign of wishing to distance himself from the Common Market issue, even to the point of reaching an agreement with Macmillan that they should refrain from discussing the EEC in any detail at their meeting in the Bahamas, scheduled for December.[72]

Having cleared the Commonwealth hurdle, the Macmillan government's EEC membership application was soon frustrated by a formal veto at the hands of General de Gaulle on 14 January 1963. For the Canadian government this was good news – British entry had been prevented and the French had shouldered most of the blame. But this was hardly a triumphant moment for Diefenbaker. Although, for the time being, Canadian interests were no longer at risk, there was every indication that Britain would make another attempt to join the EEC at some later stage. Moreover, there was no denying that eighteen months of British-EEC negotiations had soured relations between London and Ottawa, and between Britain and the Commonwealth more generally. Diefenbaker's reasons for opposing British entry had derived from deep and often unspoken anxieties about Canada's diminishing sense of Britishness. Paradoxically, the experience of discord and mutual distrust over the EEC issue merely accelerated that very process.

By 1963, the 'other Quiet Revolution' had firmly taken hold, subtly undermining the relevance and resonance of Britishness in Canadian political culture. But unlike the 'Quiet Revolution' in Quebec, it did not entail any assertive cultural revival, self-consciously shedding the trappings of an alien Britishness in favour of a new, more localized Canadian nationalism. Rather it was a more subtle process, in which long-treasured assumptions began to lose their credibility in the light of changing power relations in the world at large. In this framework, the end of empire and the British move towards Europe provoked a more immediate awareness of the changes that had been slowly undermining the foundations of Canada's Britishness since the Second World War. Above all, it was the idea that the interests of fellow 'British' countries ought ultimately to be reconcilable under a common destiny that had been shaken by the experience of Britain's EEC membership negotiations. The EEC crisis was by no means the fundamental cause of Canada's fraying ties to Britain. Nor did it resolve the fundamental dilemma of settler-colonial nationalism – how to define and elaborate an exclusive Canadian identity fully independent of its British loyalist foundations. That problem would be played out in subsequent decades in the politics of citizenship, identity, and national unity, beginning with the flag debate of 1964. Throughout these years, public discussion, reflection, and debate were driven primarily by a perceived need for a 'new nationalism which seeks to be more completely Canadian' (as Claude Ryan termed it in 1964)[73] rather than any coherent or consensual conviction about what that nationalism should entail. Public sentiment on the national question was characterized by a remarkable degree of timidity and uncertainty about what, precisely, it meant to 'be Canadian.' While this was due in part to the problems of dual ethnicity, it is insufficiently recognized how the prevailing sense of disorientation and confusion was also a powerful legacy of the unravelling of Britishness in Canadian civic culture.

Acknowledgments

Andrea Benvenuti wishes to thank the Royal Bank of Canada and the Managers of the Cyril Foster and Related Funds (Department of International Relations, Oxford University) for funding his research trip to Canada. Stuart Ward thanks the Canadian Embassy, Copenhagen, for providing financial assistance to carry out research in Ottawa in the summer of 2003 under their 'Faculty Research Program.'

Notes

1   See Chapter 3 by José E. Igartua in this volume.
2   Ibid.
3   Douglas Cole, 'The Problem of "Nationalism" and "Imperialism" in British Settlement Colonies,' *Journal of British Studies* 10/2 (May 1971): 175.

4 Eric Hobsbawm, *Nations and Nationalism since 1780: Programme, Myth, Reality* (Cambridge: Cambridge University Press, 1990), 123-24.
5 See Chapter 14 by Gregory A. Johnson in this volume.
6 Douglas Cole, 'The Crimson Thread of Kinship: Ethnic Ideas in Australia, 1870-1914,' *Historical Studies* 14/56 (1971): 523.
7 See in particular Chapter 2 by John Hilliker and Greg Donaghy in this volume.
8 Nicholas Mansergh, *The Commonwealth Experience* (London: Macmillan, 1969), 348.
9 See, for example, the essays by John MacKenzie and Dan Rebellato in *British Culture and the End of Empire*, ed. Stuart Ward (Manchester: Manchester University Press, 2001).
10 Among recent titles in a torrent of literature are R.T. Griffiths and S. Ward, eds., *Courting the Common Market: The First Attempt to Enlarge the European Community* (London: Lothian, 1996); Wolfram Kaiser, *Using Europe, Abusing the Europeans: Britain and European Integration, 1945-1963* (London: Macmillan, 1996); Jacqueline Tratt, *The Macmillan Government and Europe: A Study in the Process of Policy Development* (Basingstoke: Macmillan, 1996); N. Piers Ludlow, *Dealing with Britain: The Six and the First UK Application to the EEC* (Cambridge: Cambridge University Press, 1997); George Wilkes, ed., *Britain's Failure to Enter the European Community, 1961-1963* (London: Frank Cass, 1997); Alan S. Milward, *The Rise and Fall of a National Strategy, 1945-1963* (London: Frank Cass, 2002).
11 See Stuart Ward, *Australia and the British Embrace: The Demise of the Imperial Ideal* (Melbourne: Melbourne University Press, 2001), 57-61.
12 PRO, CAB134/1821, minutes of ad hoc cabinet meeting at Chequers, 'Europe and the Commonwealth,' 18 June 1961.
13 'Commonwealth Pilgrim's Progress,' *Economist*, 8 July 1961, 115.
14 Paul Robertson and John Singleton, 'The Old Commonwealth and Britain's First Application to Join the EEC, 1961-3,' *Australian Economic History Review* 40/2 (2000): 165-66.
15 National Archives of Canada [NAC], RG2, vol. 6177, cabinet conclusions no. 81/61, 15 July 1961.
16 UK-Canada Joint Communiqué in Cmnd 1449, *Commonwealth Consultations on Britain's Relations with the European Economic Community: Statements on Talks between British Ministers and other Commonwealth Governments* (London: HMSO, 1961).
17 PRO, FO 371/158319, Sandys to Macmillan, 15 July 1961.
18 Donald Fleming, *So Very Near: The Political Memoirs of the Honourable Donald M. Fleming* (Toronto: McClelland and Stewart, 1985), 387.
19 UK-Canada joint communiqué, 'The Common Market,' 14 July 1961.
20 Quoted in John O'Brien, 'The British Commonwealth and the European Economic Community: The Australian and Canadian Experiences,' *Round Table* 340 (1996): 486.
21 Quoted in Robertson and Singleton, 'The Old Commonwealth and Britain's First Application,' 164.
22 NAC, RG2, vol. 6177, cabinet conclusions no. 81/61, 15 July 1961.
23 NAC, RG2, vol. 6177, cabinet conclusions no. 68/61, 15 June 1961.
24 See Stuart Ward, *Australia and the British Embrace*.
25 Fleming, *So Very Near*, 390-91.
26 PRO, PREM 11/3211, 'Summary Record of Discussion at Accra,' 15 September 1961.
27 *Globe and Mail*, quoted in *The New Commonwealth*, February 1962.
28 *Vancouver Sun*, 16 September 1961.
29 *Calgary Herald*, 2 March 1961; 8 September 1962.
30 Ibid., 12 July 1961.
31 See generally editorials in the *Vancouver Sun*, 13 July 1961; *Winnipeg Free Press*, 13 July 1961; *Globe and Mail*, 12 September 1961; 14 September 1961; 15 September 1961.
32 *Ottawa Journal*, 13 September 1961.
33 Pearson, *Debates*, House of Commons, 1 October 1962, 67.
34 J.L. Granatstein, *Canada, 1957-1967: The Years of Uncertainty and Innovation* (Toronto: McClelland and Stewart, 1986), 49. See also Robertson and Singleton, 'The Old Commonwealth and Britain's First Application,' 166.
35 NAC, RG2, vol. 6177, cabinet conclusions no. 104/61, 26 September 1961.

36 Ibid.
37 PRO, DO 159/52, Amory to Joe Garner (CRO), 15 February 1962.
38 PRO, PREM 11/4016, Amory to Macmillan, 23 March 1962.
39 PRO, PREM 11/4016, 'Record of Meeting between the Lord Privy Seal, the High Commissioner, Mr. Fleming, Mr. Hees, and Mr. Hamilton in Ottawa,' 26 March 1962.
40 PRO, DO 159/52. Fleming, speech at Winnipeg, 19 January 1962.
41 Pearson, *Debates*, House of Commons, 1 October 1962, 63.
42 *Ottawa Journal*, 15 September 1962.
43 *Financial Times*, 2 July 1962.
44 Jeremy Moon, *European Integration in British Politics, 1950-63: A Study of Issue Change* (Aldershot: Gower, 1985), 201.
45 PRO, DO 159/52, Amory to CRO, 13 February 1962.
46 Quoted in PRO, DO 159/52, F.G.K. Gallagher to J.R.A. Bottomley (CRO), 26 February 1962.
47 Quoted in the *Sunday Times* (London), 8 April 1962.
48 *Globe and Mail*, 3 May 1962.
49 L.D. Wilgress, *The Impact of European Integration on Canada* (Montreal: Canadian Trade Committee, 1962), 43-44.
50 PRO, PREM 11/4016, 'Record of Meeting between the Lord Privy Seal, the High Commissioner, Mr. Fleming, Mr. Hees, and Mr. Hamilton in Ottawa,' 26 March 1962.
51 Fleming insisted that the agreement should apply to confidential as well as public statements because of the danger of government leaks.
52 PRO, PREM 11/4016, Amory to Macmillan, 23 March 1962. Amory described Diefenbaker's tactics as 'a convenient electoral stand as he can't really lose.'
53 PRO, FO 371/158328, Commonwealth consultations, 29 September 1961, quoted in Robertson and Singleton, 'The Old Commonwealth and Britain's First Application,' 166-67.
54 See for example NAC, RG2, vol. 6177, cabinet conclusions nos. 95-61, 29 August 1961.
55 As Diefenbaker explained to the visiting John McEwen, Australia's trade minister, on 16 March 1962, 'if we [the Canadian government] failed to secure what we want, the British government would then be able to say that we had our representative present and should have prevented any action detrimental to us.' See NAC, RG25, vol. 5519, file 12447/40 (pt. 49); 'Prime Minister's Conversation with Mr. McEwen, Deputy Prime Minister of Australia [and Trade Minister] on March 15 and 16 – Common Market Problems,' minutes, 21 March 1962.
56 John Hilliker, 'Diefenbaker and Canadian External Relations,' in *Canadian Foreign Policy: Historical Readings*, ed. J.L. Granatstein (Toronto: Copp Clark Pitman, 1986), 190.
57 Quoted in Granatstein, *Years of Uncertainty*, 52.
58 NAC, RG25, vol. 5519, file 12447-40 (pt. 51), record of meeting between Prime Minister Macmillan and Prime Minister Diefenbaker, Ottawa, 20 April 1962.
59 PRO, DO 159/60, Sandys to Diefenbaker, 24 July 1962.
60 British white paper, cmnd. 1805, August 1962.
61 NAC, RG2, vol. 6193, cabinet conclusions no. 73/62, 30 August 1962.
62 PRO, DO 159/55, Amory to Sandys, 6 September 1962.
63 National Archives of Australia, A3917/vol.8, meeting of Commonwealth prime ministers, 1962, PMM (62) 3rd meeting, 11 September 1962.
64 PRO, DO 159/55, Amory to Sandys, 2 October 1962.
65 PRO, DO 159/55, Sandys to Amory, undated.
66 'Communiqué Prime Ministers' Conference,' *Globe and Mail*, 20 September 1962, 7.
67 *Globe and Mail*, 20 September 1962.
68 *Vancouver Sun*, 20 September 1962.
69 *Ottawa Journal*, 20 September 1962.
70 Pearson, *Debates*, House of Commons, 1 October 1962, 64.
71 PRO, DO 159/54, Amory to Sandys, 2 October 1962.
72 PRO, PREM 11/4099, CRO to Ottawa, 30 November 1962; Garner to Amory, 14 December 1962.
73 See Chapter 14 by Gregory A. Johnson in this volume.

10

Nostalgia and National Identity: The History and Social Studies Curricula of Alberta and Ontario at the End of Empire

George Richardson

One of the most striking characteristics of the modern era has been the emergence of powerful and enduring fantasy structures of national identity that ground their emotive strength and force in the legitimizing sanction of history and tradition. But all appearances to the contrary, these structures are not timeless creations; they are the conscious creations of national elites.[1] The production of what psychoanalyst Andrew Samuels has called 'the coruscating fantasy of the nation' is a historical project that required the active participation of the state for its realization.[2] Thus, when discussing the ideal constitution for a nation-state, Jean-Jacques Rousseau could note that 'la première règle, que nous avons à suivre, c'est le caractère national: tout peuple a, ou doit avoir un caractère national.'[3] Similarly, in their analysis of national-identity formation in capitalist societies, historians Eric Hobsbawm and Terence Ranger described national identity as a 'manipulated and manufactured phenomenon.'[4] Postcolonial scholar Homi K. Bhabha makes much the same point with the assertion that 'the first duty of the state is to "give" the nation its cultural identity and above all to develop it.'[5] The association of national identity with the machinery of the state implies the need for some kind of agent to generate the mythic structure of national identity that seemed and still seems so critical to the establishment of the nation as a viable entity. In most countries that agent has been education.

Ernest Gellner speaks of national identity as the product of 'education-dependent high cultures' and Eugene Weber notes that the production of patriotism and national sentiment has been the 'greatest function of the modern school.'[6] In a Canadian context, Vincent Massey best described the connection between education and national-identity formation when he wrote in 1925 that 'in a country with so scattered a population as ours and a vast frontier exposed to alien influences the task of creating a truly national feeling must inevitably be arduous, but this is the undertaking to which our educational systems must address themselves ... To our schools we must look for the Good Canadian.'[7] But in English Canada, colonial status and the reflected glories of the imperial connection dictated that the characteristics of the 'good Canadian' remained inextricably linked with those of the 'good Briton.' Thus, writing about English Canada, Canadian historian Arthur Lower noted in 1958 that 'the wonder is that the tender plant of Canadian nationalism survived at all, for all little Canadian boys and girls have been subjected from the day on which they start school to an unending steeping in the liquid of imperialism.'[8] Comparing the mythic structure of American and Canadian identity, the literary scholar Sacvan Bercovitch concluded that although both nations developed fantasies of identity around the notion of conquest, the American ideal was imperial and independent, while the Canadian remained colonial and dependent. For Bercovitch this difference meant that Canada was condemned to be 'a country with a mythology elsewhere, systematically decentered, and characterized, accordingly, by a rhetoric of absence.'[9]

Caught in the dilemma between the lack of national identity implied by Bercovitch's 'rhetoric of absence,' yet still charged with the modernist task of manufacturing the 'good Canadian,' English-Canadian schools responded by continuing to emphasize the fundamentally British character of Canada and the sustaining force of the imperial connection. Ironically, this emphasis lasted well beyond the period in which Britain had either the capacity or the desire to act the part of mother figure to Canada's national infancy. Indeed, nowhere was the attempt to maintain the British connection in the face of radically changed circumstances more apparent than in the period from 1945 to 1970. In English-speaking Canada, the era was characterized by repeated attempts to manufacture a Canadian identity out of a nostalgic longing to preserve what remained of its colonial and imperial past and in the face of a desire to somehow control and direct those emergent forces – the growing influence of the United States, accelerating pluralism, and the rise of Quebec nationalism – that made it increasingly difficult to speak in terms of what Benedict Anderson calls the 'common imagining' of the nation. But what forces influenced the decision to situate the mythology of the nation elsewhere? How can these forces be tracked and what analytic tools are appropriate to their investigation? One important source of evidence is the Canadian school curriculum, a rich source of data for examining the changing face of the fantasy of nation. Successive provincial curricula in the postwar era present themselves in what amounts to a geomorphology of national-identity formation, each new layer or revision building on the previous stratum. Through an analysis of the changing status accorded Britain and the empire in the history and social studies curricula of Alberta and Ontario, this chapter will examine the attempt to produce a sustainable mythic structure of national identity within Bercovitch's nostalgic 'rhetoric of absence.' The analysis employed in examining the Alberta and

Ontario curricula will draw on psychoanalytic models of national-identity formation.

Psychoanalysis provides, in Anthony Elliott's terms, both a 'language' and a 'conceptual vocabulary' for relating 'the character of social institutions and the explications of social practices and processes' to the 'inner world of our most personal needs, passion, and desires.'[10] The interdependent relationship between self and society (which can be read as nation) has long been accepted.[11] Freud commented on this relationship as early as 1913 when he noted that 'our knowledge of the neurotic illnesses of individuals has been of much assistance to our understanding of the great social institutions.'[12] Speaking more directly about the relationship between the self and the nation, Carl Jung wrote that 'the "nation" (like the "state") is a personified concept that corresponds in reality only to a specific nuance of the individual psyche ... [the nation] is nothing but an inborn character.'[13] More recently, in his ground-breaking work on political psychoanalysis, Vamik Volkan asserts that the fear and hatred of the 'other' that lie embedded in the human psyche are the source of much inter- and intra-national conflict.[14] Samuels supports this contention and suggests that the fantasy of national uniqueness – a fantasy he sees as analogous to the fantasy of individual uniqueness – is at least partly the result of a kind of projection response in which 'the nation evacuates what is sensed unconsciously as its undesirable features into designated enemies.'[15]

In psychoanalytic terms, fantasy plays a pivotal role in the realization of individual identity. Briefly, fantasy acts to conceal the 'radical lack of unity' that lies at the heart of individual identity.[16] As Renata Salecl notes, 'fantasy brings consistency to our desire' to hide the incompleteness of our own identities.[17] This same 'masking' function can be seen in the role fantasies play in national-identity formation. Julia Kristeva remarks on the imagined 'cult of origins' that underlies modern nationalism, noting that recourse to originary roots as the source of national identity involves a process by which its devotees 'anxiously shelter among their own [roots], hoping to suppress the conflicts they have with them by projecting them on others – the strangers.'[18] Commenting on the notion of ideological structures as fantasy, Slavoj Zizek notes that 'the function of ideology is not to offer us a point of escape from our reality but to offer us the social reality itself as an escape from some traumatic, real kernel.'[19]

But in post-1945 English Canada, the fantasy structures of national identity and completeness that had been so tied to the imperial connection suffered from having an empty symbolic space to return to, while the vacuum left by Britain's retreat as a world power initiated a psychic crisis of identity that left its traces in the curricula of both provinces under consideration here, Alberta and Ontario. Using the tools provided by psychoanalysis, it is possible to follow the trajectory of this crisis across the history and social studies curricula of Ontario and Alberta in the pivotal quarter of a century that followed the end of the Second World War.

Drawing on psychoanalysis and postcolonial theory, Homi K. Bhabha argues that one of the consequences of imperialism has been that, in an intellectual sense, colonizing and colonized peoples have been brought together in what he terms the 'third space' – a space that is both synthetic and dynamic, one that is 'continually in a process of hybridity.' But this hybridity, Bhabha reminds us, constantly 'displaces the histories that constitute it.'[20] From this perspective, the fantasy structure of Canadian identity after 1945 was doubly challenged. Thus, although Canada's membership in the Commonwealth maintained the imperial tie, increasingly after the Second World War it was American culture and Canada's links to the American economy that came to be Canada's most critical relationship. What amounted to a doubled colonial relationship in turn doubled the problem of hybridity and further problematized the attempt to manufacture a sustainable mythic edifice of national identity.

But if the result of occupying the 'third space' was a sense of ambiguity in the post-1945 era, then ambiguity, at least in terms of Canadian identity, was given a function and a name. In this sense, the concept of the 'third space' created a kind of opportunity for an identity based on synthetic foundations, and in response to this opportunity, Canadian political elites evolved the linchpin theory.[21] Briefly, the theory held that because of its strong British traditions, and given its geographical and cultural proximity to the United States, Canada could act as a kind of diplomatic and cultural middleman between its two more powerful neighbours. The critical role of this position was to translate the economic, cultural, and diplomatic intentions of Britain to the United States, and vice versa.

The physical manifestation of the linchpin theory had been the role Mackenzie King played in bringing together Winston Churchill and Franklin Roosevelt at the Atlantic Charter Conference held off the coast of Newfoundland in 1941. Generally speaking, the conception of a linchpin role was a curious one, based on the assumption that neither Britain nor the United States were intelligible to the other, but in terms of national identity, it served two important functions. Indirectly it made a virtue out of Canada's lack of a strong identity of its own, while at the same time assigning Canada a role that increased its international status. In many ways the evolution of the linchpin theory perpetuated Bercovitch's notion of the 'rhetoric of absence' as a central characteristic of Canadian identity. Thus Canada's postwar identity was celebrated through events external to the nation (such as Commonwealth membership, UN peacekeeping missions, the cultural attainments of expatriate Canadians, and NATO involvement) much more than internal achievements (such as the building of the St. Lawrence Seaway system, the construction of the Trans-Canada Highway, the growth of the Canadian Broadcasting Corporation, or the design and construction of the Avro Arrow).

To some degree the post-1945 school curricula in Alberta and Ontario reflected this changed emphasis. In Alberta, both the 1955 and 1965 'Program of Studies' for senior high school social studies mandated that students undertake an investigation of the Cold War and of the United Nations. In fact, the external set of relationships that characterized Canada's involvement in the postwar world were added to the criteria by which Canada's status as a nation was defined. 'Since 1945,' the 1955 'Program of Studies' noted, 'Canada has played a more significant role in world politics, displaying a sense of responsibility that is the mark of a mature nationhood.'[22] What is interesting in the statement is not so much the fact of Canada's growing involvement in global issues but the evident need for validation that is implied by contextualizing internationalism in terms of nation-building. In taking a role in world issues Canada was displaying the characteristics of 'mature nationhood' as much as it was helping to resolve international conflict. As Jerrold Baker notes, 'national identity [as compared to ethnicity] is directed outward, to a community of other nations from which it seeks validation.'[23]

But as much as Canada sought external validation for its status as a full-fledged member of the international community, it was the nostalgic tie to Britain and the empire that ran through the curricula of both provinces as the dominant touchstone of national identity for most of the quarter century following the end of the war. For example, in Ontario the 1945 grade 9 history course was dedicated to the social, industrial, and political history of Great Britain from 1603 to the present. As part of that five-part course, Ontario students studied the British Commonwealth under the title of 'The Third British Empire.'[24] In a grade 10 course that focused on 'Canadian History and Citizenship,' the last of the seven aims of the course reminded teachers that they were to 'lead the pupil to see that he has duties and responsibilities towards his family, his school, his community, his province, the Dominion of Canada and the British Empire.'[25] This hierarchy of fealty left little doubt as to who merited the greatest dedication. Psychoanalytically, the external projection of the locus of national identity fits well with the notion that national fantasies involve situating oneself in terms of the desire for the approval of what Jacques Lacan termed the Big Other.[26] As Zizek notes, 'fantasy is an answer to the question[s], "What am I for the Other? What does the Other want from me?"'[27] For Jerrold Baker, these questions take on an even greater significance where national-identity formation takes place in decentred contexts. He argues that 'it is of course, in the dislocation of people ... that the affective and imaginary power of national identity emerges. The victims of the diaspora, occupation, colonization or subjection as resident minorities [desire to] appear as something more than themselves, the bearers of some ineffable substance.'[28] From this perspective the fantasy of Canadian identity was irrevocably bound up in the quest for the 'ineffable substance' to be derived from its British origins and conferred by membership in the empire. The questions Zizek poses were, in some ways, the same questions indirectly posed by the history and social studies curricula of Alberta and Ontario: 'What am I for the empire?' and 'What does the empire want from me?' While there were no absolute answers to these questions, nevertheless they clearly framed the construction of national identity during the period and, as reflected in the curriculum, they moved the locus of national identity as close to the throne as possible.

For example, in the 1945 grade 10 Ontario history curriculum noted above, Canada's gradual passage towards nationhood was described in terms of the recognition Canada received as a result of its participation in the First World War. But although it was noted that enhanced status led to an increase in Canada's trade with 'other nations,' the only specific reference in the section emphasized that 'as a result of the war, Canada has acquired a new status within the British Empire.'[29] The impression of the legitimizing power of the imperial tie is only reinforced by a listing of the steps leading to the 'achievement of nationhood.' Thus Canada's participation in the coronation of George VI is included along with the expected references to the Versailles Treaty, Canada's membership in the League of Nations, and the passage of the Statute of Westminster.[30] Significantly, well after the formation of the Commonwealth, both provinces' history and social studies curricula were framed by the discourse of empire, and any perceived gains in international status and autonomy were still measured against the yardstick of Canada's position within the imperial power structure.

Despite the curricular acknowledgment of Canada's changing role in the global community, and the new sense of self that this role gave to the Canadian identity, by and large the curriculum continued to ground Canadian nationalism in the political and cultural heritage of Britain. For example, although the 1955 Alberta 'Program of Studies' for senior high schools made the development of Canada the organizing theme for each of the three different grade levels, in many ways it was an artificial connection. At the grade 10 level students examined 'The Ancient Origins of Canadian Civilization,' but given that this involved the study of prehistory, ancient Egypt and Mesopotamia, and Greek and Roman civilization, the link to Canada seems tenuous at best. At the grade 11 level, 'The Modern Background of Canadian Civilization' was the focus, but again, the grafting of Canada onto what was essentially a course in early modern and modern European (and particularly British) history seems an awkward hybrid. The 1955 'Program of Studies' reserved an examination of Canadian issues from a purely Canadian standpoint for grade 12. But here again the context was both imperial and continental. For example, in unit 4 of grade 12, students examined 'Nationalism in the Modern World.' In the introduction to the unit, the authors noted that 'the nationalism of various peoples of the Empire was the dynamic creation of the modern Commonwealth.'[31] Viewed from this perspective, Canadian nationalism remained the product of imperial association rather than the result of any great popular longing for autonomy.

The 'understandings' set out for the grade 12 social studies curriculum in Alberta further reinforced the sense of the ambiguous nature of Canadian nationalism. The 'Program of Studies' advanced the timid observation that 'Neither Canada's historical associations with Britain nor her geographic ties with the USA have prevented the building of a Canadian nation.'[32] While the truth of such an observation is demonstrable, the sense of unease – even ambivalence – underlying the entire section seems equally clear. The final 'understanding' noted in the section bolsters this contingent and tentative sense of nationalism. Having already placed Canadian nationalism uneasily between two superpowers and implying that its creation was the product of the imperial tie, the authors concluded that 'the realization of national sovereignty has created problems of internal control and external relationships.'[33] Nationalism then, in and of itself, was presented as somehow suspect. The clear implication was that nationalism for Canada was only acceptable if it was placed within the wider (and fundamentally British) context of the empire.

The Ontario curriculum of 1955 had much the same imperial tone. In the world history courses (grades 11 and 12), teachers were reminded of the importance of instilling in students that the achievement of democracy was one of the 'crowning achievements' of Western civilization, and the necessity of showing 'what an important part England and British institutions have played in this great achievement.'[34] Thus the history and social studies curricula of both provinces framed the nation-building process and national-identity formation within the confines of the empire. But in terms of the role of education in manufacturing Massey's 'Good Canadian,' this resulted in a twofold dilemma. On the one hand, neither curriculum took the pains to elaborate what an indigenous Canadian nationalism or identity was. In the absence of such an elaboration, both continued to assert that imperial ties were the basis for Canadian identity. On the other hand, in problematizing the idea of national sovereignty itself, the Alberta 'Program of Studies' made it very difficult to investigate Canadian nationalism or Canadian national identity on its own terms.

A broader reading of the Ontario and Alberta history and social studies curricula indicates that there are three specific aspects around which the fantasy of national identity is constructed. First and foremost, the fantasy of national identity is structured around the notion of rightful inheritance. Both curricula appeal to the notion that Canadian identity is irrevocably bound to the history and achievements of Britain and the empire. But that appeal contains much more than the notion of identity conferred as a random gift. It is an earned inheritance. As a loyal and dutiful heir – an heir whose loyalty was bought at the price of blood sacrifice in two world wars – Canada was deserving of its inheritance and of the prominent position it aspired to within the imperial hierarchy. This understanding can be seen in the entire structure of the 1955 Alberta 'Program of Studies' through the historical determinism implied in the way it situates Canada as the inheritor of the whole corpus of European – and particularly British – history.[35] In the 1945 Ontario grade 13 history curriculum, the notion of earned inheritance emerges even more directly. In describing the period leading up to the declaration of the Statute of Westminster, the curriculum notes the 'debt' the empire owed Canada for the achievement of responsible government and the creation of federalism, concluding that 'it was Canada's success in these two unique experiments which established faith in their practicability in other parts of the Empire and led ultimately to one of the most interesting of modern political phenomenon, the British Empire-Commonwealth.'[36]

The second aspect of the fantasy structure of national identity erected by the Ontario and Alberta curricula was the notion of peaceful and harmonious progress implied in describing Canada's identity formation as an evolutionary process. Lacking the kind of definitive *brisure* that revolution had played in unifying France and Germany, both curricula described the emergence of Canadian national identity as a gradual and essentially natural process. This approach had two attractions. First, it implied a kind of emergent and broadly based social understanding about what the essential characteristics of the national psyche were – a suggestion that today lies at the heart of Canada's fantasy of itself as a nation built on cooperation and consensus. Second, by suggesting an evolving national identity, the exact shape of that identity did not have to be specified at any given time – avoiding what, in both curricula, clearly would have been a difficult task. As evidence of this notion of an evolutionary growth, the 1945 grade 10 Ontario history curriculum noted the 'gradual' social and economic changes in the post-Confederation era that marked Canada's 'growth towards nationhood,' while the 1955 grade 12 Alberta social studies curriculum spoke of the 'steady progress' towards independence that marked the period after 1867.[37]

The third element of the fantasy of national identity suggested by the two curricula was the notion that Canada had a 'special role' as middleman or mediator between the United States and Britain. This notion made a virtue of Canada's colonial relationship to both nations, and it can be seen as a precursor to current images of Canada as a 'middle power' whose function (and source of identity) consists in its ability to mediate between the developed and developing worlds. Both curricula emphasized the unique position Canada found itself in as a result of its historical experience with the United States and Britain, and both situate Canada as kind of social, cultural, and economic 'linchpin' between the two nations. This perception was reflected in both curricula, but the linchpin theory was perhaps most directly taken up in the 1965 Ontario grade 13 history curriculum, which noted the 'triangular relation' between the US, Canada, and Britain, typifying the portrayal of Canada's role as a middle power.[38]

In psychoanalytic terms, these three aspects of the fantasy of national identity reflect a process by which, in Renata Salecl's terms, the 'subject [or nation] endlessly searches for some point of identification with the symbolic order which would give him or her a place in the social structure which means a promise of an identity.'[39] As Étienne Balibar reminds us, this search is part of a conscious attempt to create an illusion of national self-awareness that is founded at once on historical continuity and fate. Thus the development of national identity 'consists in believing that the generations which succeed one another over centuries on a reasonably stable territory, under a reasonably univocal designation, have handed down to each other an invariant substance. And it consists in believing that the process of development from which one selects aspects retrospectively ... was the only one possible, that is, it represented a destiny.'[40]

Certainly the fantasy structure of national identity erected in the post-1945 history and social studies curricula of Ontario and Alberta can be seen as the simultaneous attempt to establish both 'the promise of an identity' and a historically grounded destiny through situating Canadian identity as closely as possible to the imperial connection. But when this attempt fails, or (as is particularly true in Canada's situation) if it is insufficiently realized as a defining fantasy, what avenues are left to the subject or the nation to define identity? It is here that selective memory comes to the aid of both the subject and the nation. For Freud, a subject in conflict could create a 'screen memory' that produced some alternative view of the past in order to mask a conflict the patient did not want to acknowledge.[41] This screen memory would subsequently act to produce a unitary and comforting sense of identity that focused on 'some "happy before" when everything was "different."'[42] Such a nostalgic conception of the past functions to mask identity conflicts and to maintain an imaginary order in which the individual (or the nation) can conceive of itself as centred and whole: in Salecl's terms, to maintain a 'space from which we could appear likeable to ourselves.'[43]

For a quarter of a century the history and social studies curricula in Ontario and Alberta were framed in the kind of nostalgic terms that Freud would typify as a screen memory. Psychoanalytically, through the retroactive construction of positive images of completeness, and in its ability to mask conflicts, nostalgic memory is an intrinsic component of individual-identity formation, and it functions in much the same way in national-identity formation. As Julian Barnes notes in his novel *England, England*: 'If a memory wasn't a thing but a memory of a memory of a memory, mirrors set in parallel, then what the brain told you now about what it claimed had happened then would be coloured by what had happened in between. It was like a country remembering its history: the past was never just the past, it was what made the present able to live with itself.'[44] An examination of the history and social studies curricula of Alberta and Ontario at the end of empire reveals a psychic crisis in both provinces in which national identity was tied to, yet separate from, the power and majesty of Britain and the empire. The fantasy of national identity was derived from the conferred status of the British and imperial connection, a 'gift' (in Homi Bhabha's terms) that the curricula of both provinces made clear was the earned and rightful inheritance of Canadians. But the unresolvable dilemma was that the imperial connection was historically bound. It was neither duplicable nor was it capable of being carried forward or transferred, and inevitably, the longer the attempt to sustain the connection, the less likely it was that some other more nationally based form of identity would develop. However, lacking any other viable source of signification or validation, even as the lived British and imperial connection grew more distant, the nostalgic fantasy structure of empire remained strong. Its persistence, as reflected in the post-1945 history and social studies curricula of Ontario and Alberta, remained as a screen memory to mask a more problematic reality that its educational elites were unable to face.

Notes

1 Benedict Anderson, *Imagined Communities: Reflections on the Origin and Spread of Nationalism*, 2nd ed. (London: Verso, 1991).
2 Andrew Samuels, *The Political Psyche* (London: Routledge, 1993), 331.
3 Jean Jacques Rousseau cited in Andrew Cobban, *Rousseau and the Modern State* (London: George, Allen and Unwin, 1964), 319.
4 Eric Hobsbawm and Terence Ranger, eds., *The Invention of Tradition* (Cambridge: Cambridge University Press, 1983), 1.
5 Homi K. Bhabha, 'Freedom's Basis on the Indeterminate' in *The Identity in Question*, ed. J. Rajchman (New York: Routledge, 1995), 178.
6 Ernest Gellner, *Nations and Nationalism* (Oxford: Blackwell, 1983), 48-49; and Eugene Weber, *Peasants into Frenchmen: The Modernization of Rural France 1870-1914* (Stanford: Stanford University Press, 1976), 332.
7 Massey cited in Charles Cochrane and William Wallace, *This Canada of Ours* (Toronto: National Council on Education, 1926), 11.
8 Arthur Lower, *Canadians in the Making* (Toronto: Longman, 1958), 350.
9 Sacvan Bercovitch, *The Rites of Assent: Transformations in the Symbolic Construction of America* (New York: Routledge, 1993), 8.
10 Anthony Elliott, 'Psychoanalysis and Social Theory' in *The Blackwell Companion to Social Theory*, ed. B.S. Turner (2nd edition, London: Blackwell, 2000), 133.

11 See for example, Erich Fromm, *Escape from Freedom* (New York: Farrar and Rinehart, 1941); Margaret Mead, 'The Study of National Character' in *The Policy Sciences*, ed. D. Lerner and H.D. Lasswell (Chicago: University of Chicago Press, 1951); and Melanie Klein, *Contributions to Psychoanalysis* (New York: McGraw Hill, 1964).

12 Sigmund Freud, *The Complete Psychological Works*, ed. J. Strachey (London: Hogarth Press and the Institute of Psychoanalysis, 1973), Vol. 13: 185-86.

13 Carl G. Jung, *Collected Works*, ed. H. Read, M. Fordham, and G. Adler (Princeton: Princeton University Press, 1977), Vol. 10: 921.

14 Vamik Volkan, *The Need to Have Enemies and Allies* (Northvale, NJ: Jason Aronson, 1988).

15 Samuels, *The Political Psyche*, 333.

16 Jerrold Baker, 'Obsessional and Hysterical Modes of National Identity,' *Journal for the Psychoanalysis of Popular Culture* 2/2 (1997): 132.

17 Renata Salecl, *The Spoils of Freedom: Psychoanalysis and Feminism After the Fall of Socialism* (London: Routledge, 1994), 87.

18 Julia Kristeva, *Nations Without Nationalism*, trans. L.S. Roudiez (New York: Columbia University Press, 1993), 3-4.

19 Slavoj Zizek, *The Sublime Object of Ideology* (London: Verso, 1994), 45.

20 Homi K. Bhabha, 'The Third Space: An Interview with Homi Bhabha' in *Identity, Community, Culture, Difference*, ed. J. Rutherford (London: Lawrence and Wishert, 1990), 210-11.

21 W.L. Morton, *The Canadian Identity* (Toronto: University of Toronto Press, 1962).

22 Government of Alberta, *Senior High School Curriculum Guide* (Edmonton: Department of Education, 1955), 123.

23 Baker, 'Obsessional and Hysterical Modes of National Identity,' 135.

24 Government of Ontario, *Courses of Study: Grades IX and X Social Studies and History* (Toronto: Department of Education, 1945), 8.

25 Ibid., 10.

26 Jacques Lacan proposed three 'registers' or orders of identity that in some ways parallel the Freudian notions of the Id, Ego, and Superego. In Lacanian terms, the Imaginary, the Symbolic, and the Real orders represent, respectively, the pre-linguistic image of wholeness in which the subject misrecognizes him/herself as autonomous and complete; the passage of the subject into the realm of society where he or she takes on social identities and seeks validation in the eyes of the Big Other; and finally, the notion that there is an unconscious 'kernel' of desire that exists as a constant and insatiable need for satisfaction. The impossibility of satisfying the demands of the Real leads us, Lacan suggests, to create compensatory fantasy structures that mask the reality of our desires. See Jacques Lacan, *Ecrits: A Selection* (London: Tavistock, 1977).

27 Slavoj Zizek, 'Fantasy as a Political Category,' *Journal for the Psychoanalysis of Culture and Society* 1/2 (1996): 84.

28 Baker, 'Obsessional and Hysterical Modes of National Identity,' 136.

29 Government of Ontario, *Grades IX and X Social Studies and History, 1945*, 18.

30 Ibid., 19.

31 Government of Alberta, *Senior High School Curriculum Guide, 1955*, 125.

32 Ibid.

33 Ibid.

34 Government of Ontario, *Courses of Study: Grades XI and XII World History* (Toronto: Department of Education, 1955), 3.

35 Government of Alberta, *Senior High School Curriculum Guide*.

36 Government of Ontario, *Courses of Study: Grade XIII History* (Toronto: Department of Education, 1945), 7.

37 Government of Ontario, *Grades IX and X Social Studies and History, 1945*, 16; Government of Alberta, *Senior High School Curriculum Guide, 1955*, 124.

38 Government of Ontario, *General and Advanced Levels of Instruction in Grade 13 History* (Toronto: Department of Education, 1965), 14.

39 Renata Salecl, 'Identity and Memory: The Trauma of Ceaucescu's Disneyland,' *Journal for the Psychoanalysis of Culture and Society* 1/1 (1996): 94.

40 Étienne Balibar, 'The Nation Form: History and Ideology' in *Race, Nation, Class: Ambiguous Identities*, ed. É. Balibar and I. Wallerstein (London: Verso, 1991), 86.
41 Freud, *The Complete Psychological Works*, 3: 307.
42 Salecl, 'Identity and Memory,' 94.
43 Salecl, *The Spoils of Freedom*, 33.
44 Julian Barnes, *England, England* (Toronto: Vintage, 1998).

11
The Persistence of Britain: The Culture Project in Postwar Canada

Paul Rutherford

Looking back, the historian Donald Creighton lamented what he saw as a lost opportunity to check American imperialism when he wrote his volume in the Canadian Centenary Series on Canada in the 1940s and 1950s. He was referring to the recommendations of the Royal Commission on National Development in the Arts, Letters and Sciences, otherwise known as the Massey Commission. In his discussion of this commission (in the chapter 'The Commonwealth in Dissolution') Creighton praised it because it had recognized that the United States, not Great Britain, or some lingering British influence, was by then the main threat to the Canadian soul. But to no avail. 'The Massey Commissioners were lone, lost voices,' he observed, 'virtually unheard of in the deaf ears and closed minds of the Government of Canada.'[1] He was wrong. At least for a time, the persistence of Britain was embodied in Canada's extraordinary culture project. Imagination had a moment of glory: There were indeed many flights of fancy that inspired conspicuous acts to the public's advantage.

By 1945 Canada was already inundated with a particular kind of culture – the culture of sentiment, sensation, sin, and above all laughter – courtesy of the United States. The voice of Frank Sinatra, the detective novels of Mickey Spillane, the zany antics of Milton Berle, radio's soap operas, baseball and boxing, Betty Grable's legs and Jane Russell's bosom – all had legions of fans across the country. Right after the war that culture had become a matter of increasing concern to social and moral authorities throughout North America. In 1951 a then largely unknown Marshall McLuhan would publish his denunciation of the popular arts, *The Mechanical Bride*, a book that accused business of financing the debauchery of humanity.[2] This was just one polemic in a much wider highbrow assault against what was called 'mass culture.' One of the longest, ongoing battles in Western civilization, at least since the late middle ages, had been the effort of the custodians of high culture to suppress the low.[3] The arrival of the new technologies of cinema, radio, and television, however, had seemingly swung the balance against authority. In the fevered minds of some champions, not just McLuhan but New York's Dwight Macdonald or the doyen of the Frankfurt School, Theodor Adorno, the final battle for the soul of humanity was already under way.[4]

Canada had some protection against the rush of the "low." There was in place a long-standing system of prevention that operated through movie censorship, customs officials, and obscenity laws. Indeed, in 1955, crime comics, mostly from the United States, were banned as an especially toxic threat to the moral health of children and adolescents. Big-city Canada was also a site for all kinds of literary, theatrical, and artistic activity, though a lot of this activity was still in the hands of amateurs.[5] The trouble was that much of this high culture was impoverished and ignored, by the general public as well as the state.

Enter Britain. This was not the Britain of postwar austerity or of the music hall and the neighbourhood pub, however. Rather it was an imagined land of Shakespeare and Shaw, the Tate, Sadler's Wells (the precursor of the Royal Ballet), and the BBC. This idealized vision of the imperial metropolis as a centre of creativity and performance was commonplace among Canada's intelligentsia, admittedly more in English than French Canada, and it found an echo among various social and civic leaders in the country's big cities. What Canada needed was polishing, an injection of real culture, an antidote to all the trash sweeping across the 49th parallel – and a succession of Britons were ready to do just that job.

A small coterie of visitors and immigrants, employed and assisted by moneyed or powerful Canadians, worked to 'civilize' a country seemingly so incomplete. Their work began just prior to the Second World War, although the various projects were not finished until the better times after 1945. Consider a few of these initiatives.

In 1938 Gweneth Lloyd and her assistant, Betty Hey Farrally, arrived in Winnipeg to set up a dance school, attracted by the enthusiasms of another recent immigrant who had been lured to the city by the prominent Richardson family to set up a physical education program. The two women came with special credentials. Both were licensed by the Royal Academy of Dance in Britain, and Lloyd was an experienced teacher with a knowledge of ballet. In the postwar years Lloyd and Farrally would pioneer Canada's first professional ballet company, the Royal Winnipeg Ballet. Their eventual success had much to do with the welcome they received from Muriel Richardson and other members of Winnipeg's social elite.[6]

Late in 1939 the Canadian government hired John Grierson, the noted British master of film documentaries, to take charge of the newly formed National Film Board (NFB), which soon became a major source of domestic and Allied war propaganda. Grierson's ability to get on with Prime Minister Mackenzie King and his aides had much to do with the success of the NFB.[7]

Out of that experience emerged a film and later an audiovisual tradition of opinionated and thoughtful productions, eventually hailed as distinctively Canadian in contrast to the mass entertainment of Hollywood.

Early in 1947, Richard Lambert, the one-time editor of BBC's magazine *The Listener* but then involved in the school broadcasts of the Canadian Broadcasting Corporation, suggested that the CBC emulate the BBC's Third Programme, a radio service geared to refined (and the task of refining) tastes. The CBC lacked the resources, never mind the will, to devote a whole network to highbrow interests, but the programmers, and in particular the corporation's erudite chairman, Davidson Dunton, believed something worthwhile was possible. So in December the CBC launched on its existing Trans-Canada Network what was blandly labelled 'Wednesday Night,' some three hours of non-commercial programming that might include learned talks, recitals, classical music, opera, and plays.[8] Here was a Canadian attempt to realize the dream of a radio that enlightened and improved, akin to that vision of the BBC held by its first director-general, John Reith. 'Wednesday Night' lasted until 1963.

Also in 1947, B. Ilfor Evans, the vice-chairman of Britain's new Arts Council, carried out a long tour of Canada, attending 109 meetings and delivering forty-nine lectures according to one count.[9] The Arts Council was a state-financed but autonomously operated agency that offered grants to organizations 'striving with serious purpose and a reasonable prospect of success to present for public enjoyment the arts of drama, music and painting,' in the words of Lord Keynes (its one-time chair).[10] Evans's promotion of the Arts Council was exactly the kind of message Canada's newly active arts lobby wanted to hear: that government had a responsibility to sponsor high culture. The British Arts Council became the model for the Canada Council, recommended by the *Massey Report* of 1951 and established in 1957.

In 1951 the administrators of Toronto's National Ballet Company hired the experienced dancer and choreographer Celia Franca, of Britain's Sadler's Wells, to become artistic director of the fledgling professional company. The three leading lights of the organizing committee, all Toronto society women, had taken counsel from Ninette de Valois, the artistic director of Sadler's Wells. She had endorsed Franca, who strove to build the National Ballet in the image of Sadler's Wells. Her company would be a grand public institution performing the European classics, such as *Swan Lake* and *The Nutcracker*, two of its early successes.[11]

Similarly the Shakespearean Festival of Stratford, Ontario, launched in 1953, was shaped by Dr. Tyrone Guthrie, a scholar and director, who came from Britain for three seasons to direct the initiative. The festival was actually started by a local citizen, Tom Patterson, who (so the story goes) had been captivated by opera in Italy and drama in England while serving overseas during the war. Guthrie produced such plays as *All's Well That Ends*

Well, *Richard III*, and *Oedipus Rex*, where he mixed Canadian and British talent, including Alec Guinness and James Mason. The Stratford Festival immediately proved both a professional and a popular success, soon winning international recognition back home, as it were, when one of its productions was invited to the Edinburgh Festival in 1956. What seemed an impossible dream had been turned into a reality: It was, as even a dour Donald Creighton admitted, an astounding achievement.[12]

These stars of these various ventures might be counted unofficial lieutenants in one last imperial enterprise that sought to establish a British kind of high culture in a fast-disappearing colony. But the true commander of such an enterprise was already a citizen of Canada – none other than Vincent Massey, later the country's first native-born governor general. Massey was very much the aristocrat, heir to a fortune, a patron of the arts, and a devoted anglophile who had served as high commissioner to London from 1935 to 1946. 'Fine chap, Vincent,' noted one English lord, 'but he does make one feel a bit of a savage.'[13] He was a natural choice to head a royal commission established by the St. Laurent government in 1949 to investigate the present and future condition of radio, television, film, the universities, and the arts in Canada. Indeed, Massey had already laid out an agenda for Canadian culture, including some version of an arts council, in a book called *On Being Canadian* in 1948.[14] He was joined on the commission by Father Georges-Henri Lévesque, dean of social sciences at Laval University; Hilda Neatby, a professor of history from the University of Saskatchewan; Norman MacKenzie, president of the University of British Columbia; and Arthur Surveyor, a francophone and civil engineer from Montreal. Except for Surveyor, it looked very much as though the ivory tower was in charge. Little wonder the Commission issued a report in 1951 that planned a culture as British as possible. The goal was the most extraordinary of the flights of fancy that excited this postwar era, at least in the realm of the arts.

The hidden agenda did not go undetected. 'The idea that by taking thought, and with help of some government subventions, we can become another England – which, one suspects, is Mr. Massey's ultimate idea – is purely fantastic.'[15] The comment came from another professor – and Canadian historian – Frank Underhill, who gave the *Massey Report* a decidedly mixed review. Massey himself dismissed the charge in a letter to Hilda Neatby.[16] In fact, critics of the commission and its report had sometimes articulated a very different concept of Canadian culture. The masters of private radio, in their representations to the commission, played out the role of the entrepreneur, eager to fashion a culture that was popular, profitable, and decidedly low. Few were quite as bold as Jack Kent Cooke, president of CKEY radio in Toronto. 'An American is basically the same as a Canadian,' he told the commission, 'motivated by the same impulse, exposed to the same influences of literature, music, the theatre, movies, and radio. In the first place, what is wrong with American material? If we are ever to have a Canadian culture, it will come as the result of full exposure to what is undoubtedly the fastest rising culture in the world to-day.'[17]

The commissioners quoted a portion of Cooke's statement in their report, along with a sneer that some of 'the wealthiest of the private radio stations have the lowest standard in programmes, and show serious neglect of their obligations as parts of the national system.'[18] For the commissioners *did* presume there was a lot wrong with both 'full exposure' and 'American material.' Demonstrating this requires a close reading of that sometimes opaque document. The political situation of the times prevented any bold expression of either anglophilia or anti-Americanism: the Canadian citizenry was in a North American frame of mind (polls in 1947 and 1950 had slightly more respondents opting for independence or union with the United States than continuing in the Commonwealth).[19] But the commission's biases were apparent. British commentators, such as Lord Keynes or T.S. Eliot, and British institutions – notably the BBC, the Arts Council, and its companion for promoting British culture abroad, the British Council – were approved, even honoured. By contrast the United States was identified as the source of 'passive entertainment,' of soap operas 'guilty of melodramatic exaggeration,' of movies that spread a false view of Canada, of 'harmful' comic books, and above all of a 'strident' advertising that debased cultural output if not the culture itself. A brief chapter on the mass media was an extended lament on the ill effects of the gramophone, the cinema, and radio upon an earlier, vibrant culture 'centred about the church, the school, the local library and the local newspaper.'[20] Running through the Report was a fear of the onset of a purely 'materialistic society,' the rise of 'mass' man, and the decline of the West into a debased state of passivity and conformity. There were times when the commissioners sounded a bit like Dwight Macdonald – indeed Underhill hoped that like-minded aesthetes north and south of the 49th parallel might unite against the perils of mass culture.[21]

The nationalism of the commission precluded any such alliance with the new Babylon. America was the main engine of both the modern technology of mass communication and the chief exponent of an aggressive commercialism. If the Report recognized the virtues of sharing in 'what might be familiarly called the American cultural output,' noting the broadcasts of Sunday symphonies for example, that was twinned with a warning: 'Our use of American institutions, or our lazy, even abject, imitation of them has caused an uncritical acceptance of ideas and assumptions which are alien to our tradition.' In the introduction to Part II of the Report, the commissioners even evoked the spectre of the Cold War, arguing that the country must attend as much to 'our cultural defences' as our 'military defences.' 'We are defending civilization, our share of it, our contribution to it,' or so went the refrain.[22] In the cultural context, though, the main enemy seemed not Soviet Russia (never actually mentioned in the Report) but rather Capitalist America. That hypothesis, by the way, was elaborated much more vociferously by another professor at the University of Toronto, Harold Innis, in his aptly entitled 'The Strategy of Culture,' a reflection on the *Massey Report*:

> We are indeed fighting for our lives ... The jackals of communications systems are constantly on the alert to destroy every vestige of sentiment toward Great Britain, holding it of no advantage if it threatens the omnipotence of American commercialism. This is to strike at the heart of cultural life in Canada. The pride taken in improving our status in the British Commonwealth of Nations has made it difficult for us to realize that our status on the North American continent is on the verge of disappearing ... We can only survive by taking persistent action at strategic points against American imperialism in all its attractive guises.[23]

The ultimate irony was that the main instrument of cultural defence would be none other than that most dangerous of technologies, television. Yes, the commission urged government to expand its subsidies to higher education so as to fortify the university, a bulwark of high culture. Yes, the commission planned a Canada Council to use scholarships to strengthen the humanities as well as to sponsor the fine arts, both crucial means of liberating Canada from its unholy dependence on the United States. But neither had the power of TV: the commission accepted the prevailing wisdom that television would exercise an extraordinary sway over the minds and mores of the future.[24] 'The combined influences of sight, sound and motion are intensified when received in the quiet of a home. There is little doubt that television is becoming as popular as it is persuasive.' The commissioners were worried, of course: The Report cited a letter by T.S. Eliot written to the *Times* of London (20 December 1950) warning of the potential harm of 'the television habit' to the mental, moral, and physical health of, in particular, children.[25] But that did not deter the desire to capture television, a strategy that inspired highbrows throughout the 1950s. The best way to 'enrich the mind and refine the taste' of the populace, to employ the language of the Report,[26] was to ensure the emergence of a public television service that was firmly modelled on the practice of the BBC.

The elitist thrust of the Report was underlined by Arthur Surveyor, the lone dissenter on the Commission, who authored a separate opinion on broadcasting. 'In Great Britain, where the funds are supplied by the owners of receiving sets, the objective is to give the people what they ought to have,' he noted; 'in the United States, where broadcasters have to pay all their expenses out of their own income, the policy is to give the audiences what they want.' The other commissioners believed that giving the people what they wanted, or thought they wanted, meant in practice allowing the advertisers, the bane of American radio, to determine and disfigure programming. So they extolled the British way of producing television because the BBC recognized the importance of education as well as its 'moral and cultural responsibilities.' These priorities had justified an 'extremely varied' kind of television programming, 'designed not only to entertain but to instruct, whether through drama, opera, ballet and music, or through lectures and commentaries.'[27] This is why the main Report not only favoured a CBC dominion in regulating TV broadcasting in Canada, even if private money might finance some TV stations, but also told the CBC to mount a determined effort to ensure quality programming.[28]

Here then was the new Church to police, and hopefully to counter, the spread of Carnival – that is, any stimulus that might excite the base instincts, the overly sentimental, the materialistic, the taste for sex, violence, or gore. In fact the CBC's masters had already begun to implement a vision of television that fitted the Massey agenda.[29] The government had turned over the making of Canadian TV to the CBC back in 1949, even before the Report arrived, and a service began, first in Montreal and Toronto, in September 1952. Chairman Dunton belonged, naturally, to that same cultural elite from which the commission had emerged. Alphonse Ouimet and Ernie Bushnell, two top CBC executives, had gone off to Britain in the 1940s to learn how to do television properly. Both would be coordinators of Canadian television in the next decade. The whole idea was to construct a service that ran against the rules of commercial arithmetic by providing program fare that served not a mass audience but an audience of minorities. So a weekly schedule in the 1950s might contain some hockey and wrestling ('La Lutte,' apparently, was very popular with women in Quebec, much to the surprise of programmers), various talk shows (initially linked to a voluntary organization), and public affairs programs (René Lévesque began his rise to stardom as host of *Point de Mire*), as well as some imported drama, a concert hour, children's programs, plays of all sorts, and homegrown and American variety shows, everything to satisfy different kinds of tastes. In particular, the CBC poured money into the production of Shakespearean plays, classical drama, operas, ballet, and theatrical works. It employed many of the actors who performed at Stratford. It hired many writers to adapt plays or produce scripts for television's theatre. It actually sponsored a ballet company, managed by a European émigré, Ludmilla Chiriaeff, who eventually founded Montreal's Les Grands Ballets Canadiens. In short, the CBC acted as one of the main patrons of the arts in the Canada of the 1950s.

There were insuperable problems, however. Right from the beginning, this Church was split by schism. There were always tensions between the centre and the periphery, between French and English, bureaucrats and producers, high and low. The very programs that attracted the most viewers and generated the most revenue – Quebec's téléromans, the anglophone variety shows, or imported American hits – were objects of disdain in some quarters, both inside and outside the Corporation. One letter-writer expressed disgust 'to see so much time, effort, [and] money frittered away on "garbage."'[30] That was just one sign of the growing disenchantment of the highbrow community by the early 1960s. There was little British material, aside from the occasional movie or newsfilm – often it seemed of one royal or another – that the CBC might use to bring a British presence into Canadian homes. Nor could the CBC reform popular tastes, especially in English Canada. There was a constant grumble from audiences about too much 'culchah' and too little entertainment on the airwaves. The owner of a private station in the Maritimes, for example, once took out a newspaper ad to apologize for being obliged to bring CBC's drama and music program *Folio* to irate viewers – 'Blame CBC,' he declared.[31] Viewers wanted more choice and more American programs: no wonder that outside antennae able to capture the signals of US stations sprouted on Canadian rooftops – an estimated 88 percent of the TV homes in the Toronto-Hamilton area by 1959.[32] That same year the producer's strike in Montreal brought another kind of surprise: researchers discovered that foreign movies, (whether from France or from elsewhere, dubbed into French), which programmers had slotted into the schedule to replace the homegrown shows, were very popular with the French-speaking audience, more so than most of the local hits.

Besides, the whole broadcasting environment soon changed. In the mid-1950s the recommendations of yet another royal commission, the Fowler Commission on Broadcasting, tried to satisfy the popular demand for choice, and opened the way to the thoroughgoing Americanization of the airwaves. Perhaps this was not surprising given that a Conservative government in Britain had just recently authorized a private, commercial television station for the first time. A new broadcasting act in 1958 stripped the CBC of its regulatory authority over the privates and of its monopoly control over television. In the next decade the public service faced escalating competition from independent private stations that used American imports to attract huge audiences. It retaliated in like fashion: indeed, when the rival CTV won the rights to carry domestic football in 1961, the CBC offered Sunday telecasts of American games. The CBC had to submit to that logic of mass communication, which it had once naïvely rejected. Three years later it was clear to one Toronto critic that both CBC and CTV now relied on US material 'to give their prime-time hours glamour, interest, and drawing power.'[33] The last great effort to replicate a BBC success proved an expensive and demoralizing flop: in 1972 CBC Drama launched *The Whiteoaks of Jalna*, a historical miniseries based on the novels of Mazo de la Roche and modelled after that superhit *The Forsyte Saga* (1967), but this much-hyped production proved so complicated and so confusing that it failed both at home and abroad to please audiences.[34] By then the amount of money and time given to the broadcast of culture had slowly waned, a victim of cutbacks and the lack of viewer interest. So too did the ideal of the British way: when, in 1972, Knowlton Nash preached the virtues of a 'programming revolution,' he and others looked to the American experience, foreseeing a kind of PBS North.

The rest of Massey's 'British' agenda suffered a similar kind of decay. The centre of the highbrow world shifted decisively from London to New York during the course of the 1950s. Right from the beginning the Canada Council looked to the experience of American institutions like the Rockefeller Foundation for guidance.[35] When incessant and exorbitant demands for money compelled the Council to investigate ballet, the council's arts administrator went first to Lincoln Kirsten, director of the New York City Ballet, for advice about what to do – another sign of how things had changed.[36] Government money and the baby boom did sponsor an enormous expansion of Canadian universities, but these became ever more American in style, substance, and personnel during the course of the 1960s. Shortly afterwards this change initiated a nationalist backlash that eventually drove the federal government to impose restrictions on the hiring of foreign (though principally American) professors.

None of which meant that this last imperial enterprise had exactly failed. By the early 1970s Canada could boast a generous Canada Council, a new National Arts Centre, three professional ballet companies, the Shakespearean and the Shaw Festivals, and new galleries, museums, and theatres, some built to celebrate the country's Centennial. In the meantime Canada's cultural project had shed its British and highbrow cast to seek, ever more desperately, the always elusive goal of cultural sovereignty. This proved no more practical than Massey's desire to make 'another England.' The goal of cultural sovereignty did justify a wealth of rules, regulations, and subsidies that guided – sometimes restricted – the production, distribution, and even the consumption of culture in Canada. But none of these brought about a utopia. Carnival had won again: a popular culture, made in the USA or imitated in Canada, remained triumphant in 1970, and for that matter, in 2000.

Let me conclude on a Freudian note. Canada's cultural project could not wholly escape its origins. It was conceived as an act of imagination and even of defiance. That legacy remained. So the project matured in ways that reflected its childhood. But, at least after the mid-1950s, the project 'grew up' in circumstances increasingly hostile to the success of any flights of fancy. What counted now was the continued existence of the project as a sign and an assertion of difference on a thoroughly American continent.

Here is a situation where appearance is reality. The much-touted goal of cultural sovereignty is one of Jean Baudrillard's simulacra, a signifier without a referent. Or, to be precise, it has become a third-order simulation that 'masks the absence of a basic reality.'[37] Vincent Massey, I imagine, would not have been amused: the culture project, however necessary to the national identity, had become a species of propaganda in an age of hyperreality.[38]

Notes

1   Donald Creighton, *The Forked Road: Canada, 1939-1957* (Toronto: McClelland and Stewart, 1976), 187.
2   Marshall McLuhan, *The Mechanical Bride: Folklore of Industrial Man* (1951; Boston: Beacon Press, 1967).
3   See, for example, Peter Stallybrass and Allon White, *The Politics and Poetics of Transgression* (London: Methuen, 1986).
4   For a sample of highbrow views, see Bernard Rosenberg and David Manning White, *Mass Culture: The Popular Arts in America* (New York: Free Press, 1957), 59-73.
5   See Maria Tippett, *Making Culture: English-Canadian Institutions and the Arts before the Massey Commission* (Toronto: University of Toronto Press, 1990).
6   Cheryl Smith, '"Stepping Out": Canada's Early Ballet Companies, 1939-1963' (PhD thesis, University of Toronto, 2000), 74-104.
7   Gary Evans, *John Grierson and the National Film Board: The Politics of Wartime Propaganda, 1939-1945* (Toronto: University of Toronto Press, 1984).
8   See Peter Stursberg, *Mister Broadcasting: The Ernie Bushnell Story* (Toronto: Peter Martin Associates, 1971), 134-37.
9   Tippett, *Making Culture*, 179.
10 Cited in the Royal Commission on National Development in the Arts, Letters and Sciences, *Report* (Ottawa: King's Printer, 1951), 375.
11 Smith, 'Stepping Out,' 105-44.
12 See Julian Park, ed., *The Culture of Contemporary Canada* (Ithaca: Cornell University Press, 1957), 175, and Creighton, *The Forked Road*, 249-51.
13 Lord Cranborne, once a secretary of state for the dominions, cited in Paul Litt, *The Muses, the Masses, and the Massey Commission* (Toronto: University of Toronto Press, 1992), 30.
14 Vincent Massey, *On Being Canadian* (Toronto: J.M. Dent, 1948).
15 Frank Underhill, 'Notes on the Massey Report,' in *Forum: Canadian Life and Letters, 1920-1970: Selections from 'The Canadian Forum,'* ed. J.L. Granatstein and Peter Stevens (Toronto: University of Toronto Press, 1972), 264.
16 Noted in Litt, *The Muses, the Masses, and the Massey Commission*, 227.
17 Cited in Claude Bissell, *The Imperial Canadian: Vincent Massey in Office* (Toronto: University of Toronto Press, 1986), 225.
18 Royal Commission, *Report*, 288.
19 Unlikely as it seems, the poll results were the same in 1947 and 1950: Commonwealth (44 percent), Independent (32 percent), Join US (18 percent). Cited in Mildred A. Schwartz, *Public Opinion and Canadian Identity* (Scarborough: Fitzhenry and Whiteside, 1967), 74.
20 Royal Commission, *Report*, 19.
21 This was Underhill's preferred solution, instead of the creation of a 'new England' or a cultural tariff. It fitted his North American perspective as well as his highbrow loyalties. See Underhill, 'Notes on the Massey Report,' *In Search of Canadian Liberalism* (Toronto: Macmillan, 1960), 212-13.
22 Royal Commission, *Report*, 14, 15, 275, 274.
23 Harold Innis, *The Strategy of Culture* (Toronto: University of Toronto Press, 1952), 19-20.
24 I have discussed this attitude towards TV in *When Television Was Young: Primetime Canada, 1952-1967* (Toronto: University of Toronto Press, 1990), 19-26.
25 Royal Commission, *Report*, 42, 413.

26 This language is embodied in the *Report*'s definition of culture: 'Culture is that part of education which enriches the mind and refines the taste.' Royal Commission, *Report*, 7.
27 Royal Commission, *Report*, 387, 47-48.
28 Witness this key recommendation: 'That the Canadian Broadcasting Corporation exercise a strict control over all television stations in Canada in order to avoid excessive commercialism and to encourage Canadian content and the use of Canadian talent.' Royal Commission, *Report*, 305.
29 The following material on CBC television is drawn from *When Television Was Young*.
30 See National Archives of Canada (NAC), RG41, vol. 206, file 11-18-11-71 for letters to the CBC.
31 Walker, Dean. 'Canada's TV Dilemma: The American Influence,' *Saturday Night*, 23 July 1960, 16.
32 International Surveys Limited, *Season Listening and Viewing Habits in Canada and Its 3 Major Markets, 1958-59*, 73
33 Dennis Braithwaite in the Toronto *Globe and Mail*, 6 May 1964, cited in E.A. Weir, *The Struggle for National Broadcasting* (Toronto: McClelland and Stewart, 1965), 382.
34 'The problem was that *Jalna* readers, who wanted their old, familiar story, were treated to an ill-conceived experiment in narrative structure complete with flashbacks, multiple plot strands, and intercut time frames, all edited in haste as the air date approached.' Mary Jane Miller, *Turn Up The Contrast: CBC Television Drama Since 1952* (Vancouver: University of British Columbia Press/CBC Enterprises, 1987), 228.
35 See J.L. Granatstein, *Canada, 1957-1967: The Years of Uncertainty and Innovation* (Toronto: McClelland and Stewart, 1986), 146-47, and Smith, 'Stepping Out,' 368-69.
36 But the actual investigatory committee also included one Briton and one Canadian. Granatstein, *Canada, 1957-1967*, 156.
37 Jean Baudrillard, *Simulations*, translated by Paul Foss, Paul Patton, and Philip Beitchman (New York: Semiotext[e], 1983), 11.
38 I have discussed this phenomenon at much greater length in 'Designing Culture: Reflections on a Post/modern Project' in *Media Policy, National Identity and Citizenry in Changing Democratic Societies: The Case of Canada,* ed. Joel Smith (Durham, NC: Canadian Studies Center, Duke University, 1998), 184-94.

12

From Guthrie to Greenberg: Canadian High Culture and the End of Empire

Allan Smith

Defined by decolonization and a sharp decline in political, economic, and military status, the end of Britain's imperial age was also signalled by a final, decisive shift in its position as cultural arbiter of the English-speaking world. That shift had, of course, come years earlier in the realm of popular culture. Unable to resist the rising tide of American activity in the new, media-based arts of the twentieth century, Britain had in fact seen its nineteenth-century success in popular fiction and the songs of the music hall all but eclipsed by the 1920s. In the domain of high culture, however, matters had gone on much as before. Covent Garden, Sadler's Wells, and the London Symphony Orchestra remained standard-setters in their fields. The work of George Bernard Shaw, Virginia Woolf, D.H. Lawrence, Edith Sitwell, Edward Elgar, Frederick Delius, Ben Nicholson, and Wyndham Lewis sustained high levels of individual innovation and excellence. Cultural life in general – the continuing presence of such luminaries as T.S. Eliot and Jacob Epstein made the point – lost nothing of its capacity to draw strength away from even the most powerful of its rivals. Ongoing accomplishment was, indeed, evident on every front, and in its clear and obvious presence the fact of enduring British supremacy in the fine, performing, and creative arts was manifest for all to see.[1]

In the 1950s, that situation too began to alter. Buffeted by the winds of change blowing through the national life at large, Britain's status as cultural leader of the anglophone world was called into question in almost every area. Funding and infrastructure were certainly weakening. Public and private patrons, their resources reduced by the continuing decline in British economic strength, were patently unable to maintain expenditures at the levels necessary to guard benchmark standards and spark fresh development. Even the Arts Council – formed in 1946 with the very purpose of making up deficiencies in private patronage – was by the early 1950s having to scale back its activities. By 1957 the funding problem was acute. Entitling its annual report for the year *Art in the Red*, the council pointed to the near crisis at hand as production standards declined, support for individual artists diminished, the talented fled abroad, and tendencies towards the commercial deepened.[2]

Importantly, too, creative renewal became an issue. Demographic accident intervened to insure that distinguished figures lost through death – Kathleen Ferrier and Dylan Thomas in 1953, Ralph Vaughan Williams in 1958 – were not in every case replaced. More critically, leading artistic producers failed to move their work beyond the confines of existing modes, styles, and preoccupations. Indeed, in remaining with the figural in painting, the classical narrative tradition in dance, and issues of class and social tension in theatre, even such strongly innovative personalities as Lucian Freud, Francis Bacon, Frederick Ashton, and the dramatists associated with the Angry Young Men experimented within frameworks defined essentially by the known and familiar.[3]

The most serious difficulty was created by the changing position of the United States. Disposing of unprecedented wealth, enriched by imports of human and cultural capital from the distressed European world of the 1930s and 1940s, enjoying the fruits of a cultural maturity that had been developing for decades, and convinced – with a conviction that gained in intensity after the onset of the Cold War – that its peculiar New World genius should find expression in high art and culture of a specifically 'national' sort, the United States was at last moving from the general acceptance of European hegemony so bemoaned by Ralph Waldo Emerson and his friends to a sharp, intense, and remarkably successful contesting of it. Evident in the physicality and radical new forms of movement that George Balanchine, Martha Graham, and Merce Cunningham were introducing to dance, to be seen in the 'national' dimension Aaron Copland and his colleagues were bringing to musical composition, a clear reality in the 'new American poetry' so closely identified with William Carlos Williams and Wallace Stevens, very much a feature of what Arthur Miller, William Inge, and Tennessee Williams were accomplishing in drama, and exhibited above all in abstract expressionism and the new sculpture of steel, iron, and angularity, the American challenge even announced itself at the heart of empire. The New York City Ballet's first British visit in 1950 was a critical and artistic success; when the Boston Symphony Orchestra toured Britain for the first time in 1952, it received an enthusiastic welcome; the West End opening in that year of plays by Williams and Clifford Odets gave American theatre a presence in Britain it had not before had; and the interest accorded American writers – the *Times Literary Supplement* devoted a special issue to them in 1954 (17 September) – made it clear that expatriate status was no longer necessary to a high British profile. Even when the attention won by the new American activity was related to what the British themselves were doing – Anthony Caro's innovations in sculpture did much to prepare the ground for a favourable reception of the new American work – that activity remained the focus of unprecedented interest and attention.[4]

Although, then, the several British accomplishments of the period – Benjamin Britten's *Peter Grimes* (1945), Graham Sutherland's success at the 1952 Venice Biennale, Kingsley Amis's 1954 reinvention of the comic novel, the extraordinary concert activity associated with the Festival of Britain (1951) and the Coronation (1953) – allowed Britain to maintain a distinguished place in the world of high culture, that place was quite substantially different from what it had been only a few years before. No longer possessing its earlier command and dynamism, facing a new, powerful, and relentlessly innovative rival, and reduced in status both absolutely and relatively, the nation was being forced to recognize that unquestioned dominance in the English-speaking world of dance, drama, music, art, and literature was no longer its to exercise.

Not all inhabitants of the English-speaking community took the measure of what was happening. Australians and New Zealanders certainly continued to orbit around the imperial sun. Significant numbers of English-speaking Canadians did too. Shaw as well as Shakespeare remained central to the concerns of the new theatre activists. Enthusiasm for the sculpture of Henry Moore – by the 1960s that enthusiasm would move the Art Gallery of Ontario towards its eventual role as the principal repository of Moore's work – strongly established itself. The attraction the London cultural scene held for young Canadians – Mordecai Richler prominent among them – remained strong. Increasingly, though, English-speaking Canadian activity in the arts reflected the fact that an important shift of force and influence was taking place. The very strength of English-speaking Canada's traditional orientation towards the British metropolis made Canadians aware of its travails and difficulties. Far, as a result, from constituting maintenance of a still vital link, the 1951 hiring of Celia Franca to head the new National Ballet – capped two years later by Tyrone Guthrie's appointment as director of the just-formed Stratford Festival – marked affirmation of one that was weakening and in decline. Struck by the difference between what lay across the Atlantic and what lay to the south, attracted by the one as the other lost strength and force, and determined to build ties with what seemed the more energetic, English-speaking Canadians opted increasingly for American ties and American ways. Even as the *Massey Report* (1951) was reminding them of the threat too close a degree of association with the American colossus posed, they found themselves caught up by, drawn to, and involved in the very significant action it seemed everywhere to be undertaking.[5]

What had, even before the war, showed signs of being a significant orientation – one thinks of American modernism's influence on the McGill poets, or John Weinzweig's early work with Howard Hanson and Bernard Rogers at the Eastman School of Music, or David Milne's encounter with American impressionism – thus took on real prominence. A new 'American' dimension certainly formed part of the burgeoning theatrical scene. Much influenced by the interest American dramatists such as Eugene O'Neill were taking in the tragic dimension of everyday life, Patricia Joudrey's *Teach Me How to Cry* (1955) drew no small part of its thematic content and dramatic structure from Sherwood Anderson, Miller, and above all Williams. The pull of Broadway attracted Robertson Davies to give his *Love and Libel* a New York staging in 1960. Len Peterson's *They're All Afraid* won first prize at the American Broadcasting Festival in 1961. With the advent of the new regional theatres in the late 1950s, orientations towards the South broadened and deepened. Directors looked to Inge as well as John Osborne; Edward Albee's provocative new drama rivalled Harold Pinter's; and the British presence shrank generally in place and importance.[6]

Evident enough in theatre, the thrust towards the American was no less clear in the developing dance world of the 1950s and 1960s. To be sure, the National Ballet retained its strong orientation towards the repertoire and style of classical dance. The older Royal Winnipeg, founded in 1938, however, left its 'British' origins behind, and – especially under Arnold Spohr after 1958 – moved decisively towards the non-narrative, plotless, event-oriented, and very physical dance associated with Graham and especially Cunningham. By the 1960s formation of the Winnipeg Contemporary Dancers, the Paula Ross Dance Company of Vancouver, and the Toronto Dance Theatre (the latter by Graham student Patricia Beatty) added to the now very evident Canadian attachment to the athleticism, naturalistic choreography, and strongly gestural movement Graham and Cunningham had done so much to promote. With Spohr's receipt of the Dance Magazine Award in 1982 – one of the premier honours in American dance – Canada's entry into the now central world to the south received an unmistakably telling mark of acknowledgement and confirmation.[7]

As English-Canadian musical composition continued its evolution, it too showed the influence of the new realities. This, ironically, was particularly clear in the view composers took of local song and melody. Moving away from the European tendency to see incorporation of these into symphonic and other work as evoking a folkish, uncorrupted, pre-industrial authenticity, composers adopted the idea – so evident in Copland – that their inclusion rather pointed to the place that a populist, frontier, democratic spontaneity and virtue had in the national life. Weinzweig's ballet suite *Red Ear of Corn* (1949) – particularly the 'Barn Dance' sequence – certainly travelled in this direction, while John Beckwith's *Night Blooming Cereus* (1953) used vernacular song and lyric material drawn from historical texts to exactly the same purpose. Recourse to 'American' innovations and techniques was very obvious, too, in compositional form and structure. A Copland-like gloss on Schönberg and Webern figured in Barbara Pentland's *Variations on a Boccherini Tune* (1948); an even more distinctly 'American' concern with tonal freedom entered her work after her 1948 sojourn with the Edward MacDowell Company in New Hampshire; and Elliott Carter's brand of pragmatic modernism was a major influence in her turn towards harmonic resilience and compositional experimentation in the 1950s and after. In Harry Somers' case, the American influence was refracted mainly through the prism of Charles Ives' and George Crumb's achievement. An Ives-like juxtaposition of tonal materials can certainly be heard in the phrasing of Somers' *North Country* (1948), while Crumb's innovative work with twelve-tone technique had a clear influence on *5 Concepts for Orchestra* (1961). Canadians were drawn in, as well, by the radical interventions John Cage was making in percussion, asymmetric rhythms, unspecified sound sources, and silence. R. Murray Schafer's increasing orientation towards sound in the natural environment, which would culminate in his *World Soundscape Project* (1969-75), reflected Cage's influence, while Schafer's written work – notably *The Composer in the Classroom* (1965) – dealt in fundamentally Cageian concepts of creative hearing and sensory awareness. With the virtual immersion of the University of Toronto's Electronic Music Studio (1959) in American-pioneered work – it operated with the heavy participation of such American composers as Jean Ivey, Pauline Oliveros, and Lowell Cross – the Canadian scene's orientation towards the vital activity on its flank made itself known in yet another quite compelling way.[8]

That the American influence should have been particularly evident in the case of poetry and fiction is not, perhaps, surprising. Long inclined to work under that influence, to cater to an American readership, and to publish in the United States, English-Canadian writers were in one dimension of their behaviour simply following a long-established tendency. Even in their case, though, new pulls and pressures were at work. Models associated with the new American poetry certainly commended themselves to Canadians with a force and urgency none of their predecessors had mustered. Not, to be sure, uniformly strong – Black Mountain's hold over the Tish poets was exceptional – that force and urgency nonetheless managed to make William Carlos Williams' poetry of process and open form a conditioning influence on the very important work Canadians were doing by the end of the 1950s. Present in Leonard Cohen's *Spice Box of the Earth* (1961), very evident in Al Purdy's *Poems for All the Annettes* (1962), and – her commitment to myth and archetype notwithstanding – a strong element in Margaret Atwood's *Double Persephone* (1962), that influence's impact on vernacular diction, syntax, and (in Purdy's case especially) rhythm recast much English-Canadian poetry in an essentially American mould.[9]

Much the same point can be made in relation to the new English-Canadian fiction. The reshaping of Jewish narrative traditions and themes evident in the work of Saul Bellow and Philip Roth certainly influenced Adele

Wiseman's *The Sacrifice* (1956) and Mordecai Richler's *The Apprenticeship of Duddy Kravitz* (1959). Sheila Watson's *The Double Hook* (1959) was wonderfully Faulknerian in its multidimensional treatment of place, perspective, and time. Alice Munro's debt to the American local colour/regional tradition – particularly the writing of the American South – was explicit. Even the deeply particularist, powerfully Jungian world Robertson Davies inhabited by the 1960s was in many of its motifs and structures a largely American artefact.[10]

In no Canadian domain was the influence of the new American centre clearer than in sculpture and painting. The angular forms and industrial materials whose use was pioneered to such an extraordinary effect by David Smith and Barnett Newman in fact provided the framework for the most innovative Canadian work of the 1950s and 1960s. Moving sharply away from the figurative sculpture still in evidence in the Art Deco period, accelerating past the concern with contoured forms and volume so evident in Moore, and, after 1960, working in New York itself, Vancouver's Robert Murray played a pivotal role in opening the way for the concern with design, materials, structure, and geometry that would be so central to the work of Robert Roussil, David Partridge, and Eli Bernstein.[11]

Canadian painting's move into American space was even more striking. By the end of the 1940s Jack Bush, Oscar Cahén, Walter Yarwood, Harold Town, and William Ronald had been fully captured by abstract expressionism's concern with colour, form, and – in its action-painting phase – spontaneity. By 1952 Alexandra Luke's Canadian Abstract Exhibition was specifying the extent to which that concern had taken hold. By 1954 Painters Eleven's first show – the group had been formed the year before – was demonstrating its impact on the artists who composed that very central group of Canadian creators. By 1956 those artists were exhibiting with the American Abstract Artists Association in New York. By 1957 New York art critic Clement Greenberg's very considerable influence in defining and promoting the new movement made its presence directly felt in Toronto through that luminary's first visit north. And by the end of the decade, the West's association with the American art community was signalled by the presence at Saskatchewan's Emma Lake Art School each summer of leading figures from the New York art scene – Newman in 1959, Greenberg in 1962, Kenneth Noland in 1963, and Jules Oliski in 1964. Affecting even artists who continued to work in a largely figurative mode – Graham Coughtry, John Meredith – the New York influence was – and remained – profound and decisive.[12]

English-speaking Canada's entry into the new cultural nexus created by Britain's fall and America's rise did not, it must of course be stressed, place it in a position of complete subordination to American paths and American ways. The fact that the community's participation in the transnational world of dance, music, art, and literature was increasingly mediated through channels supplied by US agencies and US approaches nonetheless had clear, strong, and obvious effects. Acting through the vehicle of an essentially American modernism, operating in terms of a style and aesthetic rooted in specifically American forms of innovation and experiment, and deploying techniques and methods associated with the explicitly national preoccupations of a Copland or a Mark Rothko, English-speaking Canadians produced creative work that was more and more structured in terms of the potent devices and ideas to which they were exposed on their southern frontier. Though, in consequence, what issued from their labours retained both a high degree of local content and a clear set of links to cosmopolitan concerns and interests, the materials out of which it was constructed became more distinctly 'American' with each passing year. Utilizing an American grammar, dependent on an American vocabulary, and articulated in terms of an American voice and phrasing, English-speaking Canadian achievement in fact came to operate almost entirely in terms of formal properties drawn from the American source. Alex Colville rather than Jeff Wall emerged as exemplary of community accomplishment, David Adams Richards, not Michael Ondaatje, maintained the identification, and English-speaking Canadian creative activity settled into a relationship with American techniques, approaches, and modalities at least as close and intimate as had earlier been the case with the British.

A factor of consequence in the reorientation of Canada's economic life, the end of Britain's empire thus functioned also as a key element in the refocusing of its cultural and artistic life. Depriving English-speaking Canada of a critical counterweight to American influence at precisely the moment when such a device was most urgently needed, Britain's decline in fact guaranteed that English Canada's shift into the American orbit would be both quick and complete. In marked contrast to the situation in Quebec – where language and the link to a France still dominant in its own cultural universe kept old orientations very much in being – new lines and forces took almost immediate precedence. Precipitated into the American system, thrust into a situation that compelled a viewing of the world through an American lens, functioning almost completely in the American province, English-speaking Canada's composers, painters, and poets moved to the production of work the content of whose form identified it as much a part of a world beyond its borders as it had ever been.

Notes

1 For British popular culture in the late nineteenth and early twentieth centuries, see David Vincent, *Literary and Popular Culture: England, 1750-1914* (Cambridge: Cambridge University Press, 1989); D. Birley, *Playing the Game: Sport and British Society, 1910-1945* (Manchester: Manchester University Press, 1996); and Peter Bailey, ed., *Music-Hall: The Business of Pleasure* (Milton Keynes: Open University, 1986). For the decline of that culture, and the

role American movies played in it, see Ian Jarvie, *Hollywood's Overseas Campaign: The North Atlantic Movie Trade* (New York: Cambridge University Press, 1992); Victoria de Grazia, 'Mass Culture and Sovereignty: The American Challenge to European Cinemas, 1920-1960,' *Journal of Modern History* 61/1 (March 1998): 53-87; Paul Swan, *The Hollywood Feature Film in Postwar Britain* (New York: St. Martin's Press, 1987); and Herbert Gaus, 'Hollywood Films on British Screens: An Analysis of the Functions of American Popular Culture Abroad,' *Social Problems* 9/1 (Spring 1962): 324-28. For the continuing vitality of British high culture, consult Arthur Marwick, *Culture in Britain since 1945* (Oxford: Blackwell, 1991); Robert Hewison, *Culture and Consensus: England, Art and Politics since 1940* (London: Methuen, 1995); Boris Ford, ed., *The Cambridge Cultural History of Britain*, Vol. 9: *Modern Britain* (Cambridge: Cambridge University Press, 1992); Stefan Collini, *Public Moralists* (Oxford: Clarendon Press, 1992); Samuel Hynes, *The Auden Generation: Literature and Politics in the 1930s* (London: Bodley Head, 1976); Dan LeMahieu, *A Culture for Democracy: Mass Communication and the Cultivated Mind in Britain Between the Wars* (Oxford: Oxford University Press, 1988); Peter Mandler and Susan Pedersen, eds., *After the Victorians: Private Conscience and Public Duty in Modern Britain* (London: Routledge, 1994); and Marcy Banlam and Bevis Hiller, eds., *A Tonic to the Nation: The Festival of Britain, 1951* (London: Thames and Hudson, 1978).

2 For the funding situation and the experience of the Arts Council, see 'The Arts and Literature in the United Kingdom,' in *The Annual Register … for the Year 1957,* by Ivison S. Macadam, assisted by Margaret Cleeve (London: Longmans Green, 1958), 412-64. The reference to *Art in the Red* occurs on p. 412.

3 Central institutions – Covent Garden chief among them – remained even more obviously in thrall to what one observer describes as 'safety, stasis, and compromise.' Norman Lebrecht, *Covent Garden: The Untold Story* (London: Simon and Schuster, 2000), 83. See also Ronald Hayman, *British Theatre since 1955: A Reassessment* (Oxford: Oxford University Press, 1979); John Russell Taylor, *Anger and After: A Guide to the New British Drama* (London: Methuen, 1962); Ronald Alley, *Francis Bacon* (London: Thames and Hudson, 1964); Michael Peppiatt, *Francis Bacon* (London: Weidenfeld and Nicolson, 1966); Lawrence Gowing, *Lucian Freud* (London: Thames and Hudson, 1982); Robert Hughes, *Lucian Freud: Paintings* (London: British Council, 1987); John Russell, *Lucian Freud* (London: Arts Council of Great Britain, [1974]); and Alexander Bland, *The Royal Ballet: The First Fifty Years* (Garden City, New York: Doubleday, 1981).

4 For American high culture's rise to prominence, see Lincoln Kirstein, *The New York City Ballet* (New York: Knopf, 1973); Francis Mason, ed., *I Remember Balanchine* (New York: Doubleday, 1991); Bernard Taper, *Balanchine* (Berkeley: University of California Press, 1996); Agnes de Mille, *The Life and Work of Martha Graham* (New York: Random House, 1991); Marcia B. Siegel, 'The Harsh and Splendid Heroines of Martha Graham,' in *Moving History/ Dancing Cultures*, ed. Ann Dils and Ann Cooper Albright (Middletown: Wesleyan University Press, 2001), 307-14; James Klosty, *Merce Cunningham* (New York: Saturday Review Press, 1975); Richard Kostelanetz, ed., *Merce Cunningham: Dancing in Space and Time* (Pennington, New Jersey: A Capella Books, 1992); David Vaughan, *Merce Cunningham: Fifty Years* (New York: Aperture, 1997); Aaron Copland, *What to Listen For in Music*, with a new Foreword and Epilogue by Alan Rich (originally published 1938; New York: Mentor, 1999); Arthur Berger, *Aaron Copland* (New York: Oxford University Press, 1953); Donald Allen, ed., *The New American Poetry, 1945-1960* (New York: Grove, 1960); Richard Leavitt, ed., *A Tribute to Tennessee Williams* (New York: Putman, 1978); Signi Falk, *Tennessee Williams* (New York: Twayne, 1978); Leonard Moss, *Arthur Miller* (New York: Twayne, 1967); Edward Murray, *Arthur Miller, Dramatist* (New York: F. Unger, 1967); Michael Leja, *Reframing Abstract Expressionism* (New Haven: Yale University Press, 1993); T.J. Clark, 'In Defence of Abstract Expressionism,' *October* 69/2 (Summer 1994): 28-37; Briony Fer, *On Abstract Art* (New Haven: Yale University Press, 1997), 93-107; B.H. Friedman, *Jackson Pollock: Energy Made Visible* (New York: McGraw-Hill, 1973); Diane Waldman, *Mark Rothko* (New York: Solomon R. Guggenheim Museum, 1978); Harold Rosenberg, *Willem de Kooning* (New York: Abrams, 1974); Rosalind Krauss, *Terminal Iron Works: The Sculpture of David Smith* (Cambridge, MA: MIT Press, 1971); Stanley Marcus, *David Smith: The Sculptor and His Work* (Ithaca: Cornell University Press, 1983); and E.A. Carmeau, Jr., *David Smith* (Washington, DC: National Gallery of Art, 1982).

For New York's place in the process, see Dan Wakefield, *New York in the Fifties* (Boston: Houghton Mifflin, 1992). For background to American high culture's movement abroad, see Frank Costigliola, *Awkward Dominion: American Political, Economic, and Cultural Relations with Europe, 1919-1933* (Ithaca: Cornell University Press, 1987); Emily Rosenberg, *Spreading the American Dream: American Economic and Cultural Expansionism, 1880-1945* (New York: Hill and Wang, 1982); and Frank Ninkovich, *The Diplomacy of Ideas: U.S. Foreign Policy and Cultural Relations, 1938-1950* (New York: Cambridge University Press, 1981). For the role that prosecution of the Cold War played in the process, see Serge Guilbaut, *How New York Stole the Idea of Modern Art: Abstract Expressionism, Freedom, and the Cold War*, trans. Arthur Goldhammer (Chicago: University of Chicago Press, 1984); Eva Cockcroft, 'Abstract Expressionism: Weapon of the Cold War,' in *Pollock and After: The Critical Debate*, ed. Francis Frascina (New York: Harper and Row, 1985), 125-33; Charles Thompson and Walter Laves, *Cultural Relations and U.S. Foreign Policy* (Bloomington: Indiana University Press, 1963); Philip Coombs, *The Fourth Dimension of Foreign Policy: Educational and Cultural Affairs* (New York: Harper and Row, 1964); Christopher Lasch, 'The Cultural Cold War: A Short History of the Congress for Cultural Freedom' in his *The Agony of the American Left* (New York: Knopf, 1969), 63-114; Gary Kraske, *Missionaries of the Book: The American Library Association and the Origins of United States Cultural Diplomacy* (Westport, CT: Greenwood Press, 1985); Kathleen McCarthy, 'From Cold War to Cultural Development: The International Cultural Activities of the Ford Foundation, 1950-1980,' *Daedalus* 116/1 (Winter 1987): 93-117; and Peter Coleman, *The Liberal Conspiracy: The Congress for Cultural Freedom and the Struggle for the Mind of Postwar Europe* (New York: Free Press, 1989). For American high culture in Britain, see the special issue of *Horizon* 16 (October 1947) devoted to that matter; Wyndham Lewis, *America and Cosmic Man* (London: Nicolson and Watson, 1948); Ivison S. Macadam, assisted by Hugh Latimer, *The Annual Register ... For the Year 1950* (London: Longmans Green, 1951), 396 and ibid., *1952*, 388 and 376. For Anthony Caro, see Terry Fenton, *Anthony Caro* (London; Thames and Hudson, 1986) and John Riddy, Karen Wilkin, and Ian Barker, *Caro* (Munich: Prestel Verlag, 1991).

5 For the general character of English-speaking Canada's cultural life to the 1950s, see Maria Tippett, *Making Culture: English-Canadian Institutions and the Arts Before the Massey Commission* (Toronto: University of Toronto Press, 1990). For the story in the 1950s, see Julian Park, ed., *The Culture of Contemporary Canada* (Ithaca: Cornell University Press, 1957) and Malcolm Ross, ed., *The Arts in Canada: A Stocktaking at Mid-century* (Toronto: Macmillan, 1959). For the Moore connection, see Roger Berthoud, *The Life of Henry Moore* (London: Faber and Faber, 1987), 314-17, 319. For the hiring of Franca and Guthrie, see Herbert Whittaker, *Canada's National Ballet* (Toronto: McClelland and Stewart, 1967), 18-21, and James Forsyth, *Tyrone Guthrie: A Biography* (London: Hamish Hamilton, 1976), 221-31. For the *Massey Report*, see Paul Litt, *The Muses, The Masses, and the Massey Commission* (Toronto: University of Toronto Press, 1992).

6 For Canadian poetry's link to American modernist influences, see Louis Dudek, 'F.R. Scott and the Modern Poets,' *Northern Review* 5/4 (December-January 1950-51): 23-39; Leon Edel, 'The Worldly Muse of A.J.M. Smith,' *University of Toronto Quarterly* 47/3 (Spring 1978): 200-14; Sandra Djwa, *The Politics of the Imagination: A Life of F.R. Scott* (Toronto: McClelland and Stewart, 1987); and Leon Edel, *Memories of the Montreal Group* (St. John's: Memorial University of Newfoundland, 1986). For Weinzweig, consult Peter Such, 'John Weinzweig,' in his *Soundprints: Contemporary Composers* (Toronto: Clarke Irwin, 1972), 2-29. For Milne, see Lora Senechal Carney, 'David Milne's New York,' in *David Milne*, ed. Ian M. Thom (Vancouver: Douglas and McIntyre, 1991), 37-62. For theatre, see Don Rubin, *Creeping Toward a Culture: The Theatre in English Canada since 1945* (Guelph: Alive Press, 1974) and Don Rubin, *Canadian Theatre History: Selected Readings* (Toronto: Copp Clark, 1996). Consult also Eugene Benson and Leonard W. Conolly, eds., *Oxford Companion to Canadian Theatre* (Toronto: Oxford University Press, 1989).

7 Ken Johnstone, 'Ballet,' in *The Arts in Canada: A Stocktaking at Mid-century*, ed. Malcolm Ross (Toronto: Macmillan, 1959), 54-60; Herbert Whittaker, *Canada's National Ballet* (Toronto: McClelland and Stewart, 1967); Max Wyman, *The Royal Winnipeg Ballet* (Toronto: Doubleday,

1978); and Max Wyman, *Dance Canada: An Illustrated History* (Vancouver: Douglas and McIntyre, 1989).

8 A. Walter, ed., *Aspects of Music in Canada* (Toronto: University of Toronto Press, 1969); John Beckwith and Keith Macmillan, eds., *Contemporary Canadian Composers* (Toronto: Oxford University Press, 1975); George A. Procter, *Canadian Music of the Twentieth Century* (Toronto: University of Toronto Press, 1980); and Kathleen M. Toomey and S. Willis, eds., *Musicians in Canada* (Toronto: McClelland and Stewart, 1981). Consult also Helmut Kallmann et al., eds., *Encyclopedia of Music in Canada* (Toronto: University of Toronto Press, 1981).

9 For background to English-speaking Canadian literary ties to the United States, see Tippett, op. cit., 127-55. For Cohen, see Michael Ondaatje, *Leonard Cohen* (Toronto: McClelland and Stewart, 1970) and Stephen Scobie, *Leonard Cohen* (Vancouver: Douglas and McIntyre, 1978). On Atwood, see Arnold E. and Cathy N. Davidson, eds., *The Art of Margaret Atwood: Essays in Criticism* (Toronto: Anansi, 1981), and Frank Davey, *Margaret Atwood: A Feminist Poetics* (Vancouver: Talonbooks, 1984). For Purdy, consult Sam Solecki, *The Last Canadian Poet: An Essay on Al Purdy* (Toronto: University of Toronto Press, 1999). See also Louis Dudek and Michael Gnarowski, eds., *The Making of Modern Poetry in Canada* (Toronto: Ryerson, 1967).

10 For Linda Hutcheon's location of Wiseman and Richler in 'this familiar North American vein of Jewish [writing],' see her *The Canadian Postmodern* (Toronto: Oxford University Press, 1988), 109. For Sheila Watson, consult Stephen Scobie, *Sheila Watson and Her Works* (Toronto: ECW Press, 1984) and George Bowering, ed., *Sheila Watson and the Double Hook* (Kemptville, ON: Golden Dog Press, 1985). Munro's acknowledgement – 'the writers who have [most] influenced me are probably the writers of the American South' – is in John Metcalf, 'A Conversation with Alice Munro,' *Journal of Canadian Fiction* 1/3 (Fall 1972): 54-62, 56. See also 'Alice Munro Talks with Mari Stainsby,' *British Columbia Library Quarterly* 35/1 (July 1971): 27-30, 29. For Davies and Jung, see Gordon Roper, '*Fifth Business* and That Old Fantastical Duke of Dark Corners, C.G. Jung,' *Journal of Canadian Fiction* 11 (Winter 1972): 33-39, and also Russell M. Brown and Donna A. Bennett, 'Magnus Eisengrim: The Shadow of the Trickster in the Novels of Robertson Davies,' *Modern Fiction Studies* 22/3 (Autumn 1976): 347-63.

11 Jonathan Holstein, 'Robert Murray,' *Canadian Art* 20 (March/April 1963): 114-17; Jonathan Holstein, 'New York's Vitality for Canadian Artists,' *Canadian Art* 21 (September/October 1964): 224-35; Greg Bellerby, *Robert Murray: Sculpture and Working Models* (Victoria: Art Gallery of Greater Victoria, 1983); James Patten, *Modern Metal: Roland Brener, Robert Murray, Royden Rabinowitch* (London, ON: London Regional Art and Historical Museums, 1994).

12 For abstract expressionism in Canada, see 'Canadians Abroad: Rebels in Manhattan,' *Time Canada* 67 (19 May 1956): 38; Ken Carpenter, 'The Evolution of Jack Bush,' *Journal of Canadian Art History* 4/2 (1977-1978): 124-25; Ross Fox, *The Canadian Painters Eleven (1953-1960)* (Amherst: Mead Art Museum, 1994); Margaret Rodgers, *Locating Alexandra* (Toronto: ECW Press, 1995); and Robert Bolton, *The Theatre of the Self: The Life and Art of William Ronald* (Calgary: University of Calgary Press, 1999). For Greenberg's involvement with Toronto, see Clement Greenberg, *The Collected Essays and Criticism*, ed. John O'Brian (Chicago: University of Chicago Press, 1986), Vol. 4: 323. For his Emma Lake experience, see Clement Greenberg, 'Clement Greenberg's View of Art on the Prairies,' *Canadian Art* 20 (March/April 1963): 107. For an overview of his general ideas and significance, see Robert Storr, 'No Joy in Mudville: Greenberg's Modernism Then and Now,' in *Modern Art and Popular Culture*, ed. Kirk Varnedoe and Adam Gopnik (New York: MOMA, 1990), 160-90.

13

Ontario's Agenda in Post-Imperial Constitutional Negotiations, 1949-68

P.E. Bryden

The abolition of appeals to the Judicial Committee of the Privy Council (JCPC) permanently closed an important avenue of constitutional redress for the proponents of provincial autonomy in Canada. Politicians intent on achieving a broad interpretation of the provincial powers granted under section 92 of the British North America Act (BNA Act), and a concomitantly narrow interpretation of the central powers under section 91, had found close allies on the benches of the final court of appeal in Britain. The decisions of Lord Watson and Viscount Haldane at the turn of the century had seriously limited the general power of the federal government, reducing it to use only in time of emergency, and had placed severe constraints on Ottawa's use of the trade and commerce power and the criminal law power. A less clearly biased bench in the 1930s had nevertheless been tied to the earlier decisions of the Watson and Haldane courts and had been unable to broaden the scope of the federal power sufficiently to deal with the crisis of the Great Depression.[1] The provinces, following Ontario's lead in mounting appeals and arguing effectively for a broader interpretation of provincial powers, had found a sympathetic ear at the Privy Council, and by mid-century enjoyed a breadth of jurisdiction not likely envisioned by the Fathers of Confederation.

While the JCPC was an important tool for the provinces, and particularly for Ontario, in their struggle for greater autonomy, from the perspective of the federal government its decisions were not only an impediment to legislating for the whole dominion, but also a constant reminder of Canada's continuing colonial status. In 1940 the Supreme Court of Canada decided in favour of the constitutionality of the federal government abolishing appeals to the JCPC.[2] On appeal to the JCPC in 1947, Ontario intervened, arguing that the abolition of appeals was an infringement of provincial jurisdiction over the administration of justice within the province, and a violation of its traditional right to bring civil appeals to the Privy Council as of right. The intervention had no effect on the outcome of the case, as the JCPC upheld the previous Supreme Court ruling.[3] Appeals formally ceased with the passage of the Supreme Court Act in the House of Commons in December 1949.

The decision to abolish appeals came at a time when the tools available for the exercise of provincial powers were being eroded on other fronts as well. The challenge of fighting the Second World War had created a suitable environment for the extension of federal powers. Most importantly, Ottawa moved to occupy the entire tax field in order to finance the Canadian war effort, and made it politically difficult for the provinces to recover their lost jurisdiction of direct taxation at war's end. With control over most of the tax revenue, the federal government was able to expand its de facto jurisdiction by spending in areas of clear provincial authority, most notably in areas of social security. In this environment of increasing centralization, the loss of the right to appeal decisions to the Judicial Committee took on new significance for the provinces. For Ontario, traditionally a leader in efforts to increase provincial jurisdiction and autonomy, the new reality meant that any attempt to amend the British North America Act would have to be undertaken with the utmost care. A newly weakened Ontario government struggled in the years after 1949 to define a role for itself in this post-imperial world of constitutional negotiations; without recourse to a British arbiter, resolution of conflict had to be found within Canada. In the bloody battlefield of Canadian constitutional debate, however, it was ultimately Ontario, and not the federal government, that proved up to the task of statesmanship.

Ontario had traditionally played the role of chief advocate of provincial rights within the young federation, but the circumstances of the Second World War forced a change of strategy on the part of the nation's largest province. Under the premiership of George Drew, Ontario began to deal with Ottawa not by rejecting the central government's proposals for centralization outright, but rather by offering alternative proposals of its own. At the Dominion-Provincial Conference on Reconstruction in 1945-46, Drew and his colleagues in the Ontario government sought to win favour both in Ottawa and in the other provincial capitals for their blueprint for the division of taxation and social security powers. While the conference failed to reach agreement on either the dominion proposals or the Ontario proposals, it nevertheless marked the beginning of provincial efforts to articulate a national approach to social and economic policy that would not only serve the interests of the entirety of the country but would also, from Ontario's point of view, protect the particular interests of its industrial heartland. Moving into the field of constitutional politics, however, the Ontario strategies were much less clearly defined. The renewal of efforts to patriate the constitution at first caught Ontario politicians somewhat off guard; as a result there was a partial return to the former Ontario position of outright rejection. Once it became clear that the constitution was a dilemma that would not go away, however, Ontario struggled in this area as well as in social and economic policy to initiate alternative proposals and press the other provincial governments to adopt them. The end result left the appearance that Ontario was supporting the national government, although in many ways the reverse might be a more accurate assessment.

The failure of the Reconstruction Conference in 1946 had wounded the federal government, and even years later left some members of the civil service searching for ways in which to 'recover the initiative' in federal-provincial relations.[4] Attention quickly focused on calling a conference in order to agree on a constitutional amending procedure as a way of recovering that elusive initiative. As Prime Minister Louis St. Laurent noted in his national broadcast in the spring of 1949: 'The record of Canadians in two world wars demonstrated beyond any question our ability and our capacity to bear the responsibilities of full nationhood. But our adult nationhood is not yet fully recognized in our constitution and our laws.' According to Gordon Robertson of the Privy Council office, the time was propitious for securing agreement on an amending formula, 'if, in fact, action is going to be possible at all.'[5] The prime minister was not quite so optimistic about the possibility of patriating the constitution at that time, but agreed that amending it to allow the federal government unilaterally to amend sections exclusively in federal jurisdiction would be an important first step. St. Laurent believed that the advantages to this strategy were that 'we bring back to Canada the right to amend ... we do not impinge in any way on the jurisdiction of the provincial Legislatures, [and] ... we leave to the Courts to say whether or not anything we attempted to do would impinge on a right or privilege of any Province.'[6] To this end, in the fall of 1949 St. Laurent wrote to all the provincial premiers to outline his intention 'to submit to our Parliament ... an address requesting an amendment of the British North America Act by the United Kingdom Parliament which would vest in the Parliament of Canada the authority to amend the constitution of Canada but only in relation to matters not coming within the jurisdiction of the legislatures of the provinces, nor affecting the rights and privileges of the provinces, or existing constitutional rights and privileges with respect to education and to the use of the English and French languages.' St. Laurent suggested that the amendment would 'give the Canadian Parliament the same jurisdiction over the purely federal aspects of our constitution that the provincial Legislatures already possess over the provincial constitutions, while giving both to provincial rights and jurisdiction and to the historic rights of minorities an express assurance of legal protection which we feel they should have.'[7] The proposed amendment seemed simple, straightforward, and obviously designed to correct some of the embedded inconsistencies in the existing BNA Act. The receipt of the letter in provincial capitals, however, was not met with such sanguinity.

Ontario Premier Leslie Frost had only recently assumed his position as the head of the government, but his earlier role as provincial treasurer had given him considerable experience in the area of federal-provincial relations. Although disposed to develop a more harmonious relationship with Louis St. Laurent than had been experienced between George Drew and Prime Minister Mackenzie King, Frost nevertheless approached St. Laurent's invitation to cooperate on amending the constitution with caution. The impending abolition of appeals to the JCPC cast an ominous shadow over any effort to amend the BNA Act even in part. While Frost was certain 'that no one could conscientiously object to the Parliament of Canada having a right to amend the constitution in matters which are purely of Federal concern,' he balked at the prospect of allowing the Supreme Court of Canada the authority to determine what exactly 'purely Federal concern' entailed. As Frost pointed out, 'there are conceivably some Sections of the British North America Act which in the dominion view may be matters of Federal concern only but which in the Provincial view are matters upon which the Provinces feel they should be consulted.' He therefore urged that 'no precipitous action' be taken.[8] A private conversation with the prime minister later in the week led Frost 'to believe that the abolition of appeals to the Privy Council may affect this very important side of matters more than is generally realized.'[9] As Frost noted privately, in abolishing the right to appeal to the Privy Council, the federal government secured 'complete jurisdiction.'[10] But the Ontario concerns were too late: An act of the British Parliament in late 1949 gave Ottawa the power to amend the constitution unilaterally in areas of purely federal jurisdiction.[11] Seizing the initiative would cost Ottawa, however, by antagonizing the premiers, putting federal politicians and civil servants on the defensive, and ultimately opening the door for future constitutional amendments to be spearheaded by the provinces.

Federal officials had anticipated that the two separate issues – abolition of appeals and amendment of the constitution – might become interrelated in the minds of some of the more rights-oriented provincial premiers. Robertson, recognizing that the federal government was open to the accusation that 'the court of ultimate jurisdiction is now the creature of the Dominion Government,' proposed that sections of the Supreme Court Act be written into the BNA Act stipulating the number of judges, the prerequisites of appointment, the terms of removal, and the number of judges to come from Quebec.[12] Another way of assuaging provincial fears about the extent of the power of the Supreme Court in determining constitutional jurisdiction was to force the court to follow the precedents set by the JCPC. Justice Minister Stuart Garson certainly expected that 'the Supreme Court will still be bound by the Privy Council decisions previously rendered,' but Frost felt that only a constitutional amendment could give the guarantee any real weight.[13] The Conservative opposition in Ottawa agreed, but justice critic Davie Fulton's efforts to introduce an amendment to explicitly 'preserve the principle' of *stare decisis* ('to stand by what has been decided' – the legal principle of adhering to precedents set by earlier cases) went down to defeat without a recorded vote.[14]

The more informal avenues for securing provincial protection against the federal government's possibly enormous new powers to amend seemed, by the fall of 1949, to be closed. The final venue in which the concerns of the provinces could be addressed was the full Dominion-Provincial Conference, called for early January 1950. From the federal perspective, the purpose of this conference was to 'consider: (i) a method of constitutional amendment for parts of the constitution not covered by the new Section 91(1); and (ii) desirable guarantees for the "autonomy of the provinces" and for rights *re* education and languages.'[15] How best to achieve this purpose was open to some debate, however, and was particularly affected both by the failure of previous experiments with constitutional amendment and the indecision of the prime minister. The federal politicians ultimately opted for a strategy of allowing the provincial premiers the opportunity to open discussion by explaining their own proposal for an amending formula.[16] From the provincial perspective, however, the conference was not merely about extending the amendment procedure, but also offered an opportunity to fix some of the damage that had already been done. This time, Ontario politicians made sure they were not caught off guard.

The first session of the intergovernmental meeting, held in Ottawa between 10 and 12 January 1950, was not designed to reach any conclusions on a domestic amending formula for Canada, but was rather supposed to provide the participants with an opportunity to lay out their preliminary positions. Lingering opposition to the manner in which the federal government had 'partially' patriated the constitution with the new section 91(1) infused the New Brunswick and Nova Scotia submissions; Quebec Premier Maurice Duplessis confounded his federal counterparts with his determined defence of provincial autonomy, the status of which he described as 'anything but clear.'[17] To Ontario fell the role of offering concrete proposals on how to amend the BNA Act. At the outset, Premier Frost assumed a conciliatory position, noting that 'Ontario's historical links with the British Parliament would not be weakened by determining a made-in-Canada amendment procedure.'[18] He then followed with what was the clearest proposal for moving beyond the federal amending power to adopt a more inclusive procedure. Frost proposed that the consent of the legislatures of all the provinces and the Parliament of Canada should be necessary for amendments regarding language, education, and the legislative jurisdiction of the provinces; that amendments affecting the dominion and one province should be possible with the agreement of the two governments concerned; that Parliament on its own could amend the constitutional provisions affecting the 'Executive Government of Canada and the Constitution and privileges of the House of Commons and the Senate except with respect to the representation of the provinces in the House of Commons and the Senate'; and that any other constitutional provision could be amended with the consent of not fewer than two-thirds, or seven, of the provinces.[19]

These preliminary thoughts on the amending formula were further expanded after the Ontario delegation returned to Toronto. Ontario proposed that the unilateral amending rights of the federal government exclude extending a session longer than five years except during wartime, and that unanimous consent be extended to include the amending procedure itself.[20] Over the eight months following the adjournment of the January meeting, the Ontario officials worked both alone and within the context of the standing committee of the Dominion-Provincial Conference to arrive at an agreement. On the eve of the second scheduled meeting of the conference, agreement had been reached on the classification of all but a few sections of the constitution. With the prime minister continuing to follow his strategy of allowing the provinces to decide individually the degree of provincial consent they would accept for various sorts of amendments, there was no clear direction being provided by Ottawa. The remaining areas of disagreement, however, were not insurmountable, and the Continuing Committee of Attorneys-General was charged with examining the possible solutions to the impasse and reporting back to the full conference at the third meeting, scheduled for December.[21] By December 1950, however, more pressing issues forced an abstract discussion of amending procedures off the intergovernmental agenda. The arrangements for dividing tax revenues between the federal and provincial governments were up for renewal in 1952 and needed to be negotiated; social policies first discussed seriously at the Reconstruction Conference of 1945-46 had not yet been legislated and these too needed agreement between the two levels of government. Discussion of a constitutional amending formula that would finally give Canada control over its constitutional future without recourse to an act of the British Parliament was removed to the back burner, where it would remain for another decade. Although 'partial' patriation of the BNA Act had been achieved with the federal government's unilateral 1949 amendment, the process remained far from complete. The activities of 1950, therefore, were just the first in a series of postwar constitutional failures, little more than a footnote in the history of patriation.[22]

Although nothing was gained by the provinces in terms of determining the role they could play in amending the constitution, the exercise was nevertheless an important one in identifying a role that Ontario in particular could play in the intergovernmental dialogue. Surprised by the suddenness with which appeals to the JCPC were abolished and the federal government unilaterally moved to partially patriate the constitution, Ontario officials' first response was to criticize the actions as a threat to provincial autonomy. Unable to stop the legislation from taking effect, however, the Ontario strategy quickly shifted. At the January 1950 conference, the Ontario delegation was the only one – at either the federal or the provincial level – that had prepared an alternative to and expansion of the 1949 federal amending power. With St. Laurent's decision to stay above the fray of provincial debate, the Ontario proposal became the basis of all subsequent discussion. Over the course of the next few months, it was refined to address specific concerns of other provinces, but the notes that Leslie Frost had brought to the table on 10 January 1950 remained the basis of discussion. It would have continued as the basis had talks not been aborted in the fall of 1950. While no one successfully brokered a deal, if a leadership role was played by anyone, it was Frost. This was a role that Ontario would wear comfortably.

The federal-provincial conference on constitutional amendment in 1950 ended without decision because other events, which also had an effect on the constitution but in a more concrete manner, took precedence. This would remain the case for almost two decades: While the unpatriated constitution continued to be an albatross around the necks of policymakers, pressing issues of day-to-day governance encouraged a piecemeal approach to constitutional change in lieu of an effort to attempt high-constitutional politics. Ultimately, however, the weight of individual amendments became too great, and politicians once again embarked on a course of comprehensive constitutional renewal. Ontario led the way.

When Prime Minister John Diefenbaker weighed into the constitutional impasse in 1960, he did so well aware of the difficulties inherent in both making it possible to amend the constitution in Canada, and agreeing on a formula for amendment. Feeling that it would be best to attempt the double feat one step at a time, Minister of Justice Davie Fulton accepted the advice that 'the chances of success are much greater if the conference were called for the purpose of considering the domiciling of the constitution in Canada rather than the finding of amending formula.'[23] Clearly, however, the two components of constitutional change were difficult to separate without prejudicing the process. As his letter of invitation to the provincial premiers indicated, the first anticipated step would be for the British parliament to amend the BNA Act 'at the request of the Government of Canada with the concurrence of all Provinces, to provide that the Parliament of Canada may, with the concurrence of all the Provinces, make any change to the Constitution of Canada.'[24] In other words, the first step would be to make amendment possible only with unanimity; the second step would be to devise a more acceptable formula for amendment, which would be possible only if all governments agreed. In striving to achieve patriation on any terms, the federal government's suggestion made future amendment enormously difficult.

The provinces were not about to be lured into accepting the proposed two-step process, despite Fulton's protestations that 'the general criticism which held his proposals to be too rigid did not seem to take into account ... that the concurrence of all governments would [not] be needed for every amendment.'[25] Instead, the attorneys-general agreed to open up debate over the amending formula itself, with the unsurprising result that the events of 1960 mirrored those of a decade earlier. Ontario once again produced and circulated a draft amending formula, and entertained proposals that would address the specific concerns of Quebec regarding provincial jurisdiction over property and civil rights, and the special position of Newfoundland.[26] Once again, preoccupation with the determination of taxation agreements between the two levels of government sidetracked the constitutional questions, and the efforts of 1960 were left to languish in an all-too-familiar purgatory. This time, however, the sentence was not quite so long, as Liberal Justice Minister Guy Favreau attempted to spearhead the final push to agreement in 1964. Initially successful, the Fulton-Favreau formula was a complex amending system based on the categories identified in 1950 and expanded in 1960. This attempt too, however, quickly failed when sentiment in Quebec turned against the proposal as too inflexible and unlikely to allow the more fundamental amendments necessary to protect the provincial autonomy the Quiet Revolution anticipated.[27]

Despite almost completely different actors, the efforts at constitutional renewal in 1950, 1960, and 1964 all followed a similar course. Initiated by the federal government, the meetings of attorneys-general and then first ministers ended up working from proposals put forward by the government of Ontario. At the first sign of any serious impasse, however, whether over the details of the amending procedure or as a result of public sentiment, the constitutional proposals were quickly shelved and the politicians moved on to other issues deemed more pressing. Ontario was certainly a leader in the negotiations, and the Ontario submissions were instrumental in focusing the debate. Never did the Ontario delegation attempt to shift the nature of the discussions, as defined by the federal government, from a piecemeal approach to achieving constitutional amendment, on the one hand, to a more comprehensive overhaul of the entire constitutional framework, on the other. Given the nature of Quebec's opposition to the Fulton-Favreau formula, however, it seemed that this was the structural impediment to securing agreement. It also seemed increasingly clear that while the federal government was prepared to initiate a limited evaluation of the shortcomings of the BNA Act, it was incapable of initiating a broader inquiry. This was a task that would fall to Ontario.

By the middle of the 1960s, two things were becoming clear. First, the piecemeal approach to constitutional change had failed three times in the previous fifteen years, and there was no evidence that the first ministers would get lucky on a fourth attempt. Second, negotiations over both financial arrangements and social policies, most particularly the Canada Pension Plan and the proposed national medical insurance program, were taking the constitution in directions that were causing concern in at least some of the provinces.[28] By using its power over the purse, Ottawa was exercising a level of control over areas of provincial jurisdiction that had been unheard of in an earlier time. Furthermore, the Quiet Revolution was well under way in Quebec as the spirit of *maître chez nous* was replaced with a more aggressive strategy of *indépendance ou égalité*. The strains on the existing constitutional framework were impossible to ignore; only a complete overhaul had any chance of successfully correcting all that ailed the system.

Ontario Premier John Robarts finally tired of waiting for the federal government of Lester Pearson to provide leadership, and took on the task himself. At a federal-provincial conference deadlocked over issues of higher education and the fiscal structure, Robarts reportedly 'astonished the conference' by calling for a full-blown meeting to discuss the very nature of Confederation.[29] He made clear his intention to spearhead such a discussion some months later during a visit to Montreal, and confirmed that a conference of first ministers would be convened in Ontario to discuss the future of Confederation in the speech from the throne in early 1967.[30] In the absence of leadership from the national government, it was ultimately a provincial politician who not only initiated discussion of comprehensive constitutional review, but orchestrated the event in a manner befitting a prime minister, and thus began the long process of comprehensive constitutional politics (or 'mega-constitutional politics,' in Peter Russell's formulation) within which Canada still struggles.[31]

The timing of a conference to revisit the question of constitutional amendment could not have been better, as governments wrestled separately with fiscal arrangements, health and education matters, and faced the aftermath of the failure of the Fulton-Favreau amending formula.[32] The circumstances of its organization, however, were far from normal. Pearson was taken aback by Robarts' initiative in this area, stating that 'there is no precedent for a Federal-Provincial Conference being called by a provincial government. I am certainly not one to argue that nothing can be done without a precedent, but I cannot help wondering whether this particular precedent would be wise, especially in present circumstances.'[33] Robarts attempted to 'allay any feelings of disquiet and alarm which you might hold' by stressing that his 'proposal does not infringe, nor was it intended to infringe, upon the jurisdictional authority of the Federal Government.'[34] There was no avoiding the fact that major discussions of the sort anticipated were the usual domain of the federal government; whether the intent had been to trample on the prerogatives of the federal government or not, the effect was to cast Robarts in a role that more rightly ought to have been assumed by Pearson.

Publicly, Robarts emphasized the importance of this conference for the state of the federation, and particularly for reaching a pan-Canadian understanding of the situation of Quebec. In the face of suspicions 'that Ontario and Quebec are joining together in some sort of power play to bring about changes in the terms of our Confederation,' Robarts maintained that 'there is no Ontario-Quebec axis.' Ontario had called the conference, rather, in order to facilitate open discussion 'in the widest possible context,' and reduce the sense that 'Canadians are not particularly well-acquainted with the problems of the regions of the country other than those in which they live.' He saw certain advantages to a conference with such purposes being called by a province, rather than the federal government, most significantly because the unique genesis might 'diminish the friction' that all too often developed at the more traditional federally chaired intergovernmental conferences. Moreover, Ontario was, in Robarts' mind, the obvious province to initiate a public discussion of the future of Confederation because it 'has a special role to play as an outstanding and an understanding interpreter of the view of Quebec to some of the other parts of Canada.'[35] Quebec premier Daniel Johnson agreed that 'it is only logical that an initiative of this significance be taken by a province which helped originate Confederation.'[36]

Robarts and his advisors initiated the conference, but much to the chagrin of the prime minister, proceeded to prepare for it using strategies much more commonly employed by the federal government. In the early autumn of 1967, Robarts extended an invitation to all the premiers to come to Toronto at the end of November to discuss the 'areas where each of us think our federal system could be improved ... the aims and objectives we see for the federation ... role we see for the English and French languages in this country ... [and] the machinery and structure of federal-provincial and inter-provincial relations in Canada.'[37] The invitation was, quite remarkably, followed up with visits by a delegation of Ontario officials to each of the provincial capitals to discuss preparations for the conference. This provided Ontario with an opportunity to assess beforehand what possible difficulties might arise at the conference itself, determine other possible areas for discussion, explain the anticipated publicity surrounding the conference, and get an initial impression of each province's views on the proposed subjects of discussion.[38] At home, the Ontario Advisory Committee on Confederation, whose members included historians, legal scholars, political scientists, and opinion makers, had been established years earlier to spearhead investigations into the nature of Confederation and propose changes that were deemed necessary.[39] The background papers prepared by the committee, while not necessarily reflective of the position of the government, were nonetheless the only glimpse into Ontario's own position offered prior to the opening of the conference.[40]

Pearson, who initially had anxieties about Ontario hosting a dialogue on the future of Confederation, did not change his opinion as the conference drew closer. The prime minister first refused to participate, then forced Robarts to call it an interprovincial rather than a federal-provincial conference, and finally 'persist[ed] in downgrading [it] by sending along as observers (not participants) four advisors or civil servants.'[41] But the combination of inaction and hostility on the part of the federal government was not enough to derail the conference plans. In fact, Ottawa's decision to dissociate itself from the conference left open the possibility, probably always imagined, of the provinces, and especially Ontario and Quebec, articulating a 'national' vision in the absence of any contribution from the federal government. The Ontario provincial election just six weeks before the conference opened gave some indication of the role Ontario politicians saw themselves playing in the future of the country. In an election campaign that was devoid of much grassroots participation and instead 'operated on a high level,' Robarts drove home his case for constitutional renewal and a new era of cooperation between English Canada and French Canada.[42] As one observer noted, without Ottawa's presence, the conferences' two 'principal participants' – Robarts and Johnson – could reach a 'deal between Ontario and Quebec which would have far-reaching implication.' Moreover, the provincial premiers would be speaking together for the 'national' interest, while Ottawa would become the voice of the 'federal' interest, and the two would no longer be the same.[43]

The days leading up to the opening of the conference were filled with optimistic anticipation.[44] The spirit that had motivated holding the meeting was positive, so there was no reason the result should not also be. It was lucky, however, that the conference was scheduled to last three days, as accord between the premiers was certainly not immediately apparent. In his opening remarks, Daniel Johnson indicated that profound constitutional change was necessary in order to accommodate Quebec. 'Our present constitution still contains elements which are valid for organizing Canada as a partnership of ten,' he stated, but 'we are forced to conclude that much of this other two-partner Canada remains to be invented.'[45] For other provincial premiers who were still uncertain about the necessity of a complete and dramatic overhaul of the entire constitution, Johnson's opening statement was an uncompromising line drawn in the sand. The second day of the conference opened with an even more serious rift: Robarts and Johnson disagreed over whether amendment to the constitution was sufficient or whether a complete rewriting was necessary. Robarts' statement that Ontario 'was not necessarily anxious for a complete revision' aligned him with Ernest Manning of Alberta and Joey Smallwood of Newfoundland, and threatened to break the axis. Yet the eventual relaxation of Johnson's 'hard-line' policy went further than merely mending relations with Ontario. By insisting that a solution could be achieved through a series of amendments that 'could later be consolidated,' Johnson essentially agreed that rewriting the constitution was unnecessary; when he offered a metaphor, the tension broke with laughter. 'Some people in Quebec want to divorce Canada and then remarry the same woman with a new marriage contract,' he declared. 'I want to see if we can't amend the marriage contract, rather than take the chance of a divorce and having the woman meet someone else.'[46]

Any division between Robarts and Johnson was perhaps more apparent to the reporters who were covering the conference than it was to the principal players. They had been in near-constant contact in the days leading up to the opening of the conference, and seemed to be in 'collusion' on how to handle a number of issues that arose during the discussions.[47] In any real sense, the axis was far from breaking. But the step that Johnson took towards compromise at the end of the conference was a key moment in transforming the alliance from one of two central Canadian provinces to an alliance of almost all the provinces.[48] It had been clear to observers that the provinces had similar problems with the federal government – they were, for example, unanimous in 'deploring the imposition of Medicare on them when they need money for other things'[49]; but the conference, which had been called to discuss the constitution more generally, resulted in a significant agreement to band together in the face of Ottawa's reluctance to initiate a constitutional review process. The conference was a major coup for Robarts, who received congratulations for his 'expert handling' of the 'risky venture' that, if followed by 'goodwill and continued effort,' might just save Confederation.[50] It was also a major victory for the provinces as a whole in demonstrating the viability of provincial constitutional initiatives and the benefits of provincial leadership. The ball was now in the federal court.

In a sense, Ontario had already forced the federal government's hand. The decision to hold the 'Confederation of Tomorrow' Conference, and the positive reception that decision received, had convinced Ottawa of the necessity of convening a full-blown federal-provincial conference to discuss the future of the constitution. Premier Robarts had certainly not imagined that the provinces would have the last say on the issue: As he declared after the fact, 'we believe that our decision to call the Confederation of Tomorrow Conference made it possible for the federal government, if it chose to, to resume its primary role in these matters, and I think that events have proved us to be correct.'[51] Lester Pearson, who had already been accused too often of inaction, convened what was to be the first of a series of seven first-minister constitutional conferences in Ottawa in January 1968.

Despite good intentions, the presence of the federal government at this conference, in contrast to the Robarts-convened one, seemed to loosen the alliances that had formed in Toronto. Provincial premiers, led by Joey Smallwood, seemed more ready to question the validity of Quebec's position. Even the partnership between Ontario and Quebec was strained – not because their positions had changed but rather because Quebec was lured into a head-on confrontation with the federal government. The debate between Daniel Johnson and federal Minister of Justice Pierre Trudeau, the main federal spokesperson at the conference, ended as a public and aggressive declaration of what would come to be identified as the Trudeau vision of Canada. The nationalist agenda was rejected out of hand, and the future of the French language was to be secured through individual participation in the federal system rather than collective autonomy within it.[52] The clash was the turning point: Not only did it help in propelling Trudeau into the prime minister's office two months later but, as Robarts said at the time, 'that's the end of Ontario's role as a helpful middle man. From here on in, it is going to be a battle between two varieties of French-speaking Quebeckers.'[53] Later, he noted that the 'shift in emphasis with [the] Trudeau gov't' defined the battle as 'between French Ottawa and French Quebec,' which meant that Ontario's 'role had changed.'[54]

In the years that followed, it became clear that Robarts' predictions were accurate. In the two series of conferences after 'Confederation of Tomorrow,' Ontario moved into a supporting role, first by offering proposals, then by supporting a federal position with an idea of breaking a deadlock, and then brokering the final deal.[55] However, Ontario would never again play the role of initiator. In a quite remarkable way, in the years following the end of the Second World War, Ontario had shifted its stance from one of battling the federal government for its fair share of the division of powers to one of usurping a part of Ottawa's traditional role in the national sphere. The abolition of appeals to the JCPC in 1949 brought to an end a period in which the provinces could be virtually assured of an interpretation being placed on the constitution that was favourable to them; in the years that followed, Ontario ensured that there would be a provincial voice in the determination of the shape of any new constitution. In the first round of negotiations, that provincial position was determined almost exclusively by the need to protect provincial jurisdiction in the aftermath of the assaults caused by the end of appeals and the unilateral patriation of the federal part of the BNA Act. In the second round, however, the Ontario strategy broadened to initiate a new, comprehensive attempt at constitutional overhaul, and to ensure the full participation of all the provinces. Ontario's leadership made possible the final push to full patriation after 1968. In steering the other governments in directions that made it possible to amend the constitution, Ontario was implicitly arguing that a properly functioning constitutional framework was in its own, as well as the country's, best interests. Surely this was a position that should also have been taken by national governments in Ottawa – but there, interest in regaining the initiative, approaching the issue piecemeal, and finally articulating a particular vision of French Canada, took precedence.

Notes

1 *Liquidators of the Maritime Bank of Canada* v. *The Receiver General of New Brunswick,* [1892] A.C. 437; *A.-G. Ontario* v. *A.-G. Canada (Local Prohibition),* [1896] A.C. 34; *Re: The Board of Commerce Act and the Combines and Fair Practices Act of 1919,* [1922] 1 A.C. 191; W.H. McConnell, 'The Judicial Review of Prime Minister Bennett's "New Deal,"' *Osgoode Hall Law Journal* (1968): 39-68; Paul Romney, *Getting It Wrong: How Canadians Forgot Their Past and Imperilled Confederation* (Toronto: University of Toronto Press, 1999), Chapter 11.
2 The Legislative Competence of the Parliament of Canada to Enact Bill No. 9, entitled 'An Act to Amend the Supreme Court Act,' [1940] S.C.R. 49.
3 *A.G. Ontario* v. *A.G. Canada,* [1947] A.C. 127.
4 National Archives of Canada (NAC), Louis St. Laurent papers, MG26 L, vol. 84, file: Conferences – Dominion-Provincial, vol. 1, Personal and Confidential, J.W. Pickersgill to St. Laurent, 19 July 1949.
5 Quoted in NAC, MG32 B5, vol. 138, file: Dominion-Provincial Conference (1949), Gordon Robertson memorandum, 26 July 1949.
6 NAC, St. Laurent papers, vol. 222, file: Constitutional Conference, 1950, St. Laurent memorandum, circa 19 August 1949; see also Gordon Robertson, *Memoirs of a Very Civil Servant: Mackenzie King to Pierre Trudeau* (Toronto: University of Toronto Press, 2000), 81-82.
7 NAC, Gordon Robertson papers, MG37 E87, vol. 29, file: Constitutional Conferences, 1949-1950, St. Laurent to Leslie Frost, 14 September 1949.
8 Archives of Ontario (AO), RG 3-24, premier's office papers: L.M. Frost, correspondence files, vol. 5, file: Dominion-Provincial, BNA Act (Amending), 1949, 1950, Frost to St. Laurent, 3 October 1949.
9 Ibid., Frost to St. Laurent, 7 October 1949.
10 Ibid., Frost to Judge J.A. McGibbon, 29 September 1949.
11 Geo.VI c. 37.
12 NAC, Robertson papers, vol. 29, file: BNA Act – Amendments to, n.d., 1935-1952, Gordon Robertson to Norman Robertson, 17 September 1949.
13 AO, Frost papers: correspondence files, vol. 5, file: Dominion-Provincial, BNA Act (Amending), 1949, 1950, Frost to Garson, 6 October 1949.
14 House of Commons, *Debates,* 1949, 306, 496.
15 NAC, MG32 B5, vol. 138, file: Dominion-Provincial Conference, 1949. Minutes of the cabinet committee on the Dominion-Provincial Conference, 28 October 1949.
16 On 16 December 1949, the cabinet committee on the Dominion-Provincial Conference agreed that opening positions should be provided by both federal and provincial government representatives (NAC, Paul Martin papers, MG32 B12, vol. 38, file: 3, 'Dominion-Provincial Conference on Constitutional Amendment: Procedure at Opening Session,' 16 December 1949); by December 20, St. Laurent questioned the desirability of the federal government making specific proposals at all (ibid., minutes of the cabinet committee on the Dominion-Provincial Conference, 20 December 1949); at the opening of the conference, his assistant Jack Pickersgill had finally convinced him that a federal proposal 'would simply serve as a target for attack by one or more of the premiers,' and St. Laurent allowed the provinces to take the initiative. See J.W. Pickersgill, *My Years with St. Laurent: A Political Memoir* (Toronto: University of Toronto Press, 1975), 117-18.

17 NAC, Martin papers, vol. 13, file: 3, Re Curran (legal adviser to the minister of national health and welfare) to Martin, 11 January 1950; NAC, St. Laurent papers, vol. 222, file: Constitutional Conference, 1950, Gordon Robertson, 'Notes on the meeting of the Committee of Attorneys General of the Constitutional Conference of the Federal and Provincial Governments – January 12, 1950.'

18 AO, Department of Finance papers: Dominion-Provincial Conferences, 1935-55, RG 6-41, vol. 3, file: constitutional conference of federal and provincial governments, 1950, notes on proceedings, 10 January 1950.

19 NAC, Martin papers, vol. 38, file: 3, 'A suggestion of discussion regarding a Procedure for amending the BNA Act in Canada,' by Leslie Frost, 11 January 1950.

20 Ibid., vol. 146, file: 8, 'Government of the Province of Ontario: Draft proposal to be submitted for discussion to the Committee of Attorneys General of the Conference on Constitutional amendments.' 1 March 1950.

21 NAC, Robertson papers, vol. 29, file: constitutional conference, 1950, 'Meeting of the Committee of the Whole of the Constitutional Conference of Federal and Provincial Governments,' 28 September 1950; St. Laurent papers, vol. 222, file: constitutional conference, 1950. Pickersgill to St. Laurent, 22 September 1950; AO, Department of Finance papers: Dominion-Provincial conferences, 1935-55, RG 6-41, vol. 8, file: Dominion-Provincial financial arrangements, 1941-1961. 'Proceedings of the Constitutional Conference, January and September 1950, and Meetings of the Attorneys-General, October and November 1960, on Constitutional Amendment,' n.d.

22 James Ross Hurley, *Amending Canada's Constitution: History Processes, Problems and Prospects* (Canada: Minister of Supply and Services, 1996), 30-32; Peter Russell, *Constitutional Odyssey: Can Canadians Become a Sovereign People?* (Toronto: University of Toronto Press, 1992).

23 NAC, Davie Fulton papers, MG32 B11, vol. 68, file: Constitutional Conference, memo for the minister, 23 August 1960.

24 Ibid., Fulton to Kelso Roberts, 19 September 1960.

25 NAC, Donald Fleming papers, MG32 B39, vol. 136, file: 136-6. Dominion-Provincial Conference on constitutional amendment, Ottawa, 6-7 October 1960.

26 Ibid., 'Summary of position of each province with respect to draft statement of principles circulated at the Conference on November 2nd, 1960.'

27 Gérard Bergeron, 'The Québecois State Under Canadian Federalism,' in *Quebec since 1945: Selected Readings*, ed. Michael Behiels (Toronto: Copp Clark Pitman, 1987), 178-84; Russell, *Constitutional Odyssey*, 72-75.

28 P.E. Bryden, *Planners and Politicians: The Liberal Party and Social Policy, 1957-1968* (Montreal and Kingston: McGill-Queen's University Press, 1997), Chapters 4-6.

29 John Saywell, ed., *Canadian Annual Review for 1966* (Toronto: University of Toronto Press, 1967), 76.

30 Private collection, Canadian Annual Review papers, unorganized material, 'Remarks by the Honourable John Robarts, Prime Minister of Ontario, to the Advertising and Sales Executives' Club in Montreal, Wednesday, November 23rd, 1966'; *Ontario Legislative Debates*, 18 May 1967, 3566; ibid., throne speech, 25 January 1967.

31 Peter Russell, in *Constitutional Odyssey*, contends that 'mega-constitutional politics,' or comprehensive rather than piecemeal reform, began with the discussions over the Fulton-Favreau formula (72); I see this rather as the last episode of the process begun in 1950, and the 'Confederation of Tomorrow' conference as the first stage of 'mega-constitutionalism.'

32 AO, Office of the Premier papers: Robarts, correspondence files, vol. 517, file: Provinces, Quebec, 1966-67, Ian Macdonald to Robarts, 'Discussions with Quebec People in Quebec City,' 20 March 1967.

33 AO, George Gathercole papers, MU 5311, file: Correspondence, 1965-1971, Pearson to Robarts, 26 January 1967.

34 Ibid., Robarts to Pearson, 1 February 1967.

35 *Ontario Legislative Debates*, 18 May 1967, 3570.

36 AO, Office of the premier: Robarts, correspondence files, vol. 445, file: Confederation of Tomorrow Conference – Corresp. Premiers – Ontario Government – 1967, Johnson to Robarts, 16 March 1967.

37 Ibid., Robarts to Joey Smallwood (and similar letters to all premiers and territorial representatives), 18 September 1967.
38 See, for example, ibid., vol. 444, file: Confederation of Tomorrow Conf., Ontario Gov't, Sept.-Oct. 1967, 'Notes on meeting with Premier EC Manning of Alberta,' 13 October 1967.
39 The members of the Ontario Advisory Committee on Confederation were H. Ian Macdonald, Alexander Brady, John Conway, Donald Creighton, Richard Dillon, Eugene Forsey, Paul Fox, George Gathercole, Bora Laskin, W.R. Lederman, Clifford Magone, Lucien Matee, John Meisel, R. Craig McIvor, Edward McWhinney, J. Harvey Perry, Roger Séguin, and T.H.B. Symons.
40 *Ontario Advisory Committee on Confederation: Background Papers and Reports* (Toronto: The Queen's Printer of Ontario, 1967).
41 *Globe and Mail* (Toronto), 25 September and 31 October 1967.
42 *Winnipeg Free Press*, 16 October 1967. The election was waged on such a high level, in fact, that this western newspaper characterized it as 'inaudible to people more accustomed to, say, a Saskatchewan type of election.'
43 Peter C. Newman, 'The Great Discussion about Canada's Future,' *Montreal Star*, 25 November 1967.
44 Interview, H. Ian Macdonald, 18 December 1996.
45 Private collection, Canadian Annual Review papers, press releases, 'Opening Statement by the Honourable Daniel Johnson, Prime Minister of Quebec, to the Confederation of Tomorrow Conference,' 27 November 1967.
46 Ibid., notes on the minutes of the 'Confederation of Tomorrow' Conference, 29 November 1967; Gordon Pape, 'Johnson Relaxes Hard Line Policy,' *Gazette* (Montreal), 30 November 1967.
47 *Montreal Star*, 2 December 1967.
48 Newfoundland premier Joey Smallwood remained, at the end, the only premier unwilling to accommodate Quebec's need for major constitutional reform.
49 Trent University Archives, Leslie Frost papers, 77-024, box 76, file: 8 (political correspondence, 1967), Frost to Robert Stanfield, 1 December 1967.
50 AO, John Robarts papers, Series F-15-4-3, MU 7998, box 2, file: Goldenberg, Carl, 1967-69, Goldenberg to Robarts, 4 December 1967.
51 *Ontario Legislative Debates*, 27 February 1968, 263.
52 Russell, *Constitutional Odyssey*, 79; Kenneth McRoberts, *Misconceiving Canada: The Struggle for National Unity* (Toronto: Oxford University Press, 1997), especially Chapter 3.
53 Private collection, Donald W. Stevenson papers, 'Notes for use by Don Stevenson at the Federal-Provincial Conference simulation, University of Waterloo, December 12, 1988.'
54 AO, RG 3-42, office of the premier: John Robarts, conference files, vol. 2, file: Hon. John P. Robarts, Robarts notes, n.d., but circa 1970.
55 Gathercole papers, MU 5318, file: source papers – conferences, Continuing Committee of Officials, 1968-70, drafts of Ontario's proposals, 24 June 1968; private collection, Canadian Annual Review papers, 'The Ontario Position on the spending power presented by the Government of Ontario,' 3 June 1969 and 'A Briefing Paper on Constitutional Review Activities and Discussions with the Continuing Committee of Officials,' December 1969; R. Roy McMurtry, 'The Search for a Constitutional Accord: A Personal Memoir,' *Queen's Law Journal* 81-2 (Fall 1982/Spring 1983): 28-73.

14
The Last Gasp of Empire:
The 1964 Flag Debate Revisited
Gregory A. Johnson

Most accounts of the 1964 Canadian flag debate and the subsequent adoption of the distinctive Maple Leaf flag are little more than acts of self-congratulation in which the Liberal government of the time is praised as forward-looking, progressive, and visionary in its attempt to save the country, while the Conservatives figure as reactionary fuddy-duddies stuck in an embarrassing colonialist past.[1] Liberal MP John Ross Matheson, one of the major players in the debate and the author of what one historian has called the 'definitive history' of the flag, wrote: 'This fight for a flag became a crusade for national unity, for justice to all Canadians, for Canada's dignity. The enemy was racial arrogance, the small and the mean heart! When the decision was taken in caucus to attack, [Prime Minister Lester] Pearson became David, capable of slaying Goliath.'[2] J.L. Granatstein has argued that the 'flag marked a new direction for Canada, a step into independence that ranked with the Statute of Westminster and the later patriation of the constitution.' Like Matheson, Granatstein believes that the 'flag was a deliberate gesture to Quebec that its aspirations could – with difficulty – be accommodated within Confederation and a signal to the rest of the country that great efforts were necessary to keep the nation together.'[3] Similar sentiments can be found in accounts by George Stanley, Blair Fraser, Alistair B. Fraser, and others.[4] The latest offering at the time of writing, by Rick Archbold, does little to challenge the standard view. 'The Canadian flag was chosen by a parliamentary committee,' he writes. 'The only war fought over it was a war of words. And yet it has become one of the great flags of the world ... And in fewer than forty years it has come to stand, uniquely and distinctly, for Canada. Your Canada and my Canada.'[5]

Why, given this general consensus over the apparently obvious success of the Maple Leaf flag, would one even consider revisiting the flag debate of 1964? What can possibly be discovered from reconsidering the narrowly focused, old-fashioned politics and mutterings of mostly dead white males in Canada's House of Commons some forty years ago? There are at least three reasons for a closer scrutiny of the debate. One is that a re-examination of the debate reveals a complex interplay between crass political expediency and practical national considerations in the face of the decline of the British Empire and the rise of Quebec nationalism. The debate was as much about power politics and saving Lester Pearson's career as it was about choosing a flag in order to save the nation. A second reason for revisiting the debate is to use it as a sort of test case for Eric Hobsbawm's highly praised notions about 'invented traditions.' Hobsbawm argues that the 'National Flag, the National Anthem and the National Emblem are the three symbols through which an independent country proclaims its identity and sovereignty, and as such they command instantaneous respect and loyalty.' He also notes that 'the actual process of creating such ritual and symbolic complexes has not been adequately studied by historians. Much of it is still obscure.' He goes on to speculate that 'we should expect' to see the invention of tradition 'occur more frequently when a rapid transformation of society weakens or destroys the social patterns for which "old" traditions had been designed, producing new ones to which they were not applicable, or when such old traditions and their institutional carriers and promulgators no longer prove sufficiently adaptable and flexible, or are otherwise eliminated: in short, when there are sufficiently large and rapid changes on the demand or the supply side.'[6] In this sense the flag debate was very much about inventing tradition. The rapid decline of the British Empire after the Second World War, and changing notions of what it meant to be Canadian, persuaded a growing number of Canadians of the need to create new traditions and symbols of identity – though, as this chapter will attempt to demonstrate, aspects of British-Canadian identity were alive and well. Finally, it would seem appropriate actually to measure the success of the flag against the stated intentions for adopting it in the first place. Here Pearson's objectives were not fulfilled, and in one respect the flag must be judged a failure. In an effort to unravel these matters this chapter will proceed to provide a brief overview of the 1964 debate and then an analysis of the outcomes.

The 1964 flag debate, as John Saywell noted so perceptively at the time, unfolded like a three-act play.[7] Act One opened in May 1964, thirteen months after the Liberals had returned to power promising to produce a distinctive national flag within two years. On 1 May Prime Minister Lester B. Pearson spoke to the Canadian Legion branch in Espanola, a small town seventy kilometres west of Sudbury, Ontario, in his own riding of Algoma East. He talked about the need to introduce symbols of national unity and made several references to the Canadian maple leaf. Although Pearson did not specifically spell out his intention to introduce flag legislation, reporters who attended the speech were left with the impression that he was presenting his argument for a new Canadian flag.[8] This was followed by a speech to the third Freedom Festival at the O'Keefe Centre in Toronto on 10 May, where Pearson talked about 'unity in diversity,' and, according to one report, said he 'was looking forward to the time when a Canadian flag and anthem would "erase the image and the idea of any kind of hyphenated Canadian!"'[9] Then, on 14 May, the Post Office issued a stamp featuring three maple leaves and the bilingual legend 'United – Uni' underneath it. Pearson later admitted that he had asked the Post Office to issue the stamp as a kind of trial balloon for a new flag based on a three-maple-leaf design.[10] The same day the prime minister met with a number of parliamentary press gallery reporters and announced his intention to introduce flag legislation, letting the reporters know that he favoured a three-maple-leaf design with blue borders.[11] These were mere teasers designed to sample public and press reaction. The real test came on 17 May in Winnipeg, when Pearson, with the wounded war hero John Ross Matheson in tow, addressed the national convention of the Royal Canadian Legion. 'I believe most sincerely that it is time now for Canadians to unfurl a flag that is truly distinctive and truly national in character,' he told the Legionnaires.[12] That certainly implied abandoning the Canadian Red Ensign, the modified British merchant marine flag that had served as a semi-official Canadian flag. The prime minister tried to take some of the sting out of the announcement with assurances that his government would pass a resolution that recognized Great Britain's Union Jack as the symbol of monarchy and as the emblem of Canada's membership in the British Commonwealth. The Legionnaires were not impressed. The *Globe and Mail* reported that the prime minister was 'booed and hissed' and told to 'drop dead.'[13]

The matter landed in the House of Commons two days later and, during a stormy question period, opposition leader John Diefenbaker gave the Liberals just a taste of things to come.[14] Undeterred, Pearson's cabinet approved a flag design on 26 May and two days later the government introduced a twin resolution in the House of Commons authorizing it to establish a national flag design of three red maple leaves conjoined on one stem with a white background and blue edges and to retain the Union Jack as the symbol of Canadian membership in the Commonwealth and allegiance to the Crown.[15] The resolution was a classic example of the Canadian political compromise: the adoption of a distinct national flag that could appeal to French Canadians while appearing to support the British connection by retaining the Union Jack. In parliament, the opposition recognized the resolution for what it was and pounced immediately. The prime minister, they charged, had misled Parliament and was trying to 'spread confusion and dissension across Canada.' Several prominent French Canadians, including Réal Caouette, leader of the Ralliement des Créditistes, said they would not support the Liberals if the resolution contained any reference to the Union Jack. Within days there was talk about a Liberal defeat on the flag and much speculation about whether the prime minister would have to call an election as a result.[16] Pearson decided to move ahead despite the preliminary skirmishes and on 15 June 1964 Government Order No. 44, a resolution to establish a new flag and to retain for certain purposes the Union Jack, came up for debate.

The opposition attacked the resolution before it was even read to the House. Robert Coates, the Progressive Conservative member for Cumberland, wanted the prime minister to set aside the debate and to hold a national plebiscite, and he cited as support a petition with 18,000 signatures that had been delivered to Pearson's office that morning. Then Reynold Rapp, L.J. Pigeon, and Diefenbaker took a run at the prime minister.[17] Eventually, the resolution was read and immediately attacked by Stanley Knowles, a highly respected parliamentarian and a member of the New Democratic Party (NDP). Knowles contended that since the resolution expressed two propositions it should be divided so that the mood of the House could be heard on each.[18] After considerable wrangling, the speaker of the House decided to divide the resolution. That made it easier for the French-Canadian members of the House to support Pearson's flag. An angry Diefenbaker charged the Liberals and the NDP with collusion, though there is no evidence that Knowles and the prime minister had conspired.[19]

The initial debate on the flag resolution lasted just three days, but during that time the basic positions were laid down. On the one side, of course, stood Pearson and the supporters of a distinct Canadian flag. The prime minister's favoured design was a flag with three red maple leaves conjoined on one stem with a white background and blue borders to represent a sea-to-sea motif. In a moving speech to the House of Commons, delivered on the 750th Anniversary of the signing of Magna Carta and the hundredth anniversary of the agreement between Sir John A. Macdonald and George Brown to end their antagonism in order to create the Canadian Confederation, Pearson said that a distinct flag was needed to bring Canadians closer together, to 'give us a greater feeling of national identity and unity' (thereby using older traditions in an effort to invent new ones). He tried to assure the House of Commons that he respected the Union Jack and the Red Ensign, but that the Red Ensign was the flag of the British merchant marine and similar to the flags of other British colonies. Canada's relationship to the United Kingdom had changed. Ottawa was no longer politically or legally subordinate to London, and Canadians deserved a flag that reflected that new reality. 'The time has now come,' Pearson told the House, for 'the adoption of a distinctive Canadian flag which cannot be mistaken for or confused with the emblem of any other country but Canada.' Although Pearson agreed that the past could not be ignored, he insisted that 'we have a responsibility to the present and to the future ... it is for this generation, for this parliament, to give them and to give us all a common flag; a Canadian flag which, while bringing together but rising above the landmarks and milestones of the past, will say proudly to the world and to the future: "I stand for Canada."'[20]

For John George Diefenbaker and his supporters, Pearson's flag campaign bordered on treason. Indeed, in his response to the prime minister, the leader of the opposition accused him of being tempted by the devil.[21] It is important to note that the Conservatives were not opposed to the adoption of a national flag. In the 1962 speech from the throne, Diefenbaker, then prime minister, promised a federal-provincial conference to choose a national flag.[22] What Diefenbaker and his supporters did object to was the prime minister turning his back on the past and in particular on British traditions and the British connection. Diefenbaker argued that Pearson's distinctive flag had no connection whatever to 'Canada's heritage and our past, to the contribution made by the French and by the British to the building of this nation.' So far as Diefenbaker was concerned, the Red Ensign had to form the basis of any Canadian flag, although he was prepared to stick a fleur-de-lis on the Red Ensign to represent the 'two founding peoples.'[23] Anything less would be an insult to the country and would do more to destroy than to promote national unity.[24] 'You cannot force a flag on the people of Canada and secure from them that mystic something which some ridicule as nationalism – the patriotism of men and women who love their country,' Diefenbaker told the House of Commons. 'A flag design is not a trick by which one group imposes upon others some evidence of a Canadianism that all will not accept.'[25] At the very least Diefenbaker wanted the government to hold a plebiscite on the flag question, and he implied that he would fight until the Canadian people were consulted. That was just what the Conservatives did. On 27 July the government asked for interim supply and the Conservatives began a filibuster to delay debate on the flag. Publicly, Diefenbaker said he wanted to stop 'this headstrong and stubborn rush toward the flag.'[26] To his close advisor, Gordon Churchill, he declared that his aim was 'to get the Liberal Party to vote against the Red Ensign.'[27] The curtain descended on Act One with Pearson saying that the debate over the flag had to be completed before summer recess and Diefenbaker promising not 'to retreat from our responsibilities by putting a throttle on ourselves on a matter as important as the flag.'[28]

The curtain opened on Act Two on 12 August when the House of Commons once again turned its attention to the flag. The debate continued through the long, hot summer to 11 September. During this time the same arguments were presented over and over. Tempers flared and the debate degenerated to a mudslinging contest. One of the lower points during this phase came when C.S. Smallwood hinted that the proposed new flag might be part of a communist conspiracy and threatened to release documents that would leave 'some people with red faces before we are through.'[29] It is possible that Smallwood was taunting Pearson (and other well-informed Liberals) with Elizabeth Bentley's testimony to a United States Internal Security Subcommittee in 1951 that Pearson was a communist.[30] The testimony was not yet public knowledge but the material had been passed to Diefenbaker in the 1950s.[31]

Stung by the tenacity and the effectiveness of the opposition, Pearson and the Liberals were searching for a way to get the flag out of the House even before the end of the first week of debate.[32] The prime minister wanted to refer the matter to a parliamentary committee, which would report back to the House. He met with the opposition leaders on several occasions but no agreement could be reached on time limits. Diefenbaker in particular objected to the imposition of time limits for both the committee and the subsequent debate over its report. He also demanded that 80 or 90 percent of the members of the committee had to agree on any given flag design before he would accept it.[33]

By the end of August the Liberals were in trouble. Parliament was virtually paralyzed and the government was facing growing public criticism. Walter Gordon, the minister of finance, warned Pearson that the debate could not go past the third week in September because Parliament was becoming a laughing stock and the government was being blamed for the mess.[34] John Ross Matheson, the Liberal member for Leeds and an amateur heraldist, reported to Pearson in early September that he detected a 'lack of resolution respecting the flag debate' in the Liberal caucus.[35] Tom Kent, Pearson's principal policy advisor from 1963 to 1966, later recalled that he doubted whether the prime minister, 'aging visibly and under strain,' could go on for much longer.[36]

Just when it was beginning to look as if Pearson would either have to invoke closure, withdraw the resolution, or call an election, two things happened. On 8 September NDP leader Tommy Douglas called for a truce. Enough was enough, he warned the House of Commons, because 'the real casualty in a cold war of attrition will be Parliament itself.'[37] He suggested three measures as a way out of the stalemate. One was the creation of a small committee of fifteen (seven from the government, five from the official opposition and one each from the other parties) to examine the matter with the help of heraldic experts. The second suggestion was that the committee report back to the House of Commons in sixty days or some other negotiated time frame. The third was that the party leaders meet and negotiate time limits on debate over the report.[38]

The following day Léon Balcer, the deputy leader of the Conservative party and a veteran who had served as a Royal Canadian Navy deck officer on the Atlantic convoys during the Second World War, broke with his leader and called for a compromise. Balcer told the House of Commons that both parties 'delude themselves.' On the other hand, 'it is also a delusion for the supporters of the red ensign to believe that it can be maintained without resorting to an endless filibuster.' Balcer suggested the establishment of a committee to choose a national flag based on one of the many maple leaf designs, and to fly the Red Ensign instead of the Union Jack as the symbol of Commonwealth and allegiance to the Crown.[39]

The Douglas and Balcer appeals led to a new round of meetings and on 10 September Pearson announced that the party leaders had overcome their differences and agreed to the formation of a small committee of fifteen members to choose a flag, the design of which was apparently again open for debate.[40] The seven Liberals, five Conservatives, and one each from the NDP, the Social Credit, and the Créditiste were to report back to the House of Commons within six weeks, at which time the party leaders would meet to set a time limit on debate of the report. Diefenbaker was elated. The following day he travelled to Fredericton to attend the Conservative party-sponsored 'Thinkers' conference. According to one newspaper report, he was 'trying hard to contain his joy at the derailing of the flag debate in the Commons.' 'Yesterday,' he crowed, 'we did a good job of cabinet unmaking.'[41]

Why, after insisting on large majorities and no time limits, did Diefenbaker agree to the formation of the flag committee? And why did he think he had derailed the flag and sent the government scrambling? According to Pearson, the leaders had agreed that the committee would be made up of 'impartial' members and that there would be a limit on debate if the committee brought in a 'strong report' backing a flag design.[42] It would now appear that 'impartial' and 'strong' meant different things to different people. Tommy Douglas, along with Robert Thompson, leader of the Social Credit, promised to put impartial representatives on the committee. They also believed that the committee would bring in a strong, meaning nearly unanimous, report. Diefenbaker had other plans. He said that he would not be satisfied unless at least thirteen of the fifteen members of the committee agreed on a design – a position that appears to have been based on the belief that the Liberals on the committee would support only Pearson's three-maple-leaf design. It was a bad tactical error. On 22 October, after forty-five meetings and examining thousands of designs, the committee sat down to vote (Herman Batten, who chaired the committee, did not vote).[43] It really came down to four choices: the Red Ensign, a three-maple-leaf flag, a one-maple-leaf flag, or a design containing both the Union Flag and the fleur-de-lis. The Red Ensign lost 10 to 4. The Union Jack and fleur-de-lis design was also defeated, 9 to 5. That left the three-maple-leaf and the one-maple-leaf design. The Conservatives thought that the Liberals would vote for Pearson's three-leaf design, and so decided to support the single-maple-leaf design. When the votes were counted, it was 14 to 0 in favour of the single-maple-leaf design. There was a previous agreement to vote to confirm the final selection and that vote was 10 to 4 in favour of the single maple leaf, with four Conservatives now voting against the single-maple-leaf design.[44] But the damage had been done – the Conservatives had, in Jack Granatstein's words, 'been mousetrapped.'[45] One member of the committee, Grant Deachman, said the Conservative members were 'thunderstruck' and 'cross-eyed with bewilderment and terror.'[46]

And so the curtain fell on Act Two. The victorious Liberals gathered at Mackenzie King's estate at Kingsmere (by then the residence of the speaker of the House of Commons). Apparently, after much wining and dining, the committee talked its only female representative, Margaret Konantz, into dressing up like a medium with one of the dark curtains from the windows. Someone produced a crystal ball and they tried to summon the spirit of former Prime Minister William Lyon Mackenzie King and his mother. John Matheson later wrote of the occasion: 'I think Mackenzie King smiled.'[47]

If Act Two closed with Mackenzie King smiling, Act Three opened with John Diefenbaker scowling. The committee reported to the House of Commons on 29 October and on 2 November the party leaders met to discuss the debate. Pearson later recalled that 'Diefenbaker was irritable and aggressive throughout the meeting.'[48] Diefenbaker later claimed that the Liberals had a 'secret prior arrangement' with the NDP and other third parties to out-manoeuvre the Conservatives. 'Thus,' Diefenbaker wrote, 'we could not accept the committee's report.'[49] After several weeks of considerable wrangling over procedure the opposition suddenly, on 17 November, made an uncharacteristically generous offer. If the resumption of the debate over the flag planned for 19 November could be put off for one week the opposition would finish debating the spending estimates for eight government departments. Pearson was pleased, though some of his advisors were 'mystified' over the gesture.[50] Then things turned ugly. On 23 November Tommy Douglas and Erik Nielsen, a Conservative backbencher, grilled Justice Minister Guy Favreau about someone named 'Leo' Rivard and whether there had been complaints that 'persons in high positions in Ottawa have sought to bring influence to bear by calling on Mr. Pierre Lamontagne ... in order to grant these men bail?'[51] 'Leo' Rivard was really Lucien Rivard, a Montreal drug smuggler who was fighting extradition to the United States to face narcotics charges. The opposition alleged that Rivard had friends in the Liberal party, including Pearson's parliamentary secretary, Guy Rouleau, who had tried to bribe Pierre Lamontagne, a lawyer with the United States Justice Department, into granting Rivard bail. The subsequent scandal resulted in the resignations of Favreau and Rouleau and soon there were allegations, subsequently proved correct, that the prime minister had lied to the House about his knowledge of the affair. What did this have to do with the flag? It seems to be clear that Diefenbaker wanted to use the scandals along with the flag to discredit the government, and he nearly succeeded. The journalist Richard Gwyn wrote: 'During the first days of December 1964, the Conservative party stood at the peak of its success as the Official Opposition. The Pearson Government was in a state of disarray. The Prime Minister's own image ... was being further eroded by the Conservatives' determined filibustering which threatened Pearson's brave promise of "a flag by Christmas."'[52]

Then things began to go wrong for the Conservatives. In early December, in a move that even Pearson's biographer thought was inexcusable, the prime minister tried to blackmail Diefenbaker into backing off by threatening to expose the Munsinger affair.[53] Gerda Munsinger was a German-born prostitute who had moved to Montreal. She had been a Soviet agent with underworld connections and during Diefenbaker's government she had had affairs with the associate minister of defence, Pierre Sévigny, and George Hees, the minister of trade and commerce. Pearson and Diefenbaker met and discussed the matter, at which time Diefenbaker threatened to 'expose' Mike Pearson as a communist using the Elizabeth Bentley testimony.[54] In the event, Diefenbaker did back off, and that might explain why the Conservative caucus decided, on 9 December, to continue to filibuster the flag instead of focusing all of its energy on the Rivard scandal and the so-called 'Furniture Scandal,' which broke the same day.[55]

This switch back to filibustering proved to be a bad tactical error for the Conservatives, because shortly afterwards the seemingly impossible happened: Léon Balcer broke with his leader for a second time and asked the government to apply closure to end the flag debate.[56] The Liberals hesitated but when they gave notice of closure on 11 December there was no great outcry. In fact, some newspapers, notably the *Globe and Mail*, blamed Diefenbaker for closure.[57] Government House Leader George McIlraith later said: 'I never got a word of criticism for that motion of closure, never, from anybody, in or out of Parliament.'[58]

Closure took effect on Tuesday, 15 December at 1 a.m., with each member who wished to speak being limited to twenty minutes. Near the end of the debate, the speaker of the House recognized the prime minister. One Conservative member, Eldon Woolliams, presented a motion demanding that Diefenbaker have the last word. Hugh Lawford, a member of the Liberals' legislative staff, noticed that the Woolliam's motion was typed and so must have been prepared beforehand. He concluded that the typed motion was evidence of a Conservative plot to disrupt the prime minister's speech in such a manner that one of their members would be ejected from the House so that a Red Ensign could be draped over the empty seat. In an effort to thwart the apparent plot, Lawford sent a note to Pearson suggesting that he give the last ten of his twenty minutes to Diefenbaker.[59] This led to the final confrontation between Pearson and Diefenbaker in the dying moments of the debate:

> *Diefenbaker:* The Right Hon. gentleman has done everything to divide this country.
> *Pearson:* Will the Right Hon. gentleman contain himself for two or three minutes longer and then we will vote.
> *Diefenbaker:* When the Right Hon. gentleman starts giving me advice, I say to him, You have done more to divide Canada than any other Prime Minister.[60]

At 2:13 on the morning of 15 December 1964 the speaker of the House of Commons declared that the report of the committee to adopt the single maple leaf flag had passed by a vote of 163 to 78 with 23 abstentions. The vote was more or less along party lines, with a few exceptions. Ralph Cowan, a Liberal from Toronto, voted against the government. So, too, did one NDP and three Social Credit members. The French-Canadian Conservatives, including Léon Balcer and Théogène Ricard, who had sat on the Flag Committee, voted with the government. Eight of the 23 abstentions were prairie Conservatives.[61] Two days later the House adopted the Union Jack as the Commonwealth flag.

So ended the great flag debate. But what had it all been about? Was it really a crusade for national unity in which Lester Pearson figured as the white knight who saved Canada? Or was it, as the journalist Patrick Nicholson charged, part of a campaign 'to get the Chief' and another case of poor judgment on the part of the prime minister for 'launching one of the shallow emotional issues of low priority' that wasted parliamentary time?[62] Were the Liberals hijacking the symbols of Canadian nationalism for narrow political gain? Or were there other factors and forces at work?

At the time and after, Pearson (and others) spoke of a 'flag problem' as if it were some sort of cancer gnawing away at the fabric of the nation. Matheson, for example, went so far as to write that Pearson had actually 'inherited' the flag problem, suggesting it was an issue of long standing.[63] In fact, there was no flag problem. Questions about a flag had been raised in 1925 and again in 1945. On both occasions Prime Minister William Lyon Mackenzie King had quietly shelved the issue in the face of massive opposition.[64] The matter surfaced occasionally during the 1950s and early 1960s but usually as a political football – something that could become a problem, but that was not in itself a problem. While it is true that the adoption of a new flag was part of the Liberal platform and that Lester Pearson had made a 'commitment' to the people of Canada during the 1963 election campaign to produce a new flag within two years, Pearson, as Tommy Douglas pointed out, 'made a lot of other commitments to the Canadian people on subjects that were even more important than the adoption of a national flag.'[65] The flag was not mentioned in the speech from the throne in February 1964 and the prime minister dodged the question when it was raised in the House of Commons later that month.[66] Moreover, the prime minister does not appear to have consulted his close advisers on the issue. In fact, a number of people expressed some surprise when Pearson did raise the matter.[67] Diefenbaker said he wondered 'whether what is being done is designed to distract attention, to create a diversion from the confusion and the chaos of the government in so many fields since it took office.'[68] Tommy Douglas, too, raised questions about the government's intentions. 'I think the government has put the cart before the horse,' he told the House of Commons. The leader of the NDP believed that the government should have been addressing far more important election promises, such as medical care insurance, the student scholarship program, and Canadian control over the economy.[69] Douglas was right. Canada had problems, but the flag was not one of them.

In 1963 Lester Pearson and the Liberals came to office promising 'Sixty Days of Decision.' Unfortunately the Liberals were a minority government and the Sixty Days of Decision turned into what one journalist called 'Sixty Days of Derision.'[70] By the spring of 1964 there were thirty bills listed on the order paper and Pearson seemed unable to exert any authority over the House of Commons.[71] Social Credit leader Robert Thompson said the Liberals had lost the 'fire, enthusiasm and dynamic courage' that everyone had heard so much about during the 1963 election.[72] Walter Gordon, the minister of finance, thought that the prime minister looked too weak. 'We shall have to stop changing our minds and qualifying our decisions,' he wrote to Pearson. 'It makes the government look weak and indecisive at a time when the country is calling for strong leadership.'[73] John Diefenbaker was less charitable. The Liberals, he charged, were destroying Confederation.[74]

What Pearson wanted, in the words of his biographer, was 'to pull the Canadian parliament out of the morass into which it seemed to have fallen in 1964. A new flag for Canada seemed to Mike Pearson an elixir that might transform his followers.'[75] This is not to imply that the flag was just a piece of political expediency. There is ample evidence to suggest that Pearson had been thinking of the flag since the Suez Crisis in 1956, when the Egyptians refused to allow the Canadians to participate in the United Nations Emergency force because they looked, in the styling and emblems of their uniform, too British. On that occasion Pearson had remarked, bitterly, 'What we needed was the First East Kootenay Anti-Imperialistic Rifles.'[76] A few years later he and his wife, Maryon, travelled to England by ship. As they steamed into Southampton, Maryon expressed surprise at the size of the Canadian merchant marine. When Pearson asked what she meant, she told him to look at all the Canadian Red Ensigns. The Red Ensign was the merchant flag of the United Kingdom and Pearson believed there would always be some confusion if Canada kept the Red Ensign with only minor changes in the design.[77] In Pearson's view, the 'time had come to have an emblem distinctly Canadian' and which could not be mistaken for anything else.[78]

In his memoirs Pearson did not dwell much on the decline of Britain, but it is clear that it was on his mind. He seemed to assume that the old-style British connection was gone and with it British-Canadian nationalism. A new transition had to be made, though he noted that the eventual 'Canadianization' of things 'caused more dismay, I think, in Canada than in London where it has been seen as an inevitable transition made with dignity and grace.'[79] Another observer of the Canadian scene who realized that things were changing was the historian W.L. Morton. In the summer of 1964 he surprised those attending a conference at Laval University by admitting he was experiencing 'a time of great depression.' He then went on to say: 'Slowly I had been feeling, suddenly I realized with the rush of an avalanche, and with all the clarity of loss, that the world in which I had been reared, the world by whose standards I had fitfully but not disloyally lived, the world I had bothered with and had tried to keep in modest repair, that world no longer existed. It was longer there – it had vanished. I was like a man alone in the Arctic waste, in twilight and with no landmark.'[80]

Morton, however, was not willing to cast Canada's past and its traditions into the ash bin, and he did not support the new flag. Nevertheless, that so staunch a supporter of things British could make such an admission is clear evidence that something in Canada was changing.

So too was the situation in Quebec, and Pearson was deeply concerned about developments there. The Quiet Revolution, with its *maître chez nous* ('masters in our own house') philosophy, was well under way. Pearson was impressed with the reforms and the process of modernization, but he believed that the Quiet Revolution had weakened national unity. After the spring of 1963 he became increasingly concerned about the Front de libération du Québec (FLQ), the nationalist-inspired revolutionary movement that had been engaging in terrorist activities. In January 1964 another revolutionary group, the Armée pour la libération de Québec (ALQ), raided the armouries of the Fusiliers de Montréal and stole a truckload of weapons, including machine guns, anti-tank bazookas, mortars, and rockets. Several other raids followed before the police made arrests but there was a growing sense of unease. Walter Gordon recalled that he and Pearson and others returned from an important federal-provincial conference in April 1964 'thoroughly discouraged and feeling that Canada might well be on the point of splitting up.'[81] Pearson believed that Quebec had one foot out the door of Confederation and had to be brought back in. The flag appears to have been part of the strategy to accomplish that goal. Victor Mackie, a journalist who sometimes accompanied Pearson on the campaign trail, later recalled Pearson telling him that 'I'm going to push through a flag. Got to do this to make Quebec happy.'[82]

In his memoirs Pearson claimed that 'the flag was part of a deliberate design to strengthen national unity, to improve federal-provincial relations, to devise a more appropriate constitution, and to guard against the wrong kind of American penetration. It was our purpose to develop national symbols which would give us pride and confidence and belief in Canada.'[83] This is clear evidence to support Hobsbawm's contention that 'tradition' is deliberately invented, in this case to support and foster the Canadian nation-state and to promote a hegemonic nationalism.[84] Yet, in important respects the flag did not secure Pearson's aims. In the long run the adoption of a new flag did not – indeed could not in itself – put an end to the threat of separatism in Quebec. Trudeau may have been right when he said that French Canadians did not give a 'tinker's damn' about the flag.[85] The new flag did not improve federal-provincial relations, as ongoing battles between Ottawa and the provinces indicate. And many Canadians would argue that it did not guard against the wrong kind of American infiltration. Yet, paradoxically, the flag has been an important symbol of Canadianness. Claude Ryan, who ran *Le Devoir* from 1964 until he entered politics in 1978, wrote during the debate: 'The Pearson proposal is a reaction against ... old-style nationalism. It expresses – perhaps awkwardly – a new nationalism which seeks to be more completely Canadian.'[86] In certain respects that was true but it remained to be seen how long it would take for Canadians to accept the new flag. In late April 1964, for example, Gordon Robertson, the clerk of the Privy Council, urged Pearson to settle the flag quickly 'so that any controversy can die down well before 1967, with some hope that the flag may be in general use and acceptance by that time.'[87] In retrospect it is amazing just how fast English Canadians and French-Canadian federalists, particularly the younger generation, did adopt the flag.

But what of John Diefenbaker? Why did he choose to fight the way he did on this issue and bring Parliament to a standstill? He wrote in his memoirs that he 'disagreed completely with Prime Minister Pearson's approach to the flag question.'[88] Diefenbaker did not like the fact that Pearson introduced the flag resolution without consulting the opposition or the other parties. He did not like the fact that Pearson committed the government and the Liberal party on the issue and 'boxed in the minor parties, who were afraid of an election.' And he did not like the way Pearson 'refused in every way to allow the Canadian people to decide whether they wanted to change their flag.' Diefenbaker might have paralyzed the House of Commons with the filibuster, but he claimed that was the only weapon he had.[89]

There were, however, other reasons why Diefenbaker took such a strong stance.

By 1964 Diefenbaker was increasingly seen by many in his own party as a liability. The 208 seats he won in the 1958 election – the largest majority ever won to that point in Canadian history – had been reduced to 116 seats in the 1962 election, and then to 95 in the 1963 election in which the Pearson government came to power. Thomas Van Dusen, a journalist sympathetic to Diefenbaker, later wrote that 'Conservative workers, bewildered and neglected, felt that someone owed them an explanation for what happened in the elections of 1962 and 1963 and no one was giving it to them ... Over the party hung the depression of a defeated army when victory has ceased to perch on its banner. Now, the Chief saw that even the banner was being taken away.'[90] By early 1964 old-guard Conservatives were raising questions about Diefenbaker's leadership and they even made a bid to unseat him from the party leadership during the annual convention in February 1964 at the Chateau Laurier.[91] Most of the delegates supported their leader, but there was significant opposition and there were problems with the Quebec caucus. Just as Pearson needed something to rally his party, so John Diefenbaker, too, needed an issue to rally his. There was one other reason why he was so unyielding during the flag debate: his almost pathological loathing of Mike Pearson. Diefenbaker's latest biographer, Denis Smith, has noted that Diefenbaker's 'old suspicion and jealousy of the urbane diplomat had deepened after Pearson had displaced him in power.'[92] Indeed, Diefenbaker's antipathy was so deep and so irrational that he actually believed, quite apart from losing the 1963 election, that Pearson had inappropriately taken the prime ministership away from him.[93]

But John Diefenbaker was also a great believer in the British Empire. In Michael Bliss's view, he was 'the last believer in the British Empire.'[94] For Diefenbaker, the Canadian Red Ensign was a symbol of Canada's association with the empire. In 1926 he had said: 'The men who wish to change our flag should be denounced by every good Canadian.'[95] In 1945 he told the House of Commons that in his opinion 'any flag which is determined upon for Canada must embody two ideas: one, Canada as a nation with a distinctive flag; the other, Canada within the empire.'[96] By 'distinctive,' Diefenbaker meant a flag that had to incorporate the Union Jack. He does not appear to have understood that for many French Canadians any British symbol was a symbol of anglophone oppression. For example, at a Conservative caucus meeting in August 1964, Théogène Ricard, a French Canadian loyal to Diefenbaker, spoke in support of a flag bearing a Red Ensign and a fleur-de-lis. Diefenbaker turned to another French-Canadian member and said: 'You see, that's what I mean. You go and sell it in your constituencies. It can be done.'[97] It couldn't be done, and in the end even Ricard broke with his leader and voted for the new flag.

On the other hand, it is a mistake to dismiss Diefenbaker as an old-style reactionary out of touch with his times. In hindsight, he might have *looked* like an anachronism, but Diefenbaker had his supporters.[98] Some polls suggested that only about 30 percent of English-speaking Canadians supported the Maple Leaf flag while 35 percent supported the Red Ensign (in Quebec some 69 percent supported the Maple Leaf flag).[99] Moreover, a March 1965 Gallup poll showed that, despite the flag fiasco, the Conservatives had slipped only slightly in the polls, from 32 percent to 29 percent; but so had the Liberals, from 47 percent to 45 percent. More important in the longer term was the increased press support for Diefenbaker. In 1963 only five newspapers supported the Conservatives. In the 1965 election twenty-one newspapers supported them, including the *Globe and Mail*.[100] Telling also were the results of that election. Under Diefenbaker's leadership the Conservatives fared better in 1965 (97 seats) than they had in 1963 (95 seats).[101] To be sure, the Conservatives did well in their traditional strongholds. In the Maritimes they took 10 of 12 seats in Nova Scotia, all 4 seats in Prince Edward Island and 4 of 10 seats in New Brunswick. This was to be expected. J. Murray Beck pointed out not long after the election that in Nova Scotia there was an 'Anglo-Saxon backlash, [owing to] the widespread suspicion that the government had been kow-towing to French Canada.' Beck contended that 'on this basis, many Nova Scotians explained the adoption of the new Canadian flag, a change not looked upon with enthusiasm in a province where British sentiment is still strong and where the red ensign and the Union Jack were considered to be good enough.'[102] The situation in the prairie provinces, where the Conservatives captured 42 out of 48 seats in 1965, is a bit harder to explain. But here too, according to Peter Newman, who travelled on Diefenbaker's campaign train, the Conservative leader appealed to notions of tradition: 'John Diefenbaker moves like a legend over the land' as 'the political poet who can evoke the glories of a simpler past when the Red River carts still creaked along the Battleford trail and buffalo bones littered the horizonless prairie.'[103] Diefenbaker did not often bring up the flag debate in the West; he did not have to. On the occasions he did bring it up it was to induce a vision of things to come. For example, in a speech he gave in Penticton, British Columbia, he said: 'Within two weeks after the new flag was declared officially for Canada, the Ottawa Liberal Association, the University Association of Canada came out for the abolition of the Queen ... Where will they go next? They didn't bring the flag question in front of the people in the last election. Where will they go?'[104]

The Liberals, however, having called the election in the hope of increasing their caucus to a workable majority, increased their representation, like the Conservatives, by only three seats to 131. John Matheson, one of the chief architects of the new flag, was nearly defeated in his own riding, his majority reduced from 2,214 in 1963 to 229 in 1965. Another Liberal member of the flag committee, Margaret Konantz, lost her seat in Winnipeg South. While both main parties' share of the vote actually fell between 1963 and 1965, the Liberals actually lost more than the Conservatives. The Liberal share went from 41.7 percent to 40.2 percent; the Conservative share declined from 32.8 percent to 32.4 percent. More telling is a comparison of the popular vote in Ontario, where the Conservatives took only 25 of the 85 seats, and 51 of the remaining 60 seats went to the Liberals. Yet 933,711 Ontarians voted Conservative and 1,196,349 voted Liberal.[105] Clearly there were large numbers of Canadians who wished to retain the British connection and all that it stood for. Nonetheless, Diefenbaker was that tradition's last defender in the leadership of mainstream Canadian politics, and in that sense the flag debate was the last gasp of empire in Canada. Never again would a Canadian politician go to the lengths that John Diefenbaker did in 1964 to defend symbols of the British connection. What historians are only beginning to explain is how and why the prestige and attractiveness of symbols connected to Britain and the empire deteriorated so rapidly in Canada in the late 1950s and early 1960s.

Notes

1 The New Democratic Party (NDP) held only seventeen seats in the House of Commons and so was not a major factor in the debate – though NDP leader Tommy Douglas was well respected. In this chapter I use the term 'flag debate' to include both the political debate and the choosing of the flag.

2 John Ross Matheson, *Canada's Flag: A Search for a Country* (Boston: G.K. Hall,1980), 69. John English, *The Worldly Years: The Life of Lester Pearson,* Vol. 2: *1949-1972* (Toronto: Alfred A. Knopf, 1992), 289, put the 'definitive' label on Matheson's book.

3 J.L. Granatstein, *Canada, 1957-1967: The Years of Uncertainty and Innovation* (Toronto: McClelland and Stewart, 1986), 205.

4 George Stanley, *The Story of Canada's Flag* (Toronto: Ryerson, 1965); Blair Fraser, *The Search for Identity: Canada, 1945-1967* (Toronto: Doubleday Canada, 1967), 234-47; and Alistair B. Fraser, 'A Canadian Flag for Canada,' *Revue d'études canadiennes/Journal of Canadian Studies* 25/4 (hiver/Winter 1990-91): 64-80. Other accounts include John Saywell, ed., *Canadian Annual Review for 1964* (Toronto: University of Toronto Press, 1965), 22-38 [hereafter *CAR*]; and Lester B. Pearson, *Mike: The Memoirs of the Right Honourable Lester B. Pearson,* Vol. 3 (Toronto: University of Toronto Press, 1975): 291-303. Also useful is English, *The Worldly Years,* 288-93. Diefenbaker's account is his *One Canada: Memoirs of the Right Honourable John G. Diefenbaker,* Vol. 3 (Toronto, Macmillan, 1977): 221-26. Richard J. Gwyn, *The Shape of Scandal: A Study of Government in Crisis* (Toronto: Clarke, Irwin, 1965), 45-71, contains some interesting insights by a leading journalist of the day as does Peter C. Newman, *The Distemper of Our Times* (Toronto: McClelland and Stewart, 1968), 254-64. One of the few critiques can be found in Patrick Nicholson, *Vision and Indecision* (Don Mills: Longmans Canada, 1968), 346-63.

5 Rick Archbold, *I Stand for Canada: The Story of the Maple Leaf Flag* (Toronto: Macfarlane Walter and Ross, 2002), 172.

6 Eric Hobsbawm, 'Introduction: Inventing Traditions,' in Eric Hobsbawm and Terence Ranger, eds., *The Invention of Tradition* (Cambridge: Cambridge University Press, 1983), 4 and 11. In Canada's case, the national flag arrived in early 1965. The national anthem, 'O Canada!' was approved by Parliament in 1967 but not adopted officially until 1980. As for the

national emblem, it is officially the maple leaf, though until the mid-nineteenth century it was the beaver.

7   *CAR*, 22-38.
8   See *Ottawa Citizen*, 2 May 1964, and *Globe and Mail* (Toronto), 4 May 1964.
9   *Toronto Daily Star*, 11 May 1964.
10 Pearson, *Mike*, Vol. 3: 292.
11 Newman, *Distemper of Our Times*, 256.
12 The text of the speech can be found in Lester B. Pearson, *Words and Occasions* (Toronto: University of Toronto Press, 1970), 228-32.
13 *Globe and Mail*, 18 May 1964.
14 See *Debates*, 19 May 1964, 3336-39.
15 *Debates*, 28 May 1964, 3675. The government also gave notice that it would, at the next sitting of Parliament, introduce a motion to recognize 'O Canada' as the national anthem and 'God Save the Queen' as the royal anthem. That was never acted upon.
16 *CAR*, 24.
17 *Debates*, 15 June 1964, 4289.
18 Ibid., 4293-97.
19 *CAR*, 25.
20 *Debates*, 15 June 1964, 4306-9 and 4317-26.
21 See ibid., 4326. Diefenbaker quoted a passage from the Gospel According to St. Luke referring to Christ's 40 days of temptation by the devil. Diefenbaker was fond of using Biblical passages in his speeches. Biblical symbolism carried considerable clout in early 1960s Canada.
22 John Saywell, ed., *Canadian Annual Review for 1962* (Toronto: University of Toronto Press, 1963), 34.
23 Except for a few passing references, no one appears to have given much thought to the Aboriginal peoples during the flag debate.
24 *Debates*, 15 June 1964, 4326-32.
25 Ibid., 4331.
26 Quoted in *CAR*, 27.
27 Quoted in Granatstein, *Canada, 1957-1967*, 203.
28 *CAR*, 25-27.
29 *Debates*, 27 August 1964, 7332-33. P.V. Noble was taking the same approach. See ibid., 12 August 1964, 6733 and 1 September 1964, 7559.
30 Bentley's testimony is reprinted in James Barros, *No Sense of Evil: The Espionage Case of E. Herbert Norman* (1986; New York: Ivy Books, 1987), 223-31. Most Canadian historians challenge Bentley's allegations regarding Pearson. See John English, *Shadow of Heaven: The Life of Lester Pearson*, Vol. 1: *1897-1948* (Toronto: Lester and Orpen Dennys, 1989), 303-10; and Reg Whitaker and Gary Marcuse, *Cold War Canada: The Making of a National Insecurity State, 1945-1957* (Toronto: University of Toronto Press, 1944), 422-24.
31 Diefenbaker Centre, Saskatoon, J.G. Diefenbaker papers, box 2, 008386-92. See also John English, *The Shadow of Heaven: The Life of Lester Pearson*, Vol. 1: *1897-1948* (Toronto: Lester and Orpen Dennys, 1989), 302-10. Earlier, another member of the House accused Pearson of giving in to the 'lunatic fringe.' See ibid., 26 June 1964, 4770.
32 The opposition used the tactic of debating amendment after amendment and then introducing sub-amendments.
33 See *CAR*, 29, and *Debates*, 8 September 1964, 7729-30.
34 Granatstein, *Canada, 1957-1967*, 203.
35 National Archives of Canada [NAC], Lester B. Pearson papers, MG26 K3, vol. 291, file 912.1 Policy, Matheson to Pearson, 2 September 1964.
36 Tom Kent, *A Public Purpose* (Montreal and Kingston: McGill-Queen's University Press, 1988), 341-42.
37 *Debates*, 8 September 1964, 7741.
38 Ibid., 7740.
39 *Debates*, 9 September 1964, 7791-93.
40 A description of the meeting is in Pearson, *Mike*, Vol. 3: 297.
41 *Edmonton Journal*, 11 September 1964. See also *Globe and Mail*, 11 September 1964.

42 Pearson, *Mike*, Vol. 3: 297-98.
43 The members of the committee were: Herman Batten (Liberal); Leo Cadieux (Liberal); Grant Deachman (Liberal); Jean Dube (Liberal); Hugh John Flemming (Conservative); Margaret Konantz (Liberal); Raymond Langlois (Créditiste); Marcel Lessard (Social Credit); Joseph Macaluso (Liberal); John Matheson (Liberal); Jay Waldo Monteith (Conservative); David Pugh (Conservative); Reynold Rapp (Conservative); Théogène Ricard (Conservative); and Reid Scott (NDP)
44 See Matheson, *Canada's Flag*, 133.
45 Granatstein, *Canada, 1957-1967*, 204.
46 *Ottawa Citizen*, 29 October 1964.
47 See Matheson, *Canada's Flag*, 134.
48 Pearson, *Mike*, Vol. 3: 299.
49 Diefenbaker, *One Canada*, Vol. 3: 225.
50 See Pearson, *Mike*, Vol. 3: 301.
51 Quoted in Gwyn, *The Shape of Scandal*, 12. Charles-Emile Groleau, an ex-army officer, was also named.
52 Gwyn, *The Shape of Scandal*, 67.
53 English, *The Worldly Years*, 355.
54 It is interesting to compare Pearson, *Mike*, Vol. 3: 192-98 to Diefenbaker, *One Canada*, Vol. 3: 267-73.
55 See Gwyn, *The Shape of Scandal*, 69.
56 *Debates*, 9 December 1964, 10965.
57 See the lead editorial in the *Globe and Mail*, 14 December 1964.
58 Quoted in Peter Stursberg, *Lester Pearson and the Dream of Unity* (Toronto: Doubleday, 1978), 170. See also Gwyn, *The Shape of Scandal*, 70.
59 Newman, *Distemper of Our Times*, 262.
60 *Debates*, 14 December 1964, 11136.
61 Ibid., 11138-39.
62 Nicholson, *Vision and Indecision*, 347.
63 See, for example, *Debates*, 15 June 1964, 4308, and Matheson, *Canada's Flag*, 65.
64 See J.W. Pickersgill and D.F. Forster, eds., *The Mackenzie King Record*, Vol. 3: *1945-1946* (Toronto: University of Toronto Press, 1970), 274-76.
65 See *Debates*, 16 June 1964, 4348-49.
66 See *Debates*, 21 February 1964, 92.
67 See Kent, *A Public Purpose*, 323-44; Denis Smith, *Gentle Patriot: A Political Biography of Walter Gordon* (Edmonton: Hurtig, 1973), 199; and Stursberg, *Lester Pearson and the Dream of Unity*, 155.
68 *Debates*, 15 June 1964, 4329.
69 *Debates*, 15 June 1964, 4348 and 16 June 1964, 4349. See also *CAR*, 25. To be fair, before the election Pearson said the national Medicare plan might have to be delayed until the economy improved. *Whig-Standard* (Kingston), 9 March 1963.
70 Thomas Van Dusen, *The Chief* (Toronto: McGraw-Hill, 1968), 55.
71 Newman, *Distemper of Our Times*, 255.
72 *CAR*, 15.
73 Quoted in Smith, *Gentle Patriot*, 201.
74 *CAR*, 6.
75 English, *The Worldly Years*, 288-89. See also Kent, *A Public Purpose*, 334.
76 Pearson, *Mike*, Vol. 2: 296.
77 Pearson, *Mike*, Vol. 3: 303.
78 Pearson, *Mike*, Vol. 3, 303. See also NAC, Pearson papers, vol. 291, file 912.1 Policy.
79 Pearson, *Mike*, Vol. 3, 304.
80 A.B. McKillop, ed., *Contexts of Canada's Past: Selected Essays of W.L. Morton* (Toronto: Macmillan, 1980), 255.
81 Gordon, *A Political Memoir*, 184.
82 Quoted in Stursberg, *Lester Pearson and the Dream of Unity*, 155.
83 Pearson, *Mike*, Vol. 3: 291.

84 Hobsbawm and Ranger, *The Invention of Tradition*, 13-14.
85 English, *The Worldly Years*, 291.
86 Claude Ryan, 'The Flag Dilemma,' *Le Devoir*, 15 August 1964, and *Canadian Forum* (September 1964): 128.
87 NAC, Pearson papers, vol. 3, file Canadian flag 1964-1965, Robertson memorandum for the Prime Minister, 27 April 1964.
88 Diefenbaker, *One Canada*, Vol. 3: 221-22.
89 Ibid., 222-23.
90 Van Dusen, *The Chief*, 61.
91 See Michael Bliss, *Right Honourable Men: The Descent of Canadian Politics from Macdonald to Mulroney* (Toronto: HarperCollins, 1994), 213. See also Pierre Sévigny, *This Game of Politics* (Toronto: McClelland and Stewart, 1965), 311-14.
92 Smith, *Rogue Tory: The Life and Legend of John G. Diefenbaker* (Toronto: MacFarlane, Walter and Ross, 1995), 522.
93 See Kent, *A Public Purpose*, 333.
94 Bliss, *Right Honourable Men*, 197.
95 Quoted in Newman, *Distemper of Our Times*, 254.
96 *Debates*, 13 November 1945, 2089.
97 See Matheson, *Canada's Flag*, 102.
98 See Diefenbaker Centre, Diefenbaker papers, 2nd leader of the opposition series, vols. 115-139, which contains letters of support.
99 Ryan, 'The Flag Dilemma.'
100 J. Murray Beck, *Pendulum of Power: Canada's Federal Elections* (Scarborough: Prentice-Hall, 1968), 376 and 381.
101 See Matheson, *Canada's Flag*, 5; and Bliss, *Right Honourable Men*, 213.
102 J. Murray Beck, 'The Electoral Behaviour of Nova Scotia in 1965,' in John C. Courtney, ed. *Voting in Canada* (Scarborough, Prentice-Hall, 1967), 95.
103 *Toronto Star*, 12 October 1965. The Conservatives won 10 of the 14 seats in Manitoba, all 17 seats in Saskatchewan and 15 of Alberta's 17 seats.
104 Quoted in Archbold, *I Stand For Canada*, 129-130.
105 Figures from CAR, 1965, 110.

15

'One Flag, One Throne, One Empire': The IODE, the Great Flag Debate, and the End of Empire

Lorraine Coops

> I do realize and appreciate that in any question of changing such an important symbol as a flag, it is difficult for human nature to give ready acceptance to something that is going to alter that which has been long honoured by so many.[1]
>
> – Lester B. Pearson

At the regular meeting of the Sir Robert Borden chapter of the Imperial Order Daughters of the Empire (IODE) in January 1965, Mrs. Porter, the chapter's world affairs convenor, displayed a replica of Canada's new Maple Leaf flag and read a poem that was reprinted in a local newspaper:

So many words have been spoken / So many heart strings bent,
So many persons have felt so much / That now all effort is spent.
But the traditions of the old / Must give way to the new –
A white flag with red / For the old one with blue
From picture and story / We just could not see
How such a plain pattern / Really Canadian could be
But I charge you this night / To be loyal and true
To the beautiful new flag / Now chosen for you,
By nineteen hundred and sixty-seven / May this emblem bright and clear
Fully justify the battle / On Parliament Hill last year[2]

The 'battle' Mrs. Porter alluded to was the 'Great Flag Debate' – a contest waged throughout 1964 on the floor of the Canadian House of Commons. On one side were the Liberals (recently elected to a minority government) who proposed adopting a distinctly Canadian flag with none of the British symbols that had adorned previous national banners. Leading the other side were the members of the Conservative party (ousted after six years in power) who felt the existing and widely recognized Canadian Red Ensign should receive parliamentary endorsement. These two sides represented the differing and sometimes ambivalent views of Canadians as the country continued to head away from an imperial outlook towards a more Commonwealth view of Canada's relationship with Britain.

The flag debate provides a basis from which to scrutinize Canada's growing sense of self-identity over the course of the twentieth century, a topic this chapter will examine from the perspective of an organization keenly interested in the outcome of the debate – the IODE.[3] Founded in 1900 by Margaret Polson Murray, who was inspired initially by a desire to provide field comforts to Canadian troops serving in the South African War, the IODE was, as its name implies, an exclusively female organization. It hoped, through women's patriotic service to their country, to strengthen the national bonds linking Canadians as well as to promote and secure Canada's ties with Great Britain and the empire – a vision that was in keeping with many English-speaking Canadians' sense of who they felt they were – or at least where they had come from. This feeling of connectedness with Great Britain and the empire was especially strong among the group's members: women drawn primarily from the Protestant middle and upper class.[4] However, while the IODE membership retained a strong affinity for Great Britain and the empire throughout much of the twentieth century, there was a gradual change in attitude, which coincided with a reassessment by women throughout the existing and former British colonies (as well as within Britain itself) as to their role and place in the empire. The changing Canadian perspective, especially that of Canadian women who either had, or envisioned, close ties to the British Empire, has been examined by Katie Pickles in her book on the IODE. Addressing the change in colonial identity, Pickles notes that over the course of the twentieth century 'Canada as a nation dramatically changed. From mimicking a British imperial centre in population, economics, politics and culture, Canada has moved beyond dominion status to become a globally powerful multicultural nation state, whose identity is centred in its geographical location.'[5] The activities of the IODE over this same period reflected this change, although its members were never eager to weaken – or worse, sever – ties with Canada's British past. Changes to the Canadian identity, Pickles asserts, 'are not about making a clean break from the colonial to the postcolonial, erasing past rules and dominance. Rather, change is about the perpetuation of British values and their adaptation to Canadian space. As representative of this change, the IODE has continued to argue for the importance of the tenets and institutions of British colonialism, [such as] the monarchy.'[6]

Although the IODE was ultimately unsuccessful in its efforts to maintain Canada's formal links with Britain, the privileged social position of its members did give them 'access to education boards, government and commerce,' which were important 'spaces of colonialism.'[7] Often working below the masculine colonial elite's radar, the IODE was able to pursue acceptable gendered tasks, such as offering school prizes and scholarships, in support of the organization's evolving view of Canada. While IODE school activities can readily be identified in a gendered way, scholars have recognized that simplistic definitions and distinctions of gender and empire are often insufficient to describe the colonial-imperial experience.[8] Margaret Strobel has specifically addressed the issue of women's place in the colonies, noting that while women's 'participation in the colonial process brought them benefits ... [such as] a higher standard of living,' colonial women still 'operated with institutions, cultural patterns, and personal relationships profoundly shaped by notions of male superiority ... which limited their options as women.' One option that was available was 'providing charity, a task typical of females in socially superior positions'[9] – an activity that, it might be argued, was updated by members of the IODE.

As Malia B. Formes points out, Strobel's critique 'is particularly important because [it attacks] the stereotype of the destructive European woman,' which has been so pervasive and influential in most social histories of colonialism.[10] To counteract this view, 'early feminist histories ... [devised] an opposing interpretation of [colonial women] as victims of a patriarchal imperial system constructed by European men to serve [colonial men's] own interests.' Of course, as Formes points out, women were not simply victims. Women interacted with the colonial process in a variety of ways that make it difficult to resolve 'the problem of complicity-versus-resistance in the history of imperialism.' Formes concluded in 1995 that no scholar had yet been able to provide the 'alternative approach to a colonial society ... that acknowledges its diversity, resists rigid categorizations, and conceives of power ... as a force which is dispersed throughout society and may be exercised, although unequally, by people of all statuses.'[11] Perhaps, but case studies and general critiques, at least taken together, do recognize the various and variable factors at work in colonial societies and the need to take these variables into account when writing history. Antoinette Burton reiterates Formes' theme, noting that scholars of Third-World history 'share ... a conviction (long characteristic of women's and feminist history) that the stories they excavate do not simply shed new light on national, imperial or "mainstream" accounts of modernity, but in fact require us to reconsider the inadequacy of those narratives which occlude women's participation, and even of those which acknowledge it but fail to recognise how thoroughly systems of gender, sexuality and "feminism" shaped national, colonial and anti-colonial cultures.'[12] The melding of imperialism and the person had a penetrating impact, to the point, Burton argues, that it 'has made it impossible to refute the claim that white British women's historical experience, in all its complexity and variation, was bound up culturally, economically and politically with imperial concerns and interests.'[13] Precisely how the empire impacted upon the various levels of British society is still in debate, as Burton admits when she notes that critics are right in suggesting that thus far scholars of British women have focused on the middle and upper classes, leaving some, 'like Inderpal Grewal, to call for more attention to the ways in which empire entered into and shaped the lives of ordinary women across class as well as differentially throughout the British Isles.'[14]

One group of women within Britain whose lives clearly were influenced by the empire were those women who played leading roles in the formation or initial direction of the British-based Victoria League – a group founded in 1901 and akin to the IODE. These women used their, admittedly briefer, overseas experiences to promote imperial aims and to forge their own, more active and involved place in British life – albeit for the most part within the 'safe' confines of women's separate sphere. As Eliza Riedi explains, the Victoria League was formed in part in response to efforts by colonial women's groups such as the IODE to assist in the South African War. The League was, according to Riedi, a 'predominantly female imperial propaganda society,' which aspired to be apolitical, while presenting 'itself in deliberately (but misleadingly) unassertive terms, aspiring in its constitution only to "support and assist" imperial projects,' and restricting 'its scope of action to include only "practical" work in areas that could be seen as a legitimate extension of the "domestic sphere" that Victorian ideology granted to women.' In Riedi's view, far from retiring, the Victoria League exhibited a 'fierce autonomy and [a] readiness to undertake large-scale projects, [as well as] ... innovation, both in developing new methods of propaganda and in enlarging women's imperial role. Like Antoinette Burton's 'imperial suffragists,' the League women were 'claiming their place in the Empire' and asserting the value of women's contribution to the imperial project.[15]

The League shared certain characteristics with the IODE, such as its membership profile, which was 'overwhelmingly upper and middle class.' Like the IODE, the Victoria League engaged in various educational and philanthropic activities, although Riedi asserts that the 'League specialized in turning areas of work acknowledged as "feminine" to imperial use, and in disguising the political nature of its objects under the cloak of gender.'[16] The League's aims were similar to those of other imperial and colonial organizations and included 'Anglicizing South Africa, keeping Canada British, strengthening the bonds between the self-governing dominions and the "mother country," and ensuring the maintenance of the "imperial race."'[17]

The differences between the IODE and other women's groups throughout the empire (and later the Commonwealth) illustrate that there is yet another way of looking at the interplay of gender and empire. For the IODE the promotion of imperial activities was important but not the driving principle behind the organization. Rather, IODE imperialism was always grounded in a strong sense of nationalism and citizenship, and the members' gender helped them attain their goals. Thus, as significant as the flag debate was for the IODE, it is important to recognize that flag-waving was not the only activity undertaken by the organization. From its inception at the turn of the twentieth century, the order was involved in a range of patriotic and philanthropic enterprises, most notably providing educational materials to public schools, awarding scholarships and bursaries, and promoting child-welfare issues, as well as assisting refugees and recent immigrants. As Canada increasingly separated itself from Britain over the course of the twentieth century, so too the IODE evolved, to the point that by the mid-1960s the order's activities increasingly reflected a Canadian, rather than a colonial, worldview. Members of the IODE, to varying degrees, were willing to embrace the concept of a Commonwealth of 'equal' nations. But recognition of Canada's British heritage remained an important tenet of IODE beliefs, even though by the 1960s the IODE was willing to accept the concept of 'two founding nations' and felt that the design of the Red Ensign should be modified to include both the Union Jack and the fleur-de-lis. This allegiance explains why abandoning first the Union Jack and later the Red Ensign proved so hard to do. By the early 1960s, although there was general acknowledgment among the IODE membership of the shift from empire to Commonwealth, the order could only go so far, and the choice for Canada's new flag took on almost mythical symbolism.

Historians cite various dates as marking the end of the British Empire. Within the context of Canadian history, events such as the meeting of Commonwealth leaders in London in 1926 and the passage of the Statute of Westminster in 1931 are clear indicators of a shift from the nineteenth-century empire to the twentieth-century Commonwealth. For the IODE, however, it can be argued that the empire (at least symbolically) ended on 15 February 1965, the day the Maple Leaf flag was flown for the first time on Parliament Hill. For years the IODE had lobbied to make the Canadian Red Ensign, with its combination of the British Union Jack and the Canadian Coat of Arms, the official flag of Canada – to reinforce and even entrench the British aspect of Canada's heritage within the Canadian psyche. With the raising of the Maple Leaf, the Red Ensign became relegated to the honoured past, and the IODE had little choice but to acknowledge, along with Mrs. Porter, that 'the traditions of the old / Must give way to the new.'

At the turn of the twentieth century, however, the group was not (so much) concerned that Canada's British heritage would be subsumed into a national consciousness, as that Canadians, through indifference, would permit that heritage to be frittered away. Preventing this erosion was a key motivation behind the founding of the IODE, and from the beginning the membership sought to promote patriotism and good citizenship through education and action. As part of this plan, the organization emphasized certain attitudes and activities: 'Loyalty to Canada and the Crown; Empire solidarity; knowledge of Imperial history; proper observance of historic and patriotic days; erection of commemorative monuments and plaques; [and] promotion of sound education.'[18]

British sympathies inspired IODE women to service during the First World War, at the end of which the order found itself in the enviable position of having doubled its membership and its number of chapters, garnering a significant presence across the entire country. Support for the empire and the desire to continue social, political, and economic ties with Great Britain remained integral parts of IODE philosophy and policy in the interwar era. A history of the national chapter, written in 1925, opened with a glowing tribute to imperialism; it defined the IODE as 'an organization of women in Canada, whose constructive humanitarianism has been a tremendous influence in enthusing and inspiring the women of Canada with the necessity of holding fast the glorious heritage we possess, and those British traditions so dear, so priceless and purchased by such heroic sacrifice.'[19] But the IODE was not content to bask in the never-setting imperial sun; generations of Canadians yet to come could benefit by exposure to British traditions. From its earliest years, the IODE chapters had been concerned with child welfare and education, and this interest expanded following the end of the First World War. Fundraising campaigns enabled the order to provide ongoing scholarships at university level, while members volunteered their time to ensure that young people and immigrants were educated in their duties and responsibilities as Canadian citizens. To this end, the order provided schools with what was deemed appropriate literature, pictures of the monarch and family, as well as flags – in the case of the latter, most often the Union Jack, which was the organization's official flag. The efforts of local chapters in schools across the country were duly noted at regular meetings, such as the February 1921 meeting of the Sir Robert Borden chapter in Wolfville, Nova Scotia. Commenting on the previous year's activities, the Education Committee reported that 'the spirit of patriotism in the school has received a fresh impetus in the presentation of flags from the Chapter – one for each department – with instructions from the teachers for daily salutations of the Flag by the pupils.'[20]

Canada Within the Empire, a 1939 IODE pamphlet intended to assist teachers 'throughout the Dominion, who are endeavouring to inculcate into the minds of children true patriotism and ideals dear to all Canadians,' stressed that true patriotism, as well as 'a conscious national unity,' could only be achieved if children possessed a 'knowledge of our common heritage within the Empire, the principles of justice and freedom [which would lead to] ... a basis for mutual understanding and co-operation.' Included in the pamphlet was a salute to the Union Jack: 'This is our flag. It is the Union Jack. Its colours are red, white and blue. Red is for courage, white is for purity, and blue is for truth. I will be brave; I will be pure; I will be true.' Students were to be provided with explanations on the significance and use of other flags connected with Canada, such as the White Ensign, the Canadian Blue Ensign, and the Canadian Red Ensign, but it is clear that in 1939, as far as the order was concerned, 'the Union Jack [was] the official flag of Canada, and should be the one flown in Canada.'[21]

While the IODE, at this time, had no problem deciding which flag should be the flag of Canada, at various points since Confederation, politicians, the military, as well as bureaucrats and civilians had suggested that Canada needed to possess a uniquely Canadian flag – something the Union Jack clearly was not. Prior to 1945 most Canadians would have identified either the Union Jack or the Red Ensign as *the* national flag of Canada. Technically, neither choice was correct. The Red Ensign was only officially to be flown by merchant vessels, while the Union Jack, 'although thought of as the national flag [of Britain] ... was adopted [only] informally by the public,' meaning that 'to this day, "the United Kingdom ... has no official flag."'[22] Despite its unofficial status, the Red Ensign had a long association with Canada and had been flown from the Parliament buildings from 1870 until 1902, when imperialists within the Canadian government were able to have it replaced with the Union Jack. Objections to this British emblem were raised in 1911 by Quebec's Henri Bourassa – the founder of the influential French-language newspaper, *Le Devoir* – but the Union Jack remained in place. Following the First World War, government leaders began without fanfare to find other symbols to represent official Canada. To this end in 1924 a 'new' Red Ensign, with the Canadian Coat of Arms, was unveiled and permitted for use on government buildings in foreign countries.[23]

The following year, in April 1925, the Department of Defence asked to be given a distinctive flag for the land forces. What started out as a simple request, however, became a hotly contested debate about what symbolized Canada within the empire. A committee appointed to 'consider and report upon a suitable design for a Canadian flag' might have quietly gone about its business within the context and confines of Canadian governmental bureaucracy and decided on a new flag, but members of the Toronto IODE as well as the Orange Order sent messages of protest. Under such unexpected pressure, in June 1925 Prime Minister King announced that the committee had been dissolved and no further action would be taken. Both the flag issue and Prime Minister King showed exceptional stamina, however, and twenty years later Order-in-Council PC 5888 was read to the House: 'That until such time as action is taken by Parliament for the formal adoption of a national flag ... the Red Ensign with the Coat of Arms of Canada in the fly (hereinafter referred to as "the Canadian Red Ensign") may be flown from buildings owned and operated by the federal government within and without Canada; [and] it shall be appropriate to fly the Canadian Red Ensign within and without Canada whenever place or occasion may make it desirable to fly a distinctive Canadian flag.'[24]

Once again, but more openly this time, the King government determined it 'expedient that Canada possess a distinctive national flag and that a joint committee of the Senate and the House of Commons be appointed to consider and report upon a suitable design for such a flag.'[25] By July 1946 the committee had held fourteen public sessions, considered over 2,000 flag designs, and received over 42,000 written submissions, in addition to listening to people who spoke directly to the committee members.[26] Among those organizations that presented briefs to the committee was the IODE.

Representatives of the order joined those who questioned the necessity of replacing the Union Jack with a distinctive Canadian flag. What made Canadians distinct, the IODE maintained, was their membership in the British Empire and all the 'privileges and blessings' this entailed. In a brief written by one of Canada's leading social reformers of the day, Charlotte Whitton, the national executive committee outlined why the order saw itself as a 'stake-holder' in any discussion of a distinctive Canadian flag:

> In times of peace and through two World Wars its members, for the past forty-five years, have sought to stimulate and give expression to the sentiment of patriotism which binds the women and children of the Empire around the throne and person of their Sovereign.
>
> The policy of the Order has been to promote among its members the study of the history of the Empire and of current Imperial questions; to promote unity between the motherland and the various parts of the Empire and Commonwealth; and to draw women's influence to the betterment of all things connected with the Empire. Through the study of the history and problems of the various provinces, the Order has aimed to promote a better understanding between them; and through its Educational programme, has sought to instil into the youth of Canada patriotism in its fullest sense.[27]

The order declared that the Union Jack was 'the flag of the entire British Sovereignty' and 'that any distinctive Canadian flag bear thereon always the replica of the Union Jack.'[28] In the end, Prime Minister King used the excuse that, as a unanimous decision regarding a flag design could not be reached, he did not have to accept the committee's recommendations.

So the debate over a new Canadian flag cooled down. The IODE came to the conclusion, however, that it was 'obvious from many sources that the subject of a distinctive Canadian flag will once again be brought before Parliament.' Moreover, since the 1945-46 deliberations of the flag committee had revealed that 'many elements in Canada are demanding a flag which will have no symbol of our British heritage,' the members of the national executive were in agreement 'that eventual acceptance of a distinctive flag for Canada was inevitable.' It was determined, therefore, that 'efforts must be concentrated on retaining the "one flag" of our motto, the flag of the Empire, within such a distinctive national flag.' To that end, a resolution was passed in November 1949 – on the eve of Remembrance Day – that outlined the order's plan of attack should the issue once again arise:

WHEREAS the Daughters of the Empire realize fully that the time has come when Canada, being a self governing Dominion, should have a distinctively Canadian flag, and WHEREAS the Federal Government has already taken steps by Order in Council which recognize the Red Ensign as a Canadian flag at home and abroad, BE IT resolved that the Order strongly urge the Federal Government to further implement its Order in Council by parliamentary action and proclaim the Red Ensign as the official flag of Canada.[29]

Inherent in the IODE's endorsement of the Red Ensign was the organization's initial recognition that the days of empire were coming to an end. Whereas in 1925 the order had been concerned that the Union Jack would no longer fly over Parliament as the flag of Canada, and in 1939 the educational publication *Canada Within the Empire* devoted several pages to extolling the virtues of the Union Jack, by 1949 the members, led by the national executive, were willing to support the retention of the Red Ensign as Canada's flag. This did not mean, however, that the Order was abandoning all of its own imperial trappings. As far as the National Chapter was concerned, 'The Union Jack is still and will always be the Standard of the Order ... Until such time as Parliament may designate a distinctive flag, the Chapters will follow the present policy when supplying flags to schools.'[30]

Furnishing the Union Jack to schools was one way the IODE provided subtle reminders about 'the flag issue' to a segment of the public in the years following the 1945-46 parliamentary deliberations; but the organization also pursued the political avenue, periodically refreshing the minds of elected officials about the need for British representation on the flag. Acting on resolutions passed at the national and local levels, letters were forwarded to members of Parliament as well as to editors of local newspapers. In 1953, for example, the Sir Robert Borden chapter began regular discussions of a new and 'distinctly Canadian' flag, passing the following resolution: 'Each member was requested to write to their Federal Member of Parliament, Mr. G. Nowlan, asking him to use all his pressure and power to see that the Union Jack be retained on the Flag, when such an issue arose in Parliament.'[31] In January 1954 the chapter endorsed a letter written to Nowlan by the chapter president (or regent). The flag was again the topic of the 2 March 1954 meeting, at which it was recorded that 'The Regent spoke concerning the Flag and expressed how strongly the Order felt about keeping the Union

Jack as part of a new Canadian flag – in fact, in keeping the Red Ensign as the Canadian Flag.'[32] Comments such as these indicate that while the Order was moving towards an acknowledgment of the geopolitical shift from empire alone to empire and Commonwealth, the IODE of the mid-1950s was, nonetheless, not yet ready to embrace or promote a postcolonial worldview.

Input into the flag debate – especially representations to committee members and elected officials – led to a blurring of some of the organization's founding principles. Officially – despite social, political and economic ties to a particular elite – the order was apolitical, and calls for direct political action were rarely promoted by the organization,[33] but there were exceptions. In the years after the Second World War, the IODE joined the chorus of those warning against the dangers of communism – a stance highlighted in the Spring 1952 issue of *Echoes* (the order's national magazine), where the national convenor of the anti-communism committee urged all members to 'join in the war against Communism [in] active defence of our free world.'[34] In the same issue, members were warned of another threat to Canada: the 'insidious and determined plan towards the gradual emergence of a republican state.' Evidence of this 'plot' seemed to be everywhere, and the order had been viewing 'with apprehension the attitude taken by members of the Canadian Government in the many and varied attempts to disassociate Canada from Great Britain.' The article noted that since 1946 the national chapter had sent 'many resolutions to the Dominion Government deprecating the desire to discard the Union Jack; the proposed change of "Dominion Day" to "Canada Day"; the singing of "O Canada" in place of "God Save the King"; [and] the substitution of "Canada Mail" for "Royal Mail."'[35] Given the nature and objectives of the organization in the early 1950s, it is not surprising that proposed changes to the flag, the anthem, and the renaming of Canada's national holiday roused members to action.

Although the order continued to maintain its official stance of non-involvement in matters political, many of its members clearly welcomed the election of a Conservative government in 1957. In the Autumn 1957 issue of *Echoes*, for example, there was what appeared to be a run-of-the-mill editorial urging members to exercise their right to vote in an election that was expected to be called within the coming months.[36] Although the editor maintained that 'in these words of comment there is no intention to extol or to condemn any shade of political opinion – other than Communism which we heartily condemn – or any party represented in Parliament,' implicit in her commentary is the importance of the vote as an instrument of change. 'It is a basic principle,' the editor reminded readers, 'that each member strive to be a good citizen and make her influence felt at all levels of government from the local community to the National Parliament.' The editor argued that 'a whole generation of young Canadians has grown up scarcely realizing that Dominion elections might easily mean a complete change of policy in both domestic and foreign affairs.'[37] One of the main reasons members of the order felt so favourably towards the Conservatives was because of the party's leader, John G. Diefenbaker, in whom the IODE found a champion and kindred spirit for things imperial, traditional, and British. Diefenbaker understood, they believed, the importance of maintaining strong ties to Britain and the symbols that signified this attachment.[38]

The IODE and other Conservative supporters received good news when the Conservative government was re-elected on 31 March 1958 with a massive 160-seat majority. But Diefenbaker decided to abide by the 1945 order-in-council permitting the flying of the Red Ensign on government buildings both inside and outside Canada and took no action regarding the creation of an official flag for Canada. Even an amicable invitation to tackle the issue by the then opposition leader, Lester Pearson, was not enough to stir Diefenbaker to action.[39] As Gregory Johnson notes elsewhere in this volume, 'the Conservatives were not opposed to the adoption of a national flag.' However, Diefenbaker and his supporters did object to a 'distinctive flag [that] had no connection whatever to "Canada's heritage and ... to the contribution made by the French and by the British to the building of this nation."'[40]

The Conservatives' inaction on the flag did not weaken IODE resolve, and as the country neared an expected 1962 election date the *Echoes* editor reminded members to exercise 'intelligent patriotism' when choosing among the major political parties during the next federal election.[41] Members were requested to pick up their pens as well as their ballots. At the national annual meeting of May 1961, held in Victoria, a resolution had been passed that echoed the national executive's 1949 'call to arms' in defence of the Red Ensign. The order was concerned as 'the federal government is being showered with thousands of letters urging a wide variety of design but very few who favour the Red Ensign take the trouble to write' and that given the upcoming Centennial in 1967, 'an early proclamation ... of the Red Ensign' as the official flag was crucial.[42]

The order simplified the writing process, providing a sample letter for members to send to their federal representatives. Mrs. R.D. Sullivan of Saint John, New Brunswick, copied the template word for word in her letter to her local member of Parliament, Thomas M. Bell. 'It seems imperative,' Mrs. Sullivan wrote, 'that Canada have a national flag before making preparation for the Centennial Celebration in 1967 and I strongly favour the Red Ensign as our National Flag,' since it was 'now recognized throughout the world as Canada's flag.'[43] Mrs. Sullivan received a reply from Bell a week later: he 'agree[d] that the Red Ensign should be recognized as our official flag' – an issue he would make 'every effort towards' – but cautioned his constituent that on the 'question of a national flag ... it seems impossible to obtain agreement.'[44]

The mid-summer letter-writing drive failed to generate the desired action, but a year later, less than three weeks prior to the federal election called for 18 June 1962, word came that the Royal Canadian Legion had not only passed a resolution at their annual meeting (held that year in Halifax) endorsing the Red Ensign as Canada's national flag, but had also decided to launch a campaign of its own to win government approval for the flag many veterans had marched under.[45] The news re-energized IODE members in the Maritimes. Acting on a recommendation passed a few weeks after the legion announcement, at the June meeting of the provincial executive committee the provincial secretary for New Brunswick sent the following message to the national secretary in Toronto: 'Be it recommended that a letter be written to the Dominion Command of the Royal Canadian Legion commending them on their stand to organize a publicity campaign directed at official government recognition of the Red Ensign as the Canadian flag, and pledging our support.'[46]

The federal election returned the Diefenbaker Conservatives to power, but left them with a weak minority. If the government had been hesitant to discuss the flag before, it was in no position (or likely mood) to take on such a sensitive issue now. Still, the membership of both the IODE and the Royal Canadian Legion continued to press for the flag of their choice. English-speaking Canadians were split on the issue, with some polls suggesting 'that only about 30 percent of English-speaking Canadians supported the Maple Leaf flag while 35 percent supported the Red Ensign.'[47] On occasion, proponents of the Red Ensign received additional support, such as when J. Bennett Macaulay of Sussex, New Brunswick, had his letter to the editor published in the 10 November 1962 edition of the Saint John *Telegraph Journal*. Using a style and content nearly identical to that appearing in IODE publications – a fact confirmed by the provincial president in a letter to the editor published a week and a half later[48] – Mr. Macaulay 'put forth that in our Canadian Red Ensign we have a remarkable flag that if understood and known, can be a unifying and cherished symbol for all Canadians.' In classic IODE fashion, the author then elucidated the various symbols in the flag's design, beginning 'firstly [with] the Canadian Coat of Arms' on down to 'the glorious cross of Christ.' Mr. Macaulay concluded with the by-now familiar 'caution that [the Red Ensign's] removal as Canada's national flag could only weaken the fibre, heritage and culture of Canada.'[49] The letter received resounding support not only from the provincial president, but also from 'E.S.,' whose own letter to the editor appeared the following Wednesday. Along with 'a very hearty thank-you to J. Bennett Macaulay,' the writer argued that 'It is an untruth' to say 'that Canada has no flag ... The women's organization, the IODE, I believe, accepts the Red Ensign and are for it as a group. I have always wished that they would take a stand on the matter and make themselves heard across Canada.'[50] IODE members reading this must have been both pleased and dismayed: pleased for E.S.'s unsolicited support for the Red Ensign, but dismayed that their decades-long efforts were not universally recognized.

Hopes that the Red Ensign might be entrenched as Canada's official flag received a severe setback when the not even year-old Conservative government lost the federal election of 9 April 1963. The Liberals were returned to power, and with them came party leader Lester Pearson's promise 'that Canada would have a national flag within two years of his election, in plenty of time for the 1967 centennial of Confederation.'[51] As Gregory Johnson suggests, Pearson's commitment may have been no more than an electioneering tactic.[52] Nonetheless, the IODE took the prime minister at his word, especially after he reiterated his promise in a letter to Mrs. I.M. Beattie: 'The Liberal Party in the last two electoral campaigns pledged that within two years of taking office a new Liberal Government would submit to Parliament a design for a distinctive National flag. This was one of the main points of the Party platform and as the Leader I was committed and glad to be committed by it. Since then, I have repeated on many instances in and out of Parliament that we intend to keep this commitment and that the flag design would be submitted to the representatives of the people for approval.'[53] The problem for supporters of the Red Ensign was that Pearson had already made it known that he considered neither the Union Jack nor the Red Ensign to be a suitable candidate.[54] As leader of the party in power, his status albeit achieved only with the support of the recently reconstituted New Democratic Party, Pearson seemed determined to act on his promise.

Undaunted, the IODE pressed on, distributing, shortly after the election, petition forms for members to complete and forward to the government 'regarding the Red Ensign.'[55] The summer of 1963 saw the national chapter forward to the prime minister a resolution 'unanimously adopted ... at the Annual Meeting in Victoria' urging 'the Government of Canada to retain the Red Ensign as the National Flag of Canada.'[56] Resolutions such as this were being sent, even as the national leaders made plans to hedge their bets regarding the Red Ensign. Deciding there was no point in throwing good money after bad, the national executive committee made the following recommendation, which was read at the 15 October 1963 meeting of the New Brunswick provincial executive:

> WHEREAS the question of a National flag has become a very sensitive controversial issue and thus should not be taken into the schools, and ... WHEREAS it would seem that the Canadian Parliament will make some decision in the near future in accordance with the election promise of the Prime Minister, and WHEREAS the high cost of printing folders about the Red Ensign, in colour and in quantity, might be wasted ... and WHEREAS it is felt that the Order may not be justified in pressing a political issue in the

schools, THEREFORE BE IT RECOMMENDED ... that no action be taken at the present time in designing a folder on the Red Ensign for use in I.O.D.E. adopted and assisted schools.[57]

Publicly, there was a different line, as the national chapter, in November 1963, intensified its efforts, stating that 'it was felt that the time had come to make the Order's policy for the retention of the Red Ensign known as widely as possible and to co-operate with other organizations who have the same policy, i.e., the Canadian Legion, Canadian Corps Association, Empire Clubs of Canada, Federated Women's Institutes, etc.' Fear was mounting, because, as IODE National President Pauline McGibbon emphasized, the 'Prime Minister has said repeatedly that Canada will have a new flag within two years ... [but perhaps] a flag without one reference to the founding Nations of this country.'[58]

McGibbon continued to target the Red Ensign as the goal, but her phrasing – the use of 'founding Nations' – highlighted a subtle shift that began to surface in IODE literature about this time. In the ongoing evolution of the order from an imperial to a Commonwealth outlook, there was now room to permit recognition of Canada's British *and* French heritage. The move away from an anglocentric outlook was seconded by the editor of *Echoes*, who, in the Winter 1963 issue (which featured a Red Ensign on the cover), envisioned Canadians as 'a people with diverse aims and objects united under one flag ... What better memorial to those early settlers than the shield on the Ensign? The Fleur de Lis, the Lily of France, was the emblem which the French settlers brought to Canada; The Couchant Lion, the emblem on the flag of William of Normandy, also came to us from France; the Red Lion Rampant was the emblem of Scottish Kings, and the Harp, equally ancient, is symbolic of Ireland. The Union Jack represents our link with the great Commonwealth of Nations.'[59] Naturally for its time, no reference was made to the First Nations peoples, whose traditional territories had provided the foundation upon which the 'fab four' had constructed Canada.

Recalling heritage in the order's magazine was an internal way to enthuse the membership. Outside help was also appreciated, and the provincial chapter in Fredericton received some welcome (and possibly unexpected) support in this vein from the city's mayor, who 'requested that letters go forward from the Fredericton Branch of the Royal Canadian Legion and the Provincial Chapter, I.O.D.E., asking the City Council to fly the Red Ensign from City Hall.'[60] Provincial President Mrs. Beattie wasted no time, forwarding, just two days later, a letter to Mayor Walker and the city council members informing them of the order's stance and adding that 'the Annual Meeting of the National Chapter ... will be held in Fredericton ... in May 1964. It would be most gratifying to all of the delegates to see the Canadian Red Ensign flying above the Council Chambers where the very first Chapter of our organization was formed on January 15, 1900.'[61] The city clerk replied within the week that the 'Council received a similar request from the Royal Canadian Legion and has directed that a Red Ensign be purchased and flown over City Hall.'[62]

The support of local elected officials was good news for the New Brunswick provincial chapter, providing the pro-Red Ensign side with backing that to the public appeared to be less partial than that given by organizations such as the IODE and the Royal Canadian Legion. The idea was picked up at the January meeting of the provincial executive. Believing in 'the greater influence that would be exercised through the signatures of business men,' the provincial executive passed a motion to 'have 2,300 form letters mimeographed to go forward to each Primary Chapter member. Each letter to be signed by a prominent business man in that community and forwarded ... to the local member [of Parliament] or to the Secretary of State in Ottawa.'[63] That the provincial chapter saw fit to make their request to businessmen – rather than, say, blue-collar workers – reflects the social stratum in which the members moved. IODE members from the Fredericton area represented the upper echelons of society, and would have felt as comfortable conversing with area businessmen as they had with the city's mayor. This alignment was evident when IODE delegates assembled for the 'Opening Ceremonies [of the 65th annual meeting] in the dignified and historic Legislative Assembly Chamber' in Fredericton in late May 1964. Among the dignitaries in attendance that evening were the Anglican Archdeacon of Fredericton, the province's lieutenant governor, a local member of Parliament, New Brunswick Premier Louis Robichaud, and, of course, Mayor Walker. The latter took the occasion to urge his audience to support the Red Ensign. It was 'unfortunate,' he stated, 'that a flag which has survived so much history has to be completely scrapped and that whatever Canadian flag ... is decided upon, it would seem that the Union Jack, with all its tradition and history, should have at least a small place on it.'[64] The mayor certainly favoured the Red Ensign, but his remarks indicate that he felt there was no hope of having it become Canada's national flag. All that he and other traditionalists could do was to lobby for inclusion on the new flag of some British symbol, most obviously the Union Jack.

The summer of 1964 witnessed the last great push by the IODE. Following the May national convention, 'a wire [was sent] to the Prime Minister, with copies to the leaders of the Opposition Parties, strongly urging the Prime Minister to hold a national plebiscite on whether the Canadian Red Ensign, or a flag of a new design, shall be the official flag of Canada.'[65] But no other initiative is mentioned regarding the flag in the New Brunswick provincial chapter minutes from mid-June to mid-December 1964, at which time Parliament approved the Maple Leaf design by a large margin. The IODE seems to have accepted the futility of further protest. Reaction by the

IODE to the passage of the Maple Leaf design by Parliament was uncharacteristically muted. A letter from the national secretary in Toronto to local chapter secretaries, sent less than one month after the Maple Leaf flag was first raised on Parliament Hill, contains, among other routine business, the following announcement under the heading 'Canadian Flag': 'As reported in the February letter, the National President, Mrs. D.W. McGibbon, represented the Order at the Inauguration of the Canadian Flag Ceremony in Ottawa on February 15th. Mrs. McGibbon reported that she considered it a great privilege to have been present on such an historic occasion.'[66] A 'great privilege,' perhaps, but McGibbon's presence also represented acknowledgment of the final defeat of the order's more than half-century effort to have either their first choice, the Union Jack, or their second preference, the Canadian Red Ensign, fly as Canada's flag. Similar subdued reaction was evident in Fredericton at the meeting of the provincial executive held a day after the flag-raising, where motions were carried 'that the Provincial Chapter purchase the National Flag of Canada,' and that the said 'National Flag' be displayed at chapter meetings. The words 'Maple Leaf' were not mentioned.[67]

The IODE did find some solace in that along with approval of the Maple Leaf the members of Parliament also gave their consent to allow the Union Jack to be flown on appropriate occasions in recognition of Canada's ties to Britain and the Commonwealth. More importantly for the IODE, the approval of a new flag presented a golden opportunity for the order to act upon the recommendations contained in a public-relations study commissioned by the national chapter in 1960. This study – based upon the results of a small-sample poll carried out by a Toronto advertising firm – determined that the order was 'fast approaching a vital crossroad in its long and proud history.' Public perceptions of the IODE were decidedly negative. The order's support of the Red Ensign was one reason behind this unpopular image, but equally important, as the report stated bluntly, was that 'because of [the order's] name and the circumstances of its origin at the time of the South African War, the I.O.D.E. is thought of by many Canadians as nothing more than a body of aggressively over-Anglicized women bent on denying Canada's nationhood and autonomy, and parading the British connection with unbecoming subservience.' Aside from its members, only 'a small section of the Canadian public, know that the I.O.D.E. is infinitely more than a purely patriotic organization ... [which over] the last year [1959] ... raised $1,055,327 – most of it for education, public service and philanthropies.' At best, the report continued, the public view was 'of a well-meaning association woefully out of touch with the realities of present-day Canadian thought and development.'[68]

The public-relations study presented a disturbing picture of an organization with a narrow ethnic base and a declining and ageing membership[69] which, despite a commendable tradition of community service, held views the general public considered outdated, and which made it difficult to entice young women to join the order. The report made a number of suggestions, including a name change (changing the words 'Imperial' and 'Empire') along with 'a nationally co-ordinated public relations and information program' aimed at introducing a revitalized and nationalistic IODE to the Canadian public. These were radical recommendations, however, and ones that would take many years to act upon. Discussions among the approximately 28,000 members representing nearly one thousand chapters across Canada had only reached the preliminary stage when the representatives arrived in Fredericton for the 64th Annual Meeting – just weeks before the last great push by the order to save the Red Ensign.[70] In her address to the assembled membership, National President Pauline McGibbon touched upon some of the issues raised by the public relations study, acknowledging, for example, that there were those who 'see us as an organization with an old-fashioned name and old-fashioned ideas.' McGibbon also admitted that 'perhaps we are to blame for not getting our story across to them and the public,' but countered the stereotyping of members, stating: 'Perhaps even more it is to be regretted that the average citizen does not realize that the Order is made up of outstanding women of all ages, representing many racial backgrounds. From the beginning the Order was composed of women of Anglo-Saxon, French and Jewish blood. Today, thanks to our new citizens who have joined the Order, the I.O.D.E. embraces within its membership the multiracial strains of Canada ... the I.O.D.E. sees Canada and Canadians from many points of view.'[71]

The national president's views of a diverse IODE held some measure of truth – the order had become more inclusive over the decades – but there was no denying that the words 'Imperial' and 'Empire' reminded Canadians of the past, not the present or the future. Remedying the IODE's image problems in mid-1964 – just half a year away from the parliamentary vote on a new and distinctive flag – would have to wait. The order had committed itself to the Red Ensign and required the support of all the members – something that discussing radical changes would not make easy. By 1965, however, some members of the IODE were willing to put forth (or impose) a revisionist agenda. Provincial and local chapters across Canada forwarded resolutions to the national executive with proposals ranging from replacing the Union Jack with the Maple Leaf as the order's standard through to dropping the use of a flag altogether. All the resolutions were couched in terms of patriotism, loyalty, nationalism, and tradition. It is telling, however, that many of the resolutions that called for change borrowed heavily from the results of the public relations survey. In the end, a 'Planning for the Future of the Order' committee was formed. At its annual meeting in April 1966, the national executive adopted a policy of compromise – at least for the interim. Both the Maple Leaf and the Union Jack would be present at official (and public) functions, and members of the order would again be asked to vote on the question: 'Do you wish to retain the initials I.O.D.E. if they represent a different name, such as I.O.D.E. Canada, I ... for Immigration and Citizenship; O ... for Opportunity to help those less fortunate; D ... for Dedication to the service of mankind and E ... for Education in all its phases?'[72] The membership, displaying the slow evolution in national perspective that had marked their involvement in the great flag debate, came to an agreement about the organization's name in 1972, when the order officially became simply the 'IODE,' with each letter no longer standing for anything.[73] For modern members, the transition from empire to a nation in the Commonwealth had been completed. Empire now belonged firmly to the past, and the Maple Leaf's omnipresence made this fact indisputable.

Notes

1 Provincial Archives of New Brunswick (PANB), MC200, provincial chapter, Imperial Order Daughters of the Empire (IODE), projects and service – citizenship, 84/9, MS 7/6, file: 'The Flag Controversy' (Flag Controversy), Lester B. Pearson to Mrs. I.M. Beattie, 29 May 1964.
2 Acadia University Archives, Dr. Esther Clark Wright Archives (ECWA), Acadia University, Sir Robert Borden chapter minute books (SRBC Minutes), [5] January 1965; *Acadian Recorder* (Wolfville), 14 January 1965.
3 This study uses primary sources from the New Brunswick provincial chapter and local chapters in Fredericton, New Brunswick, and Wolfville, Nova Scotia, as well as materials produced by the national chapter, based in Toronto.
4 For more on the origins and activities of the IODE see, for example, Lorraine Coops, '"Strength in Union": Patterns of Continuity and Change Within the Sir Robert Borden Chapter (IODE), 1915-1965,' *Atlantis* 20/1 (Fall-Winter 1995): 77-85; Catherine Gillian Pickles, 'Representing Twentieth Century Canadian Colonial Identity: The Imperial Order of the Daughters of the Empire' (PhD thesis, McGill University, 1996); Nancy Sheehan, 'Philosophy, Pedagogy, and Practice: The IODE and the Schools in Canada, 1900-1945,' *Historical Studies in Education* 2/2 (Fall 1990): 307-21; Sheehan, 'Tea Sippers or Crusaders? The IODE, 1900-1920' (paper presented at the Canadian Historical Association Conference, Hamilton, Ontario, 5-7 June 1987); Katie Pickles, *Female Imperialism and National Identity: Imperial Order Daughters of the Empire* (Manchester: Manchester University Press, 2002), 15.
5 Pickles, *Female Imperialism*, 3.
6 Ibid., 170.
7 Pickles, 'Representing Twentieth Century Canadian Colonial Identity,' 242.
8 See, for example, Margaret Strobel, *European Women and the Second British Empire* (Bloomington: Indiana University Press, 1991); and Catherine Hall, *White, Male, and Middle Class: Explorations in Feminism and History* (New York: Routledge, 1992), and 'Gender Politics and Imperial Politics: Rethinking the Histories of Empire,' in *Engendering History: Caribbean Women in Historical Perspective*, ed. Verene Shepherd, Bridget Brereton, and Barbara Bailey (London and Kingston: James Currey/Ian Randle, 1995).
9 Margaret Strobel, 'Gender and Race in the Nineteenth and Twentieth-Century British Empire,' in *Becoming Visible: Women in European History*, ed. Renate Bridenthal, Claudia Koonz, and Susan Stuard, 2nd ed. (Boston: Houghton Mifflin, 1987), 339.
10 Malia B. Formes, 'Beyond Complicity versus Resistance: Recent Work on Gender and European Imperialism,' *Journal of Social History* 28, 3 (Spring 1995): 631. Western women's involvement in the colonial enterprise has been characterized by a variety of sterotypes including the 'destructive woman.' These constructs are premised on concepts, for example, of British women delaying the 'progress' of the empire through their insistence on

accompanying their husbands to colonial postings and thus 'domesticating' imperialism, or as the standard-bearers of cultural imperialism imposed through Protestant missionary zeal or notions of British superiority. For discussions of constructs of colonial 'womanhood,' see, for example, Strobel, *European Women and the Second British Empire;* Kumari Jayawardena, *The White Woman's Other Burden: Western Women and South Asia during British Rule* (New York: Routledge, 1995); Margaret MacMillan, *Women of the Raj* (New York: Thames & Hudson, 1998); and Claire Midgley, *Gender and Imperialism* (New York: St. Martin's Press, 1995).

11 Ibid., 635.
12 Antoinette Burton, 'Some Trajectories of "Feminism" and "Imperialism,"' *Gender and History* 10, 3 (1998): 563.
13 Ibid., 560.
14 Ibid., citing Grewal, *Home and Harem: Nation, Gender, Empire and Cultures of Travel* (Durham, NC: Duke University Press, 1996).
15 Eliza Riedi, 'Women, Gender, and the Promotion of Empire: The Victoria League, 1901-1914,' *The Historical Journal* 45/3 (2002): 572-73.
16 Ibid., 577-78.
17 Ibid., 578.
18 Vera Eaton Longley, *A History of the Sir Robert Borden Chapter I.O.D.E.* (Wolfville: self-published, 1962), 2.
19 *The Imperial Order of the Daughters of the Empire: Twenty-fifth Anniversary History* (n.p.: n.p., 1925), 4.
20 ECWA, Acadia University, SRBC minutes, 7 February 1921.
21 *Canada Within the Empire* (Toronto: Imperial Order Daughters of the Empire, 1939), 5.
22 Alistair B. Fraser, 'A Canadian Flag for Canada,' *Revue d'études canadiennes/Journal of Canadian Studies* 25/4 (hiver/Winter 1990-91): 68. John Ross Matheson, the Liberal MP given the task of selecting a flag design, used similar words when explaining the Union Jack to the House. See House of Commons, *Debates*, 16 December 1964, 11, 251. For the technicalities of who should fly what flag and when, see Fraser, *The Flags of Canada*, <www.fraser.cc/FlagsCan>; Auguste Vachon, 'Choosing a National Flag,' *The Archivist* 17/1 (January-February 1990): 8-10; and Matheson, *Canada's Flag: A Search for a Country* (Boston: G.K. Hall, 1980).
23 The summary in this and the following paragraph are drawn from Fraser, 'A Canadian Flag for Canada,' and *The Flags of Canada*, Chapter 5.
24 Matheson, *Canada's Flag*, 40, and House of Commons, *Debates*, 1 October 1945, 593.
25 Motion moved in the House of Commons, 8 November 1945, as cited in Matheson, *Canada's Flag*, 41, and House of Commons, *Debates*, 8 November 1945, 1,932.
26 Matheson, *Canada's Flag*, 62.
27 PANB, flag controversy, 'Bases for a Brief to the Special Parliamentary Committee on the Flag,' enclosure with letter from Marjorie Smart, National Secretary, IODE, 17 January 1946.
28 Ibid.
29 ECWA, Acadia University, Sir Robert Borden (Wolfville) chapter papers, 10 November 1949.
30 Ibid.
31 See reference in ECWA, Acadia University, SRBC Minutes, [5] December 1961.
32 Ibid., March 1954.
33 For example, in the minute books of the Wolfville chapter from 1915 to 1965 only one mention is made concerning the exercising of the members' franchise. A letter from the provincial chapter in June 1957 stated that 'all members should exercise their franchise in the coming election and encourage others to do the same.' ECWA, Acadia University, SRBC Minutes, [4] June 1957.
34 For a discussion of the IODE's 'war on communism' see, for example, Pickles, *Female Imperialism*, Chapter 7, and *Echoes* 206 (Spring 1952): 13.
35 Mrs. B.B. Osler, 'Dominion – or Just a Sublime Joke?' *Echoes* 206 (Spring 1952): 43.
36 An election had just been held on 10 June 1957, but resulted in a shaky minority government with 112 Conservatives facing a combined opposition of 153 members. The *Echoes* editor felt it wise to inform her readership that 'to most observers this latter circumstance

indicates clearly that another Dominion election will be held in the not far distant future.' [Zoë Pauline Trotter], *Echoes* 228 (Autumn 1957): 3. An election was held on 31 March 1958.

37 [Trotter], 'Editorial,' *Echoes* 228 (Autumn 1957): 3.

38 In a campaign speech in Saskatchewan in 1926, Diefenbaker declared: 'I want to make Canada all Canadian and all British! The men who wish to change our flag should be denounced by every good Canadian.' Margaret Wente, ed., *'I Never Say Anything Provocative': Witticisms, Anecdotes and Reflections by Canada's Most Outspoken Politician – John G. Diefenbaker* (Toronto: P. Martin Associates, 1975), 79, 80. In November 1945 Diefenbaker told the House: 'In my opinion, sir, any flag which is determined upon for Canada must embody two ideas: one, Canada as a nation with a distinctive flag; the other, Canada within the Empire.' Matheson, *Canada's Flag*, 46.

39 Matheson, *Canada's Flag*, 65-67.

40 See Chapter 14 above. Johnson also notes that, too late perhaps, 'In the [September] 1962 speech from the throne Diefenbaker ... promised a federal-provincial conference to choose a national flag.'

41 [Zoë Pauline Trotter], 'Editorial,' *Echoes* 244 (Autumn 1961): 3.

42 Mrs. H.G. Chant, 'Report on the 61st Annual Meeting,' *Echoes* 244 (Autumn 1961): 46.

43 PANB, Flag Controversy, Mrs. R.D. Sullivan to Honourable Thomas Bell, 3 July 1961. The use of a 'form letter' was also suggested at the New Brunswick annual provincial meeting of 12 April 1961 'so that [members] might know the type of letter to write.' See under PANB, MC 200, M51 A15, 'Red Ensign,' minutes – provincial executive committee (NB executive minutes).

44 PANB, flag controversy, Thomas M. Bell to Mrs. R.D. Sullivan, 10 July 1961.

45 *Telegraph Journal* (Saint John), 7 June 1962.

46 PANB, flag controversy, Mrs. J.A. Mersereau to Mrs. H.G. Grant, 26 June 1962. Mrs. Mersereau received a reply several weeks later informing her that the national chapter had complied with her request: Mrs. F.C. [Helen] Woolley to Mrs. J.A. Mersereau, 10 July 1962.

47 Johnson, Chapter 14 above.

48 See PANB, flag controversy, Mrs I.M. Beattie, 'Letters to the Editor,' *Telegraph Journal*, 19 November 1962, in which she states: 'I might add, that the information contained in Mr. J. Bennett Macauley's [sic] letter last Saturday was also presented to our Provincial Annual Meeting in Fredericton last April in an article prepared by a member of the Order in the province.'

49 Letter to the editor from J. Bennett Macaulay, *Telegraph Journal*, 10 November 1962. Macaulay almost certainly had some tie to the IODE, though one this author is unaware of at present.

50 Letter to the editor from E.S., Newcastle, *Telegraph Journal*, 14 November 1962.

51 Fraser, *Flags of Canada*, Chapter 5 (webpage 16).

52 Johnson, Chapter 14 above.

53 PANB, flag controversy, Lester B. Pearson to Mrs. [I.M.] Beattie, 29 May 1964.

54 Pearson's reasons for rejecting the Red Ensign and the Union Jack are given in House of Commons, *Debates*, 15 June 1964, 4308-9, 4317-14.

55 PANB, flag controversy, Mrs. J.A. Mersereau to Mrs. J. William Murray, 17 April 1963.

56 PANB, flag controversy, from an apparent form letter mailed to provincial chapter presidents, under the heading 'Madam Regent,' signed by Mrs. D.W. [Pauline M.] McGibbon, 15 November 1963.

57 PANB, NB executive minutes, 15 October 1963.

58 McGibbon to 'Madam Regent,' 15 November 1963.

59 *Echoes* 253 (Winter 1963): 3.

60 PANB, NB executive minutes, 19 November 1963.

61 PANB, flag controversy, Mrs. I.M. Beattie to Mayor William T. Walker and members of the city council, 21 November 1963.

62 PANB, flag controversy, H.P. Gough to Mrs. I.M. Beattie, 27 November 1963. At the next executive meeting Mrs. Beattie reported that the legion had purchased the flag and had presented it to the city council. PANB, NB executive minutes, 21 January 1964.

63 PANB, NB executive minutes, 21 January 1964.

64 May G. Bray, '64th Annual Meeting in Fredericton,' *Echoes* 256 (Autumn 1964): 10-13. The mayor continued his personal crusade less than two weeks later at the June 1964 meeting of Canadian Federation of Mayors and Municipalities in Regina, where he sent a telegram to the prime minister appealing to him to 'DELAY DECISION ON FLAG.' Mayor Walker wrote to Mrs. Beattie about the telegram, adding that a motion respecting the flag was discussed heatedly at the meeting, but 'no action could be taken because the delegates had received no official authority prior to the meeting.' PANB, flag controversy, Wm. T. Walker to Mrs I.M. Beattie, 10 June 1964.

65 PANB, NB executive minutes, 16 June 1964.

66 PANB, flag controversy, Mrs. F.C. [Helen] Woolley to chapter secretaries, 5 March 1965.

67 PANB, NB executive minutes, 16 February 1965.

68 PANB, MC200, public relations, M84/242, 'A Public Relations Study of the I.O.D.E.'

69 IODE membership statistics are given in Pickles, *Female Imperialism*, 28-29, Table 1.1. IODE numbers held stable in the low- to mid-30,000 range until the early 1960s, but dropped at a faster rate beginning in the mid-1960s.

70 Membership numbers from ibid.; chapter statistics as reported in *Echoes* 244 (Autumn 1961): 47.

71 May G. Bray, '64th Annual Meeting in Fredericton,' 45.

72 PANB, flag controversy, national executive committee agenda, 6 April 1966.

73 See Pickles, 'Representing Twentieth Century Canadian Colonial Identity,' 233-34.

16
More Royal than Canadian? The Royal Canadian Navy's Search for Identity, 1910-68
Marc Milner

From the time of its inception in 1910 until its formal demise by Act of Parliament on 1 February 1968, the Royal Canadian Navy (RCN) suffered from an identity crisis. Outwardly the navy's problem was one of form and appearance: a shared British White Ensign, British uniforms and heritage, common ship types, and some shared personnel and accents. On the face of it, this was not a major problem at all. After all, Canada was a formal ward of the British Empire until 1931 and after that a member of the British Commonwealth. Even during the grim days of armed forces unification in the 1960s Canada had its share of 'Highland' and Royal regiments, formal scarlet uniforms, and British military forms in drill, custom, and ceremony. Yet few would have thought of the Canadian army as 'British' – least of all the army itself, which had participated in two world wars not only to fight its country's enemies, but also to demonstrate its uniqueness.

For many contemporaries, however – and modern historians – the RCN's problems went much deeper than flags, ceremonies, and uniforms. Indeed, through much of its fifty-eight-year history the RCN not only looked British, but as an institution it identified itself primarily as British: as part of the brotherhood of the sea and of the imperial navy tradition. In the early years of its life, when Canada too was demonstrably British and still comfortable with that image, the RCN's identity problem was not serious. However, as Canada came of age in the mid-twentieth century, the RCN failed to move with the times. It may well be that the RCN's failure to identify itself as 'Canadian,' rather than 'Royal,' led ultimately to its extinction in 1968. If this is true, then the problem of identity within the RCN over its fifty-eight-year lifespan is of more than passing academic interest.

The notion that failure to adapt leads to extinction is not a new one. And like the dinosaurs, or the ice-age megafauna that came after them, it is also true that there probably was not much that the RCN could do to avoid its ultimate fate. The intractable problems of attitude and personnel that seem to have sealed the RCN's doom in the two decades after 1945 had roots that were set deep into the institution during the first – very difficult – thirty-five years of its existence. The problem of identity that arose for the navy in its early history stemmed from two general factors: The RCN was too new and too small to establish its own identity, and the Royal Navy was too venerable and too big to avoid smothering the RCN in its embrace.

Sir Wilfrid Laurier, the prime minister who founded the RCN in 1910, understood the relationship between size and national identity well enough. His plan called for a fleet of five cruisers and six torpedo-boat destroyers: a tidy little squadron capable of effective patrolling off Canada's coasts. More importantly, such a fleet was large enough to require the establishment of training schools for both officers and ratings. Although clearly some advanced training would have to be done in imperial naval establishments and ships, the intent was to 'grow' Canadian officers for the new Canadian service. Laurier's plan was therefore for more than just a Canadian fleet; he wanted to build a Canadian service. To achieve that distinction he wanted francophones to be able to take the entrance exams in French and he wanted a distinct naval ensign for the new service. The 'impracticality' of a bilingual service killed plans for the entry of unilingual francophones. And although the governor general and Laurier's cabinet approved a distinct RCN ensign in the form of the traditional White Ensign with a green maple leaf centred on the cross of St. George, 'One fleet, one flag!' was the response from London. And so for the next fifty-five years the RCN sailed under British colours. The one concession to the new navy was the addition of 'Canadian' to the traditional prefix 'His Majesty's Ship.' 'The four letters look strange,' the Halifax *Herald* opined when HMCS *Niobe* arrived in October 1910, 'but we may get accustomed to the change.'[1]

In the end, the only enduring legacies of Laurier's naval scheme were the institution itself, the Royal Naval College of Canada, and the two aged cruisers *Niobe* and *Rainbow*, which were acquired for training purposes in 1910. They came with British officers and crews. When Sir Robert Borden's Conservatives won the 1911 election and committed themselves to sending money to help build the imperial fleet rather than invest in their own, the RCN atrophied. Classes continued at the RNCC, putting young Canadians through and into the RN for further training: *Niobe* rotted alongside the wharf at Halifax while *Rainbow* enjoyed a more active life policing the seal industry on the west coast. Most Canadians who joined the lower deck quickly deserted, while the British ratings on loan pined for repatriation.

The First World War demonstrated the need for a Canadian navy. Although the imperial fleet was there in 1914 when the initial threat from enemy cruisers was greatest, when the U-boats arrived in 1917 and 1918, the Canadian government could not get even timely intelligence out of the Admiralty. The Americans sent some modest assistance, but the U-boat crisis made a naval convert out of Sir Robert Borden. By 1918-19 Borden was planning a substantial fleet, and hoped that the Jellicoe Commission would give him the right model. But in the end Borden's navy came to nought as well. The disarmament conference in Washington in 1921-22 rather eliminated the need for maintenance of large naval forces, while postwar recession and a change in government did the rest. Mackenzie King, never enamoured of the 'militaristic fashions of European states,' carved the navy budget to the bone. Most of the fleet was cast off, the RNCC and ratings' entry school were closed, and the institution put on life support. Through much of the 1920s it was down to two destroyers and a couple of armed trawlers. And at the height of the Great Depression in 1933 the general staff proposed to the government that the navy be abandoned altogether. Modest expansion followed in the late 1930s, when under Mackenzie King's guidance the RCN expanded to six modern destroyers – on the cusp of being a national service, but also on the cusp of another great war.

As Bill Glover has argued, such a tiny fleet was hardly the stuff of an independent national service.[2] It was just too small to maintain the training and educational infrastructure needed to give the RCN a definite Canadian flavour. Even getting Canadians to join was a major problem. Throughout the 1920s some 75 percent of RCN personnel were on loan from Britain. In the 1930s that figure was reversed, but one suspects that naturalization to Canadian citizenship had much to do with it.[3] Moreover, the navy operated from those quintessentially British bastions of Halifax and Victoria, and most of the officers – even those from the Province of Quebec – were Anglicans – the official naval religion, if there was one.[4] Annual fleet exercises were held alongside the RN, and a typical officer's career path led him through a rotation of Canadian and imperial postings. Canada may have become a fully independent nation in 1931, but the navy was wholly tied to the 'one flag, one fleet' concept. Not surprisingly, such an insecure service could only find legitimacy through its association with the RN.

This British connection went deep. In the absence of a Canadian naval college, newly enlisted RCN officer candidates, typically eighteen years old, were sent overseas to be trained in RN establishments, only returning to the RCN after five years. 'In other words,' as Glover observed, 'what is widely recognized as the most important formative period of a person's life was spent in the bosom of the RN.' Moreover, as Glover asserts, 'Trained within the imperial navy environment, for the most part politically unaware, and unable to think for themselves, as officers in a Canadian navy they got off to a poor start.'[5] Thus was the senior leadership cadre of the post-1945 navy, and indeed the navy's whole conception of itself, formed. Given the tiny size of the RCN it's not clear how it could have been otherwise.

It is generally accepted that two naval traditions emerged in Canada from the Second World War and that the Battle of the Atlantic from 1939 to 1945 was the formative national naval experience. In time, the complex experience and legacy of that war shaped the navy as an institution and brought it and the nation closer together. However, the path to that reconciliation was not smooth, and its hazards and challenges proved to be the RCN's undoing.

During the Second World War two Canadian navies were built, and they fought, side by side, for rather different objectives. The professional RCN used the war as an opportunity to advance its long-husbanded plans for a proper fleet of real warships – ultimately aircraft carriers and cruisers, supported by a large flotilla of fleet-class destroyers.[6] Serious and ambitious planning in that direction started in November 1940 and was sustained with but one short interval throughout the war. Even the Admiralty understood that the RCN was using the war to elevate itself from obscurity, and it aided and abetted the Canadians as it could. Indeed, the final securing of both cruisers and aircraft carriers was done through RN-RCN collusion, using the British government to pressure Mackenzie King to do more by taking over large warships that the British could not man.

Mackenzie King was aware of the games the RCN was playing, and worked through 1944 and 1945 to trim its ambition. Nor was everyone in the navy's senior leadership enamoured with things British. Admiral Percy Nelles' replacement as Chief of the Naval Staff (CNS) at the end of 1943 was Vice Admiral G.C. Jones, who, along with a small faction of naval staff officers, had become stridently anti-British by late in the war. They had grown utterly frustrated with trying to deal with the Admiralty on technical matters, and bitter about the way the RCN had been 'used' in the Atlantic war by the RN. For example, while the RCN drove its fleet hard in 1942 without much call for refit and training, the British found the time to modernize and train their own vessels. It was under Jones that the RCN abandoned its reliance on the RN's *King's Regulations and Admiralty Instructions* as the guidelines for service management and adopted the new *King's Regulations for the Canadian Navy*. And both Jones and his immediate successor, Rear Admiral H.E. Reid, sought to move the RCN into the United States Navy camp late in the war and during the first few postwar years. They succeeded in shifting communications procedures and some key equipment systems to US Navy (USN) norms. In addition, the naval air service sought, ultimately successfully, to bring RCN aviation into line with that of the USN in equipment and procedures. However, the Jones camp was soon replaced by a very pro-British generation of senior officers – most of whom had served at sea in or alongside RN ships during the war.[7]

In the meantime, the small-ship convoy-escort war went on, using auxiliary warships hastily built for war service, manned by 'Hostilities Only' reserve personnel, and operated and commanded by retired naval officers recalled to active service. Once this 'Sheep Dog Navy' was up and running, regular-force RCN personnel – always a very small cadre – concentrated on their normal routine of big-ship time, professional courses, and service in the new, larger ships acquired as the basis of the postwar navy. Personnel in the Sheep Dog Navy preferred to keep their distance from regular RCN and RN bases and officers, and prided themselves on a rough-and-ready seamanship and professionalism that got the job done with a minimum of fuss. Senior British officers commented often on the unruliness and occasionally unkempt appearance of Canadian sailors and ships, but the reservists observed that they were there to help win the war, not chart a career path.

The rejection of the reservist's war by the professional RCN was particularly pronounced after 1943,[8] in part because the new, proper warships began to appear in service, and because the regular-force cadre of the RCN remained very small. In December 1944, when the total strength of the RCN was 92,931 (3,000 lower than its wartime peak), only 1,026 officers and 3,296 ratings were regular force. The balance – some 88,500 – were reservists.[9] So the Sheep Dog Navy became very much identified as the nation's navy. At its peak strength in late 1944, the Canadian Navy was as large as the Royal Navy of 1939, and the RCN ended the war as the third-largest navy in the world (behind the USN and the RN) in terms of overall numbers of ships and personnel. During the war it undertook myriad tasks, but by far the most important – and the one that captured public imagination at home and attention abroad – was the defence of North Atlantic convoys. At its height in 1944 the RCN provided close escort for the main Atlantic trade convoys from New York to Britain, and some 40 percent of the anti-submarine warfare (ASW) vessels in UK waters. By the summer of 1944 the Admiralty was thinking about withdrawing virtually all its ships in the Atlantic and sending them to the Far East, leaving the RCN to run the show. This was the achievement and legacy of the Sheep Dog Navy: this was Canada's formative national naval experience.

In the post-1945 period the national naval experience and the RCN's own ambitions clashed and combined. The government was prepared to let the RCN keep most of its wartime acquisitions, including one aircraft carrier and several squadrons of aircraft, but the long-term commitment of the government to such a navy was doubtful at best. Clearly, as Borden had discovered by 1918, so Mackenzie King realized by 1945 that Canada needed some kind of proper navy. The essential difference between 1918 and 1945 is that in the Second World War Canada had an enviable national naval experience: a kind of 'people's navy,' which had done great and memorable things (not unlike the Canadian Corps in the First World War). Many Canadians saw little of the professional RCN in this. In fact, even in 1945 MPs were complaining in the House of Commons that the professional service was still characterized by 'slavish conformity to the traditions of the Royal

Navy.' As one MP observed in late October, 'I think we have reached the time when we must realize that Nelson is dead.' Even Brooke Claxton, minister of national defence, recalled that in the immediate postwar period 'the senior officers of the Navy were way out of line not only with Canadian sentiment, but with the feeling of junior officers, petty officers and ratings of *our new* Navy.'[10]

The RCN met the postwar challenge initially by buying into the national naval tradition exemplified by the Sheep Dog Navy. During 1946-47 the RCN shifted its fleet-planning focus from carrier-based strike forces to a large, modern escort and anti-submarine navy. In doing so they did not wholly adopt the Sheep Dog legacy. Instead, the navy identified itself primarily with the offensive anti-submarine warfare forces of the late-war period, the hunter-killer forces, rather than the close-escort role. This was a vital step in defining a Canadian role and fleet structure for the Canadian navy.[11] The Cold War helped this process by thrusting Canada back into an alliance virtually identical to that which had fought the war, and therefore back into a similar naval function. These were concepts that the government would accept, even to the point of maintaining the aircraft carrier in a new anti-submarine and fleet air-defence role. Only the cruisers got lost in the shuffle, and they were replaced by a large new fleet of St. Laurent Class destroyer escorts: distinctively Canadian vessels.

But building a new kind of fleet did not mean a sea change in attitudes. The clash came when the professional RCN tried to reassert its ties with the imperial navy, and when British-trained officers tried to operate postwar ships – crewed in large part by veterans of the Sheep Dog Navy who stayed on after the end of hostilities – like British ships of a bygone era. The result was a series of mutinies in 1948, when rather pompous and martinet-like officers alienated portions of three ships' companies. All three mutinies were simple refusals to respond to calls to work, and lock-downs of messes. All three were resolved without incident. But they led to a commission of enquiry, under the direction of Rear Admiral R. Mainguy, which reported in October 1949. By then Brooke Claxton, the minister of national defence, had already had several run-ins with the senior naval staff over trying to get the 'Canadian' back into the Royal Canadian Navy. When Rear Admiral Harold T. Grant became chief of the naval staff in September 1947 he sought to check the navy's drift into the clutches of the USN and bring it back into the fold of the imperial fleet. Grant soon re-established the practice of sending all RCN midshipmen to the RN for their final training, ordered the removal of all 'Canada' flashes on uniforms, ordered all flag officers to remove buttons that bore the word 'Canada,' and struck all maple leaves from the funnels of the fleet.

Not surprisingly, Grant's testimony before the Mainguy Commission into the mutinies of 1949 reflected this sentiment. Wearing 'Canada' flashes on the shoulder, 'looks like hell on any officer,' Grant confided, 'I refuse to wear it consistently myself ... I think it ruins the uniform.' Having already been ordered by the minister of national defence to reinstate maple leaves on ships' funnels, the chief of naval staff was not prepared to go any further: 'If they do not like it and still want to put "Canada" on we will take the maple leaf off and put "Canada" on the seat of their pants.' Grant went on to add that 'I think Canada makes enough damn noise in this world without doing anything about it' – which seems to have been the basic thrust of his displeasure over the trappings of identity.[12] Not surprisingly, Grant was 'furious' over the report of the Mainguy Commission.[13] Its essential finding was that the culture of the regular navy was out of sync with that of the ordinary citizens – and veterans of the Sheep Dog Navy – who now filled the messdecks. 'An opinion is widely held amongst many ratings and some officers that the 'Nelson Tradition' is overdone,' the final report observed, 'and that there is still too great an attempt to make the Canadian Navy a pallid imitation of the Royal Navy.'[14] Grant blamed the 'drunkenness and lack of discipline' among the many re-enlisted reservists for the problems. They, he said, had 'undermined the entire Navy.'[15]

There was an element of truth in Grant's position. The RCN's basic problem in 1948-49 was rapid expansion and weak leadership, not slavish adherence to Nelsonian traditions. But the postwar problem also spoke of a clash of cultures between the more casual North American attitudes of the general Canadian population and the more rigid 'pusser' ('government-issue' in naval slang) pre-war traditions of the RCN's officer corps. Grant's testimony to the Mainguy Commission was proof of the problem. As the Mainguy Commission observed, 'Many of the men examined said in varying ways that they felt they were cogs in a machine, whereas they would have liked to have been, in however humble a capacity, partners in a common enterprise.'[16] As a concession, the Naval Board authorized 'Canada' flashes for the 'cogs' of the lower deck on 4 January 1950 – Claxton had to intervene to extend the order to officers as well, including the chief of the naval staff, on 20 January. In October 1950 the navy also introduced 'Battle of the Atlantic Sunday' as its official 'feast day.' The initial date chosen seems to have had more to do with the customary celebration of Trafalgar Day than with any date particularly significant in the Battle of the Atlantic. Therefore, in 1951 the special day was moved to the first Sunday in May to commemorate the victory over the U-boats in 1943. This was an important beginning of national and distinct consciousness. Other issues, such as messing arrangements, pay, allowances, leave, dress regulations, and grievance procedures raised by the Mainguy Commission were also addressed.

But just how far the old navy was prepared to go remains a moot point. A decade later William Pugsley observed that 'the "artificial distance" [between officers and men] mentioned in the Mainguy Report still exists today' – and this was after Mainguy himself had succeeded Grant as CNS (1951-56). Pugsley conceded, however, that although the artificial distance remained, the barrier between messdeck and wardroom was porous, with something like half of the RCN's officers having come up from the lower deck. This was bound to have a 'Canadianizing' effect on the navy. And although until the late 1950s junior-officer training was still finished with the RN, these young men seem to have had no problem with national identity. Indeed, the enormous Cold War expansion of the navy, from an interim-force personnel strength of barely 6,000 to more than 20,000 by 1960, took it to its largest-ever strength in peacetime, and it drew thousands of Canadians into short- and long-term associations with the service. Nothing like that had ever happened before. It is arguable, therefore, that the RCN was going through a de facto Canadianization in the 1950s – whether it liked it or not.

But it is not clear that the culture and the senior cadre of the RCN were moving as fast as the country itself in shedding their Britishness. The officers who were needed to support the expansion of the navy came not only from the Canadians of the lower deck, but many – including key senior staff officers – came directly from the RN and the British merchant service. They, and the British-trained and educated RCN senior-officer cadre, helped maintain the patina of the imperial fleet. Charles Westropp, one of many young officers recruited from the British merchant service in the 1950s, was immediately struck by how 'British' the RCN was, especially when compared to the RN personnel with whom he had trained. Moreover, by the late 1950s many of the key senior posts in Ottawa were held by RN officers who had transferred to the RCN after the war, while most among the old navy had a 'mid-Atlantic' accent that seemed affected and foreign to the average Canadian. Arguably none of this would have mattered had the RCN been willing to see itself solely as an instrument of the Canadian government, had it made a concerted effort to move with the country in its social and intellectual development, and had it been able to keep its internal problems quiet – and, it might be added, had the navy of the early 1960s been in the hands of better-skilled and more politically astute officers. It failed on all counts.

It seems that the RCN of the early Cold War had a demonstrable propensity to see itself primarily as part of the international brotherhood of the sea – if perhaps not distinctly British. Two incidents are suggestive here. In 1952 the carrier *Magnificent* was training with the RN on NATO exercises in the Mediterranean when a coup in Egypt overthrew King Farouk. *Magnificent* happened to be lying in Istanbul roads, along with the British fleet, when orders were received for 'all British ships' to proceed to Malta. Tension had already been running high over the Suez Canal and the British were planning military action. Canada's position in all this was markedly different from Britain's, and Canadian diplomats in Turkey were keen not to see *Magnificent* steam off with the rest of the British fleet. Captain Ken Dyer, her commanding officer, was clearer in his duty, and a compromise was reached whereby the British ships departed several hours ahead of *Magnificent* – which in turn was followed by a number of USN warships. The carrier may well have been serving under British operational command at the time, and therefore obliged to respond to such orders. But the Suez business was not a NATO problem, it was a British one, and Canadian diplomats were not pleased with Dyer's decision to sail.[17]

Dyer was involved in the more serious and more familiar case of 'independent' naval action during the Cuban Missile Crisis of October 1962. As flag officer, Atlantic coast, Dyer sailed the fleet and cooperated with the USN in naval operations during the crisis while the Diefenbaker government in Ottawa opted for a policy of inaction. The RCN prided itself for years after for 'going to war' while the federal government dithered, but Dyer played a dangerous game. Everything he did was entirely within the letter of the law of both his command responsibilities and existing international defence agreements, but the spirit of the RCN's action was completely beyond what the government was prepared to accept. Diefenbaker's government, itself in a precarious state, took no action against the RCN. However, Pearson's newly elected Liberals did, starting in 1963. And it is hard to shake the echo of Charles Lynch's comment, reported in *Time* magazine in August 1964, that one of the key objectives of the Liberals' policy of unifying the armed forces was 'getting the Navy.'[18]

While historians still have not tackled just why Pearson's Liberals might have had such an animus against the RCN, the lingering problem of identity clearly played a role, and perhaps the key one. In April 1963 Lester Pearson's Liberals came to power promising 'sixty days of decision' on domestic, economic, and defence issues. Faced with a rising population and pressure for increased social spending, and a Quiet Revolution in Quebec, Pearson's Liberals pursued a distinctly Canada-first policy. Social change, full integration of French Canada into the Confederation, and a new flag were high on the agenda. So, too, was the financial crunch in defence, and its now complex and rather muddled command structure. Finally, as Canada intervened increasingly in support of UN peacekeeping missions, there was some urgency in the need to differentiate Canadian forces from those of Britain, the old colonial power.

Just what the new minister of national defence, Paul Hellyer, thought of the navy prior to assuming his portfolio remains unclear. However, the RCN's problems of identity were in the news in the late summer of 1963 when Commodore James Plomer, recently retired, unburdened himself publicly about the problems of the service. His basic complaint was that the RCN was run by an old-boys' club of prewar RN-trained officers who looked after each other. Plomer charged that they had, to a man, failed to act on either the spirit or the letter of the *Mainguy Report*. The officers responsible for provoking the mutinies had all been promoted, most notoriously Rear Admiral Jeffrey Brock, who was now flag officer, Atlantic coast. This 'uniformed Tammany Hall' had virtually come to see the RCN 'as their own private property.' Worse still, perhaps, as the navy had expanded through the 1950s these officers had clung tenaciously to their British roots. '[T]his childish obsession with the pomp of a bygone age is far stronger in the RCN,' Plomer charged, 'than in any other modern navy.' As evidence of all this Plomer cited his recent experience serving on the Naval Board, which during the Cuban Missile Crisis had devoted most of its effort to a new book on ceremony and summer uniforms for WRENs.[19]

Plomer's charges were later effectively dealt with by the navy, but not before Hellyer deemed it his duty 'to find out first hand if the situation was as bad as alleged.'[20] It was the RCN's great misfortune that the first place Hellyer visited was the east coast, and the command of Rear Admiral Brock, a martinet who had cultivated the worst affectations of an RN officer. Brock relished the pomp and circumstance of an admiral's command. Just about everything he did to impress his new minister backfired, from the traditional mess dinners with polished silver on Irish linen and squads of properly attired stewards, to the thoroughness with which Hellyer's bed was turned down and his pyjamas laid out. As Hellyer recounted in his memoirs, 'Old World hospitality was only made possible by treating ordinary seamen as lackeys ... Such practices seemed an abuse of indentured labour reminiscent of the dark ages ... by the time I returned to Ottawa I knew I had my work cut out for me. The navy was going to need a lot of modernization to make it contemporary.'[21]

In the battle over unification that followed, Hellyer's toughest opposition came from the RCN, much of it public and openly hostile. The last chief of the naval staff, Admiral Herbert S. Rayner, opposed Hellyer's unification plans internally and was 'prematurely retired' at the end of July 1964. Hellyer told Brock on 5 August that he, too, would be 'retiring' early – but gave him until November to get things sorted out in Halifax and find a successor. British-born Commodore Fraser Harris, the Assistant CNS (Air and Warfare), went before he was pushed, resigning on 19 August still some eight years before his retirement was due. Brock arranged for Rear Admiral Bill Landymore to replace him in Halifax. Landymore was a gruff, opinionated, direct sailor, with none of Brock's pretence and none of his British affectation. He proved to be Hellyer's nemesis in the increasingly bitter and very public battle over unification.[22]

While Landymore settled into his job the first solid evidence of the future manifested itself. On 15 February 1965 the RCN replaced its White Ensigns with the new Maple Leaf flag. For most naval personnel there was a real sense of loss, but it was tempered by 'a new obligation happily undertaken.' After all, fifty-five years earlier Laurier had tried to secure a distinctive ensign for the navy, and it had taken another Liberal government to make it happen. But a new flag was the easy part. As Hellyer's scheme of unification became clearer, so too did the depth and bitterness of naval opposition. Everyone except Hellyer thought that the whole thing would stop short of full integration, at least until June 1965 when Hellyer announced his intention to introduce a single uniform and rank structure for the army, navy, and air force alike (the ranks used being those of the army) by 1 July 1967 – the hundredth anniversary of Confederation. Hellyer had consistently promised that the essential elements of tradition would not be tampered with, but now it was clear that naval ranks and uniforms would be forfeit to his scheme. This exploded in the navy like a bomb, and Landymore now advised his personnel to debate and critique policy publicly. In this he was aided and abetted by an old-boys' network, led by Brock, which pounded the government relentlessly over the need to maintain naval identity. Hellyer saw Landymore's action as insubordinate and possibly mutinous behaviour.

The matter came to a head in the spring and summer of 1966. In April, in response to naval opposition to the proposed changes, the minister's office told the *Globe and Mail* that 'sailors don't just scrub decks and set sail now, they're skilled men and the old attitude of officers just doesn't fit. We're trying to change that.' Landymore flew to Ottawa in a boiling rage demanding an apology. He got none. Hellyer's position seemed to soften in the early summer of 1966, when it was announced that Highland regiments in the army would keep their distinctive elements of dress. It was therefore with some optimism that Landymore responded to Hellyer's summons to Ottawa on 12 July 1966. When Landymore raised the issue of naval identity, Hellyer refused any concessions. When Landymore then asked that everyone in the RCN be allowed to resign with honour and without financial penalty, Hellyer declined and, instead, demanded Landymore's retirement. When Landymore refused, he was told simply that he would be retired early. When Landymore steamed out of Hellyer's office he found the west coast admiral, Mickey Stirling, in the outer office: he had come to resign.

Unlike Brock, who was given months to settle his affairs, Landymore had four days. On 16 July 1966 he was given a hero's send-off in Halifax. But the battle was not quite over. In August Hellyer unveiled the new uniform: a bottle-green imitation of the US Air Force uniform, which pleased the air force and was not unduly offensive to the army. Hellyer later admitted that it was not 'as classy as the existing naval officer's uniform' and – perhaps less genuinely – that 'the more I thought about it the more it bothered me.' But it did get soldiers and sailors out of the rough serge and bell-bottoms that had reduced the other ranks to 'second class citizens in a country that claimed to be democratic.' Not surprisingly, the prospect of looking like the USAF did not go down well in the navy. The issue – and the bitter debate over identity – came to a head in Halifax in September 1966 when Hellyer visited the navy again. There, in a room packed full of serving officers, Hellyer was asked a formal question by Lieutenant Commander Nigel Brodeur, the grandson of Canada's first naval minister. Brodeur prefaced his question by quoting from Hellyer's own 1964 white paper on defence, which said that '"esprit de corps" by nature is associated with ship, or corps, or regiment or squadron, as well as with service. There is no thought of eliminating worthwhile traditions.' 'What better traditions,' Brodeur asked, 'have the Navy, Army and Air Force than their names, the names of their units and the heritage of uniforms worn by Canadian officers and men who gave their lives for their country?' Hellyer responded by simply charging the navy with a belief that their uniform was ordained by God. The comment sparked a near riot.

The bitterness and acrimony of the debate intensified over the next six months, but by the end of 1966 the act of unification, Bill C243, had passed second reading. It cleared the House in May 1967 and was put into effect on 1 February 1968. On that day the Royal Canadian Navy, the Royal Canadian Air Force, and the Army ceased to exist. They were replaced by a unified command and a series of functional commands, with the fleet falling within something with the Orwellian moniker of 'Maritime Command.' Naval uniforms disappeared formally on 1 July 1970. The navy salvaged only a few vestiges of its former identity. The 'HMCS' prefix was retained for ship names, and the sea-going branches were spared the embarrassment of having to adopt an army rank structure (which would have had ships commanded by Lieutenant Colonels and Colonels and squadrons commanded by Brigadiers).

What followed from unification was two decades of chaos before a distinctive Canadian navy re-emerged from its Babylonian captivity in bottle-green air-force uniforms and organizational muddle. Arguably, it emerged a much smarter, fully 'made-in-Canada' navy, well attuned to the domestic political and social winds, and happy with its own identity. Some would argue that the navy needed the hard medicine of unification and 'banishment' in order to find its true place as a Canadian service. Still others contend that that process was already well underway in the late 1950s, and that the navy would have gotten there without Hellyer's 'help.' Regardless of how that issue is resolved, it is clear that the Canadian navy, taking its lead from the federal government, has tied itself to the coat-tails of the new imperium. Its stated objective is to try to stay apace with the cutting edge technology being developed by the USN, in part so that it can carve out a niche for itself as a key interface between the USN and other navies. Over the last few years Canadian frigates have been fully integrated into USN carrier battlegroups in the Persian Gulf area, with more to follow. For some this is a very disturbing trend. But it seems we are still a long way from singing the praises of John Paul Jones, or hanging portraits of Farragut or Dewey in the wardrooms of the fleet. So far, so good.

Notes

1 Quoted in Marc Milner, *Canada's Navy: The First Century* (Toronto: University of Toronto Press, 1999), 22.
2 William Glover, 'The RCN: Royal Colonial or Royal Canadian Navy?' in *A Nation's Navy: In Quest of Canadian Naval Identity*, ed. Michael L. Hadley, Rob Huebert, and Fred W. Crickard (Montreal and Kingston: McGill-Queen's University Press 1996), 71-90.
3 David Zimmerman, 'The Social Background of the Wartime Navy: Some Statistical Data,' in ibid., 256-79.
4 When Ralph Hennessy told his father in the, 1930s that he wanted to become a naval officer, his father – a Roman Catholic – marched him down to the nearest Anglican Church and had him baptized. Hennessy retired as a vice admiral. Interview with Vice Admiral Hennessy, April 1998.
5 Glover, 'The RCN: Royal Colonial, or Royal Canadian Navy,' 77.
6 See Alec Douglas's seminal article, 'Conflict and Innovation in the Royal Canadian Navy, 1939-1945,' in *Naval Warfare in the Twentieth Century*, ed. Gerald Jordan (New York: Crane Russak, 1977), 210-32.
7 For a discussion of RCN connections with the USN in the immediate post-1945 period see Marc Milner, 'A Canadian Perspective on Canadian and American Naval Relations since 1945,' in *Fifty Years of Canada-United States Defense Cooperation: The Road from Ogdensburg*, ed. Joel J. Sokolsky and Joseph T. Jockel (Lewiston, NY: Edwin Mellon Press, 1992), 145-74.
8 Marc Milner, *The U-Boat Hunters: the Royal Canadian Navy and the Offensive Against Germany's Submarines* (Toronto: University of Toronto Press, 1994), epilogue.
9 See figures in Marc Milner, *Canadian Naval Force Requirements in the Second World War*, Extra Mural Paper no. 20 (Ottawa: Operational Research and Analysis Establishment, NDHQ, December 1981), 47.
10 Quoted in Milner, *Canada's Navy*, 185, emphasis added.
11 See Jan Drent, '"A Good Workable Little Fleet": Canadian Naval Policy, 1945-1950' in *A Nation's Navy*, 205-20.
12 Quoted in Glover, 'The RCN: Royal Colonial or Royal Canadian Navy,' 72. Earlier in the same testimony Grant had said: 'These young fellows like to go around strutting themselves with "we won the war, we are quite something," but they are not something and until they prove that they are something I don't believe in giving them any advertisement at all.'
13 Commission of Enquiry, *Report on Certain 'Incidents' Which Occurred on Board HMC Ships* Athabaskan, Crescent *and* Magnificent, *and Other Matters Concerning the Royal Canadian Navy* (Ottawa: Queen's Printer, 1949).
14 Quoted in Milner, *Canada's Navy*, 193-94.
15 Ibid., 194.
16 Ibid., 175.
17 The basic facts are in J.D.F. Kealy and E.C. Russel, *A History of Canadian Naval Aviation* (Ottawa: DND, 1965), 83. Information on the diplomatic tension is courtesy of Pat Ryan.
18 'Defense: Sounding Brass,' *Time* (28 August 1964): 10.
19 See 'The Gold-Braided Mind Is Destroying Our Navy,' *Maclean's* (7 September 1963): 22-23, 44-50.
20 Paul Hellyer, *Damn the Torpedoes* (Toronto: McClelland and Stewart, 1990), 62.
21 Ibid., 60-62.
22 The account that follows is a condensation of Chapter 13 of Milner, *Canada's Navy*.

17
Technology and Empire: The Ideas of Harold A. Innis and George P. Grant

R. Douglas Francis

'Minerva's owl begins its flight only in the gathering dusk.' Hegel's observation was noted by Canadian intellectuals Harold Innis and George Grant in their studies of modern culture within Western civilization. Innis used Hegel's reference to Minerva's owl as the title and theme of his presidential address to the Royal Society of Canada in 1947, a paper often seen as Innis's first foray into his communication studies. Upon quoting Hegel, Innis went on to assess the significance of Hegel's observation for the modern age: 'Hegel wrote in reference to the crystallization of culture achieved in major classical writings in the period that saw the decline and fall of Grecian civilization. The richness of that culture, its uniqueness, and its influence on the history of the West suggest that the flight began not only for the dusk of Grecian civilization but also for the civilization of the West.'[1] George Grant also quoted Hegel's comment in his first major publication on technology and the modern age, *Philosophy in the Mass Age*, published in 1959, a study in which Grant contrasted ancient and modern philosophies. Having quoted Hegel's reference to Minerva's owl, Grant, like Innis, went on to explain the significance of Hegel's comment for the current period. 'What [Hegel] means is that we take thought about the meaning of our lives when an old system of meaning has disappeared with an old society, and when we recognize that the new society which is coming to be raises new questions which cannot be understood within the old system.'[2]

It is significant that both Innis and Grant saw meaning in Hegel's comment for their own age, the post-Second World War era. Both saw their own age as one of profound change when Minerva's owl was once again taking flight. Both men were thinking of this change in much broader terms than the 'End of Empire.' Innis saw it in terms of the fall of Western civilization; Grant in terms of the disappearance of a (Protestant) Christian-based culture in North America with the onslaught of a secular mass society. In a revealing address given by Innis sometime during the Second World War entitled 'This Has Killed That,' he noted the significance of the First World War as signalling the collapse of Western civilization, and searched for the roots of that collapse: 'In attempting to suggest the background of this collapse of modern civilization we may well ask what has happened which brought to an end about a century of comparative peace from the end of the Napoleonic Wars to the outbreak of the first Great War. Are there any signs within the last twenty-five years before the outbreak of the first Great War which point to the dangers of collapse?'[3] Yet both of these Canadian thinkers also saw the changes going on in their own times as being tied to the rise and fall of empires. Both wrote major works in which 'empire' is a prominent term in the title: Innis's *Empire and Communications* (1950), and Grant's *Technology and Empire* (1969). While the end of the British Empire is clearly not the focus of either study, both were premised on an assumption that sometime in the twentieth century the British Empire fell, to be replaced by an American Empire, and that this transition was part of a broader change that had a profound impact on modern Western civilization, particularly in North America and especially for Canadians. This chapter explores the ideas of Harold Innis and George Grant on the role that technology played on the fall of the British Empire and the rise of the American Empire, and the implication of this transition for Canada.

The focus of Harold Innis's studies – *all* of his studies, I would argue – was the rise and fall of Western civilization. This is clearly most evident in his communication studies, but it is equally the focus of his *History of the Canadian Pacific Railway* (1923) and in his so-called 'staple studies.' And throughout all of his studies, he was interested in understanding the role that technology played in the rise and fall of Western civilization. The place of empires was of secondary importance to civilizations, the role of the former often implied rather than discussed. Even *Empire and Communications* seems to be incorrectly titled, since the focus is on the role of communication technology on the rise and fall of civilizations – from Egypt and Babylonia to Greece, Rome, and Europe – as opposed to empires. For example, in his preface, Innis acknowledges the works of Kroeber, Mead, Marx, Spengler, Toynbee, and others on 'the significance of communication to modern civilization,' and claims that his own study was an attempt 'to work out its implications in a more specific fashion and to suggest the background of their volumes. The twentieth century has been conspicuous for extended publications on civilization which in themselves reflect a type of civilization.'[4] It is almost as though Innis felt that, since the series of lectures that made up the book were given as the Beit lectures on imperial economic history, therefore the book should have the word 'empire' in the title. Yet such an explanation is too simplistic. Clearly Innis saw a significant link between the rise and fall of civilizations and the role of empires, including the link between the British Empire and Western civilization. In his introduction to *Empire and Communications*, he attempted to make the link. He argued that one of the characteristics of Western civilization in the twentieth century was a concern for 'the role of economic considerations in the success or failure of empires.' He associated this particular economic perspective with our modern interest (indeed obsession, in Innis's view) with the history of the British Empire. 'Recognition of the importance of economic considerations is perhaps characteristic of the British Empire and it will be part of our task to appraise their significance to the success or failure of the British Empire and in turn to the success or failure of Western civilization.' He then went on to note the difficulty of achieving historical objectivity when such 'obsessions' predominated: 'A citizen of one of the British Commonwealth of Nations, which has been profoundly influenced by the economic development of empires, who has been obsessed over a long period with an interest in the character of that influence, can hardly claim powers of objectivity adequate to the task in hand ... Obsession with economic considerations illustrates the dangers of monopolies of knowledge and suggests the necessity of appraising its limitations. Civilizations can survive only through a concern with their limitations and in turn through a concern with the limitations of their institutions, including empires.'[5] Thus, Innis saw the British Empire playing an economic role in the history of Western civilization.

Here was the link to technology in Innis's thinking. It was the superior technology of the British, arising out of the Industrial Revolution, that enabled Britain to amass the most powerful empire of the world, thus making it by the nineteenth century the imperial centre of Western civilization. To explain how British imperial dominance occurred within the North American context was the purpose underlying his study of the Canadian Pacific Railway and his staple studies. In *A History of the Canadian Pacific Railway*, Innis argued that the significance of the CPR lay in enabling Britain to extend its sphere of influence in the western interior beyond the river valleys that had previously been the main arteries of communication and trade, and in turn enabled 'the spread of Western civilization over the northern half of the North American continent.'[6] But already he saw the impact of the railway and of imperial dominance as being much more than of a physical nature. For the railway was more than a mechanical device. It represented a mindset or *mentalité* that was technological, and as such, representative of the dominant paradigm of thought of the British Empire and therefore of Western civilization. That mindset was the tendency to measure everything in economic, quantitative, mechanical, or mathematical terms – as profits, material goods, and power. It was this 'technological mentality' that, he argued, made Western civilization dominant, that enabled Britain to be the imperial centre of that civilization, and that kept Canada tied to the British Empire, and through the empire linked to Western civilization.[7]

Innis was interested in discovering the roots of British imperial dominance in North America, and found it in the early fur trade and fisheries. The technological superiority of European civilization – in terms of machinery and manufactured goods but also a more aggressive approach to the exploitation of natural resources – enabled Europe to dominate the Native civilization of North America. As he outlined in his conclusion of *The Fur Trade in Canada*:

> The history of the fur trade is the history of contact between two civilizations, the European and the North American, with especial reference to the northern portion of the continent. The limited cultural background of the North American hunting peoples provided an insatiable demand for the products of the more elaborate cultural development of Europeans. The supply of European goods, the product of a more advanced and specialized technology, enabled the Indians to gain a livelihood more easily – to obtain their supply of food, as in the case of moose, more quickly, and to hunt the beaver more effectively ... [But] the new technology with its radical innovations brought about such a rapid shift in the prevailing Indian culture as to lead to wholesale destruction of the peoples concerned by warfare and disease.[8]

Innis also argued in his fur trade and cod fisheries studies that within the rivalry of the European powers to gain the upper hand in North America, the British ultimately prevailed because of their imperial might, based in turn on technological superiority gained through their priority in industrialization. Thus, by the time that Innis was ready to embark on his communication studies (around 1940), he had come to associate British imperial dominance in the nineteenth century with the country's technological advancement, which in turn accounted for Britain being the centre of Western civilization.

What his communication studies illuminated about empires and their decline were two key ideas: the role that communications technology played in the rise and fall of all civilizations throughout time, including most importantly the rise and fall of Western civilization; and the means by which the United States supplanted Britain as the imperial centre of Western civilization. Innis had discovered a pattern in the rise and fall of civilizations. He believed that a civilization rose to prominence as a result of a superior form of communications technology that enabled the dominant elite within that civilization to establish a 'monopoly of knowledge,' and thus to control the thought patterns of people under the elite's control. He noted that each form of communications technology was oriented towards either time or space – in Innis's terminology, they were either 'time-biased' or 'space-biased.' Communications media that were durable and difficult to transport, such as stone, clay, or parchment, were time-biased, whereas those that were light and easy to transport over long distances, such as paper and papyrus, were space-biased.[9] By 'bias' Innis meant more than a simple preference for one type of technology over the other. He argued that civilizations oriented towards time or space created a dominant paradigm of thought – a monopoly of knowledge – that in most cases prevented counter-values or alternative social structures from emerging. As well, the principal medium of communication favoured one particular group within that civilization – the group that controlled the technology of communication – which maintained its power by preventing the emergence of any alternative communications technology that could threaten it. The oral tradition, for example, enabled the Spartan oligarchy to prevail; writing on papyrus benefited the Roman imperial bureaucracy; parchment allowed the medieval clergy and the Roman Catholic Church to monopolize knowledge in the Middle Ages; by contrast, Gutenberg's mechanical print fostered the vernacular and allowed the monarchs of nation-states to consolidate their power and, through the merchant class, create vast empires. Newspapers, a hybrid of the printed word and electronic media, particularly the telegraph, enabled empires to extend over vast distances and yet be easily controlled by an imperial centre. It was the success of newspapers in Britain that enabled the country to extend its empire around the world by the nineteenth century.

Yet Innis discovered that there was a paradox. The monopoly of knowledge that enabled a civilization to achieve physical and cultural greatness, and the empire at the centre of that civilization to maintain dominance, also led to the inevitable demise of that empire and ultimately to the civilization of which the empire was a part, since it did not allow for the rise of new ideas required for renewed growth. This was the point, Innis observed, when Minerva's owl took flight to a new centre of cultural creativity. This new centre was invariably a nation on the margin that had developed a superior form of communications technology. Innis noted the different centres that Minerva's owl had 'visited' in the West: 'Since its flight from Constantinople Minerva's owl has found a resting-place only at brief intervals in the West. It has flown from Italy to France, the Netherlands, Germany and after the French Revolution back to France and England and finally to the United States.'[10]

Exactly when Minerva's owl had taken flight from England to the United States, Innis did not say. He did believe, however, that the transition had a great deal to do with the two world wars. These wars, however, were more reflective of, and a result of, a fundamental change in a communications technology, which in this case (in Innis's view) was that of newspapers. In an article entitled 'The Newspaper in Economic Development,' Innis noted that the advent of newspapers in Britain in the seventeenth century had resulted in political partisanship, political corruption, and the rise of advertising. The British Parliament had responded by temporarily restricting the freedom of the press. As a result, newspaper editors fled Britain. One of those editors, Benjamin Harris, fled to the United States where, in 1690, he started the first newspaper in America, *Publick Occurences*.[11] The beginnings of newspapers in America coincided with an improvement in print technology, when pulpwood replaced rags as an easier and, more importantly, more economical way to make paper. Two centuries later, the cost of materials was still falling: The cost of newsprint declined dramatically from 8.5 cents a pound in 1875 to 1.5 cents per pound in 1897.[12] In one of those familiar sweeping statements characteristic of Innis, he noted: '"Taxes on knowledge" in Great Britain prior to 1861 restricted the development of newspapers, favoured a monopoly of *The Times*, reduced the demand for rags, and accelerated development of newspapers in the United States.'[13] With cheaper newsprint came the rise of the penny press, with its emphasis on sensationalism, especially war news. Innis noted how first the Crimean War and especially the South African War had helped British newspaper magnates such as Lord Northcliffe to achieve a monopoly over the newspaper world. The Spanish-American War did the same for Hearst and Pulitzer with their chains of newspapers in the United States.[14] Cheaper newsprint also meant fiercer competition, with a resulting dependency on advertising as a means to sell papers.[15]

These changes benefited the United States because of the easy access that American newspaper entrepreneurs had to sources of inexpensive pulp and paper, especially in northern Ontario and Quebec. As well, the American newspaper industry benefited from railways that crisscrossed the United States for quick, easy, and wide distribution across the continent, telegraph service for news transmission, and, in the twentieth century, the radio as a source of information. Innis pointed out the myriad ways that the advent of newspapers, and the changes in technology within the industry, affected modern society, culture, and mentality:

> The concentration of the natural sciences on the problems of physics and chemistry concerned with speed reflects the influence of the newspapers. Educational systems and literacy have been subject to their influence directly and indirectly. Speed in the collection, production and dissemination of information has been the essence of newspaper development. Widening of markets, the effectiveness of competition, lowering of costs of production, the spread of the price system, the evolution of a sensitive monetary structure and the development of equilibrium economics have followed the development of the newspaper. By its drive for the use of small coins it has acted as a spearhead in penetrating to lower incomes. In its

effective use of advertising in the selection and exploitation of news, it developed a medium for the advertising of goods. The lifting power of advertising increased from patent medicines to automobiles. The influence of newspapers on communication and transportation has varied with waves of technological advance. Increase in sensitivity in the price system has varied with the efficiency of adaptation of technological improvements. Economic analysis has become more complex and confused. The conservatism of knowledge which resists the impact of improvements in communication breaks down in a conservatism of confusion.[16]

Innis believed that, due to the rapid changes in communications technology in the modern age, no sooner had Minerva's owl set down in the United States as its new resting place with the advent of newspapers than this 'newspaper civilization' had entered its concluding phase in the 1920s. Part of the explanation was the rise of a new communications technology, the radio. But more importantly, in keeping with his wider understanding of the pattern behind the rise and fall of civilizations throughout time, it was due to the monopoly of knowledge engendered by newspapers that new ideas, counter to those of the newspaper lords and their political lackeys (who monopolized the thinking of the time), were prevented from emerging. Ironically, he noted, 'the American faith in the freedom of the press had been one of the biggest "barriers" in the way of the American people achieving their freedom.'[17] Innis was just beginning to study the implications of the change, and the flight of Minerva's owl once again, when he died prematurely. He did appear to think that Canada was the next creative centre upon which Minerva's owl might rest.

Innis believed that the decline of the British Empire and rise of the American Empire did have serious repercussions for Canada. It had altered the country's economy from staples in demand in Britain, such as timber and wheat, to other staples desired by the United States, such as pulp and paper and minerals. Since the transportation system in Canada in the nineteenth century had been geared to trade with Britain, the rise of American dominance of the Canadian economy necessitated a fundamental change in Canada's transportation network. As well, since the staples in demand for the American market – namely pulp and paper, and minerals – tended to be concentrated in Ontario and Quebec, the new economy pitted central Canada against the hinterlands of the West and the Maritimes to a greater degree than had previously been the case. The advent of radio aided regional politicians and thus contributed to increased regionalism as well. Furthermore, Canadian dependency on the American economy had led inevitably to Canadian subservience to American foreign policy. The only hope of offsetting this American dominance, he believed, was for Canada 'to call in the Old World to redress the balance of the New, and hope that

Great Britain will escape American imperialism as successfully as she herself has escaped British imperialism.'[18] Thus, clearly for Innis, the end of the British Empire and the advent of the American Empire had dramatic implications for Canada that he found most distressing, but equally it had serious repercussions for the survival of Western civilization, since he believed that Minerva's owl's days of flight in the West were numbered.

Like Innis, George Grant also saw the British Empire as assisting Canada in offsetting the pull of the American Empire in the twentieth century. This need for balance – the old North Atlantic Triangle – was all the more imperative after the Second World War, Grant believed, as the world divided itself into two armed camps dominated by two superpowers. He saw these superpowers as great continental empires that would dominate the regional or territorial land masses adjacent to their own borders: the United States in North and South America and the Pacific; the USSR in Central Europe and Asia. There was still, however, a third empire – the British Empire or Commonwealth – that was different from the other two in that it was a maritime empire with possessions around the world; thus it could balance the two opposing continental empires in geopolitical terms. It would serve Canada's interest, Grant argued in a little pamphlet published in 1945 entitled *The Empire, Yes or No?*, to support the Empire-Commonwealth as the only means to prevent a conflict between the superpowers, a conflict that would take place 'on our own soil.' He reasoned: 'As our north and south connections run to the U.S.A., so they run across the Pole to Moscow. As our east and west connections join us together, so they carry us towards Siberia and Asia in the east and to Great Britain and Europe in the west. We would be at the very centre of the conflict between two great continental empires. It is clearly in our most direct and immediate interest to prevent that. If we do not, we will be caught like the nut in the nutcracker.'[19] Furthermore, as an independent nation without the British Empire-Commonwealth, Canada would eventually become absorbed by the United States, or, at least, become its satellite, an argument that had been made by Grant's grandfathers, George Munro Grant and George Parkin, as English-Canadian imperialists in the late nineteenth century.[20]

But in Grant's mind the British Empire and Commonwealth stood for much more than just a geopolitical counterpull to the two superpowers. Again, in keeping with the perspective of his grandfathers, he saw the British Empire-Commonwealth as a great liberal, moral, and spiritual force in the world: the only great world organization that was based on the free association of nations, one that was based on the rule of law rather than the rule of force, the only world power committed to assisting 'backward people towards political democracy and economic maturity,' and the heart of Western Christian civilization. As Grant put the ultimatum to Canadians in *The Empire: Yes or No?*:

We cannot judge the British Commonwealth from our petty interests alone (however well these are satisfied), but on the highest criteria of political morality. For today in the modern world, with it more than with any other political institution, lies the hope of Christian man, of ethical man, of man the reasonable, moral being who stands before God and history ... [I]f we believe in Christian man, the finest flower of all that Western civilization has produced, then there can be no doubt that our chief hope in the survival of such values is in the survival of the British Commonwealth. Canada has a vital responsibility. Canada must choose.[21]

Thus for Grant in 1945, association with the British Empire-Commonwealth was both the means by which Canada could survive independently of the United States, and the reason *why* it should, since as part of this liberal, moral, and spiritual organization, it offered an alternative to the more radical, materialistic, and power-hungry American empire.

In Grant's mind, this was the battle between the philosophy of the ancient and the modern worlds that he outlined in *Philosophy in the Mass Age* (1959). Britain had remnants of the ancient world through its association with European civilization; the United States, as a society cut off from the Old World and populated initially by Puritans who rejected ancient Greek philosophy in favour of a New World Christian faith, did not. If Canada severed its ties with Britain and its Empire-Commonwealth, it lost its lifeline to Western civilization and the tradition that was a part of that connection. By the mid-1960s, Grant believed that lifeline was gone, because Britain no longer played an important role in the Canadian consciousness. Britain had ceased to be a world power that gave Canada a role in the world as a member of its Empire-Commonwealth; and the American empire had, through technology and economic ties, absorbed Canada within its orbit. Thus both the means and the reason for Canada's existence, as set out in *The Empire: Yes or No?*, had disappeared; Grant could only lament the loss of his nation. He saw the defeat of John George Diefenbaker in the 1963 election as the symbolic act of denouement, but Diefenbaker's defeat was only an inevitable result of the triumph of the American empire, thanks to the nation's technological dominance. To those who objected to the term 'empire' in association with the United States, as being an antiquated term reminiscent of past ages when empires were associated with colonial possessions, Grant argued that 'an empire does not have to wield direct political control over colonial countries. Poland and Czechoslovakia are as much part of the Russian Empire as India was of the British, or Canada and Brazil of the American. An empire is the control of one state by another. In this sense, the United States of America has an empire.'[22]

What made the American Empire so insidious compared to the British Empire was not the fact that it had possessions but that it was able to dominate those possessions to a degree impossible for the British Empire in the past due to advances in technology. That technology was more than machines or industrialization; it was for Grant (as for Innis) a mindset. Fundamental to that mindset was a faith in progress through technology. This was a liberal concept that went against Canadian conservatism. With the triumph of the liberal belief in progress, Canadian conservatism was impossible. 'As Canadians,' Grant wrote with lament, 'we attempted a ridiculous task in trying to build a conservative nation in the age of progress, on a continent we share with the most dynamic nation on earth.' It was technology, and the philosophy of liberalism that fostered it, that defeated Canada. 'Our culture floundered on the aspirations of the age of progress. The argument that Canada, a local culture, must disappear can, therefore, be stated in three steps. First, men everywhere move ineluctably toward membership in the universal and homogeneous state. Second, Canadians live next to a society that is the heart of modernity. Third, nearly all Canadians think that modernity is good, so nothing essential distinguishes Canadians from Americans.'[23]

What he had come to realize by the time he finished *Lament for a Nation*, however, was that liberalism and technology were not unique to the American empire but actually went hand and hand with *all* empires, including the British Empire. 'Great Britain was the chief centre from which the progressive civilization spread around the world. Politically it became the leading imperial power of the West.' This imperial dominance only occurred once Britain abandoned its conservative ethos for a liberal tradition that upheld the freedom of the individual, and that believed history was on its side. 'As Plato saw with unflinching clarity,' Grant wrote, 'an imperialistic power cannot have a conservative society as its home base.'[24] Looked at from this perspective, Grant's lament for the disappearance of Canada as an alternative, conservative nation to that of the dominant liberal nation of the United States on the North American continent, was a lament for something greater that had been lost much earlier than the mid-twentieth century: a conservative tradition within Western civilization. That had ended within the British tradition with the advent of the British Empire itself. Conservatism was an impossible – because incompatible – philosophy in the modern liberal world of technology and imperialism. Hence the title of Grant's greatest and most profound collection of essays, which addressed this larger issue: *Technology and Empire* (1969).

In *Technology and Empire*, Grant no longer talked about a British Empire versus an American Empire. He simply talked about empires within Western civilization, characterizing them as the centres of technological dominance. The United States was only the most recent and most technologically advanced of imperial centres, and thus able to dominate others – even the entire world – to an extent that Britain never could in its day. But the ambition was the same, since it was intrinsic to empires to dominate; and the means were also the same, through technology. As Grant noted: 'Imperially we [North Americans] turn out to the rest of the world bringing the apogee of what Europeans first invented, technological civilisation.' He explained further: 'Western technical achievement has shaped a different civilization from any previous, and we North Americans are the most advanced in that achievement ... Through that achievement we have become the heartland of the wealthiest and most powerful empire that has yet been. We can exert our influence over a greater extent of the globe and take a greater tribute of wealth than any previously. Despite our limitations and miscalculations, we have more compelling means than any previous for putting the brand of our civilisation deeply into the flesh of others.'[25]

What were the implications for Canada living next door to the heartland of imperial technological dominance? That was the question Grant attempted to answer in his essay 'Canadian Fate and Imperialism' in *Technology and Empire*. He began by noting that a 'central aspect of the fate of being a Canadian is that our very existing has at all times been bound up with the interplay of various world empires.' Those empires – the French and the British – were 'north-western empires' as opposed to Mediterranean-based empires. What distinguished these northerly empires from the more southerly ones, according to Grant, following Hegel, was their unique brand of 'secularizing Christianity.' This secularizing Christianity had its roots in the seventeenth century 'in England and its empire,' through a 'union of the new secularism and Protestantism.' It manifested itself in capitalism, and capitalism was the economic ideology behind technology and imperialism. It was this capitalistic ethos that took hold in North America. The United Empire Loyalists who fled the United States in the War of Independence imbibed this ethos also, only they 'were not so given over to modernity as were the leaders of the U.S.' This meant that English-speaking Canada had at least 'some roots with tradition, even though that tradition was the most modern in Europe up till the eighteenth century.' Still, that difference was in detail only, 'not in any substantial way which questioned that modernity.' He noted this as a corrective to those who had dismissed *Lament for a Nation* as simply 'nostalgia to the British empire and old fashioned Canada.'[26]

Now Grant realized that the imperial scramble for colonial possessions in the last half of the nineteenth century – even of the British Empire – was 'modern man (man as Hobbes has said he is) realizing his potentialities. The culmination of that European process was the war of 1914.' That war was a pure-and-simple imperial war, although cloaked at the time in the guise of freedom and justice (which he earlier had been naïve enough to accept). 'When one thinks what that war was in fact being fought about, and the slaughter of decent men of decent motive which ensued, the mind boggles. As that war spelled out the implicit violence of the West, it also spelled out Canadian fate.' That 'fate' was to confront the modern American technological empire as it wreaked havoc on the world, as evident in the Vietnam War, without any counterpull to offset Canadian absorption into the American leviathan. And as a predominantly liberal country (under Liberal rule) that had 'bought into' the American mythology of progress through technology, Canada was ill-prepared to see the American leviathan for what it was: imperial dominance and tyranny. As Grant lamented: 'Our modern way of looking at the world hides from us the reality of many political things; but about nothing is it more obscuring than the inevitable relation between dynamic technology and imperialism.'[27]

Grant presented the dilemma that the Canadian fate held for Canadians: 'To live in a world of these violent empires, and in a satellite of the greatest of them, presents complex problems of morality.' Grant was referring specifically to the Vietnam War. Having accepted the American way of life, Canadians also accepted American liberal values, including the belief that Americans were fighting in Vietnam to save liberal democracy in the Western world. In this respect, the Vietnam War was as much Canada's war as America's: 'It is being done by a society which more than any other carries the destiny of the West, and Canadians belong inevitably to that destiny.' For Grant, who deeply opposed that war, it meant a profound sense of alienation – an inability any longer to love one's own country or civilization. 'Surely the deepest alienation,' Grant realized, 'must be when the civilisation one inhabits no longer claims one's loyalty ... Indeed the depth of the alienation is seen in the ambiguity of the words "one's own."' He gained a faint glimmer of hope in realizing that Canada was still independent enough not to send troops to fight in Vietnam; but that was little solace upon realizing that behind 'the small practical question of Canadian nationalism is the larger context of the fate of western civilisation. By that fate, I mean not merely the relations of our massive empire to the rest of the world, but even more the kind of existence which is becoming universal in advanced technological societies. What is worth doing in the midst of this barren twilight is the incredibly difficult question.' [28]

In the space of two decades, George Grant had gone from seeing the British Empire as a great noble, liberal, spiritual, and moral force in the world, which offered Canada the means to be an independent nation on the northern half of the North American continent, to seeing it as a power-hungry, materialistic, and amoral entity, the originator of the modern liberal, technological empire, of which the United States was the most recent offspring. The British Empire was responsible for the loss of Canadian independence and the country's absorption into the American empire. Thus, both Harold

Innis and George Grant died sick at heart that the end of the British Empire sealed the fate of Canada as a nation, and even more, sealed the fate of Western civilization. The End of Empire saw Minerva's owl take flight 'in the gathering dusk.'

To what extent did Innis's and Grant's ideas reflect and/or contribute to a Canadian perspective on the British Empire and its decline in the postwar era? Innis's communication studies, couched in a cryptic writing style, made his views of interest to only a coterie of his followers. On the other hand, his significant influence in the Canadian academic community and among government officials, especially having served on the prestigious Royal Commission on National Development in the Arts, Letters, and Sciences, gave his ideas tremendous leverage. And Innis's uneasiness about the implications for Canada of the shift in the Western world from one of British dominance to one of American dominance was characteristic of many Canadians in the era after the Second World War. Innis's famous adage that in the short space of a few decades 'Canada went from colony to nation to colony' captured the deep concern of many Canadians in the mid-twentieth century as Canada increasingly came under the dominance of the United States, not unlike its colonial position under Britain.

Unlike Innis, George Grant was well known among the educated English-Canadian population through his weekly book reviews in the 1950s, his lecture series on the Canadian Broadcasting Corporation (CBC), and especially as a result of the publication of his popular and controversial *Lament for a Nation*. Grant's 'lament' was for the 'death of Canada,' not for the end of the British Empire, but, as already noted, the end of the British Empire had, in Grant's estimation, a great deal to do with Canada's demise as an independent nation and its incorporation into the American Empire. Grant's views encapsulated the concern that many Canadians felt in the 1950s and 1960s as the United States came to dominate all aspects of Canadian life. So in their own ways, Innis and Grant contributed to the mid-century debate on Canada's destiny, especially vis-à-vis the United States, and expressed the sentiments of a number of Canadians (as noted in several chapters in this collection) on the serious implications of the end of the British Empire for the future of Canada.

Acknowledgments
I want to thank the Killam Foundation for a Killam Resident Fellowship in the Fall of 2000, during which time I wrote this chapter.

Notes

1 Harold A. Innis, 'Minerva's Owl' in *The Bias of Communication* (1951; reprinted Toronto: University of Toronto Press, 1991), 3.
2 George P. Grant, *Philosophy in the Mass Age* (1959; reprinted Toronto: Copp Clark, 1966), 5-6.

3   Harold A. Innis, 'This Has Killed That,' *Journal of Canadian Studies* 12/5 (Winter 1977): 3.
4   Harold A. Innis, *Empire and Communications* (1950; reprinted Toronto: University of Toronto Press, 1972), i.
5   Ibid., 3-4.
6   Harold A. Innis, *A History of the Canadian Pacific Railway* (1923; reprinted Toronto: University of Toronto Press, 1971), 287.
7   For a discussion of the theme of power as related to technology in Innis's writings, see R. Douglas Francis, 'The Anatomy of Power: A Theme in the Writings of Harold Innis,' in *Nation, Ideas, Identities*, ed. Michael D. Behiels and Marcel Martel (Toronto: Oxford University Press, 2000), 26-40.
8   Harold A. Innis, *The Fur Trade in Canada* (1930; reprinted Toronto: University of Toronto Press, 1973), 388.
9   The best summary of Innis's theories on communications media is still James W. Carey, 'Harold Adams Innis and Marshall McLuhan,' *Antioch Review* 27 (Spring 1967): 5-39.
10 Innis, 'Minerva's Owl,' 30.
11 Harold A. Innis, 'The Newspaper in Economic Development,' in *Political Economy in the Modern State* (Toronto: Ryerson Press, 1946), 8-9.
12 Innis, *Empire and Communications*, 161.
13 Innis, 'Technology and Public Opinion in the United States,' in *The Bias of Communication*, 160.
14 Innis, 'On the Economic Significance of Cultural Factors,' in *Political Economy in the Modern State*, 94.
15 Innis, *Empire and Communications*, 161.
16 Innis, 'The Newspaper in Economic Development,' 32-33.
17 Innis, 'Technology and Public Opinion,' 187.
18 Innis, 'Great Britain, the United States, and Canada,' in *Staples, Markets, and Cultural Change: Selected Essays of Harold A. Innis*, ed. Daniel Drache (Montreal and Kingston: McGill-Queen's University Press, 1995), 287-88.
19 George P. Grant, *The Empire: Yes or No?* (Toronto: Ryerson, 1945); excerpt reprinted in *The George Grant Reader*, ed. William Christian and Sheila Grant (Toronto: University of Toronto Press, 1998), 46.
20 On parallels in the ideas of George Parkin Grant and his grandfathers, George Munro Grant and George Parkin, see William Christian, 'Canada's Fate: Principal Grant, Sir George Parkin, and George Grant,' *Journal of Canadian Studies* 34/4 (Winter 2000): 88-104.
21 Grant, *The Empire: Yes or No?*, 49-50.
22 George Grant, *Lament for a Nation: The Defeat of Canadian Nationalism* (Toronto: McClelland and Stewart, 1965), 8 fn.
23 Ibid., 68, 54.
24 Ibid., 73.
25 George Grant, 'In Defence of North America,' in *Technology and Empire: Perspectives on North America* (Toronto: House of Anansi, 1969), 16, 15. It is interesting to note that when referring to civilization in general or in the context of Western civilization, Grant uses what he saw to be the British spelling of the word ('civilisation'); when referring to the American form of civilization, and particularly in a negative context, he uses what he saw to be the American spelling.
26 George Grant, 'Canadian Fate and Imperialism,' in *Technology and Empire*, 63, 65, 66, 68.
27 Ibid., 69, 70, 72-73.
28 Ibid., 73, 74, 76, 78.

18
Petitioning the Great White Mother: First Nations' Organizations and Lobbying in London

J.R. (Jim) Miller

On the prairies, First Nations' public ceremonies, such as those associated with commemoration of treaty making, always include an element that seems jarring, even anachronistic. Veterans and elders pray and raise flags to start the day's observances, but among the flags that are ritually run up the improvised poles, the Union Jack seems strangely out of place to observers from outside the First Nations' community. However, the raising of Britain's venerable pennant is neither anachronistic nor out of place for First Nations, given their long-standing and still vibrant sense of kinship with the Crown, including what scholars would refer to as the Crown in right of the United Kingdom. This tie was established and grew strong in the eighteenth century, the product of both Aboriginal approaches to external dealings and First Nations' well-developed strategic sense. It played a role through the nineteenth and twentieth centuries both in treaty making and lobbying for imperial support for First Nations' causes. Most recently and most noticeably, it was a prominent element in the hectic campaigning for and against the patriation of the Canadian constitution, which led to the adoption of a new constitutional package in April 1982. In other words it persisted beyond the 'End of Empire,' the period when both Britain's imperial reach and grasp came to an end. Only very recently have there been signs that Aboriginal groups' penchant for lobbying in London might give way to another form of international activity. Surely any tradition such as this lobbying – petitioning the Great White Mother – is worthy of investigation.

Aboriginal leaders' use of terms such as the 'Great Father' or the 'Great White Mother' is easily explained. Within First Nations communities, interactions almost invariably took place between kin. In societies whose fundamental organization was usually by clan and family, ties of kinship were not only important; they were vital to the conduct of relations of various kinds. It was essential to be in a familial relationship of some kind in order to conduct business with other people in these communities. Examples of the importance and use of kin ties are many and varied. The elaborate alliance system that developed in the northeast woodlands in the seventeenth and eighteenth centuries – the Covenant Chain of the League of the Iroquois and their allies – was a bewildering network whose links were characterized by family relationships. Some paired links in the chain related as parent to child, while the relationships between others were fraternal (or sororal), and still others were typified by a purported relationship of uncle to nephew or niece.[1] Each and every one of those different familial links was a metaphorical description of the nature and quality of the relationship: those between brothers were links between equals; but those between father and child, or between uncle and nephew, connoted an inequality in power and status between the two. Much of this relationship was, in the language of anthropologists, 'fictive,' meaning that it was imputed to the parties metaphorically, as a way of describing and facilitating their relationship.

Other examples of the use of kinship in relationships with Aboriginal peoples can be found in the North American fur trade and in treaty making in the West. As is well known, European male traders often took Native partners, and Native families were often pleased to see their daughters enter a relationship with the newcomers who had the coveted trade goods. Among the reasons for the formation of these fur trade family units was the reality that in Aboriginal society kinship links facilitated trade. The European trader who married a Cree woman would automatically have a network of trading partners, while the bride's family would enjoy preferred access to that trader and to the company for whom he worked.[2] Finally, in the making of the numbered treaties of the latter decades of the nineteenth century, the use by both government and Aboriginal negotiators of familial imagery is striking. Treaty commissioners such as Alexander Morris talked repeatedly of how the 'Great Queen Mother' desired good for her 'Indian children' and wished to provide for them from her 'bounty and benevolence,' and a suspicious Cree leader, Mistahimusqua (Big Bear), assured the government representative that 'I am not an undutiful child,' even as he was rebuffing the commissioner's efforts to get him to sign a treaty in 1876.[3]

If use of the language of kinship and family was universal in Aboriginal relations, an agreed understanding of the meaning of familial terms was often not. Indeed, one of the striking features of commercial and diplomatic relations between the representatives of the Crown and First Nations in Canadian history is the way in which the Europeans over time lost their understanding of how the terminology worked. In the early phases, when the Europeans were represented in their dealings with First Nations by the likes of Sir William Johnson, himself married into the Mohawk nation of the Six Nations Iroquois, the newcomers could use and parse the terms of kinship with all the skill and subtlety of the First Nations' leaders from whom they had learned to do so. However, a century later, by the time both government treaty commissioners and First Nations were passing terms like

'Queen Mother' and 'Indian children' across the negotiating table, it is clear that the Euro-Canadians no longer understood completely what the First Nations meant by familial terms. When government representatives referred to the Queen's 'Indian children' in the 1870s treaty talks, the reference was invariably followed by some comment that assumed the subordination of First Nations to the government. This stood in dramatic contrast to First Nations' usage, for their references to themselves as 'children' never occurred in a context that implied subordination and obedience to the 'Queen Mother' and her government in Ottawa. When First Nations leaders used this terminology, they did so within a First Nations cultural context, a set of social assumptions that treated children as distinct individuals who enjoyed a great deal of autonomy and who could count automatically on the love and protection of their parents.[4] Over time the meaning of the language of kinship and family changed, but what remained constant was the predominance of such language.

If describing the British monarch as the Great White Mother can be understood against the backdrop of Aboriginal insistence on having relations take place within a framework of kinship, real or fictive, why did some leaders consider it necessary to take their petitions to the Great Father or Queen Mother in London themselves? Here the explanation is found in the Native leaders' perception of how critical the Crown's response was to their well-being, and in their desire – a desire that grew ever stronger over time – to avoid intermediaries who they feared would muffle or distort their message. The first major example of petitioning the Crown, Mohawk chief Joseph Brant's pilgrimage to London in 1775-76, illustrates both the importance of the crisis and the desire to transmit the message clearly. The strategic context for the expedition was the American War of Independence, and the tactical context was the recent death of Joseph Brant's brother-in-law, Sir William Johnson. The onset of the rebellion cast into doubt both the future of the League of the Iroquois and the security of their lands south of Lake Ontario, directly in the path of the expansionist American colonists, with whom they had had uneasy relations for some time. For security they had relied on imperial instruments such as the Royal Proclamation of 1763, which forbade all settlement beyond a defined western boundary and restricted entry to the interior for trading purposes to those merchants who obtained a licence from the governor in advance of their foray into Indian Country. Even with the protection of the Royal Proclamation, First Nations in the period after 1763 saw settler pressure on their lands constantly increase. In this situation they relied on William Johnson, superintendent if the Northern Department of the Indian Department that Britain had created in 1755, to try to restrain the land-hungry Americans. Johnson was motivated both by personal inclinations and by his official duty to do what he could to protect the territorial interests of these First Nations. He was a trader and large landowner in the Mohawk River valley, a man who depended on good relations with Indian peoples in order to promote his own interests. He was also married – married in the Iroquois fashion, at any rate – to Molly or Mary Brant, the remarkably talented and courageous Mohawk Clan Mother who was sister to the then-young Joseph Brant. In addition to these ties of self-interest and family, it was Johnson's responsibility as the effective head of the Indian Department in the region to try to conciliate Indian communities and retain their alliance with Britain if possible, or, failing that, their neutrality in any quarrel in which Britain might become involved. Johnson had a remarkable career between his appointment in 1755 and his death in 1774, largely succeeding in maintaining the alliance system in which the League of the Iroquois were such a vital link.

Johnson's death immediately cast into doubt the foundations on which many Mohawk, such as the Brants, had built their strategy. In the War of Independence, the Mohawk and the other nations in the Iroquois confederacy were pressed to support Great Britain militarily. However, they were understandably concerned about Britain's reliability. If they fought with Great Britain against the colonists, would Britain support their territorial claims and help to defend their lands? It might have been possible to rely on assurances from a trusted figure such as Sir William Johnson if he were still alive. However, he was gone, and the young Joseph Brant took it upon himself to go to London in the winter of 1775-76 in search of reassurances about British intentions towards its Indian allies.

Joseph Brant and another Mohawk man travelled to London in the company of Guy Johnson, a nephew of the late Sir William who was in search of his uncle's office as Indian superintendent. In an interview with the colonial secretary, Lord George Germain, Brant outlined the objective of his mission: 'I have come over on purpose to be informed of the real motive which ocasioned the unhappy dispute subsisting twixt Brittain and her American Colonies, as numbers of Rebbles were amongst the Indians circulating various reports which if they had believed would in all probability have ocasioned unhappy consequennces. Therefore, [I] begg of your Lordship to inform me of your Intentions respecting the Quelling those disputes, as I mean to return and use my utmost endeavours in favor of Government.'

Lest the colonial secretary too easily miss the point and leap to the conclusion that the Mohawk, at least, would support the Crown in the war, Brant continued with grievances and concerns for which he needed reassurances. The previous year the Mohawk had assisted in the defence of Canada but had not received any credit for their contribution. He also impressed on Germain that 'notwithstanding our Attachement to Government we had suffered greatly in our Lands, which had been taken wrongfully away from us, and would be very glad to know, if His Majesty meant to redress the Mohawks respecting said lands.'⁵ Germain was satisfyingly forth-coming. He informed Brant that he was aware of the Mohawk's recent military contributions and grateful for them. And 'he said respecting the Lands which was wrongfully taken, he knew every circumstance that I related to be true, but on account of these disputes, they could not attend to them but that I might rest assured as soon as the troubles were over, every grievance and complaint should be redressed and he hoped the Six Nations would to fulfill their engagement with Government as they ever had done, and in consequence of which, they might rest assured of every support England could render them.' Joseph, not surprisingly, took this assurance as a guarantee that, if the Iroquois supported Britain against the American rebels, the United Kingdom would defend the Indians' lands against American invasions and ambitions. Accordingly, Joseph 'thanked him in the name of the Six Nations and acquainted him that he might depend they would fulfill their engagement with Government.'

This pilgrimage to London proved far more satisfactory to Brant and the Mohawk than its aftermath. In addition to obtaining what he took to be Britain's commitment, he had pledged Six Nations support. Moreover, he had been received at Court by George III – an event that seemed to affect him positively and permanently – and been lionized in London society.⁶ Back in North America Brant found that he could not deliver fully on his promise to Germain. Thanks in no small part to the exhortations of Molly and Joseph Brant, the Mohawk swung loyally and tenaciously to support the British alliance, and the Seneca, Cayuga, and Onondaga somewhat less enthusiastically did as well.⁷ However, the Oneida and Tuscarora, who had close ties to Congregationalists in the Thirteen Colonies because of the ministrations of missionaries among them, were sympathetic to the rebels. The result of the division of opinion was the extinguishment of the League Council fire, signifying the end – temporarily as it later proved – of the Iroquois Confederacy.

At war's end, it hardly mattered whether an Iroquois nation had fought with Britain or sympathized with the rebels, because all members of the league found their territorial interests surrendered or ignored. Joseph Brant charged that 'the King had "sold the Indians to Congress."'⁸ Another disillusioned Iroquois leader was even more scathing: 'The King surely would not pretend to give the Americans that which was not his to give; and [he] would not believe that the Americans would accept that which the King had not power to give. They were allies of the King, not subjects; and would not submit to such treatment ... If England had done so it was an act of cruelty and injustice and capable only of *Christians*.'⁹ Britain obtained lands north of Lakes Ontario and Erie from the Mississauga and created reserves near Belleville and Brantford for their Iroquois allies. However, the sense of betrayal remained strong among leaders such as Joseph Brant.

Because of these developments Joseph Brant undertook a second trip to petition the Crown in 1785. This journey merely deepened Mohawk disillusionment. For one thing, in contrast to the 1775-76 pilgrimage, which British officials had facilitated because they were eager to obtain solid Iroquois support in the war, Joseph found this time that Indian Department officials tried to dissuade and ultimately prevent him from sailing from Quebec. It was only with persistence and dissembling that he got to Britain at all.[10] More serious was the fact that although Joseph was received at Court and made much of, he was unable to obtain even a promise of British redress of losses, including territorial losses, that the Mohawk had suffered during the war, or to secure guarantees of imperial support in the event of conflict between the Indians and the United States. He was well received by the king and Queen, consorted uproariously with the Prince of Wales (who took him to some places 'very queer for a prince to go to'), and was invited out by many people.[11] And, while he and his sister Molly had their personal claims compensated, and Joseph would eventually be placed on half-pay pension, the larger strategic question of what Britain would do in the event of hostilities between the United States and the First Nations was not satisfactorily resolved. The written words of Colonial Secretary Lord Sydney were facile but vacuous. Referring to commitments to compensation for individuals, Sydney claimed they signalled good will for the future, but he refused to be more specific or concrete about what assistance the future might hold:

> This liberal conduct on the part of His Majesty, he trusts, will not leave a doubt upon the minds of his Indian allies that he shall at all times be ready to attend to their future welfare; and that he shall be anxious, upon every occasion wherein their happiness may be concerned, to give them such farther testimonies of his royal favour and countenance, as can, consistently with a due regard to the national faith, and the honour and dignity of the crown, be afforded to them.
>
> His Majesty recommends to his Indian allies to continue united in their councils, and that their measures may be conducted with temper and moderation; from which added to a peaceable demeanour on their part, they must experience many essential benefits, and be most likely to secure to themselves the possession of those rights and privileges which their ancestors have heretofore enjoyed.[12]

A disappointed and disillusioned Joseph Brant returned to North America shortly after receiving this weak response from the colonial secretary.

The next phase of pilgrimages to London was different in character from Brant's, reflecting the enormous changes that occurred in Native-newcomer relations in British North America between the late decades of the eighteenth century and the middle years of the nineteenth century. Joseph Brant's journeys to the imperial capital had been motivated by strategic concerns. The next phase of journeying to London, which began in the 1850s and continued into the twentieth century, was also motivated on the First Nations' side by concerns about their lands. But in the later period they had no diplomatic and military quid pro quo with which to try to negotiate with imperial officers. The diplomatic-military frontier between First Nations and Europeans in Canada had ceased to exist with the end of the War of 1812. It was replaced by an agricultural frontier in which First Nations were regarded as an obstacle to settlement and development, rather than a potentially valuable asset in strategic calculations. In this changed relationship, neither the imperial Crown nor colonial legislatures had much interest in safeguarding Aboriginal lands. Worse still, the advent of colonial self-government meant that First Nations were largely abandoned by Britain to the tender mercies of settler societies. The consequences of this transition – a shift from a military to a settlement relationship – was a concerted campaign by the local farmers and developers to dispossess First Nations of their lands and change them culturally through extensive campaigns of attempted assimilation that would last from the 1830s to at least the 1970s.[13]

This altered relationship, now in the context of a poisoned colonial atmosphere, was the background for forays such as that of the redoubtable Nahnebahwequa in 1859-60. Nahnebahwequa, also known as Catherine Bunch Sonego or Catherine Sutton after her marriage to the English immigrant William Sutton, was a well-connected Mississauga woman who grew up on the Credit Mission near Toronto.[14] The niece of Mississauga Methodist clergyman and chief Peter Jones (Kahkewaquonaby, Sacred Feathers), she was closely associated with Canadian Methodism throughout her life. She met her husband through the English wife of her uncle, and she and William Sutton lived for a number of years at Credit Mission, where Catherine also acted as a Methodist instructor. In the 1840s she and her family lived near Owen Sound, where they were granted 200 acres by the Chippewas of Newash, and in the early 1850s they were at Garden River near Sault Ste Marie, a centre of intensive Christian evangelization. After a sojourn in Michigan from 1854 to 1857, they returned to Owen Sound, where they discovered that their land had been taken by the Indian Department in the surrender of the Bruce peninsula, and put up for sale. Furthermore, the Department denied Nahnebahwequa an opportunity to purchase when she sought to get their land back. When Nahnebahwequa and two Indian men, one of them a chief, pursued the matter with the Indian Department in Toronto, a bureaucrat told her that 'Indians where [*sic*] not allowed to Purchase Land.'[15] No satisfaction was to be obtained from officialdom in the settler society of Ontario. A petition to the provincial legislature by the three would-be Indian purchasers proved unavailing, and, to add insult to injury, Nahnebahwequa found that the arguments the Indian Department

gave for not permitting her to acquire her lands kept shifting. They culminated in a contention that she was no longer an Indian because she had
married a 'white man.' Incensed by the treatment she had received, she
determined to take her search for redress to London and the Queen. As her
petition put it: 'I am an Indian woman born of Pagan Parents but brought
up under religious instructions. My Father and Mother [were] full Blood
Indians and my forefathers fought and bled for the British Crown, and the
Representatives of Briton have repeatedly told our Fathers that they [were]
the Friends of the Red Men and would continue to be, as long as the grass
grew and waters continued to flow. [B]ut for the last Quarter of a Centuary
[there has] been a strange way of showing it.'[16] Perhaps the Queen, a wife
and mother herself, would prove more sympathetic than the hard-hearted
men in the Indian Department in Toronto.

Authorized by chiefs to represent their land claims, too, and assisted fi-
nancially by sympathetic Quakers in New York, Nahnebahwequa made her
way to Britain in 1860. With support from prominent figures in the Aborigines Protection Society, she secured an audience with Victoria in June
1860. The Queen was favourably impressed. 'She speaks English quite well,
and is come on behalf of her Tribe to petition against some grievances as
regards their land,' Her Majesty noted.[17] Although no immediate action was
taken, promises apparently were made, and the Queen did prevail on her
secretary of state, the Duke of Newcastle, to hear the petition of the other
claimants when he accompanied the Prince of Wales to British North America
later in 1860. The petitioners made an impressive case to Newcastle, but,
again, no action ensued. Methodists who were sympathetic to the Indian
cause, several of the claimants being prominent Methodist converts, strongly
suspected that the good that the Indians' interview and petition accomplished with the colonial secretary was offset by the pernicious influence of
R. Pennefather, an Indian Department official who had previously resisted
the claims and who, as secretary to the governor, accompanied Newcastle
everywhere during the prince's tour of the colony.[18] Only Nahnebahwequa
received her lands, apparently as the result of a commitment by Victoria
herself; the other dispossessed claimants got no redress. Nahnebahwequa
spent the last few years before her death in 1865 campaigning against the
settler mindset, publicly characterizing 'their ideas of justice' as 'might makes
right' and describing as 'wholesale robbery and treachery' the government's
efforts to acquire Manitoulin Island from First Nations who had been promised it in perpetuity in 1836.[19]

The other high-profile effort by First Nations to petition the Crown directly for redress from settler rapacity originated in British Columbia in the
first decade of the twentieth century. Indeed, early twentieth-century British Columbia in disturbing ways resembled the situation in mid-nineteenth-

century Canada West (Ontario) that had produced Nahnebahwequa's expedition. The indigenous population of the Pacific province had been overtaken numerically in the 1880s by non-Native settlement, and First Nations' control of their lands and activities from then on was steadily more circumscribed by the presence of non-Natives and the imposition of laws created by the provincial legislature they dominated.[20] Land matters in British Columbia were complicated by the fact that very little of the province was covered by treaties between the Crown and First Nations. Aside from fourteen small pockets on Vancouver Island for which treaties had been negotiated by Governor James Douglas in the 1850s, and the northeast corner of the province, which was embraced by Treaty 8 (1899), British Columbia consisted of unsurrendered First Nations' land. However, the legal status of the lands – or what a twenty-first century authority would regard as their unsurrendered status – did not prevent British Columbians from usurping and appropriating lands, waterways, and natural resources of all kinds. In the British Columbia case, the situation became more entangled by an imbroglio that had developed between Ottawa and Victoria after British Columbia entered Confederation in 1871. To put the matter simply, the province systematically opposed and frustrated federal efforts to regularize the anomalous situation of Indian lands from the late 1870s onward. The federal government, which had become a notorious victimizer of First Nations itself in most other parts of the country, found itself outdone in uncharitable and punitive treatment of Indians in the Pacific province by the settler government that administered matters there.

Eventually, the response of some First Nations in British Columbia was to seek redress elsewhere for most of three decades by petitions and representations to both Victoria and Ottawa, but these efforts always proved unavailing, principally because of the intransigent attitudes of the province. By the middle years of the first decade of the twentieth century, some First Nations leaders had had enough. In particular, Coast Salish groups on Vancouver Island and the mainland began to organize to project their claims beyond Victoria and Ottawa to London.[21] Taking advantage of a fortuitous visit to Victoria by Prince Arthur, Duke of Connaught, nephew of King Edward VII, the leadership of the Cowichan, a Salish group on southern Vancouver Island, presented an address of welcome that emphasized their ties to the Crown, their affection for the late Queen Victoria, and their allegiance to the new occupant of the throne:

> We the undersigned chiefs of the Cowichan Indian tribe, representing about seven hundred people, desire to express our sincere gratitude to Your Royal Highness for this unexpected pleasure of seeing a member of the royal family.

By our first governor, Sir James Douglas, we were told of Her Most Gracious Majesty, the late Queen Victoria, whom we learned to love as a mother, and whose memory we revere with unspeakable devotion.

Whilst we still mourn the death of our beloved Queen, we nevertheless rejoice that in her noble son, King Edward VII, she has found a worthy successor – long may he reign ...[22]

Other preparations for a foray to London included a series of potlatches, the sharing ceremonial of Northwest Coast peoples, that were used to build solidarity among First Nations and support for the trip to Britain. Three chiefs – Joseph Capilano (Kayapálanexw), a Squamish; Basil David, a Shuswap; and Chillihitza (Chief Charlie), an Okanagan – were selected for the delegation, and a line of argument agreed upon. To the immense frustration of the local press, the Salish leadership refused until just before their departure to divulge the contents of the message they intended to deliver, a strategy apparently adopted to build press interest and prevent government from thwarting their mission by countering their arguments in advance. After a large parade in Vancouver, the chiefs and their interpreter boarded a transcontinental train for the long journey to Montreal and connections with an ocean liner that carried them to the United Kingdom.[23]

After some setbacks, the three chiefs succeeded in laying their views before the 'Great White Chief.'[24] Their arrival in London had coincided with the King's absence on a hunting excursion, but His Majesty agreed to see them first thing upon his return to the capital, not long before the chiefs were scheduled to depart on their return voyage. Their formal message reiterated the theme of allegiance ('We bring greetings to your majesty from thousands of true and loyal hearts'), explained briefly the way in which their land rights had been ignored ('in British Columbia the Indian title has never been extinguished, nor has sufficient land been allotted to our people for their maintenance'), threw their cause on the Crown's mercy ('We are persuaded that your majesty will not suffer us to be trodden upon or taken advantage of'), and asked for an investigation of their grievance: 'We cannot tell your majesty all our difficulties, it would take too long, but we are sure that a good man, or some good men, will be sent to our country who will see, and hear, and bring back a report to your majesty.'[25] As had been the case with Nahnebahqequa, though, little concrete action was to flow from the appeal, despite its careful preparation and staging.

The aftermath of the Salish chiefs' trip might not have included effective action, but it did pave the way for important political developments among British Columbia's First Nations. According to an unverified version of Chief Joseph Capilano's recollections, 'we talk with King and at end he shake my hand hard and ... pat my right shoulder three times so ... and say, "Chief we see this matter righted, but it may take a long time, five years perhaps" ...

King he received me like a brother chief and very kind.'[26] The three chiefs' recollections of Edward VII's expressions of sympathy and what they reported as his assurances about their case became a source of political strength and confidence to Salish and other groups in the Pacific province.[27] Moreover, the efforts at political unification among British Columbia's First Nations that had preceded the trip continued after the chiefs' return. The 1906 pilgrimage to London is generally regarded as part of the consciousness-raising and coalition-building that were forces behind the emergence in 1916 of the Allied Tribes of British Columbia, the first major pan-Indian political movement in a province marked by the large number and heterogeneity of its First Nations.[28] In this sense, the 1906 trip can legitimately be seen as the harbinger of an increasing emphasis on political topics and tactics among First Nations in Canada, an emphasis that also manifested itself in future ventures to the imperial capital by First Nations delegations.

Although First Nations delegations continued to head to London from British Columbia and other parts of Canada,[29] eventually the focus of the effort shifted to Ontario, more particularly to the Six Nations near Brantford.[30] The Six Nations community that produced an international campaign for recognition of their status as a sovereign people was unique among First Nations in Canada. The members of the Iroquois Confederacy had been allies of first the Dutch in the seventeenth century, and then of the British. According to the Iroquois view of the history of their interactions with the newcomers, their relationship with the strangers was both recorded and symbolized by the *gus wenta*, or two-row wampum. Wampum belts were used for a variety of purposes, among them to record and archive important discussions and agreements with other groups. The *gus wenta* contained symbols – two parallel canoes – that stood for a relationship of allies and equals who would forever respect the autonomy of the other group. When the American War of Independence ended badly for Britain and its Iroquois allies, tensions between them rose dramatically. Those Iroquois who had fought with Britain were angry at their ally's blithe surrender of their territorial rights in the peace settlement. To conciliate the Iroquois and avoid further complications with the young United States, Britain acquired lands from the Mississauga on which they could settle both their Aboriginal allies, such as the Iroquois, and non-Native allies who wished to escape the republic. Significantly, the grant by which Governor Frederick Haldimand conveyed land to the Six Nations referred to their role as 'His Majesty's allies.'[31]

The usefulness of the Six Nations in the eyes of the imperial government ended with the War of 1812, in which they again fought with the British. After the Rush-Bagot Convention ushered in enduring peace between British North America and the United States, the Six Nations were no longer valued for their military contribution. The Six Nations land-base shrank, in part because the imperial and colonial administrations showed little disposition to protect it from the covetousness of developers and settlers. The community was divided deeply between religious traditionalists and Christians, and also between those who believed in Iroquois sovereignty and others who preferred to work within the framework of Canadian law, including the Indian Act. In the late decades of the nineteenth century and early decades of the twentieth, there was growing polarization between supporters of hereditary governance and proponents of elective institutions – the Indian Affairs Department favouring the latter. Although there was not exact congruence between religious traditionalists and supporters of hereditary government or Iroquois sovereignty, there was a high degree of correlation.

Relations between the Six Nations and the federal government were seriously strained at the end of the First World War when Parliament amended the Indian Act to permit involuntary enfranchisement at the behest of the Department of Indian Affairs. Enfranchisement was the mechanism by which a male with the legal status of an Indian gave up that status and became a Canadian citizen. Efforts to persuade First Nations to enfranchise voluntarily had been going on since 1857, but without much visible success, and by 1920 the government was prepared to adopt sterner measures. The 1920 amendment that authorized involuntary enfranchisement at the will of the Indian Affairs minister joined with disputes over governance to provoke a showdown with the Six Nations that quickly expanded into a full-blown confrontation over the issue of Iroquois sovereignty.[32]

The leading spirit in the movement that became the Iroquois sovereignty campaign was Deskaheh, or Levi General, a follower of the traditional longhouse religion and ally of hereditary governance in the Six Nations. Disgruntled at Indian Affairs' rejection of the case for recognition of Iroquois sovereignty, and irritated by the passage of the involuntary enfranchisement provision in 1920, Deskaheh and his followers took their case to London and George V in the summer of 1921. As they had during the Ottawa phase of their campaign for recognition, the advocates of sovereignty showed themselves adept at generating and exploiting newspaper publicity to further their cause, even though the British government was not prepared to support them. Deskaheh, for example, gained a sympathetic hearing from journalists in the imperial capital, much to the annoyance of senior officials of the Department of Indian Affairs. The publicity and a change of Canadian government in late 1921 from the Unionists to Mackenzie King's Liberals resulted in the repeal of the 1920 involuntary enfranchisement amendment of the Indian Act. This paved the way for another attempt, again futile, to gain recognition of Iroquois sovereignty from Ottawa in 1922.

Deskaheh, his advisors, and his supporters among the hereditary-government element, next determined upon a more ambitious gambit. While they had been negotiating with the Canadian government in 1922-23, they had also been seeking international support. When the Dutch government agreed to support them internationally, Deskaheh broke off talks with Ottawa. He would take the search for recognition of the Six Nations as a sovereign people over the heads of Ottawa and London; with the support of their first European ally, the Netherlands, they would seek recognition in the recently created international body, the League of Nations. When the Dutch representative to the League forwarded the Iroquois petition, without committing his government to verifying or supporting its claims, both Canada and the United Kingdom took defensive action. The Canadian government prepared a reply asserting that the Iroquois were British subjects, and that, therefore, whatever complaints they had were a domestic Canadian matter. For its part, the British Foreign Office made it clear through the Dutch ambassador in London that Britain disapproved of the Dutch action and that the Netherlands, as an imperial power itself, might find that the action it had taken would come back to haunt it at Geneva. These steps seemed successful; by the summer of 1923 it was obvious that the Iroquois petition was going nowhere with the League.

As part of the campaign, Deskaheh in the summer of 1923 made the usual pilgrimage to London, en route to Geneva. As was becoming usual with First Nations from Canada, Deskaheh took some pains to arouse press interest in the matter, issuing a pamphlet and provoking significant journalistic comment in the United Kingdom. At the League, Deskaheh initially confronted a procedural stone wall: no member state had asked that the Iroquois petition be put on the agenda, and therefore it would not be discussed. However, by the spring of 1924 the Iroquois sovereigntist had persuaded a striking group of League representatives, who were former colonies of major powers, to support his case. It was reported that the delegates from Persia, Estonia, Ireland, and Panama were all sympathetic to the initiative. And it was lost on no one that all four of these states were former or actual colonies themselves. At this point the British Foreign Office weighed in heavily, telling the quartet of 'minor powers' that their proposed 'interference' in British and Canadian affairs was 'impertinent.'[33] This had the desired effect, and the four feisty states abandoned their support of Deskaheh and the Iroquois.

Defeated in Geneva, Deskaheh and his supporters once more turned to London. In the autumn of 1924 Deskaheh appealed to George V for justice for the Iroquois, only, as usual, to see his request referred to Ottawa and the unsympathetic ears of the Department of Indian Affairs. The death of Deskaheh in June 1925 removed the energetic Iroquois leader from the struggle, but it did not end the crusade. In the summer of 1930, another group of Iroquois made their way to London in pursuit of claims both for recognition of their sovereignty and redress for what they claimed was

Indian Affairs' mismanagement of their funds. Once again, they employed the tactics that had been developed over several similar forays: they enlisted the support of prominent Britons and staged colourful incidents that captured press attention for them and their cause. The Iroquois, in full regalia, were entertained for tea on Westminster Terrace by sympathetic members of parliament, and 'the historic pipe of peace was produced and handed around.'[34] Labour MP Fenner Brockway pursued their cause with British officialdom, and found their demands, as usual, spurned. Another sympathizer who asked for a hearing was told 'that as the matters referred to in your letter lie within the exclusive competence of His Majesty's Government in Canada, the Secretary of State cannot see his way to receive the deputation or to take any action in regard to these matters.'[35]

Although the Iroquois campaign during the 1920s had a quixotic and futile quality, its significance nonetheless was considerable. The effort was the culmination of a tradition of petitioning the Crown in London that went back at least a century and a half, to the days when Joseph Brant had sought a British commitment to defend Six Nations' territorial interests in return for military support from the Iroquois during the War of Independence. During the nineteenth century the pilgrimages continued, but now they often focused on land-related questions. The cause that took petitioners to London now might be grievances of individuals, such as Nahnebahwequa or the Salish chiefs who attended the court in 1906, and the kinds of strategic considerations that motivated Brant were no longer in evidence. One other change that occurred in the practice of petitioning the Crown was increasing First Nations' reliance on publicity to advance their cause. That had been evident in the preparations in British Columbia in 1906, when the departing chiefs arranged for a parade in Vancouver that attracted considerable attention. Seeking out publicity was a tactic even more in evidence in the struggles in the 1920s to advance the cause of Iroquois sovereignty.[36] Now the argument was not, as it had been in Brant's day, that strategic necessity required British support of the Iroquois. Rather the contention was that the Iroquois and the British had always been allies, that Iroquois sovereignty had never been surrendered or extinguished, and that Britain ought, as a simple measure of justice, to help the Iroquois secure recognition of their sovereign status. And, of course, by the 1920s First Nations' use of publicity to attract attention to their cause and embarrass the government back in Canada had become very pronounced. By the time of the Statute of Westminster, many Aboriginal political organizations in Canada had become quite sophisticated in their tactics of petitioning the Crown.

It was the reliance on publicity and media manipulation that was most obvious in the last chapter of this saga of First Nations' pilgrimages to London: the lobbying efforts carried out in the campaign over constitutional renewal in 1979-82. In 1976 a Parti Québécois government had been elected in Quebec dedicated to achieving sovereignty for the province, and Canadian Prime Minister Pierre Elliott Trudeau was determined to frustrate that goal, preferably by renewing the Canadian constitution with a made-in-Canada amending formula and an entrenched bill of rights that would guarantee both basic civil and democratic rights, and minority linguistic rights. The struggle over constitutional renewal went on from 1977 until early 1982. Throughout this period, Aboriginal leaders, especially the leaders of the status-Indian organizations, whose national representative was known as the National Indian Brotherhood (NIB), sought to become involved in the process in order to advance their own agenda. As early as 1978 the NIB insisted that Aboriginal organizations must play a prominent role in the constitutional talks and that any new constitution must guarantee Aboriginal and treaty rights. If these things did not occur, the NIB warned, they would go to the United Kingdom to ask Queen Elizabeth II to stop the constitutional patriation process.[37] One of the reasons for this stance, according to the president of the Indian Association of Alberta, was a concern 'that treaty rights may not be safeguarded by a new constitution and that the ending of Canada's colonial status could also mean the ending of the Indian people's special relationship with the Crown.'[38] When the NIB leadership became convinced that they were not going to achieve meaningful participation in the constitutional talks, they dispatched a large delegation to London in the spring of 1979. The government of Joe Clark found itself faced with the question of what advice to give the British government on how the delegation should be received. Even though Queen Elizabeth had been the recipient of a carefully negotiated political speech in Alberta when touring Canada in 1973, and a large delegation had gone to Britain in 1976 and had an audience on the centenary of the signing of Treaty 6, the Clark government advised Britain that the Queen not meet the delegation. But the two hundred people in the delegation met with various politicians, especially from the opposition, and once again captured enormous publicity for their cause.[39] Although the Clark government promised that Aboriginal leaders could attend constitutional talks as participants rather than observers, the Trudeau government, which returned to power early in 1980, reneged. Worse still, the eagerness of the re-elected Trudeau to complete constitutional renewal meant that Aboriginal issues were going to be deferred to a later round of constitutional talks, after the concerns of Quebec had been addressed.

Aboriginal leaders resisted the constitutional juggernaut both through protest in Canada and initiatives in Britain. In the autumn of 1980 the NIB determined on a widespread lobbying campaign in Britain, and succeeded as early as November of that year in getting a hearing by the Foreign Affairs Committee of the British House of Commons. Unfortunately for the Canadian Aboriginal cause, the Committee's report, issued in January 1981, declared that Crown treaty obligations had been transferred to Canada, although no one seemed entirely certain when and how that had occurred. The organizations continued to lobby in London, but their efforts were hampered by a breakdown in the common front they had hammered together for their submission to the Foreign Affairs Committee. Part of the problem was that the Aboriginal movement in Canada was divided among the Inuit Council on National Issues; the Native Council of Canada representing the Métis and non-status Indians; and the National Indian Brotherhood, representing status Indians. The NIB, the largest and best organized of the three, was having its own internal problems, with differences over strategy being only one of the sources of division. In spite of these difficulties, it appeared that progress was made in Canada early in 1980, when the government and NIB seemed briefly to agree on a formula of words for the new constitution that said 'The aboriginal and treaty rights of the aboriginal peoples of Canada are hereby recognized and affirmed.' However, this entente fell apart, too, because of western provincial opposition, and the various Aboriginal groups repaired once more to London in the spring and summer of 1981. In the autumn, the climactic First Ministers Conference on the constitution notoriously betrayed the Aboriginal organizations by, initially, dropping the proposed entrenchment of 'aboriginal and treaty rights,' and, when there was an outcry over this duplicity, agreeing to restore the clause with the critical limiting adjective 'existing' before 'aboriginal and treaty rights.'[40] That and the failure to include Quebec in the final deal in November 1981 left the supposed triumph of constitutional renewal a shambles.

In addition to public agitation aimed at the politicians, the Aboriginal organizations also entered the courts to try to frustrate the Canadian government. Unfortunately, they did not manage to maintain a common approach in their litigation. The Indian Association of Alberta chose to challenge the decision of the Foreign Affairs Committee, arguing that the Crown in right of Britain retained obligations to Aboriginal organizations. The British Columbia and Saskatchewan First Nations organizations, on the other hand, chose to argue merely that Aboriginal agreement was a necessary condition for patriation of the constitution. Alberta lost in the court of first instance, but in December the Court of Queen's Bench, or, more specifically, its chief justice Lord Denning, granted them leave to appeal. However, Denning eventually ruled that it was, as the British government maintained, the Crown in right of Canada that now bore responsibility to Aboriginal groups.[41] Frustrated and disappointed in court, the Aboriginal groups now swung their attention to Westminster, where the Canada Bill, which embodied the cobbled-together deal on constitutional renewal, was to be debated. The organizations scored a moral victory, inasmuch as their parliamentary champions delayed passage for a time and the debates in both Commons and Lords focused overwhelmingly on Aboriginal issues.

However, the Canada Bill passed, and the Queen in April 1982 signed the new constitutional provisions in Ottawa. Aboriginal organizations, as well as the premier of Quebec, boycotted the signing, and the Native groups declared 17 April a day of mourning. The patriation story was another disappointing chapter in the lengthy saga of pilgrimages by Aboriginal people to Britain.

Although the reasons that Aboriginal organizations, especially First Nations, had for taking their cause to London and the monarch were clear and understandable, the practice never produced much satisfaction for them. In their cultural and diplomatic world, the tie to European powers such as the United Kingdom was fashioned as personal and familial, and they regarded their link to the king or queen as an important symbol of their relationship to the monarch's people. However, on the British side, where relations with First Nations leaders and individuals were always fashioned within a framework of constitutional parliamentary government, the links existed for *raison d'état*, and there was nothing familial or personal about them. Accordingly, the British government, in spite of the honeyed words spoken on some occasions by the king or queen, treated the relationship as instrumental and the interests of the Aboriginal petitioners as a relatively low priority. Over time, Native leaders from Canada began to adjust to that harsh reality, reaching out to opposition politicians, to media outlets that could publicize their cause and perhaps shift politicians' attitudes, and finally, to international organizations such as the League of Nations that might, if they could not deliver redress, at least embarrass the British and Canadian governments into taking corrective action. The constitutional campaign from 1977 to 1982 certainly revealed the limitations of the strategy of petitioning the Queen. For Britain, if not formally and fully in relation to Canada until 1982, empire had ended decades earlier. Entanglements with Aboriginal groups in Canada, aside from colourful opportunities during royal visits to the dominion, were an inconvenience and encumbrance.

Certainly First Nations leaders have learned the lesson. If the Crown is no longer the answer, perhaps an international forum is, or so both First Nations intellectuals and political leaders seem to think. Recently, efforts by some First Nations leaders have focused on talks in Geneva, where a Working Group on the Draft Declaration of Indigenous Populations, a subgroup of the United Nations Human Rights Committee, has been wrestling with the question of Aboriginal peoples' place in the world. And when Matthew Coon Come became grand chief of the Assembly of First Nations in 2000, he promised his followers that he would, if necessary, take their grievances to the United Nations to embarrass Ottawa into doing right by First Nations. The pilgrimages continue, but now, as with so much else in Canadian life, they are to New York, or sometimes Geneva, rather than to London.[42]

Acknowledgments

This chapter was prepared with the assistance of a Standard Research Grant from the Social Sciences and Humanities Research Council of Canada. Its preparation was immensely facilitated by the work of research assistant Christa Nicholat.

Notes

1 The most comprehensive coverage of this complex matter is found in the Covenant Chain trilogy of Francis Jennings, *The Invasion of America: Indians, Colonialism, and the Cant of Conquest* (Williamsburg, VA: University of North Carolina Press, 1975); *The Ambiguous Iroquois Empire: The Covenant Chain Confederation of Indian Tribes with English Colonies from Its Beginnings to the Lancaster Treaty of 1744* (New York: W.W. Norton, 1984); and *Empire of Fortune: Crowns, Colonies, and Tribes in the Seven Years' War* (New York: W.W. Norton, 1988).

2 Sylvia Van Kirk, *'Many Tender Ties': Women in Fur-Trade Society in Western Canada, 1670-1870* (Winnipeg: Watson and Dwyer, [1980]), especially Chapters 2-3.

3 Alexander Morris, *The Treaties of Canada with the Indians* (1880; reprinted Saskatoon: Fifth House, 1991), 193.

4 John L. Tobias, 'The Origins of the Treaty Rights Movement in Saskatchewan,' in *1885 and After: Native Society in Transition*, ed. F. Laurie Barron and James B. Waldram (Regina: Canadian Plains Research Center, 1986), 248.

5 National Archives of Canada [NAC], MG11, CO 42, vol. 87, 221, Joseph Brant's notes of speech; original spelling retained. I have suppressed some of the exuberant upper-casing in this document.

6 See the account in Isabel Thompson Kelsay, *Joseph Brant, 1743-1807: Man of Two Worlds* (Syracuse, NY: Syracuse University Press, 1984), 161-71, and an example of the lionization, James Boswell's gushing account of 'Joseph Thayendaneken, The Mohawk Chief' in *London Magazine* (July 1776).

7 Barbara Graymont, 'The Six Nations Indians in the Revolutionary War,' in *Sweet Promises: A Reader on Indian-White Relations in Canada*, ed. J.R. Miller (Toronto: University of Toronto Press, 1991), 94-96.

8 Quoted in Robert S. Allen, *His Majesty's Indian Allies: British Indian Policy in the Defence of Canada, 1774-1815* (Toronto: Dundurn, 1993), 56.

9 Quoted in D.C. Scott, 'Indian Affairs, 1763-1841,' *Canada and Its Provinces*, ed. A. Shortt and A.G. Doughty (Toronto: Glasgow Brook, 1914), Vol. 4: 708.

10 See CO 42, vol. 17, 188-93 and 208-9.

11 William L. Stone, *Life of Joseph Brant* (1838; reprinted St. Clair Shores, MI: Scholarly Press, 1970), Vol. 2: 249-60.

12 Lord Sydney to Joseph Brant, 6 April 1786, quoted in ibid., 256.

13 This process is traced in J.R. Miller, *Skyscrapers Hide the Heavens: A History of Indian-White Relations in Canada*, 3rd edition (Toronto: University of Toronto Press, 2000), parts 2 and 3.

14 The biographical details come principally from Donald B. Smith, 'Nahnebahwequay,' *Dictionary of Canadian Biography* (Toronto: University of Toronto Press, 1976), 9: 590-91. I have also benefited from reading papers by Ian Radforth, 'Performance, Politics, and Representation: Aboriginals and the 1860 Royal Tour of Canada'; and by Celia Haig-Brown, 'Missions and Canadian National Identity: Nahnebahweaqua in the Struggle for Justice' (paper presented at a conference on 'Missions and Canadian National Identities,' York University, Toronto, 27 February 1999).

15 NAC, RG10, Records of the Department of Indian Affairs [RG 10], vol. 2877, file 177, 181, petition of Catherine Sutton. Internal evidence indicates that this petition was prepared in 1859 or 1860 (she says she's been married twenty years; *DCB*, 9: 590, says she married in 1839), likely for presentation in England ('but let the British Government order a thorough investigation of all Indian afairs [sic]').

16 Ibid.

17 Quoted in *DCB*, 9:591.

18 See *The Christian Guardian's* editorial of 5 September 1860, in Conrad Van Dusen, *The Indian Chief: An Account of the Labours, Losses, Sufferings, and Oppression of Ke-zig-ko-e-ne-ne (David Sawyer), a Chief of the Ojibbeway Indians in Canada West* (London: W. Nichols 1867),

144. See, too, the *Guardian's* editorial of 30 January 1861 charging that Indian Department officials deliberately manufactured a misleading image of the Indians by having them parade before the Prince and Newcastle 'every where as savages. They were instructed to present themselves half-naked, with painted faces, feathers in their hair, the most grotesque forms of savage dress, and with every appearance of savage ferocity. The effect of all this would be to make the Duke feel that lands could be no use to them, and that they were incapable of valuing or improving that which might be conferred upon them' (ibid., 147-48).

19 Quoted in *DCB*, 9: 591.

20 The literature on this depressing process is extensive, but a good beginning can be made by referring to Robin A. Fisher, *Contact and Conflict: Indian-European Relations in British Columbia,* 2nd edition (Vancouver: University of British Columbia Press, 1992), especially Chapters 7-8; and Paul Tennant, *Aboriginal Peoples and Politics: The Indian Land Question in British Columbia, 1849-1989* (Vancouver: University of British Columbia Press, 1990), especially Chapters 1-7.

21 There was an unsuccessful effort to see the king in 1904, when two chiefs from the interior, accompanied by an Oblate priest, failed to get an audience with Edward VII. See R.M Galois, 'The Indian Rights Association, Native Protest Activity and the "Land Question" in British Columbia, 1903-1916,' *Native Studies Review* 8/2 (1992): 6-7.

22 *Victoria Daily Colonist,* quoted in Daniel P. Marshall, *Those Who Fell From the Sky: A History of the Cowichan Peoples* (Duncan, BC: Cowichan Tribes, 1999), 147. I am indebted to my colleague Keith Thor Carlson for bringing this source to my attention.

23 Tennant, *Aboriginal Peoples and Politics*, 85; Marshall, *Those Who Fell*, 147-48.

24 London *Daily Telegraph,* 25 August 1906, reprinted in Victoria *Daily Colonist,* 31 August 1906.

25 'Indians' Petition to King Edward,' Victoria *Daily Colonist,* 6 July 1906.

26 'A Mirror of Joe Capilano,' in Carolyn Thomas Foreman, *Indians Abroad, 1493-1938* (Norman: University of Oklahoma Press, 1943), 211. Unfortunately, this work has no references that would permit verification of the author's sources. According to other authorities, the delegation were told 'to present their claims to the Canadian Government and if they then received no satisfaction, their complaints would be dealt with further' in *Native Rights in Canada,* ed. Peter Cumming and Neil Mickenberg (Toronto: Indian-Eskimo Association of Canada in association with General Publishing, 1970), 188.

27 Marshall, *Those Who Fell*, 157-58.

28 Galois, 'The Indian Rights Association,' 7-8.

29 See correspondence concerning a trip by three Dakota from Oak River in Manitoba in the summer of 1907, for example, in NAC, RG10, vol. 4035, file 311, 256. The purpose of the trip is not clear from official records.

30 Both the governor general's office and the Department of Indian Affairs reacted with alarm in August 1906, when a group from the Six Nations were reported to be on their way to England 'with the hope of seeing the King.' NAC, RG 10, vol. 3099, file 301, 224. J. Hanbury Williams to deputy superintendent general of Indian Affairs, 8 August 1906. All concerned relaxed when it turned out that the group was merely part of a hired entertainment troupe. The reason for their leaders' return to London two years later is unclear.

31 Quoted in E. Brian Titley, *A Narrow Vision: Duncan Campbell Scott and the Administration of Indian Affairs in Canada* (Vancouver: University of British Columbia Press, 1986), 112.

32 The issue is well covered in Titley, *A Narrow Vision,* Chapter 7; Richard Veatch, *Canada and the League of Nations* (Toronto: University of Toronto Press, 1975), Chapter 7; and Joëlle Rostkowski, 'The Redman's Appeal for Justice: Deskaheh and the League of Nations, '*Indians and Europe: An Interdisciplinary Collection of Essays,* ed. Christian F. Feest (Lincoln: University of Nebraska Press, 1989), 435-53. I have also benefited from Donald B. Smith, 'Onondeyoh: The Grand River and Toronto Backgrounds of Fred Loft (1861-1934), an Important Early Twentieth-Century First Nations Political Leader' (paper presented at the Conference on 'Twentieth-Century Canadian Nationalisms,' Massey College, Toronto, 18 March 2001).

33 Quoted in Titley, *Narrow Vision,* 123.

33 *Peterborough Examiner*, n.d. (The item was datelined: 'London, June 24'), in RG 25, vol. 1573, file 673 (1930).

34 Ibid.

35 Ibid., H. Tait, to J.R. Ockleshaw-Johnson, 8 July 1930. According to Titley (*A Narrow Vision*, 129-31), Ockleshaw-Johnson was a British adventurer who interested himself in the Iroquois cause until they grew suspicious of his aims and severed their connection with him.

36 For example, see Rostkowski, 'The Redman's Appeal,' 444-45.

37 The Aboriginal role in the patriation process is well covered in Douglas E. Sanders, 'The Indian Lobby,' in *And No One Cheered: Federalism, Democracy and the Constitution Act*, ed. Keith Banting and Richard Simeon (Toronto: Methuen, 1983), 301-32. I have also benefited from an unpublished paper by Michael D. Behiels, 'Aboriginal Nationalism in the Ascendancy: The Assembly of First Nations' First Campaign for the Inherent Right to Self-Government, 1968-1987' (paper presented at the Conference on 'Twentieth-Century Canadian Nationalisms,' Massey College, Toronto, 18 March 2001). See also Tony Hall, '"What are We, Chopped Liver?" Aboriginal Affairs in the Constitutional Politics of Canada in the 1980s,' in *The Meech Lake Primer: Conflicting Views of the 1987 Constitutional Accord*, ed. Michael D. Behiels (Ottawa: University of Ottawa Press, 1989), 423-56; and Michael Woodward and Bruce George, 'The Canadian Indian Lobby of Westminster, 1979-1982,' *Journal of Canadian Studies* 18/3 (Autumn 1983): 119-43. Also instructive are Peter Jull, 'Aboriginal Peoples and Political Change in the North Atlantic Area,' *Journal of Canadian Studies* 16/2 (Summer 1981): 53-68; and Simon McInnes, 'The Inuit and the Constitutional Process,' ibid., 68-80.

38 Joe Dion, quoted in Sanders, 'The Indian Lobby,' 304.

39 Ibid., 305-6.

40 Douglas E. Sanders, 'Prior Claims: Aboriginal People in the Constitution of Canada,' in *Canada and the New Constitution: The Unfinished Agenda*, Vol. 1, ed. Stanley Beck and Ivan Bernier (Montreal: Institute for Research on Public Policy, 1983), 227-28.

41 *R. v. Secretary of State for Foreign and Commonwealth Affairs, ex. P. Indian Association of Alberta* [1982] 1 QB 892 (C.A.).

42 Marie Battiste and James Sa'ke'j Youngblood Henderson, *Protecting Indigenous Knowledge and Heritage: A Global Challenge* (Saskatoon: Purich, 2000), especially 1-6 and 251-61.

Contributors

Andrea Benvenuti is a member of the School of Political Science and International Studies, University of Queensland.

Phillip Buckner is a professor emeritus at the University of New Brunswick and a senior research fellow at the Institute of Commonwealth Studies at the University of London.

P.E. Bryden is an associate professor in the Department of History at Mount Allison University.

Lorraine Copps is a public relations associate, JSTOR, New York City.

John Darwin is Beit University Lecturer in the History of the British Commonwealth at Neffield College, Oxford University.

Greg Donaghy is the head of the Historical Section, Foreign Affairs Canada.

R. Douglas Francis is a professor of history at the University of Calgary.

John Hilliker is the former head of the Historical Section, Foreign Affairs Canada.

José E. Iguarta is in the Département d'Histoire, Université du Québec à Montréal.

Gregory A. Johnson is based at the Centre for Global and Social Analysis at Athabasca University.

Steve Koerner is a private scholar based in Victoria, British Columbia.

J.R. (Jim) Miller holds the Canada Research Chair in Native-Newcomer Relations and is a professor of history at the University of Saskatchewan.

Marc Milner is a professor and chair of the history department at the University of New Brunswick.

Bruce Muirhead is a professor in the Department of History, Lakehead University.

George Richardson is in the Faculty of Education at the University of Alberta.

Tim Rooth is a professor in the Department of Economics at the University of Portsmouth.

Paul Rutherford is a professor of history at the University of Toronto.

Allan Smith is a professor of history at the University of British Columbia.

Gordon T. Stewart is the Jack and Margaret Sweet Professor of History at Michigan State University.

Stuart Ward is in the Department of English at the University of Copenhagen.

Index

wars, 3; American War of Independence, 302-4, 309; communications and, 289-90; Vietnam War, 296. *See also* Suez Crisis; World War I; World War II
Wedgewood-Benn, Anthony, 144-45
West Germany, 153, 155, 158
white dominions. *See* settler countries
Whitney, John Hay, 107
Whitton, Charlotte, 258
Wilgress, L.D., 112, 175
Wilson, Harold, 35; Wilson administration, 34-36, 136-48

Winnipeg Free Press [newspaper], 55-56, 61
Winters, Robert, 30
women: in colonial societies, 253-54, 268n10. *See also* Imperial Order Daughters of the Empire
Woodbury, Willoughby, 101
World War I, 4, 18, 19, 94, 256, 295-96; Royal Canadian Navy, 273-74
World War II, 4, 17, 20-21, 94; effect on Canada-US relations, 96, 101, 174; extension of federal powers, 217; Royal Canadian Navy, 274-76, 278